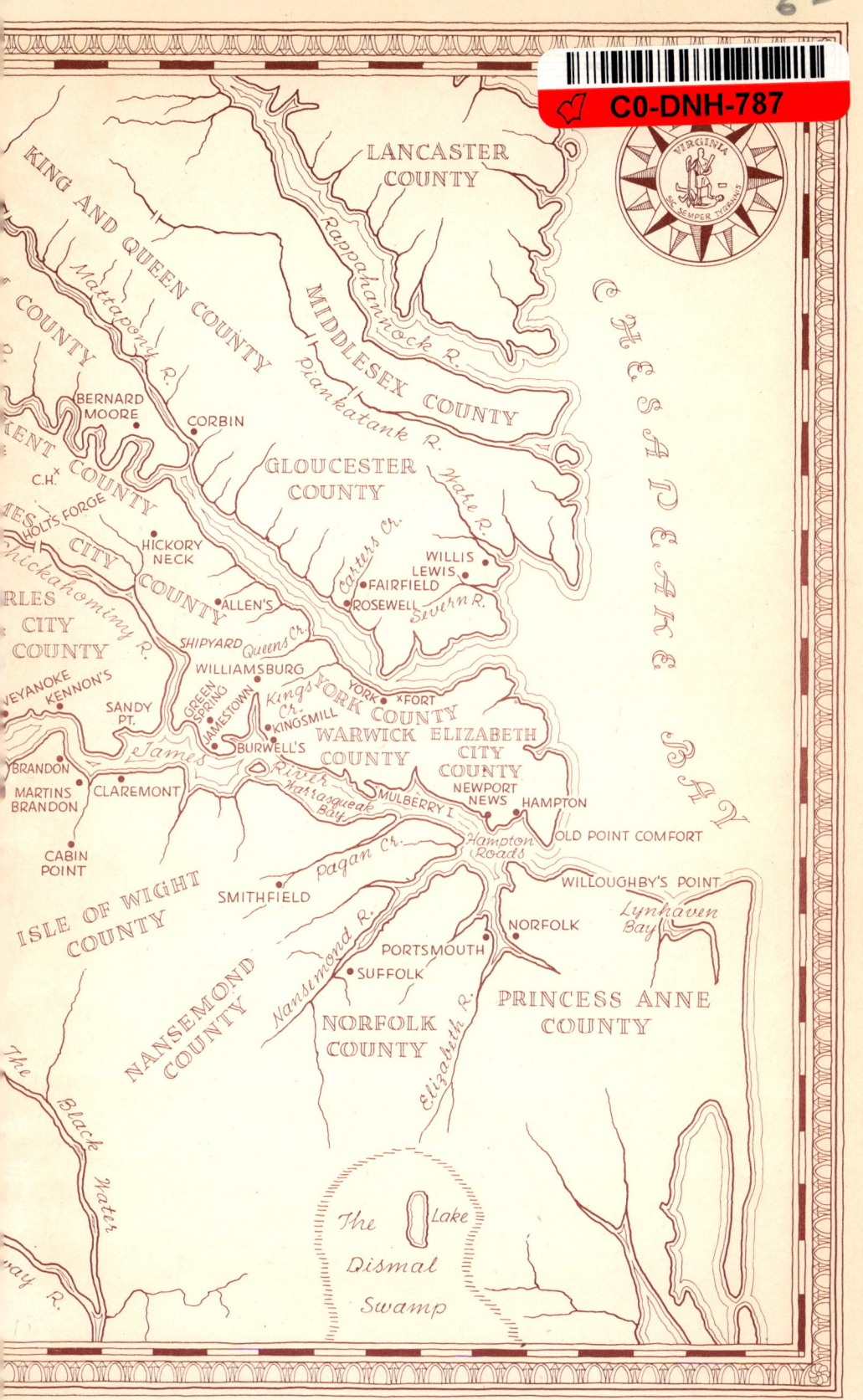

JEFFERSON

WAR AND PEACE

1776–1784

Books by Marie Kimball

JEFFERSON: THE ROAD TO GLORY

JEFFERSON: WAR AND PEACE

THE MARTHA WASHINGTON COOK BOOK

JEFFERSON. By Houdon

JEFFERSON WAR AND PEACE 1776 to 1784

by

Marie Kimball

Coward-McCann, Inc., New York

COPYRIGHT, 1947, BY MARIE KIMBALL

All rights reserved. This book, or parts thereof, must not be reproduced in any form without permission.

Published simultaneously in the Dominion of Canada by Longmans, Green & Company, Toronto.

Designed by Robert Josephy

MANUFACTURED IN THE UNITED STATES OF AMERICA

VAN REES PRESS · NEW YORK

Author's Note

The author wishes to express her very great thanks to the Alderman Library of the University of Virginia for the unstinting generosity with which it has made available its books, its microfilms, and its manuscripts to a person whose admiration for Jefferson and his university is her only claim to such consideration. She is also deeply indebted to the American Philosophical Society, which has likewise most kindly put all its similar facilities at her disposal.

Her particular thanks are due to the John Simon Guggenheim Memorial Foundation. By awarding her a fellowship for the years 1945-46 and 1946-47 it has made the writing of this book possible in these difficult times.

Contents

I.	The Empire of Liberty	3
II.	Europe Comes to Jefferson	18
III.	Governor of Virginia	46
IV.	The Conquest of the West	78
V.	Jefferson's Second Term	96
VI.	The Parricide Arnold	125
VII.	The Burdens of State	152
VIII.	Between Invasions	175
IX.	Phillips and Cornwallis	203
X.	Retirement and Vindication	237
XI.	The Notes on Virginia	259
XII.	The Darkest Year	306
XIII.	The Leader of Congress	324
XIV.	Farewell to America	352
	Notes	363
	Index	391

Illustrations

Jefferson, by Houdon	*Frontispiece*
Baron von Riedesel, from a portrait in the possession of the Riedesel family Facing page	34
William Phillips, by Francis Cotes	35
George Rogers Clark, by Matthew Harris Jouett	90
Benedict Arnold, from the engraving after Pierre Eugène du Simitière	91
Baron von Steuben, by Ralph Earl	140
Lord Cornwallis, by Thomas Gainsborough	141
Banastre Tarleton, from the mezzotint after Sir Joshua Reynolds	188
Jefferson's bust of Lafayette, by Houdon	189
Marquis de Marbois, from the engraving after the portrait at Versailles	258
The Natural Bridge, from the engraving in the *Columbian Magazine*, September, 1787	259
Buffon, by Houdon	282
John Sullivan, by John Trumbull	283
Marquis de Chastellux, by Charles Willson Peale	302
Jefferson's portrait of Washington, by Joseph Wright	303

JEFFERSON

WAR AND PEACE

1776-1784

I. The Empire of Liberty

THE ADOPTION of the Declaration of Independence on July 4, 1776, represents a milestone in the career of Thomas Jefferson in more ways than one. It marked not only the culmination of his increasing efforts on behalf of the colonies from the tyranny of British rule, but it gave him liberty, at last, to turn his attention to the problems facing his own Virginia and enabled him to devote the powers of his exceptional mind to their solution. That rare phenomenon, a prophet in his own country, he was destined to lead his people out of the morass of surviving feudalism in which the late eighteenth century still found them floundering. For the next five years, indeed almost until the moment he sailed for France as Minister Plenipotentiary, the best of his energies were to be dedicated to the service of his state and to the enlightenment of his compatriots.

During this brief period he swept away the lingering inheritance of centuries of darkness. Through "the generous energy" of his mind, he bestowed upon Virginia, and through her upon all the United States of America, an ideal of freedom such as man had hitherto not dreamed of. His revisal of the laws of Virginia anticipated all that we like to think America stands for, and which we, in turn, seek to confer upon those countries of the world which, rightly or wrongly, we consider benighted. Firm in the belief that "Almighty God hath created the mind free and manifested His supreme will that free it shall remain by making it altogether insusceptible of restraint," he laid a foundation "for a government truly republican." By his statute for religious freedom he freed his country from the bonds of an abysmal bigotry, by abolishing entail and primogeniture he eradicated "every fibre of ancient or future aristocracy," by his revision of the laws concerning crime and punishment, he abolished forever the grosser forms of cruelty that have distinguished man's inhumanity to man, and by his reformation of the educational system he made the written word intelligible to millions who had hitherto not been thought to have the right to such a boon. Jefferson's dream of empire was, indeed, not a physical but rather a spiritual one—the empire of liberty, as he described it to that other empire builder, George Rogers Clark.

During the summer of 1776 Jefferson continued a faithful if somewhat impatient member of the Continental Congress, then in session at Philadelphia. He served, as usual, on various committees, but curiously enough, was not appointed to the one designated to draw up the Articles of Confederation. Indeed, those three outstanding men, Jefferson, Franklin, and Adams, who had lent the brilliance of their minds to the Declaration of Independence, were notable for their absence on this body. It was composed of a representative from each of the states and proved to be a group of minor characters, as far as statesmanship was concerned. Thomas Nelson was appointed for Virginia. To the conservative John Dickinson of Pennsylvania, the man who had opposed independence to the bitter end, fell the task of draughting a scheme of confederation. The articles, written in his hand, which he finally produced on the twelfth of July, 1776, met with an indifferent reception. They had, as Edward Rutledge observed at the time, "the vice of all his productions to a considerable degree; I mean the vice of refuting too much."[1] And this proved to be true.

To how great an extent Jefferson took part in the discussions concerning the articles of confederation is not definitely known, for the Journal of the Congress does not report such details. John Adams, however, made certain brief notes on the debates in the Committee of the Whole during that July and quotes Jefferson as speaking up very decidedly on certain occasions. Jefferson, likewise, made notes on those earlier debates of the committee, which he incorporated in his "Autobiography." He goes into considerable detail reporting the remarks of such persons as John Adams, Franklin, Chase of Maryland, James Wilson, Dr. Rush, and others. He does not, alas, quote Mr. Jefferson.

These observations, along with those made by Adams, are one of our chief sources of knowledge of the opinions advanced by the various delegates, and of the states they represented, concerning questions of such moment as taxation, representation, the Indians, and western land. There were disputes and arguments in profusion. Small wonder Adams was led to observe, as quoted by Jefferson: "Reason, justice and equity never had weight enough on the face of the earth to govern the councils of men. It is interest alone which does it, and interest alone which can be trusted."[2] There is a slight note of weariness—weariness of the bickering and human frailty—with which Jefferson brings these notes to a close: "These articles, reported July 12, '76, were debated from day to day and time to time for the next two years. ... Maryland alone held off for two years more, acceding to them March 1, '81, and thus closing the obligation."[3]

Jefferson was, however, appointed on various other committees, such as that for Indian affairs, the one to draw up rules for the government of Congress, that for the Philadelphia prisoners reportedly about to be released from jail, the one for encouraging Hessian soldiers to desert, the committee on gold and silver coins—to mention a few of them. With Adams and Franklin, he was likewise appointed on a committee "to prepare a device for a seal for the United States of America." Each of these gentlemen had an idea to offer. Each proposed an allegorical or biblical subject. Jefferson suggested the children of Israel in the wilderness, led by a cloud by day and a pillar of fire by night; on the reverse side the figures of Hengest and Horsa, the chieftains who led the first Saxon bands to settle in England about the year 445. Adams and Franklin asked Jefferson to combine his ideas with those of his colleagues. This he did in a rather elaborate design. For the arms he proposed a shield with six quarterings, denoting the six countries from which America had drawn her settlers. The shield was to be placed within a red border with thirteen escutcheons linked together by a gold chain. Each of these was to bear in black the initials of the thirteen confederated states. The goddess of liberty was to support the shield on one side, the goddess of justice on the other. The crest was to be the eye of Providence in a radiant triangle, with the glory extending beyond the figures. The motto was *E Pluribus Unum*. On the reverse was Pharaoh in a chariot pressing through the divided waters of the Red Sea. Rays from a pillar of fire beamed upon Moses, who stood on shore with raised hand. Franklin's motto, "Rebellion to tyrants is obedience to God," adorned this side.

Although the committee reported on the tenth of August, nothing was done about the matter. It was revived in March 1779, but once more it was allowed to die. Not until June 17, 1782, was the seal we all know finally adopted. It is based, in part, upon a design suggested by Sir John Prestwich to John Adams, then in London. All that remains of Jefferson's seal is the motto with which we are familiar on every coin we handle, *E Pluribus Unum*.

The summer of 1776 was proving a trying one to Jefferson and his colleagues from Virginia. Torn between their desire to assist in creating a united nation and their eager concern over the future of Virginia—the first colony to undergo the metamorphosis of becoming a state—it was at times difficult for them to remain in Philadelphia. "We are in confusion beyond parallel," Edmund Randolph wrote from Williamsburg at this time. "No government is in existence but such as is vested in the hands of the Convention."[4] Richard Henry Lee felt so strongly that, after having introduced his famous resolutions of June 7 declaring "these United Colonies are, and of right ought to be, free and independent states," he set out on the thirteenth for Richmond in order to lend a hand in the determination of the new form of government.

Without doubt Virginia was politically the most advanced of the colonies. As early as May 15, 1776, the Virginia Convention had instructed its delegates in general congress to propose to that respectable body to "declare the United Colonies free and independent states, absolved from all allegiance to, or dependence on, the Crown or Parliament of Great Britain; and that they give the assent of this Colony to such declaration."[5] Having thus declared its independence, the next step was to frame a constitution. A committee of twenty-eight, including men of such distinction as Henry Lee, Robert Carter Nicholas, Archibald Cary, Patrick Henry, Edmund Randolph, Richard Bland, Thomas Ludwell Lee, John Page, and George Mason was appointed to prepare it.

We are left in no doubt that Jefferson desired with all his heart to be in Richmond at this time. Although it was impossible for him yet to know what had happened on the fifteenth, he was fully aware of the sentiment prevalent in Virginia. On the sixteenth he wrote Thomas Nelson, "... should the Convention propose to establish now a form of government perhaps it might be agreeable to recall for a short time their delegates. It is a work of the most interesting nature and such as every individual would wish to have a voice in."[6] The Virginia Convention was deaf to any such suggestion, however—if indeed it was made.

Nothing daunted, Jefferson proceeded to prepare an outline of a constitution for his native state. Although at this time, and for years afterward, he was of the opinion that this Virginia Convention had not the right to adopt a constitution, inasmuch as the establishment of a state government was not a question before the people when the delegates to the convention were elected, Jefferson did not let this deter him. He circumvented this belief by casting his constitution in the form of "a bill for new modeling the form of government, and for establishing the fundamental principles thereof in the future."[7] This work was accomplished between the twenty-seventh of May, the day on which resolutions of the Virginia Convention reached the Continental Congress, and the middle of June, when Jefferson turned his mind to forming the Declaration of Independence. The main features of this constitution have been outlined and discussed in the first volume of this biography, *Jefferson: The Road to Glory*.[8]

Jefferson consigned his paper to the care of George Wythe, who, like Richard Henry Lee, was taking leave of absence from Congress to attend the Virginia Convention. He sent it, as he says, "on the mere possibility that it might suggest something worth incorporating into that before the Convention. He [Edmund Pendleton] informed me afterwards by letter that he received it on the day on which the Committee of the Whole had reported to the House the plan they had agreed to; that that had been so long in hand, so disputed inch by inch, and the subject of so much altercation and debate, that they were worried with the contentions it had produced, and could not, from mere lassitude, have been induced to open the instrument again; but that, being pleased with the Preamble to mine, they adopted it in the House, by way of amendment to the Report of the Committee; and thus my Preamble became tacked to the work of George Mason." [9]

The Virginia Constitution was adopted on June 29 after a battle royal between the conservatives, led by Robert Carter Nicholas, and the radicals, under the banner of Patrick Henry. " 'Tis very much of the democratic kind," wrote Richard Henry Lee in describing the outcome, "although a Governor and second branch of legislation are admitted, for the former is not permitted voice in legislation, he is in all things to be advised by his Privy Council.... Both Houses of the Legislature are to be chosen by the whole body of the people.... The Judges and other great officers of State are to be chosen by joint ballot of both houses.... These are the outlines of our political machine, which I hope is sufficiently guarded against the Monster Tyranny." [10] He adds in a letter the following month: "... the inclosed form of government will show you that this country has in view a permanent system of liberty." [11]

Jefferson refused to accept this constitution as the final solution, however, and his mind continued to be occupied with the problem for many years. A whole section of the *Notes on Virginia* is devoted to an analysis and criticism of it. "This constitution was formed when we were new and unexperienced in the science of government," Jefferson writes there. "It was the first, too, which was formed in the whole United States. No wonder then that time and trial have discovered very capital defects in it." [12] Chief among the half-dozen objections to it which he elaborates in the *Notes* was what he considered an unequal system of representation—that the Senate was "too homogeneous with the House of Delegates," and that "all the power of government, legislative, executive, and judiciary, result to the legislative body." [13]

Jefferson's term as delegate to the Continental Congress was due to expire on August 11. Although he had indicated his desire not to be reappointed, the Virginia Convention on June 20 had elected him for another year. It was a commitment he did not feel able to fulfill. More pressing duties were awaiting him in Virginia. Late in July he asked permission of the Virginia Convention to leave Philadelphia and return home, where a very sick wife was much in need of the comfort of his presence. He wrote Edmund Pendleton, the President of the Convention: "I am sorry the situation of my domestic affairs renders it indispensably necessary that I should solicit the substitution of some other person here in my room. The delicacy of the House will not require me to enter minutely into the private causes which render this necessary. I trust they will be satisfied. I would not urge it again, were it not unavoidable. I shall with cheerfulness continue my duty here till the expiration of our year, by which time I hope it will be convenient for my successor to attend." [14]

Not wishing to leave the Congress without a stanch and vigorous advocate of the Virginia interests, on July 29 he addressed an urgent letter to his coadjutor, Richard Henry Lee. "The minutiae of the Confederation have hitherto engaged us," he writes, "the great points of representation, boundaries, taxation, etc., being left open. For God's sake, for your country's sake, and for my sake, come. I receive by every post such accounts of the state of Mrs. Jefferson's health that it will be impossible for me to disappoint her expectation of seeing me at the time I have promised, which supposed my leaving this place on the 11th of next month.... I pray you to come. I am under a sacred obligation to go home." [15]

It was not until September 3, after an extensive settlement of his affairs, that he was able to leave Philadelphia. He traveled along the fertile valley of the Susquehanna, through Lancaster and York to Frederick. On the seventh he crossed the "Potowmack," as it was still called, and arrived at Monticello two days later. The rest of the lovely, lazy September days were passed in quiet domesticity on his mountaintop. Another bricklayer, Randolph Johnson, was engaged to further the laying of the brick in the main body of the house, then under construction. A fawn was bought for the park, meetings were held with Dr. Gilmer and others concerning the powder money being raised in Albemarle.

These idyllic days came to an end on September 28. On that day

Mr. and Mrs. Jefferson, with their little daughter Martha, now three years old, set off for Williamsburg. After a brief stay there and a consultation with Dr. Brydon concerning his wife's health, Jefferson took his family to The Forest, Mrs. Jefferson's home before her marriage. On the twenty-eighth of October Wythe wrote: "... make use of the house and furniture. I shall be happy if anything of mine can contribute to make your and Mrs. Jefferson's residence in Williamsburg comfortable." [16] That the Jeffersons moved into the ample if undistinguished brick house facing the Palace Green, seems evident from a subsequent letter of Wythe, written a few weeks later, in which he says: "...the conveniency of my house, servants, and furniture to you and Mrs. Jefferson add not a little to their value in my estimation." [17] Here they remained until early December.

The Jeffersons' stay in the Wythe house seems to have been a short one. Although it is not definitely known when Wythe left Congress, it was apparently in December. He wrote on November 18 that he was ready to return to Virginia whenever he was needed for the revision, but in the meantime, he said, "I purpose to abide here if the enemy do not drive me away." [18] He is known not to have been in Philadelphia on January 4, 1777. On December 4 Jefferson notes in his account book that he "pd for carting furniture to Pinkney's 4/"; also that he "took two rooms of Pinkney. No rent agreed on. He pays £25 for whole tenement. If I give him half of this it will be plenty." On the seventh he "gave servants at Mr. Wythe's 14/ and left with Mrs. Drummond for Mr. Wyth 30/." The following day the family started for home by way of Eppington.

At this time, unknown to Jefferson, the Continental Congress had taken the following action: "Agreeable to the order of the day, Congress proceeded to the appointment of commissioners to the court of France. Resolved that three be appointed. The ballots being taken, Mr. Franklin, Mr. Deane, and Mr. Jefferson were elected.... Resolved that an express be sent to Mr. Jefferson to inform him of his appointment and that a copy of the resolve for secrecy be at the same time transmitted to him, and that he be requested to inform the President at what time and place the vessel shall meet him." [19] The purpose of the mission was "to negotiate a treaty of alliance and amity and peace with the court of France." [20]

On September 27, Richard Henry Lee wrote Jefferson from Philadelphia: "The plan of foreign treaty is just finished, and yourself with Dr. Franklin and Mr. Deane now in France, are the trustees to execute this all important business. The great abilities and unshaken virtue, necessary for the execution of what the safety of America does so capitally rest upon, have directed the Congress in their choice; and though ambition may have no influence in this case, yet that distinguished love for your country that has marked your life, will determine you here. In my judgment, the most eminent services that the greatest of her sons can do America, will not more essentially serve her and honor themselves than a successful negotiation with France. With this country everything depends upon it." [21]

The news reached Jefferson in Williamsburg as he was about to take his seat in the House of Delegates. There can be no doubt that the temptation was somewhat akin to those with which Mephistopheles sought to seduce Faust. Visions of European travel which had filled his mind as a youth rose once more before him. This time it would be shared with a loved one. For three days Jefferson hesitated, weighing every aspect of the question. Should he, could he, abandon his cherished and carefully developed plans for the reform and betterment of his Virginia? Should he risk the very frail health of his wife?

By the eleventh he had come to his conclusion. He wrote John Hancock, the President of the Continental Congress, on that day: "Your favor of the 30th together with the resolutions of Congress of the 26th ult. came safe to hand. It would argue great insensibility in me could I receive with indifference so confidential an appointment from your body. My thanks are a poor return for the partiality they have been pleased to entertain for me. No cares for my own person, nor yet for my private affairs, would have induced one moment's hesitation to accept the charge. But circumstances very peculiar in the situation of my family, such as neither permit me to leave nor carry it, compel me to ask leave to decline a service so honorable and at the same time so important to the American cause. The necessity under which I labor and the conflict I have undergone for three days, during which I could not determine to dismiss your messenger, will I hope plead my pardon with Congress." [22]

When the General Assembly met on October 12, the day following this important decision, it was as though a thunderbolt had struck it. With a determination that left the easy-going Virginians aghast, Jefferson promptly seized the leadership, as he had previously done when many of these same men constituted the House of Burgesses. It became plain that the Declaration of Independence, the breaking of all ties with England, was not the culmination of all that he and his associates had been struggling for during the last decade. In Jefferson's opinion it was the commencement of revolution—a social revolution as well as a political one. With fire in his eye and a noble purpose in his heart, he set about destroying much that his countrymen held dear in the way of privileges and much that they accepted or ignored in the way of archaic and inhuman laws. In return he gave them much that he conceived to be for the good for their souls, for the benefit of posterity, and for the glory of mankind.

No one has expressed Jefferson's purpose more ably than he himself. He was persuaded, as he says, "... that our whole code [of law] must be reviewed, adapted to our republican form of government, and now that we had no negatives of councils, governors, and kings to restrain us from doing right, it should be corrected, in all its parts, with a single eye to reason and the good of those for whom it was framed." [23] The moment the House and the committees were organized, Jefferson introduced certain bills which he considered of primary importance, "selecting," as he says, "points of legislation prominent in character and principle, urgent, and indicative of the strength of the general pulse of the reformation." [24] These bills dealt with the establishment of courts of justice intended to supersede those under the royal government, with the removal of the capital from Williamsburg to Richmond, and with the naturalization of foreigners. They embraced likewise such heretical proposals as the bill to revolutionize the laws concerning the inheritance of property, thus destroying the cherished principle of entail, and the passionately disputed bill for religious freedom.

Ideas as radical as these were no proper provender for a legislature of Virginia planters. In championing this bill, as well as the one abolishing entails, Jefferson engaged in one of the most bitter struggles of his career and won for himself more enemies than by any other act in his long and eventful life. The progressive element was well entrenched in the Assembly, however; and, although the conservatives again called to the colors such able veterans as Robert Carter Nicholas and Edmund Pendleton, it was of no avail. The bill ending entails became law on October 23, eleven days after its introduction. The "Bill for Establishing Religious Freedom" was not to be so quickly disposed of. With its proud overture, from which we have already quoted, it was hotly debated at every session of the Assembly from 1776 until 1779, when it was finally and victoriously written into the book as "The Statute of Virginia for Religious Freedom."

"So far," Jefferson observes, "we were proceeding in the details of reformation only." His next work was to introduce a bill quite as unpalatable. This was for the complete revision of the laws of the state. It was passed on October 25. On November 5 the Senate and the House balloted on their respective nominees for the committee to undertake this task, and it was "resolved that Thomas Jefferson, Edmund Pendleton, George Wythe, George Mason, and Thomas Ludwell Lee, Esquires, be appointed a committee to revise the laws of this commonwealth." [25] Mason and Lee resigned very shortly. The work of revisal thus fell to the lot of the three other men.

The revisal has been fully discussed by the author in *Jefferson: The Road to Glory*.[26] It has been pointed out how Jefferson by these revolutionary October bills bestowed upon his fellow Virginians a freedom such as they had never visioned, and perhaps never desired. Some time in this year of 1776 he had jotted down certain notes endorsed only, "scraps early in the revolution." They were apparently from his speeches before the House of Delegates during these momentous debates. He had written, "The care of every man's soul belongs to himself. But what if he neglect the care of it? Well, what if he neglect the care of his health or estate, which more nearly relate to the state? Will the magistrate make a law that he shall not be poor or sick? Laws provide against injury from others, but not from ourselves. God himself will not save men against their wills." [27] Wise beyond the number of his years, Jefferson in this October set about showing his countrymen how they might care for their souls, whether they willed it or not.

The revisers met in Fredericksburg on January 13. It was a question whether to "abolish the whole existing system of laws and prepare a new and complete institute, or preserve the general system and only modify it to the present state of things." [28] The conservative Pendleton, "contrary to his usual disposition in favor of ancient things," was disposed toward the former proceeding. As he practically withdrew from the conferences before long and became a figure to whom the other two men occasionally deferred, Jefferson and Wythe were able to carry on the work according to their own ideas. These involved changes of the most fundamental character, changes destined to alter the very fabric of the life and customs in Virginia.

To Jefferson fell the revision of the criminal code. The resulting bill, eradicating the incredibly brutal survivals of an archaic conception of criminal law, is a monument to his humanity. It was also he who proposed and successfully fought for the abolition of the time-honored law of primogeniture. Three other proposals made at this time, which he describes as "a systematical plan of general education," likewise testify to his enlightenment and to his eagerness for disseminating the democracy in which he so ardently believed. These are the "Bill for the More General Diffusion of Knowledge," "For Amending the Constitution of William and Mary College," and "For Establishing a Public Library." All were bitterly contested as another onslaught on the citadel of wealth and privilege. Who could expect a Tidewater aristocrat—for such these people considered themselves—to step down from his pedestal in favor of persons of "genius and virtue" from the mountains or the lands beyond? Who could expect him to concur in such sentiments as introduce the bill proposing universal education? "Whereas it is generally true," writes the idealist that was Jefferson, "that people will be happiest whose laws are best, and are best administered, and that laws will be wisely formed, and honestly administered, in proportion as those who form and administer them are wise and honest; whence it becomes expedient for promoting the public happiness that those persons whom nature hath endowed with genius and virtue should be rendered by liberal education worthy to receive, and able to guard, the sacred deposit of the rights and liberties of their fellow citizens, and that they should be called to that charge without regard to wealth, birth, or other accidental condition or circumstance." [29]

To carry out his ideas, Jefferson's bill provided that the state should be divided into hundreds. In each of these a school was to be built, so located that the children might attend daily. "At every one of those schools shall be taught reading, writing, and common arithmetic, and the books which shall be used therein for instructing the children to read shall be such as will at the same time make them acquainted with Graecian, Roman, English, and American history. At these schools all the free children, male and female, resident within the respective hundred, shall be entitled to receive tuition gratis for the term of three years, and as much longer at their private expense as their parents, guardians, or friends shall think proper." [30] This bill was not acted upon until 1796, and then not adopted as introduced. The proposal that such children of the indigent "whom nature hath fitly formed and disposed to become useful instruments for the public, should be sought for and educated at the common expense of all" was one which required many years for assimilation.

The bill for amending the constitution of the College of William and Mary, "to enlarge its sphere of science and to make it in fact a University," was the second step in Jefferson's educational revolution. The college was, as he observed, "an establishment purely of the Church of England; the Visitors were required to be all of that Church; the Professors to subscribe to its Thirty-nine Articles; its students to learn its catechism; and one of its fundamental objects was declared to be to raise up Ministers for that Church." [31] In his bill Jefferson states that "the experience of near one hundred years hath proved that the said college, thus amply endowed by the public, hath not answered their expectations, and there is reason to hope that it would become more useful if certain articles in its constitution were altered and amended." [82] The youthful reformer goes on to declare that it now "becomes the peculiar duty of the Legislature, at this time, to aid and improve the seminary in which those who are to be the future guardians of the rights and liberties of their country, may be endowed with science and virtue, to watch and preserve the sacred deposit." [83] With this end in view, Jefferson placed the affairs of the college under the control of a board of five visitors appointed annually by joint ballot of both houses of the Assembly. These men were to "be deemed the lawful successors of the first trustees, and invested with all the rights, powers, and capacities given to them, save only so far as the same shall be abridged by this act, nor shall they be restrained in their legislation by the royal prerogative or the laws of the kingdom of England; of the canons or the constitution of the English church." [84] Jefferson went even further in abolishing the school of theology and in proposing that henceforth instead of the president and six professors, as licensed in the original charter, there be eight. In place of "teaching the Hebrew tongue and expounding the holy scriptures, explaining the commonplaces of divinity, and controversies with heretics," these gentlemen were to teach such revolutionary subjects as "the laws of nature and of nations, fine arts, law, mathematics, civil and ecclesiastical history, medicine, natural philosophy and natural history, as well as ancient and modern languages." In short, Jefferson proposed to create an institution in all essentials the counterpart of a modern university.

The work of revisal continued through the years 1777 and 1778. The last meeting of the revisers took place in Williamsburg in February 1779, when they "examined critically our several parts, sentence by sentence, scrutinizing and amending until we had agreed on the whole. We then returned home and had fair copies made of our several parts." [85] It was not until June 18, 1779, after Jefferson had already been installed as governor, that the committee presented the report of their work to the Assembly. It was accompanied by a letter signed by Jefferson and Wythe: "The committee appointed in pursuance of an act of General Assembly, passed in 1776, intituled 'an Act for the revision of the laws,' have according to the requisitions of the said act gone through that work and prepared 126 bills, the titles of which are stated in the enclosed catalogue. Some of these bills have been presented to the House of Delegates in the course of the present session, two or three of them delivered to members of that House at their request to be presented; the rest are in the two bundles which accompany this; these we take the liberty of presenting through you to the General Assembly...." [36]

The Assembly proved somewhat apathetic to the enthusiasm of the revisers. Increasingly involved in a multitude of internal problems, to say nothing of the war, it displayed a far less passionate desire to reform its complacent constituency. "The Speaker laid before the House a letter from the Governor and George Wythe,..." the *Journal of the House of Delegates* tells us, "the said letter was read, and together with the said list and copies ordered to be referred to the consideration of the next session of the Assembly." [37] It was not until 1784 that the report of the revisers was printed. In the session of the legislature in 1785 and 1786, 56 of the 126 bills with amendments were finally written into the statute books.

Looking back on his eager and enthusiastic activities of this period from the distance of nearly a decade, and the vantage point of another world, Jefferson was able to answer the queries of a Dutch friend, the Comte van Hogendorp, with modesty and with the detachment of mature years. "If you had formed any considerable expectations from our revised code of laws, you will be much disappointed," he writes. "It contains not more than three or four laws which could strike the attention of a foreigner. Had it been a digest of all our laws, it would not have been comprehensible or instructive but to a native. But it is still less so, as it digests only the British statutes and our own acts of Assembly, which are but a supplementary part of our law. The great basis of it is anterior to the date of the Magna Charta, which is the oldest statute extant. The only merit of this work is that it may remove from our bookshelves about twenty folio volumes of our statutes, retaining all the parts of them which either their own merit or the established system of laws required." [38]

II. Europe Comes to Jefferson

IN THE YEARS immediately following the outbreak of the Revolution, Jefferson was to enjoy one of the most stimulating and agreeable experiences of his life. In his early manhood, as we have seen, he had been preoccupied with dreams of European travel. Now Europe was to come to him, bringing him some of the treasures and many of the pleasures he had long envisioned. It was to come, first, in the persons of Philip Mazzei and Carlo Bellini, two Tuscan gentlemen who were henceforth to become an integral part of the Virginia scene. France came with the arrival of the Chevalier d'Anmours, the first French consul to Virginia, and later with the Marquis de Chastellux. Finally, there were the German officers of the so-called "Convention Troops," lodged in Albemarle County after the defeat of Burgoyne. These were General von Riedesel and Jefferson's particular favorites, Baron von Geismar and Jean Louis de Unger, a young lieutenant of the Brunswick troops.

Jefferson clutched at Europe when it came to him. There was much these cultivated and agreeable men, trained in the courts of their respective countries, had to give him—and much they were to receive in return. To find a man of Jefferson's caliber in what was to them a wilderness, was a revelation. Jefferson, in turn, made them intimates of his own home and introduced them to his circle of friends in Albemarle. If they could not bring the architecture, the painting, and the sculpture Jefferson was later so profoundly to admire, they did bring ideas which gave rise to the philosophical conversations in which he was fond of indulging. Above all, they brought their music, "an enjoyment the deprivation of which with us cannot be calculated," as Jefferson said to Bellini.

We have no description of the appearance of these men. We know little of their way of life or their actions, except for General von Riedesel. They live in no memoirs and in no travel notes. Mazzei was the only one of them who wrote down his recollections, and that when he was so well advanced in years that the figures who wander through his early life are given only a chance phrase. All we know of them is, for the most part, through their correspondence with Jefferson, whom they found quite as remarkable as he found them. Except for the Italians, who continued to live in Virginia or have some connection with it, friendships destined to endure for years were crowded into a few brief months. This was particularly true of the German officers who arrived in Virginia in January 1779. Jefferson seems to have met them almost immediately and entered into the most friendly relations. Riedesel and Geismar lived near by, but De Unger's letters are dated *"Aux Barraques,"* where the troops were quartered, a couple of hours' ride away.

The year these men spent in Albemarle before being exchanged was a particularly busy one for Jefferson. The work on the revisal was being concluded, and in June he was elected governor. All spring there was a constant going and coming between Monticello and Williamsburg. On February 9 Jefferson left for Elk Hill, where he spent some time, and reached Williamsburg on the twentieth. Mrs. Jefferson appears to have remained at home with Martha and six-months-old Polly. By the ninth of March Jefferson was back at Monticello for nearly two months, a period which doubtless marked the flowering of his new friendships. It was at this time that the Jeffersons, General von Riedesel, and General Phillips, whom Jefferson describes as "the proudest man of the proudest nation on earth," and who was later to repay Jefferson's kindness with typical British rudeness, were calling and dining back and forth—a time when officers, even though prisoners of war, were treated as gentlemen, and when war had not yet become quite the contest in bestiality which was to mark it in the twentieth century. Jefferson took the stand, as he wrote Phillips, that "the great cause which divides our countries is not to be decided by individual animosities. The harmony of private societies cannot weaken national efforts." [1]

On May 2 Jefferson was once more at Elk Hill, and on the eighth of the month he took his seat in the House of Delegates. He was not at Monticello again until July 31, when he and his family stayed there for nearly two months while John Page, the lieutenant governor, acted in Jefferson's place. When he returned to Williamsburg, on September 27, he found himself so completely engrossed in the duties of his office that he did not leave the capital again for over a year, except for a flying trip to Monticello at the end of February 1780.

If we have no descriptions of the German officers, except that of their extraordinarily gay appearance in blue regimentals with bright red facings and silver frogs, broad lace upon their hats and coats, one of them has given us a picture of the Jefferson household at this time. It was sent to Jefferson on December 1, 1780, by Jacob Rübsamen, a German who had a powder mill at Manchester. He had seen it in a Hamburg newspaper which had been received by one of the prisoners at the Barracks. "My only recuperation at present," writes this unnamed officer, who may very well have been Geismar or De Unger, "is to learn the English language. I have free access to a copious and well-chosen library of Colonel Jefferson, Governor of Virginia. The father of this learned man was also a favorite of the muses. There is now a map of his of Virginia extant, the best work of the kind. The Governor possesses a noble spirit in building. He is now finishing an elegant building projected according to his own fancy. In his parlor he is erecting in the ceiling a compass of his own invention by which he can know the strength as well as the directions of the winds. I have promised to paint the compass for it. He was much pleased with a fancy painting of mine.... As all Virginians are fond of music, he is particularly so. You will find in his house an elegant harpsichord, pianoforte, and some violins. The latter he performs well upon himself, the former his lady touches very skillfully, and who is in all respects a very agreeable, sensible, and accomplished lady." [2]

Philip Mazzei may be said to represent the advance guard of the European invasion of Virginia. His arrival preceded the actual outbreak of the Revolution by several years. He came to Virginia late in November 1773. Jefferson speaks of him as "well informed and possessed of a masculine understanding." He may be described as something of a revolutionist, not inciting revolutions but infected with the ideas that culminate in them. He was a man who had led and was to continue to lead an adventurous life. Without ever becoming a person of real consequence himself, he was useful to others and enjoyed the confidence of many of the leading figures of his day. For some years before coming to Virginia he had lived in London. There, in 1766, he made the acquaintance of Benjamin Franklin, Thomas Adams of Williamsburg, and other Americans, chiefly from Virginia. Mr. Adams, he writes, "being a close friend of Jefferson, made it possible for Mr. Jefferson and me to know a great deal about each other some years before we actually met." On his arrival in Williamsburg, Mazzei was immediately taken into Jefferson's circle—indeed, he stayed at the house of Jefferson's brother-in-law, Francis Eppes.

It was Mazzei's intention not only to export wheat and other articles, but to introduce into Virginia the cultivation of the grapevine, a project in which Jefferson was deeply interested. To find land suitable for this purpose he started with Adams on a journey to Augusta County, beyond the Blue Ridge. Here Adams had recently purchased a large tract of land where he proposed to settle. En route the men stopped at Monticello for several days. "We arrived in the evening," Mazzei writes, "and the following morning while the others were still asleep, Jefferson and I went to take a walk in the neighborhood. He took me to the home of a poor man who owned a cabin and about 400 acres of land, which bordered on his own.... As Mr. Jefferson ... had much more land than he needed, he said he would give me a tract of 2000 acres. By the time we returned home, everyone was up. Looking at Mr. Jefferson, Mr. Adams said: 'I see by your expression that you've taken him away from me. I knew you would do that.'" Thus Jefferson acquired a new and congenial neighbor, one who was later to be influential in introducing him to "the circle of literati" whose society he enjoyed in Paris.

With the hospitality characteristic of eighteenth-century Virginia, Jefferson invited Mazzei to stay at Monticello while he was getting established. Mazzei responded by creating a situation which his host had doubtless not foreseen. He returned to Williamsburg to get his possessions, which included a traveling companion, Mrs. Martin.

He married her and brought her and her daughter along. The angelic Mrs. Jefferson, as Mazzei calls her, refused to be dismayed; her husband, however, after a proper acquaintance with the lady, was led to one of the rare discourtesies he is known to have uttered, by referring to her as "that bitch." [3]

Mazzei set about clearing his land and building his house, which he named "Colle." Jefferson, he tells us, "assumed the task of supervising the execution of my plans." [4] Whether Jefferson designed the house for him, as he later did for many of his friends, is speculative. There was a center building with four smaller ones forming a quadrangle, two of them octagonal in shape, surmounted by a cupola. Here Mazzei lived for four years, in almost daily communication with Jefferson concerning political and agricultural matters. "We agreed," says Mazzei, "to announce through the newspapers the publication of a periodical, by which we aimed to show the people the true state of affairs.... As I knew the views of the cabinet at the Court of St. James and particularly of the persons involved, I was to write the articles in my native tongue, and he [Jefferson] would translate them into English.... After he had translated a few numbers of my periodical, he asked me to write in English, explaining that he would correct me whenever necessary. I was afraid that the work of translating had bored him, but he assured me to the contrary, saying: 'You have a way of expressing yourself in your own tongue which I cannot translate without lessening the effect.' So I wrote in English. By the time he got through making the corrections on the first sheet, it looked as if a plague of flies had settled on it. But soon there were fewer corrections." [5]

Meanwhile viniculture was not lost from sight. Mazzei had brought with him a number of Tuscan laborers who cleared the land and planted vines, both imported and selected stock of native wild grapes. In November 1774 there was a proposal to form a company for the making of wine and olive oil, both of which had long been, and continued to be, schemes on which Jefferson laid much stress. The backwash of the Revolution, however, destroyed this plan. The fall of 1778 found Jefferson offering Mazzei the post of Virginia's economic agent in Europe, which he accepted, and what might be called the Italian interlude came to an end.

That Jefferson's early enthusiasm for Mazzei did not continue unabated, that the European mission may have been a way of taking care of a neighbor who had become difficult, we may gather from a remark to Madison made when Mazzei returned briefly to Virginia, a few years later. "I am induced to this quick reply [to your letter]," Jefferson writes, "by an alarming paragraph in it, which is that Mazzei is coming to Annapolis. I tremble at the idea. I know he will be worse to me than a return of my double quotidien headache." [6]

Meanwhile, when the brig which Mazzei had purchased and sent to Leghorn with a cargo of wheat returned to Virginia, it brought Carlo Bellini and his wife. He was a friend of Mazzei, a former official in the tax office, who likewise sought to improve his fortunes by coming to the New World. With Mazzei and his wife, the Bellinis found shelter under the hospitable roof of Monticello when they first arrived. A friendship in which both delighted sprang up between Jefferson and the warmhearted Italian, a friendship that was to endure until Bellini's death in 1804. The letters they exchanged during Jefferson's residence in Europe are the only ones known in which he is addressed not with the usual and formal "Sir," but by his given name—as "My dearest Thomas" or "My most esteemed friend and patron, Thomas." Not even John Page ventured more than "My dear Jefferson." In return Jefferson assured Bellini, "You are often the object of my thoughts and always of my affection."

Bellini lived with Mazzei at Colle for some time. The establishment was broken up, however, when Mazzei went to Europe; and Bellini removed to Williamsburg, where he had been appointed the first professor of modern languages at the College of William and Mary. He "knew French very well," Mazzei tells us, "and had a smattering of German and Spanish." In May 1778 he had likewise been named French Secretary to the Council. The Latin of the members may have been excellent, but their French seems to have left much to be desired. In view of the "increasing commerce and intercourse with the French nation and often receiving and sending despatches of the greatest importance in that language," the notice of his appointment reads, "the Executive power has been repeatedly embarrassed as the members of it are not accurately acquainted with the French tongue."

Jefferson seemed to turn to Bellini when he wanted to unburden his heart. It was to him that he addressed his famous letter: "Behold me at length on the vaunted scene of Europe!" in which he describes "how this new scene has struck a savage of the mountains of America."[7] This in reply to Bellini's graceful challenge: "To pay compliments to a philosopher of your dignity would be equal to blasphemy; therefore I adopt the sincere American style, persuaded and convinced that even though you were Minister Plenipotentiary of the Supreme Being, you would not change your manner of thinking, neither would you be other than Thomas Jefferson."[8]

That this friendship did not cool with the years, that Jefferson preserved his feeling for this amiable man, is expressed in a letter written from Monticello twenty-five years after their first meeting, in response to one from Bellini: "It recalled to my mind many very dear scenes which passed while we had the happiness of possessing you here. Events have separated the actors and called them to other stages; but neither time, distance, nor events have weakened my affection for them. The portrait of one of them [Mrs. Bellini] which you propose to gratify me with, would be placed among my most precious reliques. But why, my friend, separate yourself from the portrait till you go to rejoin the original? Then, if I am living, let it dwell with me till I can join you all."[9]

Jefferson's Italian portrait gallery would not be complete without the mention of Giovanni Fabbroni, a man whom Jefferson apparently never saw yet with whom he corresponded intermittently for forty years. He is characterized in the *Enciclopedia Italiana* as "*homo politico & poligrafo*," who was an agent in Paris and London for the Grand Duke Leopold of Tuscany and was subsequently made an honorary professor at the University of Pisa. Mazzei tells us that when he was in Tuscany in the summer of 1773, preparing to leave for America, he was approached by two young men who wanted to go with him. One was Signor Giovanni Fabbroni, a youth of twenty-one. "I was favorably impressed by his appearance," says Mazzei.

"I was struck by his knowledge and even more by his sound reasoning powers, especially considering his age....[10] The next time I saw him, I told him that Mr. Thomas Jefferson, a Virginian of great ability, an encyclopedist, most distinguished in the pure sciences and in law, who had learned our language by himself without ever having heard it spoken, would greatly enjoy the company of a cultured young Tuscan; and that that fact would give him, Fabbroni, an opportunity to succeed in America. But since I wished to ship a cargo of grain to Leghorn as soon as I reached Virginia, I thought it best to await my further instructions... and he could join me on the return trip of that ship."[11]

As things turned out, Fabbroni never came to America. Shortly after his conversation with Mazzei he had been introduced to the Grand Duke of Tuscany by the Abbot Fontana, a distinguished physicist, and the Grand Duke had taken the youth, whom he considered of unusual ability, into his service. Despite this, his correspondence with Jefferson gives the impression that the two men were well acquainted. Fabbroni was the first European with whom Jefferson entered into an exchange of scientific ideas by letter, as he was later to do with many of them. The majority of those extant, and they are few in number, were written between 1776 and 1779, when Fabbroni was in Paris. They are sometimes in English, sometimes in Italian. Whether Jefferson met him when he went there in 1784 is not known. In 1786 he was residing in Florence, and Jefferson wrote him to secure for George Wythe a history of the Taliaferro family, into which Wythe had married, along with a coat of arms, a commission which he executed.

The first letter of the correspondence which is preserved, so far as is known, is one from Fabbroni written from Paris on September 15, 1776. It presupposes an earlier one from Jefferson. "'Tis needless to tell you that the present troubles of America postponed the return of Mr. Mazzei's vessel to Virginia [and] deprived me also of the pleasure of the kin [kind] offers you were so good as to make me. I was not a little chagrined to find myself all at once bereft (at least for some time) of the hopes of seeing that fine country, the fertility of which can be equaled by nothing but the magnanimity of its inhabitants. I hope you will let me know the particulars of the present war as far as they relate to your welfare, which your silence and that of my friends in that country has made me vastly uneasy about. Yet in so good a cause as that of liberty, there can be no doubt but event[s] will be crowned with success.... I wraite [write] you at present from Paris where any service to you I hope you will command me...." [12]

Jefferson did not reply to this letter until June 8, 1778, and he used the occasion to give the young man the account of "the particulars of the present war" which he desired. "We discover," he writes, "that our enemies have filled Europe with Thrasonic accounts of victories they had never won and conquests they were fated never to make. While these accounts alarmed our friends in Europe, they afforded us diversions. We have long been out of fear for the event of the war. I enclose you a list of the killed, wounded, and captives of the enemy from the commencement of the hostilities at Lexington, in April 1775, until November 1777, since which time there has been no event of any consequence. This is the best history of the war that can be brought within the compass of a letter. I believe the account to be near the truth, though it is difficult to get at the numbers lost by the enemy with absolute precision.... I think that upon the whole it [our loss], has been about one half the number lost by them.... This difference is ascribed to our superiority in taking aim when we fire, every soldier in our army having been intimate with his gun from his infancy. If there could have been a doubt before as to the event of the war, it is now totally removed by the interposition of France and of the generous alliance she has entered into with us."

Fabbroni was apparently a fellow music lover, for Jefferson now proceeds to unburden his heart on that subject. It must be born in mind that this was the period of ascendancy in Italian music, and that, with the exception of Mozart and one or two other German composers, it was mostly Italian music with which Jefferson was familiar. "If there is a gratification which I envy any people in this world," he writes, "it is to your country its music. This is the favorite passion of my soul, and fortune has cast my lot in a country where it is in a state of deplorable barbarism. From the line of life in which we conjecture you to be, I have for some time lost the hope of seeing you here. Should the event prove so, I shall ask your assistance in procuring a substitute, who may be proficient in singing, etc., on the harpsichord. I should be contented to receive such an one two or three years hence, when it is hoped he may come more safely and find here a greater plenty of those useful things which commerce alone can furnish." [13]

Jefferson goes on to tell Fabbroni how it is his ambition to employ among his domestic servants those who, in addition to their regular duties, could play various orchestral instruments. "Without meaning to give you trouble," he continues, "perhaps it may be practicable for you, in ordinary intercourse with your people, to find such men disposed to come to America. Sobriety and good nature will be desirable parts of their characters. If you think such a plan practicable, and will be so kind as to inform me what will be necessary to be done on my part, I will take care that it shall be done...."

This letter unfortunately never reached Fabbroni. It suffered from the misfortunes of war and was intercepted by the British. Thus Jefferson's plan was never realized, and the correspondence on scientific and philosophical subjects never developed, although the two men occasionally wrote each other over a period of years.

On the conclusion of the Treaty of Alliance with France, the question of representatives of that country to the various states came up. On July 27, 1779, Gerard, the French Minister to the United States, addressed a letter to the President of Congress enclosing an appointment of the Chevalier d'Anmours as Vice-Consul to the State of Virginia.[14] He had already occupied the post of consul in Maryland. On November 23 Jefferson wrote the Speaker of the House of Delegates, saying: "There is reason to believe that the appointment of a Consul to reside in this state on the part of his most Christian Majesty either has been already or will shortly be made. I must submit to the General Assembly the expediency of considering whether our laws have settled with precision the prerogatives and jurisdiction to which such a person is entitled by the usages of nations; and putting the office on the footing they would wish it to rest." [15]

The Chevalier, however, had ideas of his own on these matters—or perhaps represented those of his government in regard to extra-territorial rights. He lost no time in making them clear. On December 8, in a letter to Jefferson, he enclosed a memorial stating his position in no uncertain terms. The peremptory and uncompromising tone of his communication is no doubt due largely to his lack of familiarity with the niceties of expression of the English language.

"I have the honor of informing Your Excellency, and the honorable House of Assembly," he writes, "that, having lately received a commission that appoints me Consul of France for his most Christian Majesty in the State of Virginia, I accept with the highest degree of pleasure. . . .

"I have the honor to subjoin to this letter, a memorial containing some eventual demands in favor of his Majesties subjects, and the French nation in general that do, or will hereafter, reside in Virginia. . . .

"I will always be ready to answer any objections that might be made to them. Yet as an entire mistake of principles as well as of motives might give room to form some which I apprehend, I choose to answer them before they are made, by an ample explanation of my motives.

"The reason why I demand that French subjects that are settled, or will hereafter settle in Virginia, be entirely submitted to the Consuls of France is that, being under their direct administration, the conduct of those same subjects would be more known to them; and by that means they would be more able to stop or prevent an immensity of dissentions which might arise from the difference of languages, manners, etc., and propagate those ancient national prejudices which every true patriot endeavors to wipe off.

"The reason why I demand some privileges in favor of those same subjects is to render that authority and administration agreeable and advantageous to them, at the same time that those same privileges would be useful to the trade of both nations. For foreign merchants will always prefer to trade with those countries where they shall be certain to find a protector, immediate and strict justice, and privileges with security for their ships and commercial operations.

"If I demand that the Government of Virginia would make all possible and proper regulations to stop all desertions and prevent emigrations from France and her possessions, it is not only because I think it an act of justice, but also because I conceive it to be one of prudence. By the nature of things every man will emigrate from every other country but France will diminish the number of the enemies of America; from France it would lessen the number of her friends, and such friends, that will always be ready to take up arms in her defense...." [16]

If Jefferson was stunned by these frank observations, we do not know it. His reply does not appear to have been preserved. He submitted the memorial to the House of Delegates, where it was referred to the Committee of the Whole, "on the bill for the protection and encouragement of the commerce of nations acknowledging the independence of the United States of America." [17] Three weeks later, on December 30, Jefferson issued the following proclamation: "Whereas the General Assembly by their act entitled 'An act for the protection and encouragement of commerce of nations acknowledging the independence of the United States of America' have authorized the Executive to receive and admit into this commonwealth a Consul or Consuls from any state which shall have acknowledged the independence of the United States of America, have given them jurisdiction to determine all controversies between the subjects or citizens of their own state... and His Most Christian Majesty, our great and good ally, having been pleased after declaring and supporting our independence, farther to manifest his willingness to cultivate friendship, commerce, and free intercourse with these states, by establishing consuls to be resident therein, and hath appointed the Sieur Chevalier D'Anmours to exercise that office within this commonwealth—I have therefore thought fit, by and with the advice of the Council of State, to declare that the said Chevalier D'Anmours is received within this commonwealth as Consul... and that he is entitled to all the exemptions, prerogatives, and jurisdictions belonging to the said office...." [18]

Despite this somewhat formidable entrance into Virginia and despite the fact that he was at times rather difficult to handle, Jefferson found D'Anmours a sympathetic companion. It was the familiar tie of books, of similar literary and philosophical tastes, that drew them together. D'Anmours's "hobby horse," as he wrote, was natural history. Already on September 6, 1779, Richard Henry Lee had written Jefferson a letter introducing the Chevalier: "I have had the pleasure of being acquainted with this gentleman since early in the year 1777, and I have found in him the same unshaken attachment to our cause in times of its great depression as others are willing to show in the day of its prosperity. The goodness of the Chevalier's head is by no means inferior to that of his heart, few men having more knowledge of books and the world than he possesses. It gives me pleasure to introduce such a person to your acquaintance."[19]

An introduction such as this was the open sesame to Jefferson's heart and to the familiar life at Monticello. There are, alas, very few tangible remains of their intercourse. Jefferson was, unfortunately for us, not in the habit of commenting on his companions or friends of every day in writing to others. There is, however, an interchange of letters between the two men preserved among the Jefferson papers. From them we learn that they were on terms sufficiently friendly for D'Anmours to have stayed at Monticello at a time when Jefferson appears to have been absent. D'Anmours writes him from there on October 25, 1780, on his way to Baltimore through Charlottesville and Winchester.

"It will appear to you very strange," he says, "that I should communicate political news from this place where I expected to hear of none out of the usual sort. Yet I have one which, though it may at first seem rather extraordinary, is not altogether quite improbable.

"Yesterday, after I had finished my letter to Mrs. Jefferson, I went to dine with Dr. Gilmer. In the evening, just as I left the town, I overtook a British officer who was riding the same road I did. As he heard me speak French to my servant, he addressed me in that language and asked me what news? I told him what I knew. He then asked me where I thought General Clinton was? I answered him in New York. He then told me that that same day they had received news at the Barracks that he was gone to Halifax on account of a French fleet having landed at Annapolis in the bay at [illegible] with a view of attacking the first of three places. The following circumstances immediately occurred to my mind and may serve as a basis for the reliability of that intelligence...."

D'Anmours proceeds to theorize for several pages on the probable activity of the fleet. He then continues: "You will learn from my letter to Mrs. Jefferson how I was punished for having neglected the advice you gave me of getting a good dinner before I went to Mr. [illegible]. This is the only instance of inhospitality I ever met from Virginians, and another proof that national virtues as well as others, though ever so general, have their exceptions. I leave Montecielo today to continue my journey by Staunton and Winchester to Baltimore." [20]

Jefferson's reply, dated November 30, 1780, is of interest from several angles. "I received your favor from Baltimore," he writes, "and shall carefully attend to the notifying you of the arrival of any fleet here from your nation, or other circumstance which I may think interesting to you. The enemy have left us, as you will before have heard. Though I do not wish for new occasions of calling together my countrymen to try their valor, yet I really wish, as they were called together, the enemy had stayed to give them a little exercise and some lessons in real war. Were it not that an invasion of our State at Portsmouth shuts the only door of our commerce, I had rather fight our share of them than send 300 miles to seek them in a climate more fatal than the sword.

"I am at present busily employed for Mons. Marbois without his knowing it, and have to acknowledge to him the mysterious obligation for making me much better acquainted with my own country than I ever was before. His questions as to this country, put into my hand by Mr. Jones, I take every occasion which presents itself of procuring answers to. Some of them, however, are to never be answered till I shall [have] leisure to return to Monticello, where alone the materials exist which can enable anyone to answer them.

"I am exceedingly anxious to get a copy of 'Le Grande Encyclopédie,' but am really frightened from attempting it through the mercantile channel. Dear as it is originally and loaded as it would come with the enormous advances which they lay on under pretext of insurance on it, etc. ... You once thought that some means might be fallen on of effecting this importation by some vessel of war, and perhaps of making the remittance in tobacco in the same way. Should any such occur, I shall be greatly obliged to your availing me of it and will surely answer every engagement you may make for me." [21]

Whether D'Anmours exerted himself to get the *Grande Encyclopédie* we do not know. Surprisingly enough, it is not listed in Jefferson's manuscript catalogue of his library of 1783, nor is it among the books sold to the Library of Congress in 1815. In any case, it was not until twenty-four years later that there again seems to have been an exchange of letters between Jefferson and D'Anmours, although the account book shows that in March 1784 Jefferson sent him £17/16/6 to pay for twelve silver spoons. On September 30, 1804, D'Anmours broke the long silence by writing his old friend and patron. Time and circumstances had altered both their lives, and the free interchange of ideas of the past was no longer possible.

"If the hurricane that has so much agitated the ocean of the Political World since I had the pleasure of seeing you last on the borders of the Atlantic," D'Anmours writes, "have not entirely erased from your memory the features of a man you always treated with a distinguished kindness, you will perhaps hear with a smile of satisfaction that that man is still alive, and still full of the same sentiments of attachment and respect with which you inspired him from the first instant of his acquaintance with you. Retired from public affairs ever since the death of the last and most unfortunate of the Kings of France, I have also at the same time withdrawn from the active part of society, and from my retreat in the bosom of the immense forests of Louisiana have remained a [illegible] and almost indifferent spectator of the scenes that have been acted in the theater of the world. ..." [22]

Jefferson, now President of the United States, did not reply until six months later. A brief note of acknowledgment was dispatched on March 29, 1805, and with that all communication between them ceased.

The arrival in Albemarle of the Convention Troops, four thousand in number, marked the coming of another phase of European culture.

The troops consisted of six English regiments, with a detachment of a seventh, five regiments of Brunswick dragoons, in addition to Hessian artillery and a battalion of grenadiers.[23] Perhaps by their very strangeness and difference in language, the German troops seem to have dominated the scene. To this day the prisoners of that period are referred to in Albemarle County as "the Hessians." In their coarse linen jackets and overalls, with knapsacks containing their regimental coats, they were a familiar sight to the natives. The English Major General Phillips was at first in command of the troops, but he was shortly succeeded by General von Riedesel, a genial veteran of the Seven Years' War. It was not long before he was on terms of friendship with the Jefferson household.

His advent in Charlottesville coincided with the moment Mazzei was preparing to leave on his European mission. Colle was for rent. Mazzei tells us that Jefferson had already rented it while Mazzei was in Williamsburg to "four young officers who had been taken prisoners. One of them was German and the others English." When General von Riedesel arrived, he "felt that the young men could easily find accommodations elsewhere; while he, aside from his advanced age [he was fifty-one years old at the time] and his duty to remain near his troops, which were quartered in the neighborhood, was expecting his wife that same evening, with their two children, and he had no place in which to shelter them."[24]

The young officers, of course, agreed to letting the General have the house, and here he established himself with his family. Mme. von Riedesel with her children had made the perilous voyage across the Atlantic, had been with her husband in Canada, then followed him to Cambridge, where he was a prisoner. Finally, after a harrowing journey of seven hundred miles in the dead of winter, she arrived in Virginia in January 1779. It proved to be anything but the paradise she, as well as the troops, had been led to expect. It was a winter most unusual for that country, when it lay buried under feet of snow. "There could not have been a more unlucky concurrance of circumstances," writes Jefferson, "then when these troops first came. The Barracks were unfinished for want of labor, the spell of weather the worst ever known within the memory of man, no stores of bread laid in, the roads, by the weather and number of wagons, soon rendered impassable." [25]

Colle proved too small for the General's family, which included adjutants, secretaries, and servants. Another building, with a long central hall and rooms on each side, was erected before long. Every day there gathered about his hospitable table his adjutants, Captains von Poellnitz, Cleve, Burchsdorff, Gerlach, Willoe, and von Geismar, along with Lieutenants Freeman and De Unger, and Chaplain Mylius, all of whom were acquainted with Jefferson. Owing to the scarcity of provisions, the General decided to invest in cows, hogs, and chickens in true country style—something that would have been quite out of the question in Europe—so that, he says, his place looked more like a peasant's farm than the residence of a general.

Not long after the arrival of the Convention Troops an attempt was made to effect their removal from Albemarle County. It was largely a question of politics. Jefferson was quick to take up the prisoners' cause, not for personal reasons, as he says he had "carefully avoided conversation with them on public subjects," but because of the true spirit of humanity that marked his conduct on similar occasions. The draught of the long letter he addressed to the Governor of Virginia on March 27, much interlined and rewritten, shows the importance he attached to the matter and the careful thought he gave it. "A report prevailing here," he writes from Albemarle, "that in consequence of some powers from Congress, the Governor and Council have it in contemplation to remove the Convention Troops, either wholly or in part, from their present situation, I take the liberty of troubling you with some observations on that subject." After hoping "that they will acquit me of impropriety in the present representation," he discusses in detail an article in the Saratoga Convention which stipulates that the officers shall not be separated from their men. "But," he asks, "are they [Congress] so far lords of right and wrong as that our consciences may be quiet with their dispensation? ... As an American I cannot help feeling a thorough mortification that our Congress should have permitted an infraction of our public honor; as a citizen of Virginia, I cannot help hoping

BARON VON RIEDESEL. From a portrait by Bach in possession of the Riedesel family. (*Reproduced from* The Pageant of America. *Copyright, Yale University Press*)

WILLIAM PHILLIPS. By Francis Cotes. (*Courtesy of the Frick Art Reference Library*)

and confiding that our Supreme Executive, whose acts will be considered as the acts of the Commonwealth, estimate that honor too highly to make its infraction their own act...."

Jefferson devotes several pages of his letter to the question of provisioning the troops and pointing out how their present situation is ideal in this respect. He likewise argues against the extravagance of moving officers and men, once the former have found comfortable quarters at great expense and barracks already built for the latter. "The environs of the barracks are delightful," he continues, "the ground cleared, laid off in hundreds of gardens, each enclosed with its separate paling; these well prepared and exhibiting a fine appearance. General Riedesel alone laid out upwards of two hundred pounds in garden seeds for the Germans only.... Their poultry, pigeons, and other preparations of that kind present to the mind the idea of a company of farmers, rather than camp of soldiers. In addition to the barracks built for them by the public, and now very comfortable, they have built great numbers for themselves, in such messes as fancied each other; and the whole corps, both officers and men, seem now happy and satisfied with their situation. Having thus found the art of rendering captivity itself comfortable, and carried it into execution at their own great expense and labor, their spirits sustained by the prospect of gratifications rising before their eyes, does not every sentiment of humanity revolt against the proposition of stripping them of all this? ... Is an enemy so execrable that, though in captivity, his wishes are to be disregarded and even crossed? I think not. It is for the benefit of mankind to mitigate the horrors of war as much as possible. The practice, therefore, of modern nations, of treating captive enemies with politeness and generosity is not only delightful in contemplation, but really interesting to all the world, friends, foes, and neutrals...." [26]

The Convention prisoners were not disturbed. There is no doubt that Jefferson was influential in the decision reached. The removal of the English prisoners in March 1781, when the British were pressing inland into Virginia, had of course nothing to do with the proposal of two years earlier.

The Riedesels received a warm welcome from the Jeffersons, and the two families soon became fast friends. Indeed, we shortly find Jefferson doing small errands for Mme. von Riedesel in Williamsburg, such as having eight silver spoons made and "note, I delivered him 17½ oz. of silver for her." He bought a calfskin from Major Lewis for her at the same time he got one for himself, and he even went so far as to sell her his pianoforte, for which the General agreed "to give me £100." [27]

General von Riedesel belonged to one of the wealthiest and most prominent families in central Germany. He had won distinction in his own right. His wife, in addition to her literary gifts, possessed a voice of unusual beauty, and it is not difficult to imagine that she was a valued addition to the musical Jefferson circle. In her memoirs Mme. von Riedesel tells a story of how a countryman arrived with butter at Colle one day while she was singing. When she had finished he asked her to sing the song over again. Jokingly, she asked what he would give her for doing so, and the man replied: "Two pounds of butter." The baroness sang on and on, to the man's entrancement. The next morning he appeared at Colle with five pounds of butter, along with his wife, in order that she too might enjoy the miracle of this song.

Mrs. Jefferson seems to have taken a particular fancy to Mme. von Riedesel and her children, one of whom was about the age of "la jolie Patsy," as Baron de Unger referred to the eldest Jefferson daughter, then between six and seven years old. Some time after he had left Virginia, Riedesel wrote Jefferson: "The little ones are all well and have not yet forgot the amiable Mrs. Jefferson, which, permit me to say for children, is no small proof of the impression her kindness had made." [28] During the months Jefferson was at Monticello, before removing to Richmond as Governor, there was much entertaining back and forth between the two families, including also General Phillips, who had rented "Ned Carter's place," Blenheim, near by. Little Patsy was sometimes formally included in the party, as when General Phillips writes: "Major General Phillips sends his compliments to Mr. and Mrs. Jefferson, requests the favor of their company at dinner on Thursday next at two o'clock to meet General and Mme. de Riedesel. Major General Phillips hopes Miss

Jefferson will be permitted to be of the party to meet the young ladies from Colle. Blenheim, Sunday evening, April 11, 1779." [29]

These happy times came to an end when Jefferson was elected Governor. On July 4, 1779, he wrote Riedesel, as we have seen, that "condolations would be better suited to the occasion, not only on account of the labors of the office to which I am called, and its withdrawing me from retirement, but also the loss of the agreeable society I have left, of which Mme. de Riedesel and yourself were an important part. Mrs. Jefferson in this particular sympathizes with me, and especially on her separation from Mme. de Riedesel...." [30]

At the same time he wrote General Phillips, "The appointment which has drawn me from the society of my late neighbors, in which character I with pleasure considered yourself, General and Mme. de Riedesel, for that cause as much as for any other is not likely to add to my happiness. The hours of private retirement to which I am drawn by nature ... and which would again join me to the same agreeable society, will be the most welcome of my life...." [31]

In the fall of 1779 General von Riedesel left for New York, where he expected to be exchanged—an event that did not take place, however, until a year later. On December 4 he sent Jefferson a letter of farewell and appreciation, the first of four which were dispatched in the course of the year. "I should consider it an instance of ingratitude," he writes, "to leave Virginia without repeating to you my heartiest thanks for every mark of friendship which you have so kindly testified to me from the first moments of our acquaintance, and for the assistance and hospitality which you have shown our troops under my command since you have assumed the government of Virginia. I beg you will be assured I shall ever retain a grateful remembrance of them and deem myself singularly happy, after this unnatural war is ended, to render you any service in my power as a token of my regard for you and your family.... Mme. de Riedesel's best compliments to Mrs. Jefferson, whose very amiable character and the many proofs we have experienced of her friendship can never be effaced from out of our memory...." [32]

Another letter followed, on March 30, 1780, announcing the birth of a fourth daughter to the General and his wife instead of the much-desired son. On May 13 Jefferson sent his condolences on this event, bringing the friendly interchange of letters to a close. "The little attentions you are pleased to magnify so much," he concludes, "never deserved mention. My mortification was that the peculiar situation in which we were, put it out of our power to render your stay here more comfortable.... Opposed as we may happen to be in our sentiments of duty and honor, and anxious for contrary events, I shall nevertheless sincerely rejoice in every circumstance of happiness or safety which may attend you personally. And when a termination of the present contest shall put it in my power to declare to you more unreservedly how sincere are the sentiments of esteem and respect (wherein Mrs. Jefferson joins me) which I entertain for Mme. de Riedesel and yourself." [33]

Among the young men who accompanied General von Riedesel as adjutants, Jefferson found two unusually congenial. With each he formed a friendship that lasted long after they had left the United States. Both were professional officers, but both seem to have been men of peculiar sensibility and charm. One was Baron von Geismar; the other a young lieutenant, Jean Louis de Unger. We have, unfortunately, only the most fragmentary record of the latter, only a few letters that bear testimony to a friendship once flourishing. From them we may gather that the young man was of a thoughtful disposition and that he and Jefferson were in the habit of indulging in "attic conversations," as had Jefferson in his youth when himself the protégé of an older man.

De Unger's stay in Albemarle was to be brief, as was that of the other German officers who were Jefferson's friends. In November 1780, when the Convention Troops were about to be removed from the vicinity of Charlottesville owing to the threat of an invasion, he wrote appreciatively, almost plaintively, to his patron and friend:

Aux Barraques
Ce 13me du Novembre
Comme nous avons reçu les ordres de quitter cette place j'ai cru qu'il dût être un de mes premiers devoirs de vous rendre mes remerciements pour toutes les marques de bienveillance dont il vous a plût

me daigner, et de vous demander très humblement la continuation de vos bonnes graces.... Je vous prie d'être assuré que je suis incapable d'oublier toutes les bontés dont il vous a plût m'honorer pendant notre séjour en Virginie; et quoique il y a beaucoup des personnes qui perdent en quittant cette province, ma perte est la plus considérable lorsque je serai privé (peut-être pour jamais) de la satisfaction de converser avec une personne en qui se trouvent toutes les qualités qui peuvent donner de l'estime et d'affection. Quel bonheur serai-ce pour moi, si à la place ou nous allons être conduite, je trouverais un bienfaiteur comme vous! Ce serait un bien qui me donnerait en quelque façon du soulagement. Il ne me reste qu'à adresser à la providence les voeux les plus sincères pour vous et votre chère famille....[34]

At the same time De Unger returned to Jefferson's library, through Dr. George Gilmer, a mutual friend, *"les livres qui m'ont fait passer bien des jours agréablement et utilement."* These included *"Cours de Mathématique de Bezout,* 6 vols., *Boileau,* Works, 2 vol., Plays of Vanbruck, 2 vol., Candide, 1 vol., *Contes Moreaux de Marmontel,* 3 vol."[35]

De Unger's prospects brightened after the writing of this letter. On November 25 he dispatched another one to the Governor saying: *"Maintenant un exchangement de quelques officiers vient de se publier, parmi quel nombre ma personne a le bonheur de se trouver; cela m'oblige de répéter mes protestations et prendre pour une seconde fois et peut-être pour jamais mon adieu de vous, Monsieur, une personne que je ne perderai jamais de souvenir."*[36] He then asked Jefferson for a pass which would permit him to carry with him the servant and secretary he had brought from Germany.

The pass was granted, and Jefferson, busy man that he was, took time to send a personal word with it. "The letter which covers this being of a public nature," he writes, "I wished to acknowledge separately the many things personally obliging to me expressed in your two letters. The very small amusement which it has been in my power to furnish, in order to lighten some of your heavy hours, by no means merited the acknowledgment you make. Their impression must be ascribed to your extreme sensibility rather than to their weight. My wishes for your happiness give me participation in your joy at being exchanged—sensibly, however, allayed by a presentiment of the loss I shall sustain. ... When the course of events shall have removed you to distant scenes of action where laurels not tarnished with the blood of my country may be gathered, I shall urge sincere prayers for your obtaining every honor and preferment which may gladden the heart of a soldier. On the other hand, should your fondness for philosophy resume its merited ascendancy, is it impossible to hope that this unexplored country may tempt your residence by holding out materials wherewith to build a fame founded on the happiness, and not on the calamities, of human nature? Be this as it may, whether philosopher or soldier, I wish you many felicities." [37]

No further word passed between the two men until toward the close of January 1788, when Jefferson received a letter from Salzliebenhalle in Germany. It was primarily a letter to recommend to Jefferson's attention a man who had served in the Revolution as *"port-enseigne"* and now eager to emigrate to America and settle in Virginia. It is a graceful letter, but all we learn of De Unger or his activities after leaving the United States is that the ruler of Brunswick had been pleased to promote him to a captaincy on his return. Jefferson's reply recalled their days together in distant Albemarle. A vision of the parlor at Monticello, his wife at the pianoforte, the young officers with their musical instruments, wide-eyed Patsy looking on, must have risen before his eyes as he wrote: "I retain a strong remembrance of the happy moments in which you participated, and to which you contributed so much, at Monticello." [38] One more letter from De Unger, in which he *"demande respecteusement pardon à votre Excellence de ce que j'ai desiré, si long temps à lui exprimer les sentiments de gratitude avec lesquels j'ai reçus la gracieuse reponse dont elle a daigné m'honorer en datte du 16me Février,"* [39] and the two men passed from each others' lives. Time, distance, variety of interests, and occupation had taken their toll.

When Mazzei speaks of renting his house to four young officers, before General von Riedesel's occupancy, he mentions one of them, a young German, "who, aside from being a most charming youth, played the violin very well, and, as Jefferson played the violin passably, he wished to have him near by." [40] The probabilities are that this "charming youth" was the Baron von Geismar. Color is lent this idea by a phrase in the farewell letter he wrote Jefferson when he left Albemarle in February 1780 to be exchanged in New York: "Doriano has all my music for you." Jefferson seems to have valued him above all the other friends he made among the German officers and to have found him more sympathetic in spirit.

In 1788, when planning a continental tour for young Thomas Shippen of Philadelphia and Edward Rutledge of South Carolina, Jefferson sent them to see his old friend, now stationed at Hanau, near Frankfurt am Main. The letter Shippen wrote Jefferson from Geneva on the twenty-second of September of that year, after having been with Geismar, gives us an excellent idea of that amiable gentleman. "I have omitted until now," says Shippen, "and am very much ashamed of it, how much I owe to your excellent friend Baron de Geismar, and to you, Sir, for having procured for me his acquaintance. It would have been impossible for a man to receive a long-absent and much-beloved brother with more cordiality or friendship than I received from that gentleman. He introduced me to the Court of Hesse-Cassel as his friend, showed me everything that was to be seen in or near Hanau, and behaved in every respect with the greatest possible attention and amiability. It was not among the least of his recommendations to me that he loved and respected you, as he often assured me he did without bounds.... His sentiments do alike honor to his head and his heart, and his conduct seems to have been always in union with them. How he has been able, in a military life and under a despotic government, to preserve his principles so pure, so free, and so liberal, is alike surprising and honorable to his character. But you know much better than I do his merits." [41]

Within a few months of his arrival in Paris, Jefferson happened to meet Baron de Waltersdorff at Franklin's house in Passy. The Baron was about to set off for a visit to the Court of Hesse-Cassel. Geismar's name very naturally came up, as he had been at that court before coming to America, and De Waltersdorff wrote his address on a slip of paper, still preserved. Within a few days, remembering

Geismar's final adjuration, "Adieu, be my friend, do not forget me and persuade yourself of my devotion," Jefferson was dispatching a letter to "*Monsieur le Baron de Geismar, Capitaine et Gentilhomme de la cour au service de S.A.S^m Monseigneur le Landgrave et Prince Héréditaire de Hesse-Cassel, à Hanau, par Frankfort sur le Main.*" "An unfortunate change in my domestic situation by the loss of a tender companion," Jefferson writes, "who joined me in esteeming you, occasioned me to wish a change of scene, and to accept an appointment which brought me to this place and will keep me here some time. Since your departure from America I have been altogether uninformed of your history. I am sure I need not tell you that the regard I entertain for you has rendered that interesting to me. A vague report of your death, which was never so authenticated as to command belief but which has not been authentically contradicted, has particularly occasioned me to wish a line from yourself. Till this or some other assurance of your still being on this side of the Styx, I shall indulge no further the feelings of friendship which would render my pen more diffuse." [42]

The letter duly reached its destination. On March 28 Geismar replied how delighted he was to hear from his old friend, of whom he had already had news through Baron de Waltersdorff, "*qui a passé à notre cour.*" It is a long, friendly letter, covering five pages in Geismar's all but illegible script, assuring Jefferson that he is very much in this world. He apologizes for writing in French, saying that he can still read and speak English, but he has quite lost his former facility with the pen.

Six months later, after a disclaimer that "you are now too distant from America to be much interested in what passes there," Jefferson proceeded to send Geismar news of the country he had seen in the making—of the United States of America of which Jefferson was so justly proud. "From the London Gazettes and the papers copying them," he writes, "you are led to suppose that all there is anarchy, discontent, and civil war. Nothing, however, is less true. There are not, on the face of the earth, more tranquil governments than ours, nor a happier and more contented people.... Their hatred against Great Britain, having lately received from that nation new cause and new aliment, has taken a new spring." Turning to personal matters, and once more giving expression to his deep attachment to Geismar, he continues: "Among the individuals of your acquaintance, nothing remarkable has happened. No revolution in the happiness of any of them has taken place, except that of the loss of their only child to Mr. and Mrs. Walker, who, however, left them a grandchild for their solace, and that of your humble servant, who remains with no other family than two daughters.... The character in which I am here at present confines me to this place, and will confine me as long as I remain in Europe. How long this will be, I cannot say. I am now of an age which does not easily accommodate itself to new manners and new modes of living, and I am savage enough to prefer the woods, the wilds, and the independence of Monticello to all the brilliant pleasures of this gay capital. I shall, therefore, rejoin myself to my native country, with new attachments, and with exaggerated esteem for its advantages; for, though there is less wealth there, there is more freedom, more ease, and less misery. I should like it better, however, if it could tempt you once more to visit it; but that is not to be expected. Be this as it may, and whether fortune means to allow or deny me the pleasure of ever seeing you again, be assured that the worth which gave birth to my attachment, and which still animates it, will continue to keep it up while we both live." [43]

This was a period of long intervals between letters. No means of speeding communications between friend and friend had yet been dreamed of. On December 6 Geismar again dispatched a long letter telling of a visit from the Marquis de Lafayette the preceding summer. "*Ma situation me fait douter,*" he continues, "*que dans cette vie j'aurais encore le plaisir de passer quelque temps à Monticello.*" He does hope, however, to spend a few days in Paris before long and renew their acquaintance there. "*Je vous prie, Monsieur, de me rappeler à Miss Jefferson, laquelle, peut-être ne se souviendra plus d'un prisonier qui l'a eu souvent sur les bras.... Gardez moi la continuation de votre amitié et bonté et sois persuadé que je ne* [illegible] *jamais de vous apartient.*" [44]

Three years later an opportunity for a meeting finally arose. On March 18, 1788, Jefferson wrote Geismar from Amsterdam: "Having been called hither, my dear friend, by business and being somewhat at liberty as to my return, I propose to go along the Rhine as far as Strasbourg before I turn off to Paris. I shall be at Frankfort probably between the first and fifth of April. If your residence is still at Hanau, I know you will meet me at Frankfort. I shall be at the Rott in [*sic*] house tavern. ... If you will lodge here a note of your address, I will contrive to see you. This pleasure has had its share in determining my return to Paris by this route, though I am very apprehensive you will have removed with your court from Hanau to Cassel." [45]

The four days which the two friends spent together in the beautiful Rhineland, with the breath of spring in the air, are described in another chapter. On his return to Paris Jefferson wrote exultantly: "I take the first moment to inform you that my journey was prosperous, that the vines which I took from Hochheim and Rüdesheim are now growing luxuriantly in my garden here, and will cross the Atlantic next winter, and that probably if you ever revisit Monticello, I shall be able to give you there a glass of Hock or Rüdesheimer of my own making." [46]

Jefferson and Geismar continued to correspond for another year or more, until the eve of the former's departure for America. In the winter of 1788-89, Jefferson went to great pains to make a drawing of a phaeton for Geismar. The infinite trouble he took in executing any commission, however slight, is well revealed in his letter of February 23, 1789. "You have had great reason, my dear sir," he writes, "to wonder that you have been so long receiving an answer to your request relative to the drawing of a cabriolet and phaeton. Your object was to have such drawings as that a workman could work by them. A painter's eye draught would not have answered this purpose; and, indeed, to be sure of having them done with the accuracy necessary to guide a workman, I could depend on nobody but myself. But the work was to be done principally in an open court, and there came on between two and three months of such intense cold as rendered this impossible. Since the season has become milder I have devoted such little scraps of time to this object as I was master of, and I now enclose you the drawings. They are made with such scrupulous exactness in every part that your workman may safely rely on them...."

Much of the letter is missing, and only a small portion of the drawing is preserved. As always, Jefferson sends his friend the latest news from America, "that our new Constitution will begin in March and with an almost universal approbation. In order to reconcile those opposed to it, a declaration of rights will be added. General Washington will undoubtedly be President." After announcing his own imminent return to America, Jefferson goes back to their common bond, music, and concludes: "I enclose you a pretty little popular tune which will amuse you for a day or two." [47]

With Geismar's letter of thanks, dated April 16, 1789, Jefferson's association with the Europeans he had known during the Revolution comes to an end. Within six months he was on the ocean, bound for home. He was never to return to Europe, as he had expected to do. Becoming more deeply involved in domestic politics with every day, Jefferson's correspondence with figures of the past languished. His mind was fixed on the future.

III. Governor of Virginia

JEFFERSON WAS elected governor of Virginia on June 1, 1779, not long after he had entered upon his thirty-sixth year. He was chosen over his boyhood friend, John Page, lieutenant governor under Patrick Henry, and over Thomas Nelson, who subsequently became governor. The following day the youthful executive appeared before the legislators to express his thanks. He stood in the great pilastered hall of the House of Delegates which had served the burgesses so many years and had now become the seat of this democratic assemblage. On a raised platform at the semicircular end of the room sat the Speaker, arrayed in the formal gown prescribed for the occasion. Around the hall in a double row, seated on benches covered with green serge and adorned with scarlet gimp, were his peers, their heads covered. The members of the old, established families appeared in the fashionable dress of the period. Those from more distant countries, we are informed, came in "boots, trousers, Indian leggings, great-coats, the usual coat, and short jackets. In other words, each one wears what he pleases." [1]

Jefferson, in powdered wig and suitable costume, began to speak. "Gentlemen," he said, and there was the arresting quality in his voice that was familiar in his pen, "the honor which the General Assembly have been pleased to confer on me, by calling me to the high office of Governor of this Commonwealth, demands my most grateful acknowledgments, which I desire through you, gentlemen, to tender them with the utmost respect. In a virtuous and free state, no rewards can be so pleasing to sensible minds as those which include the approbation of our fellow citizens. My great pain is lest my poor endeavors should fall short of the kind expectations of my country. So far as impartiality, assiduous attention, and sincere affection for the great American cause shall enable me to fulfill the duties of my appointment, so far I may with confidence undertake; for all beyond I must rely on the wise counsels of the General Assembly, and of those whom they have appointed for my aid in those duties...." [2]

Never was a man more warmly welcomed to office than was the distinguished author of the Declaration of Independence. Letters of congratulation from his old friends poured in. The first governor's popularity had long since waned. Virginia was ready for a change of leadership. "I will not congratulate you, but my country," wrote William Fleming, a college friend. "It will break in on your domesticity," he added prophetically, "and you will find it a troublesome office during the war." [3] John Page, who had been defeated for the office by only six votes, hastened to add his words of congratulation, which called forth a reply, both grateful and heartfelt, from his old friend. "It has given me much pain," Jefferson says, "that the zeal of our respective friends should ever have placed you and me in the situation of competitors. I was comforted, however, with the reflection that it was their competition, not ours; and that the difference of the members which decided between us was too insignificant to give you a pain, or me a pleasure, had our dispositions towards each other been such as to admit those sensations. I know you too well to need an apology for anything you do, and hope you will forever be assured of this." [4]

Richard Henry Lee, ten years older, wise in the ways of the world, and Jefferson's stanch coadjutor in the long struggle for independence, wrote enthusiastically: "I shall rejoice at the reputation which your administration may derive from the combined application of ability, industry, and the truest affection for our country and its cause. Every good Whig will wish success to a governor whose principles of action are not the incentives of whim, or the support of partiality; but who is influenced by motives of sound whiggism, which I take to be those of genuine philanthropy." [5] St. George Tucker added his high hopes of the new administration in a letter addressed to Theoderick Bland, Jr.: "I wish his Excellency's activity may be equal to the abilities he possesses in so eminent a degree. In that case we may boast of having the greatest man on the continent at the helm." [6] Virginia was prepared for a brilliant administration.

Jefferson could not have come to this office at a more unhappy time. That he was aware of this is evident in his replies to other letters of congratulation such as that to General von Riedesel, in which he remarks that "condolations would be better suited to the occasion." [7] Similarly, he wrote Richard Henry Lee within a fortnight of his election: "I received your letter and kind congratulations, for which I return you my thanks. In a virtuous government, and more especially in times like these, public offices are, what they should be, burdens to those appointed to them, which it would be wrong to decline, though foreseen to bring with them intense labor and great private loss." [8]

It is doubtful, however, whether Jefferson quite realized how great his burdens were to be. He was, of course, familiar with many of the problems, both military and economic, which had been facing Virginia since her emergence as a state. This is attested not only by his correspondence of 1776-79, but by his activity on numerous committees in the House of Delegates. His name is to be found on every one of importance. At each session of the Assembly during these years we find him serving on anywhere from twelve to twenty-four committees. The number of reports and bills drawn in his hand is legion. Indeed, he may be said to have had complete ascendancy over the Assembly during this period. Gradually and inevitably he had attained the power and the popularity which had been Patrick Henry's in such full measure, as the embodiment of the interests of the poor and the lowly, of what today we like to call the "little man." As such, as the living symbol of the rising tide of democracy, he had been elected governor of Virginia.

In this post Jefferson found himself playing quite a different role from that of reformer and leader of the radical party in the legislature. His situation proved to be anything but an enviable one. The men who framed the Virginia constitution, all too familiar with misuse of power in the persons of the royal governors, had created an office in which the governor of the state was little more than an executive officer. As was the case in practically all the newly formed states, the governor was hedged about with restrictions inspired by memories of abuses too lately suffered to be forgotten. "He shall," the Virginia constitution reads, "with the advice of a Council of State, exercise the executive power of government according to the laws of the Commonwealth; and shall not, under any pretense, exercise any power or prerogative by virtue of any law, statute or custom of England.... The Governor shall not prorogue or adjourn the Assembly during their sitting, nor dissolve them at any time." [9]

"After creating the office of governor," Edmund Randolph philosophizes, "the Convention gave way to their horror of a powerful chief magistrate without waiting to reflect how much stronger a governor might be made, for the benefit of the people, and yet be held with a republican bridle." [10] The Convention, however, was in no mood to take chances. They likewise established a council similar to that under the royal government, but without its judicial and legislative aspects. "A Privy Council or Council of State," it was decreed, "consisting of eight members, shall be chosen by joint ballot of both Houses of Assembly, either from their own members or the people at large, to assist in the administration of government." [11]

Theoretically an advisory body, the Council actually dominated and ruled the state at this period. The governor's position was that of chairman of the Council, carrying out its decisions, rather than that of an independent executive advised by Council. Jefferson's respect for law would not permit him to deviate from this conception of the division of functions, even in a crisis, when it not only became a calamity for Virginia that he clung so closely to the letter of the law, but reacted on his own reputation. He may well be said to have been a sacrifice to his principles, a victim of the new conception of government he was pioneering. The Assembly and the Council had been chosen as representatives of the people to carry out their will. It was the governor's duty to see that this was done. Before his term was over, however, Jefferson was to learn that no matter what the theories, no matter what the letter of the law, he, not the Council, not the legislature, not the constitution, was to be held responsible when disaster struck. With the crescendo of war, his conception changed. From the moment of Arnold's invasion, his policy was to change. He seized the helm with a grasp of iron which did not relax until his term expired.

In the winter of 1776 an incident had occurred that confirmed Jefferson in his views of the powers of the executive. During the dark days of December of that year, the House of Delegates, sitting as a committee of the whole, had resolved that "whereas the present imminent danger of America, and the ruin and misery which threatens the good people of this Commonwealth, and their posterity, calls for the utmost exertion of our strength, ... it is become necessary for the preservation of the state that the usual forms of government should be suspended during a limited time, for the more speedy execution of the most vigorous and effectual measures to repel the invasion of the enemy." [12] The bill then proceeded to enumerate certain measures the governor was empowered to take. The Senate, more cautious than the House, on the same day substituted for the words "the usual forms of government should be suspended" the phrase, "additional powers be given the Governor and Council."

Jefferson leaves us in no doubt as to how he viewed these proceedings, and how impossible it would have been for him ever to have considered exceeding the executive power as outlined in the constitution. Writing in the *Notes on Virginia*, he observes: "In December 1776, our circumstances being much distressed, it was proposed in the House of Delegates to create a *dictator*, invested with every power legislative, executive, and judiciary, civil and military, of life and of death, over our persons and over our properties.... One who entered into this contest from a pure love of liberty, and a sense of injured rights, who determined to make every sacrifice, and to meet every danger, for the re-establishment of those rights on a firm basis, who did not mean to expend his blood and his substance for the wretched purpose of changing this matter for that, but to place the powers of governing him in a plurality of hands of his own choice, so that the corrupt will of no one man in future oppress him, must stand confounded and dismayed when he is told that a considerable portion of that plurality had meditated the surrender of them into a single hand, and, in lieu of a limited monarchy, to deliver him over to a despotic one." [13]

As governor, Jefferson suffered two misfortunes that were almost catastrophic to his career. First, he was elected after the people had been through three years of the agony of war. Secondly, he left office a few months before the victory of Yorktown—an event that would have shifted the emphasis on his governorship from one of supposed incompetence to that of spectacular success.

Jefferson inherited certain problems from his predecessor. He likewise acquired new ones, appalling in number and magnitude. His legacy from the first governor of the state was an exhausted treasury, a currency that was depreciating with every day, a population unable to pay the heavy taxes, and an army that was nonexistent, as far as the defense of Virginia was concerned.

The financial situation of the state was deplorable from every angle. It became increasingly desperate in the months following Jefferson's election, and through no fault of his. The treasury was practically empty. There was very little specie available. The more paper money the overworked presses printed, the more rapidly its value declined. From his retirement in Henry County, Patrick Henry wrote bitterly to his successor: "... I have had many anxieties for our commonwealth, principally occasioned by the depreciation of our money. To judge by this, which somebody has called the pulse of the state, I have feared that our body politic was dangerously sick. God grant it may not be unto death. But I cannot forbear thinking, the present increase of prices is in a great part owing to a kind of habit, which is fostered by a mistaken avarice and, like other habits, hard to part with. For there is really very little money hereabouts.... But tell me, do you remember any instance where tyranny was destroyed and freedom established on its ruins, among a people possessing so small a share of virtue and public spirit? I recollect none, and this, more than the British arms, makes me fearful of final success without a reform...." [14]

A glance at Jefferson's pocket account book tells the story of Virginia's financial disintegration. Prices show a gradual and continued rise during 1777 and 1778, especially in wages and in "storebought" goods. Local produce, which is likely to play a large role in personal accounts, remained almost stable. Thirteen chickens still cost

13 shillings, and 15 shillings would still buy 15 pounds of venison for the Jefferson household. By June 1779 all values were in a state of chaos. We find Jefferson paying £5/2 for having his horses shod, whereas in January 1778 the same service had cost 30 shillings. On June 21 he bought two china bowls for £29, and on the twenty-fourth he paid £24/12 "for cap wire, thread and needles" for his wife. The twenty-ninth found two pounds of tea, which had been priced at 50 shillings in 1778, selling for £36. The governor's salary, originally fixed at £1,000, as it became obviously "necessary to vary the stipends of the officers in the civil department of the government," was raised to £1,500 in October 1777, and the following October to £3,000. In May 1779 this was so inadequate that the Assembly voted the chief magistrates £4,500, and the next October increased it to £7,500.[15]

In a frantic attempt to find money for Continental requisitions, as well as funds for running the state, the legislature, under both Henry and Jefferson, resorted to the time-honored method of legislatures under such circumstances: the imposition of increased taxes. The people in a large number of cases, however, were in no position to pay them. Thus of the taxes due in the fall of 1779, sixteen of the seventy-three counties of which Virginia was then composed paid none at all. Nine other counties made a token payment but returned no assessments, and still another eight neither paid anything nor returned assessments.

The military situation that faced Jefferson was an equally gloomy one. During the first years of the Revolution the theater of war had been largely confined to the northern colonies. Virginia had loyally complied with the demands of the commander in chief that her men and matériel be diverted to the armies there engaged. Some six months before Jefferson came into power, however, a change occurred in the British policy concerning the war. The surrender of Burgoyne at Saratoga and the evacuation of Philadelphia by Lord Howe had been bitter blows to British prestige. Without abandoning the war in the north, a vigorous southern campaign was determined upon. The royal governors of Georgia and South Carolina, who had returned to England, whispered of easy success in this sparsely settled territory. The further and not unreasonable hope was entertained that it would be possible to work northward from such a base, putting the rich and proud state of Virginia under British domination. A force of 3,500 men was detached from Clinton's army and sent to Georgia under the command of Colonel Archibald Campbell. Success was swift. Savannah fell on December 29, 1778. Augusta was taken the following month. It now became clear to the Americans that this was not an isolated raid, but a carefully planned, and thus far successful, campaign. Some thousands of men were consequently shifted from the Continental Army and sent south. Virginia was required to furnish an additional quota of men, arms, and supplies to the army of the Southern Department. There was no one left for the defense of the state except the halfhearted, untrained, and poorly equipped militia.

This was to prove a sorry bulwark. Although as early as May 9, 1777, Jefferson, with William Fleming and Carter Braxton on the committee, had drawn a bill providing against invasions and insurrections,[16] which was essentially one for organizing the militia, he himself had little confidence in it. That same month he wrote John Adams: "Our battalions for the Continental service were some time ago so far filled as rendered the recommendation of a draught of the militia hardly requisite, and the more so as in this country it ever was the most unpopular and impractical thing that could be attempted. Our people, even under the monarchial government, had learned to consider it the last of all oppressions."[17] Similarly, in August of the same year, Joseph Jones, uncle of James Monroe, was telling Washington: "... such is the present disposition of the people of Virginia, neither Captain Monroe, nor any other officer preserving the character a gentleman ought to support, can recruit men. Some men have indeed been raised, but by methods I could not recommend and I should be sorry he should practice."[18] This, then, was the situation which confronted the governor of peace-loving, agricultural Virginia as the Revolutionary War progressed.

In May 1779, during the last weeks of Patrick Henry's administration, the British made their first bold raid on Virginia. A fleet under the command of Admiral Sir George Collier sailed unopposed into Hampton Roads and anchored on the ninth of the month. Meeting with but feeble opposition—Fort Nelson on the west bank of the Elizabeth River, the chief defense of Norfolk, Portsmouth, and the state Navy Yard at Gosport, was totally inadequate—Collier and General Matthews, in command of the troops, seized Portsmouth and used it as a base for sending out raiding parties to capture or destroy whatever came their way. The little town of Suffolk in nearby Nansemond County, situated close to the confluence of all the navigable waters of the county, was the chief storehouse for the military and naval supplies of the state. As soon as news of the arrival of the British was known, the militia of Nansemond was summoned. Few in number, pitifully armed if at all, they were no match for the enemy. Suffolk was burned to the ground, the supplies destroyed or carried off. Not satisfied, the British remained in Virginia sixteen days, destroying public and private property with an impartial hand, committing "ravages and enormities, unjustified by the usage of civilized nations," as Jefferson wrote the president of Congress.[19]

Virginia was totally unprepared. "Did the enemy know how very defenseless we are at present," St. George Tucker wrote shortly after the event, "a very small addition to their late force would be sufficient to commit the greatest ravages throughout the country. It is a melancholy fact that there were not arms enough to put in the hands of the few militia who were called down on the late occasion; of those which were to be had, a great number were not fit for use. Nor was there by any means a sufficiency of ammunition or camp utensils of any kind. In short, never was a country in a more shabby situation; for our fortifications and marine, on which more than a million have been thrown away, are in no capacity to render any service to us, nor have we any standing force to give the smallest check to an approaching enemy."[20]

Thus Virginia had the first taste of war upon her own soil. So intense was the hostility to the British and their manner of conducting warfare that, on the twentieth of the month, the General Assembly resolved "that the Governor and Council be desired to remonstrate with the commanding officer of the British troops now in the state, against the cruel and barbarous manner in which he is waging war against the good people of this commonwealth, by prosecuting it with fire and every other cruelty unknown to civilized nations by custom or law." [21]

This was the scene in Virginia when Jefferson was chosen governor. His election could not have been an entirely unexpected honor. The constitution provided that no man could serve for more than three consecutive terms of one year each, and Patrick Henry was concluding his allotted span. Jefferson was easily the most prominent man in politics and, as we have seen, the standard bearer of the progressive, new party which he had led to power. At the moment of his election he was engaged in the final phases of the revisal of the laws of the state. He had spent the early spring at Monticello, busy with this work, but left home on the first of May to take his seat in the legislature. Going by way of Elk Hill and spending the night of the fourth with his cousins at Tuckahoe, he reached Williamsburg on the seventh. He notes in his account book that he "took seat in house" on the eighth, five days after the legislature had convened. Mrs. Jefferson and the two little girls appear to have remained with her family at The Forest, for a letter to John Page from her husband written nine days after his election says: "A desire to see my family that is in Charles City carries me thither tomorrow, and I shall not return until Monday. Mrs. Jefferson, I believe, will not come shortly to town." [22] His account books show that these visits took place frequently during the long, hot summer—on May 21, June 4, July 2, and 22, until the family went to Monticello for seven weeks on August 3.

Thus there was no illumination of the city, no welcoming committee to meet the new governor at the edge of the town, as there had been in the days of the royal governors. As simply as he was later to become President of the United States, Jefferson rode up to the palace, as it was still called, where as a young man he had been a familiar of that most cultivated and enlightened gentleman, Governor Francis Fauquier. Here he established bachelor's quarters with one Carter as steward, shortly succeeded by a certain Thompson. It was not until the last days of September that Mrs. Jefferson and her two little daughters joined her husband at the palace. They lived there until April 1780, when the capital was removed to Richmond and the family had to find a new residence in what was little more than a hamlet with "scarce one comfort of life," as a contemporary tells us.

This move had been proposed by Jefferson as early as 1776 in a revolutionary bill which provided suitable structures to house separately the various branches of the new government—the executive, legislative, and judicial. It was the first time such a thing had been contemplated in either Europe or America and constitutes another of Jefferson's important contributions. The bill was not passed at the time; but a subsequent one embodying the same features was introduced by his friend John Harvie three years later and became law. The removal was anything but popular with the members of the legislature. "I understand the Assembly, after finishing many nothings," Archibald Cary wrote Jefferson on December 18, 1779, "are this day to adjourn, and, nothwithstanding several attempts to prevent, are to meet at Richmond in May. Have they determined on which hill to build? Until that is done no private buildings will go on, and, of course, so much the longer will those who are obliged to attend public business be put to inconvenience. I understand many of the great officers intend to resign, no great mark of patriotic spirit I confess." [23]

At the spring session of the legislature in 1780 it was determined to erect the public building on Shockoe Hill. A committee of nine men, headed by Jefferson, was appointed to act as the directors of the public buildings. This was an opportunity according to Jefferson's heart. He immediately turned his fertile mind to the problem. A series of drawings for extending the town of Richmond, for the halls of justice, and for the governor's mansion were the result of his cogitations.[24]

Although the legislature had decreed that a governor's house should be built "in a handsome manner, with walls of brick or stone, and porticoes where the same may be convenient or ornamental, and with pillars and pavements of stone," [25] it was a long time before anything of the sort was carried out. Meanwhile Jefferson, once more pioneering, once more sacrificing his personal comfort to his principles in advocating the removal, was obliged to find such quarters as he could.

It has not been generally known where Jefferson lived in Richmond while governor. Usually it has been assumed that he resided in the simple frame house which is known to have been in existence and occupied by Governor Harrison in December 1781. A glance at Jefferson's account book of 1780, however, shows that on April 17 he "got possession of Colonel Turpin's house." Thomas Turpin was Jefferson's uncle. His seat was in Goochland, near Fine Creek, the early home of Jefferson's father. Like many of his contemporaries, he was something of a speculator in land. When the city of Richmond was platted, he purchased lot No. 367, just south of the existing governor's house.[26] He also owned considerable property to the north and east of the area that became Capitol Square when this plot was laid out in 1780.[27] There is still extant in the state archives some correspondence between Jefferson and his uncle concerning the amount to be paid for the rent, and as to whether it was to be paid by him or by the public. Jefferson fixed 8,000 pounds of tobacco as a suitable sum. The colonel considered this too modest. After his retirement as governor, Jefferson laid the matter before his successor in a letter dated August 7, 1782. "On removal of the seat of government," he writes, "I engaged his [Turpin's] house on the hill. A house having always been found for the governor, I took it for granted that the rent of that would be considered as a public charge, though from the nature of my application to Col. Turpin I became personally liable to him. I flatter myself it will still be the opinion it should be paid by the public...." The following year the question was taken up by two referees, Thomas Prosser and William Hay, who certified "that Col. Turpin should be paid for the rent of his Brick House and garden at the rate of £100 per annum."[28] This is the first intimation we have that a brick house existed at this early period when Richmond was largely an assemblage of wooden shacks. As throughout his life, the young governor took pains to live with such elegance as circumstances would permit.

From the palace at Williamsburg, which was henceforth to be neglected and serve various utilitarian purposes, were shipped no less than 4 dozen "packages," as the inventory calls them. There were 3 crates of dressing tables, 14 containing dining and tea tables and a "tea kitchen." There were likewise 2 desks, one "covered with green cloth," 2 book cases, a large number of chairs of various kinds, numerous looking glasses, 4 cases of chandeliers, 2 cases and barrels of lamps, 1 case of "beds, etc.," and seven of glass and china. Also listed are "2 pictures, 6 large pictures, 17 prints," Venetian blinds, and a variety of household utensils from a spinning wheel to meat hooks, jack, and crane.[29]

On arriving in Williamsburg, the methodical Jefferson had at once ordered an inventory of the contents of the palace made by William Goodson and Humphry Howard. It must be remembered that the majority of the furnishings which made the palace so luxurious in the days of the royal governors, and which have been re-created in the recent restoration, were the property of the governors themselves. This applies to most of the pictures, the books, the hangings, the silver, and some of the mirrors and furniture. When Patrick Henry became the first governor of the state, he was voted $1,000 to make the palace habitable. Much of what was bought was in bad condition at the close of his three terms.

In the inventory made for Jefferson, the furniture is not listed according to rooms, as is usual, and the descriptions are of the most meager sort; but we can picture him living among no less than scores of mahogany chairs with hair or leather bottoms (the twelve "best," along with six elbow chairs were covered with crimson damask); some fifteen mahogany tables, described as dining, pembroke, and card tables; a marble sideboard; with sixteen scripture prints and a dozen others different in character adorning the walls, along with numerous looking glasses in gilt frames. The family dined off "blue and white dishes" or "red and white ditto," and there were delft plates and cups for special occasions. No mention is made of the fabrics which hung at the windows, or of the curtains which draped the six beds. We are told only that one set was of "green worsted, wanting vallons, top, and headpiece."

From the very first moment of holding office, Jefferson was dogged by misfortune and assailed by problems of the most vital character. The very crops failed that year, and we find him writing the president of Congress that if Virginia is to supply the necessary amount of flour to the Convention troops, it will be necessary to send in 10,000 barrels of seed for the next year's planting.[30] To judge by the ceaseless stream of letters that henceforth flowed from his pen,[31] Jefferson's days were spent in the council chamber in neverending conference with his advisers. From his correspondence and his other writings of this period, certain questions emerge as having been most urgent and as having engaged all the energies and powers of his mind. These were the constant necessity of raising money, the levying and supplying of troops, and the question of western boundaries, which involved the problem of the Indians. Ominously overshadowing all was the matter of the defense of Virginia.

Desperate as was the financial situation of the state, Jefferson was at first not without hope of ameliorating it. An obvious, and apparently fruitful, source of revenue appeared to be the confiscation and sale of British property. As early as October 1777 he had drawn a bill for "sequestering British property, enabling those indebted to British subjects to pay off such debts." As adopted it read:

"Whereas divers persons, subjects of Great Britain, had during our connection with that kingdom acquired estates, real and personal, within this Commonwealth, and had also become entitled to debts to a considerable amount, and some of them had commenced suits for the recovery of such debts before the present troubles here interrupted the administration of justice....

"Be it therefore enacted by the General Assembly that the lands, slaves, stocks, and implements thereunto belonging within this commonwealth, together with the crops now on hand, or hereafter to accrue, and all other estate, of whatever nature, not herein otherwise provided for, of the property of any British subject, shall be sequestered into the hands of commissioners to be appointed from time to time by the governor and council for each particular estate, which commissioners shall have power, by suits or actions to be brought in the manner of the proprietors, to receive and recover all sums of money hereafter to become due to the said proprietors of such estates....

"And be it further enacted, that it shall and may be lawful for any citizen of this commonwealth owing money to a subject of Great Britain to pay the same, or any part thereof, from time to time, as he shall think fit, into the said loan office, taking thereout a certificate for the same in the name of the creditor ... and shall deliver such certificate to the governor and council, whose receipt shall discharge him from so much of the debt...." [32]

Five days before Jefferson's election as governor the Assembly took a further step toward confiscation. It was enacted that "all property real and personal within this commonwealth, belonging at this time to any British subject, or which did belong to any British subject at the time such escheat and forfeiture (as before mentioned) may have taken place, shall be deemed to be vested in the commonwealth, the lands, slaves, and other real estate by way of escheat, and the personal estate by forfeiture." [33]

A final measure to rid the state of the last remnants of the British scourge was contained in the proclamation issued by the new governor at the direction of the Assembly in its June session. After rehearsing the provisions of the act concerning escheats and the banishment of British subjects, it states: "I have thought fit, by and with the advice of the Council of State, to issue this my proclamation hereby strictly charging and commanding all persons coming under any one of the descriptions of said act, and now being within this commonwealth, to be and appear before me in Council, at Williamsburg, on or before the seventeenth day of August in this present year in readiness to depart the commonwealth in such manner as shall then be prescribed to them, as they will answer the contrary at their utmost peril. And I do moreover charge and inform all officers, civil and military, and all other good citizens of this commonwealth, to apprehend and carry securely to the commanding officer of the militia of some county within the commonwealth all such persons, whom after the said day they shall find lurking or being therein.... And I do farther prohibit all persons so described from entering into this commonwealth during the continuance of the present war with their Prince, under color of any commission, passport, license, or other pretense whatsoever, and do publish and make known to such of them as shall presume to violate this prohibition, that they shall be deemed and dealt with as spies wheresoever they be taken...." [34]

Jefferson had great hopes of these measures. A few days after his inauguration he wrote William Fleming: "... the sale of British property take place, and our tax bill put on a better footing. These measures I hope will put our finances into a better way and enable us to co-operate with our sister states in reducing the enormous sums of money in circulation. Every other remedy is nonsensical quackery." [35]

His optimism was, alas, not justified. Four months later he was addressing the speaker of the House of Delegates in quite a different vein. Resolutions from Congress had been received requesting additional supplies of money. Jefferson writes: "The General Assembly in considering this subject will naturally cast their eyes on the funds already provided for the supply of their public treasury. As a principal branch of these was in some degree under the care and direction of the executive, I mean the proceeds of the estates of British subjects, it becomes my duty to guard the assembly against relying on their calculations for any great and immediate supplies from hence. Facts have come to our notice which give great reason to believe that the traverse and other pleadings justly allowed by the law for saving the rights of those who have real or probable appearance of right, is perverted to frustrate or delay its effects, by being put in on grounds either frivolous or false, and by that means throwing the subject into a course of legal contestation which, under the load of business now on the docket of the General Court, may not be terminated in the present age. ... I thought it my duty to guard the General Assembly against any deception in their expectations from these funds, that no disappointments may accrue in the measures they shall be pleased to adopt." [36]

Although the power of taxation and of issuing money resided in the Assembly, it is significant to note what measures were taken in regard to the currency during Jefferson's administration. It was, of course, impossible for him not to have been consulted regarding them and not to have had knowledge of what was going on. Here again he inherited a situation that was almost hopeless. In June 1775, during the so-called interregnum, Virginia had started on the inevitable but perilous path of issuing paper money. She continued to do so with increasing celerity and in ever greater amounts until the collapse of 1781. Before Jefferson came to office the situation was already the cause of great anxiety to the leaders of the new Virginia government. In November 1778 we find Richard Henry Lee writing the governor: "Division among ourselves and the precipice on which we started with our paper money, are, I verily believe, the sources of their hope [i.e. early conquest by the British]. The former is bad, but the latter is most seriously dangerous! Already the continental emissions exceed in a sevenfold proportion the sum necessary for medium; the state emissions added greatly increase the evil. It would be well if this were all, but the forgeries of our currency are still more mischievous. They depricate not only by increasing the quantity, but by creating universal diffidence concerning the whole paper fabric. In my opinion these miscreants who forge our money are as much more criminal than most other offenders, as parricide exceeds murder.... I hope, Sir, you will pardon so much on this subject, but my anxiety arises from the clear conviction I have that the loss of our liberty seems at present more likely to be derived from the state of our currency than from all other causes." [37]

In May 1779, shortly before Jefferson took office, an act had been passed repealing "so much of an act as makes it penal to offer or pay, ask or receive, more in paper bills of credit of this commonwealth or Congress, for any gold or silver coin, or more in the said paper bills for any property, real or personal, than is asked or offered in gold or silver." [38] The floodgates were thus opened. Prices advanced beyond bounds as the value of money decreased with each day. "The inundation of money appears to have overflowed virtue, and I fear will bury the liberty of America in the same grave," writes Richard Henry Lee to George Mason on June 9. "The demon of avarice, extortion, and fortune-making seizes all ranks.... I well know that much of this will in all countries take place in time of war, but in America, unfortunately at this time, nothing else is attended to." [39] Jefferson, recognizing the certain signs of disaster, was moved to communicate with Lee on the seventeenth. "It is a cruel thought that when we feel ourselves standing on the firmest ground, in every respect," he observes, "the cursed arts of our secret enemies, combining with other causes, should effect by depreciating our money, what the open arms of a powerful enemy could not. What is to be done? Taxation is become of no account.... I own I see no assured hope but in peace, or in a plentiful loan of hard money." [40]

In May of the next year a determined attempt at stabilization was made. The legislature passed "an act for calling in and redeeming the money now in circulation, and for emitting and funding new bills of credit according to the resolutions of Congress of the eighteenth of March last." [41] The state quota of Continental money, some $200,000,000, as well as all the state money then in circulation, was to be called in and destroyed. The taxes due in August and September 1780 were to be "applied for the purpose of calling in and destroying said money." A new system of taxes and tax collection "on all and every article of property," the details of which need not concern us here, was instituted with what seemed every safeguard. As "the exigencies of war" required the further emission of paper money, until "the act for calling in and redeeming the money now in circulation... shall have its operation," the treasurer was empowered to "issue treasury notes in dollars for any sum or sums which may be necessary..., not to exceed 2,000,000 pounds." These were redeemable "in Spanish milled dollars, or the value in gold or silver at the rate of 1 for 40, at the Treasury of Virginia on or before the last day of December 1784." [42] A fund for the redemption of these bills was to be provided by a tax of one shilling for every glass window of every inhabited house in the commonwealth in the month of September 1781, and for the following three years. Taxes on conveyances and mortgages, on tobacco, on rum and other spirits were likewise provided. A further safeguard was supposedly insured by the clause that "if the events of war should render any of the aforesaid funds unproductive, then the capitol and palace in Williamsburg and the public lands in James City and on the Eastern Shore" were to be sold.[43]

By October 1780 it was apparent that the measures taken had been of no avail. The situation was even more serious. Another act was passed for "procuring a supply of money for the exigencies of war." This time the treasurer was empowered to issue notes in dollars not to exceed 6,000,000 pounds, "unless seen necessary," in which event the limit was to be 4,000,000 pounds more. The problem of finding means to redeem this money was passed on to the next Assembly. Meanwhile a new tax on lands, slaves, and other property was "hereafter to be imposed." [44]

In the next session of the legislature, the following March, all paper money issued by Virginia as well as by Congress was declared legal tender. The value of money, or the lack of it, had by now become fantastic. The Assembly likewise authorized the treasurer to issue "notes in dollars to the value of 10,000,000 pounds"; and, if that proved insufficient, the governor, with the advice of Council, was empowered "to emit more to the extent of 5,000,000 pounds." There was nothing left but to pledge "the public faith" for the redemption "of all sums of money issued under this act, on or before the thirtieth day of December 1792, by fair and equal assessment upon the whole property of this commonwealth." [45] Two months later 20,000,000 more pounds were authorized, and once more the public faith was pledged to redeem it before the last day of December 1794.

By 1781 the situation was hopeless. The legislature, in session in November of that year, after Jefferson's retirement, decreed that the "paper money heretofore issued by this state shall cease to be a tender in payment of any debt or contract whatsoever." As Edmund Randolph truly observed, Virginia "had clung to paper money with the affection due to an old servant, though impaired in strength. Depreciation was lamented, but we could recount some of the most brilliant exploits of the Revolution, achieved by armies which depended on paper money, and we were infatuated with a whimsical gratitude for it." [46]

A problem rivaling the financial one in gravity and complexity was that of the raising and supplying of troops, both for the Continental forces and for the state. This dual need, and the dual organization involved, offered pitfalls without end for the executive, for the Assembly, and for all concerned. The ensuing confusion is reflected in an interchange of letters between Washington and Jefferson in November 1779. Washington writes from West Point on November 5 of that year: "I would take the liberty of addressing a few lines to your Excellency respecting such officers and privates of Bland's and Baylor's regiments of Dragoons and of Harrison's artillery as belonging to the state of Virginia. Their situation is really disagreeable and discouraging.... It is said that under the idea of their not having been originally a part of the troops apportioned on the state in September 1776, the state provision for clothing and bounty for re-enlisting their men is not to be extended to them, or at least that is a doubtful point. This is the source of great uneasiness and indeed of distress among them, and it is the more felt as most of the states ... have made no discrimination between officers and men belonging to them, in the same predicament, and those who were explicitly assessed on them as their quota; but, on the contrary, have permitted them to participate in every benefit and emolument granted others of their troops." [47]

Jefferson took up the matter in a long letter on the twenty-eighth. "Your Excellency's letter on the discriminations which have been heretofore made between the troops raised within this state, and considered part of our quota, and those not so considered, was delivered to me four days ago. I immediately laid it before the Assembly, who thereupon came to the resolution I now do myself the honor of enclosing to you.... It would be a great satisfaction to us to receive an exact return of all the men we have in Continental service who come within the description of the resolution, together with our state troops in Continental service...." After listing certain ones, he continues: "A return of all these would enable us to see what proportion of the Continental Army is contributed by us. We have at present very pressing calls to send additional numbers of men to the southward. No inclination is wanting in either the legislature or executive to aid them or strengthen you, but we find it very difficult to procure men." [48]

The upshot was a resolution by the Assembly providing "that all officers and soldiers, being citizens of this Commonwealth, belonging to any corps or Continental establishment, and not being in the actual service of any other state, shall hereafter be entitled to all state provisions, clothing, bounty, and other emoluments, either in land or money, which have or shall be allowed to those belonging to the line of the state, although such officers and soldiers do not immediately serve therein." [49]

In May 1779 Jefferson had been one of a committee for establishing a Board of War. It consisted of five men chosen by joint ballot of both houses of the Assembly. Its duties consisted in superintending and managing "all matters and things within the department of war, and all persons holding office or performing duties within that department." At least once in two months the members of the board were to examine "the condition of the military stores and provisions in the several magazines." [50] The board proved cumbersome. Instead of facilitating action, it was just another body to be consulted and taken into consideration. After a brief existence it was abolished in May 1780, "for the purpose of introducing economy in the various departments of government, and for conducting the public business with the greatest expedition." [51] The governor was authorized to appoint a commissioner of war in place of the board. Colonel George Muter was named to the place and was shortly succeeded by the able Colonel William Davies.

When Jefferson assumed the governorship, the military situation in Virginia was becoming ominous. The state had contributed fifteen regiments to the Continental line at the beginning of the war, and the remnants of these were joined by the two state regiments in 1778. How wise Virginia had been to give so unstintingly of her men and resources was a question that must often have arisen in the minds of those responsible. In a letter to Samuel Huntington, president of Congress, concerning the detention of certain Continental arms by the state, Jefferson not only justifies the action, but stresses Virginia's unquestioning eagerness to do her full share toward the common good. "This state in an early part of the present contest," he writes, "raised at first two, and soon afterwards seven, battalions for its particular defense. Finding, however, that the dangers of our being invaded became less, our legislature made a tender of these battalions to the Continental service. The tender was accepted of by Congress only on condition that we would permit them to carry their arms with them. They were accordingly marched to the grand army, time after time, as we could get them armed. I think this condition was dispensed with as to two battalions only, which Congress, induced by their increasing wants of men, permitted to march on without their arms. This is one of the articles of debit in our account of arms against the Continent.... Since this, however, at different times and for different corps, many smaller parcels of arms have been lent to Congress by us. It is a fact, which we are to lament, that, in the earlier part of our struggles, we were so wholly occupied by the great object of establishing our rights, that we attended not at all to those little circumstances of taking receipts and vouchers, keeping regular accounts, and preparing subjects for future disputes with our friends. If we could have supported the whole Continent, I believe we should have done it, and never dishonored our exertions by producing accounts; sincerely assured that in no circumstances of future necessity or distress, a like free application of anything theirs would have been thought hardly of, or would have rendered necessary an appeal to accounts...." [52]

With the majority of her forces thus engaged in the Continental service, the defense of Virginia rested on the militia. This time-honored institution, the backbone of the military system of Virginia since the time of the earliest settlers, proved to be a questionable reliance at this period. Although recognizing its inherent defects, Jefferson appears to have accepted it without question. Washington, on the other hand, as early as October 6, 1776, wrote Patrick Henry of his "want of confidence in the generality of the troops," particularly in the militia "who, as soon as they are firmly fixed in camp, are impatient to return to their own homes, and who from utter disregard of all discipline and restraint among themselves are but too apt to infuse the like spirit into others. The evils of short enlistments and employing militia to oppose against regular and well-appointed troops, I strongly urged to Congress before the last army was engaged.... Besides the militia being altogether unfit for the service when called into the field, we have discovered from experience they are much more expensive than any other kind of troops, and that the war could have been conducted on more moderate terms by establishing a permanent body of forces who are equal to every contingency, than by calling in the militia on imminent and pressing occasions." [53]

The militia was composed, nominally, of "all free male persons, hired servants, and apprentices between sixteen and fifty years of age," with certain exceptions, such as the governor, Council, judges, keepers of public jails, and a few others. Each county lieutenant, colonel, lieutenant colonel, and major was to "appear on his respective musterfield ... accoutered with a sword. ... Every captain and lieutenant with a firelock and bayonet. ... Every noncommissioned officer and private with a rifle and a tomahawk, or good firelock and bayonet with a pouch and horn, or a cartouche or cartridge box. ... If any soldier be certified to the court martial to be so poor that he cannot purchase such arms, the said court shall cause them to be procured at the expense of the public. ..." [54] As time went on more and more men, either through not possessing arms or being unable to purchase them, seemed willing, if not to brand themselves as "poor soldiers," at least to have their arms furnished at public expense. Shortly it was enacted that "the soldiers of such militia [i.e. the divisions called up], if not well armed, shall be furnished with the arms and ammunition of the county, and any deficiency in these may be supplied by the public magazines, or if these admit not of that delay, by impressing arms and ammunition of private property." [55]

Under the constitution, the governor might "embody the militia with the advice of the Privy Council, and when embodied, shall alone have the direction of the militia under the laws of the country." [56]

In the *Notes on Virginia*, Jefferson gives the total number of the militia, from the returns of 1780 and 1781, as 49,971 men, 18,828 of whom were from "between the Blue Ridge and the Tide Waters." [57] It was supposedly organized into battalions of not more than 1,000 or less than 500 men, "if there be that many in the country." In these words resides the tragedy of the Virginia militia. It is impossible for anyone who thinks in terms of the populous northern colonies such as Massachusetts or New York to realize how sparsely Virginia was settled and how scattered were her inhabitants.

"The people of this country are dispersed over a great extent of land," Richard Henry Lee had written of his native state, and never was it described in words more true. It was a lonely country, a country of vast plantations and few settlers. The plantations were self-sufficient with slaves trained in the various crafts necessary to keep them going. Until the Revolution, the only town except Norfolk that could possibly merit the name of a city was Williamsburg, the capital, itself no more than a village.

Immediately following Collier's raid, an "act for the better regulation and discipline of the militia"[58] was rushed through the Assembly, along with an "act for raising a body of volunteers for defense of the state."[59] The enlistment of 4,560 volunteers was authorized, to serve until "one month after the enemy shall have withdrawn from the Commonwealth." Throughout the spring session of the legislature one act after another was passed in an effort to raise sufficient infantry, cavalry, and militia "for better defense of the commonwealth and providing a force sufficient to repel any hostile invasion." Bounties were increased and every possible inducement offered. Finally it was decreed that the delinquent counties should draught every twenty-fifth man of the militia to serve for eighteen months.

There is ample evidence that military service was none too popular with the militia, that it lacked the "military ardor which is of the utmost moment to an army," as Washington remarked.[60] "Such is the tardiness of people to engage in the military," wrote Richard Henry Lee to Jefferson in October 1779, "that we have yet but obtained two men in Westmoreland upon both the acts 'for raising a body of troops, etc.,' and that 'concerning officers, soldiers, sailors, and marines.'"[61] Similar complaints came from almost every county. It was no unwillingness to serve their country that brought about this condition, but rather the reluctance to leave their farms and their families exposed to the dangers to which their isolated position subjected them. As Edmund Randolph observed at the time, "there were other forcible reasons which detained the militia at home. The helpless wives and children were at the mercy not only of the males among the slaves, but of the very women who could handle deadly weapons; and these could not have been left in safety, in the absence of all authority of the masters, and of union among neighbors." [62]

In the western counties there was the additional and ever-present peril of brutal attack by the Indians; on the eastern seaboard the danger of raids by the British. How serious this was we gather from a letter of Richard Henry Lee to Samuel Adams. It is dated June 18, 1779, and written from his home, Chantilly, on the Northern Neck. "I am this moment returned from an expedition with our militia," he says, "to prevent the further ravage of a set of Tory miscreants from New York who have clubbed their force for the purpose of plunder and revenge... most excellent agents of George the Third! They landed 60 men where there was no force collected to oppose them, and burnt the warehouses on Wicomico River with between two and three hundred hogsheads of tobacco, and three private houses, carrying off a gentleman from one of them with several slaves from the neighborhood. Finding the militia were assembling, they embarked and disappeared, declaring their purpose was to burn every warehouse on Potomac River. This discovery of their intention will I expect defeat their design.... These wretches have it in their power to create us great expence and much trouble, pierced as we are in every part with waters deep and broad, without marine force sufficient to oppose even this contemptible collection of pirates. We are compelled to such frequent calls upon the militia as to injure greatly the agriculture of the country, without effectually answering the purpose of defense." [63]

Collier's incursion into Virginia having proved a raid and not the long-feared invasion, the legislature apparently took heart. At the October session, 1779, a new policy was adopted. The executive was empowered to send to the aid of North Carolina militia to the extent of 1,500 men and "so many of the state troops as can be marched thither according to the terms of their enlistments, or are willing to march." [64] A wave of economy likewise swept over the Assembly, prompted in part by the financial situation of the state. Almost all the acts for increasing the armed forces passed in the last session were rescinded. The body of cavalry that had been ordered raised was reduced to three troops, to be retained in the service of the state. The same action was taken in regard to the regiments of infantry, previously authorized. Only one regiment instead of three was to be raised for the western frontier. Unconsciously, but all too well, the state was preparing for a successful invasion of the British under the leadership of Benedict Arnold.

The navy was also to suffer at the hands of this fall legislature. With the creation of the great western counties, the Tidewater no longer had a majority of representation in the Assembly. It was as difficult for the men "from the mountains" as it is for the average person not familiar with the topography of Virginia, to realize how open to invasion, how difficult of defense the state was. The Virginia shore is a lacework of bays, rivers, and creeks which taunted the defenders and lured the enemy. The wide waters of the Potomac, the Rappahannock, and the York rivers, of the James, lifeline of colonial Virginia, were an ever-present invitation to the British to send their heavily armed and heavily manned ships into the interior for the conquest and the humiliation of the lordly state of Virginia.

Each of the seaboard states was, of course, obliged to establish and maintain a navy of its own at this period. With this in view, the Virginia Convention, in May 1776, had created a board of commissioners "to superintend and direct the building of all vessels whether such are employed for the immediate annoyance of the enemy or for expediting the transportation of troops over rivers." [65] Two row galleys were to be built at once for the defense and protection of Northampton and Accomac counties. When the first Virginia Assembly met in the fall of 1776, it ordered the building of two frigates, to carry 32 guns, 4 galleys mounted with proper cannon, and empowered the commissioners to raise a force not exceeding 1,300 men, exclusive of officers.[66] Toward the close of Henry's governorship the navy is said to have consisted of 17 ships, 15 brigs, 19 schooners, 15 galleys, 2 armed pilot boats, and 2 barges.[67] In the last weeks of his administration came Collier's raid on Norfolk. A triumphant letter from Collier to General Sir Henry Clinton describes the destruction of a "great number" of the "rebel ships and vessels." [68] From a list among Jefferson's unpublished papers headed "A State of the Armed Vessels of Virginia, October 30, 1779," we learn that the navy at that time consisted of 12 ships of different sorts, bearing 88 guns and manned by 343 seamen.[69] It was a pathetically inadequate little fleet to pit against the British Navy.

No one was more aware of the importance of a navy to Virginia than Jefferson, and no one was more conscious of its shortcomings. Richard Henry Lee, at that time chairman of the Marine Commission, shared these views and could not have been a more ardent protagonist. "In Virginia we have properly two frontiers," he wrote Jefferson at this time, "one bordered by the wilderness, the other by a sea. Into both of these issue savages, and into the latter the most savage.... I suppose that the shores of Virginia washed by navigable waters exceed a thousand miles. Almost the whole of this must be come at through a passage of 20 miles, which neglected, leaves us vulnerable through so great an extent of coast. Reason points out the remedy.... I know from good information," he continues, "that these pirates express fear of the Maryland galleys, while they deride and scoff at our marine force. In these lower counties of the Northern Neck our situation is really distressing—exposed by being on the water at a distance from any marine protection, a dispersed militia without arms or ammunition, puts it in the power of these buccaneers to infest and injure us without danger of punishment." [70]

Jefferson's reply, hitherto unpublished, states his position in no uncertain terms. It likewise gives us a glimpse of the politics within politics existing at that time. He writes from Williamsburg on July 17, 1779: "In order to render our miserable navy of some service, orders were some time ago issued for two galleys on the seaboard of the Eastern Shore to join the others; another galley, heretofore stationed in North Carolina (if not purchased by that government as proposed by our Assembly), will be called into the bay. It seems we have few or none which can ride on the middle grounds. It is therefore in contemplation to keep them about the North Cape for the protection of the North Channel and for the purpose of descrying such hostile vessels coming into the bay as they may be competent to attack. From a very early period of this contest it has been my uniform opinion that our only practicable defense was naval, and that though our first efforts in that way must be small and would probably be unsuccessful, yet that it must have a beginning, and the sooner the better. These beginnings have indeed been unsuccessful beyond all my fears, but it is my opinion we should still persevere in spite of disappointment, for this plain reason that we can never otherwise be defended. Impressed with the necessity of this kind of defense, the assembly as long ago as October 1776 were prevailed on to direct two frigates and two large galleys to be built. Being ignorant of these things myself, but having great confidence in the British experience on the water, the proposition only referred as to the frigates to their method and as to the galleys to the Philadelphia plan. I left the House soon after; some members, vain enough to suppose they could correct errors in the construction of British vessels, got the plan changed. Their plan was again ventured to be improved on by the Navy Board, and the event was £100,000 laid out to not a shilling's benefit. I believe now we should be gainers were we to burn our whole navy and build what we should be able on plans approved by experience and not warped to the whimsical ideas of individuals who do not consider that, if their projects miscarry, their country is in a manner undone. I am in hopes that Congress are about to correct their long-continued habits of neglect to the trade of these southern states and to send us some aid." [71]

A few days before writing this to Lee, Jefferson had addressed a letter to the governor of Maryland declining, from necessity, to buy two galleys which had been offered to Patrick Henry, while governor, in February 1778. "I am to return you thanks," he writes, "for your obliging offer of a preference in the purchase of your two galleys; but it happens that we cannot become purchasers, having already full as many as we can either man or maintain. We think the defense of our bay so important that we would spare nothing to effect it within the compass of our abilities. We trust the same opinion prevails with you, so great a part of your state lying adjacent to the bay and its waters; and of course that strong motives of expediency must have induced you to propose to lessen your force there. The late depredations on our coast and captures in the bay have put us on the greatest exertions we can make to put our little fleet into order for action. The force, however, must be small to which that is competent." [72]

"The late depredations," which refer, of course, to Collier's raid, had, alas, not proven a sufficient warning to the legislators. What remained of the navy was subjected to a drastic reorganization undertaken by the Assembly in the fall of 1779. The Navy Board had already been discontinued in the spring session. Its duties were to be performed by the boards of war and trade.[73] On November 27, George Mason reported for the Committee of Ways and Means "on certain necessary economical regulations" affecting both the army and the navy, to which the committee had agreed. "The deranged state of the army, and the ruinous situation of the navy," the report read, "hath greatly enhanced the expense of maintaining the one and subtracted from that little defense which was expected to be derived from the other; whilst the accumulated charge of both creates an article of expenditure which hath already reduced your finances to difficulty, and is too enormous to be supported." [74] On the thirtieth the House resolved itself into a committee of the whole and recommended the resolutions which were to stop recruiting, reduce the number of officers and commands, and to a great extent disband the navy. It was written into the statutes that "the Ships *Tartar* and *Dragon,* and the galleys *Henry, Manly, Hero, Page, Lewis,* and *Safeguard,* be no longer retained as part of the Virginia Navy.... That the ship *Thetis,* the brig *Jefferson,* the *Accomac* and *Diligence,* galleys, and the *Liberty* and *Patriot,* boats, be retained in the Virginia Navy; and that the *Gloucester* be also retained as a prisonship ... that the ship *Tempest* be retained til the *Thetis* be ready for sea, and then be disposed of ... that a third boat such as *Liberty* or *Patriot,* to serve as a lookout boat, be procured." [75]

In all this, of course, Jefferson took no actual part, except insofar as he was consulted by individual members of the Assembly or by the various committees. That their action was contrary to his belief and judgment is obvious from the foregoing discussion. That he did not merely bow in acquiescence is witnessed by the many memoranda among his unpublished papers, from which we cannot escape the conclusion that his mind was never at rest concerning these problems, nearly insoluble, presented by the armed forces and by the navy.

The fall of 1779 saw certain minor crises arising in Virginia, ominously foreshadowing what was to come. On June 19 Jefferson had written John Jay, the president of Congress: "Our trade has never been so distressed since the time of Lord Dunmore as it is at present by a parcel of trifling privateers under the countenance of two or three larger vessels who keep our little naval force from doing anything." It was impossible for a note of resentment not to enter into his next words: "The uniform train of events which during the whole course of this war we are to suppose has rendered it improper that the American fleet or any part of it should ever come to relieve or countenance the trade of certain places, while the same train of events has as uniformly rendered it proper to confine them to the protection of certain other parts of the continent, is a lamentable arrangement for us. The same ill luck has attended us as to the disposition of the prizes taken by our navy.... A British prize would be a more rare phenomenon here than a comet, because the one has been seen but the other never was." [76]

By November the depredations on both sea and land had reached such a point that Jefferson issued the first of many proclamations for which he was to become famous, laying an embargo on the export of foodstuffs. "Whereas the exportation of provisions from this state will be attended with manifest injury to the United States," the proclamation reads, "by supplying the enemy and rendering it difficult for the public agents and contractors to procure supplies for the American troops ... I have therefore thought fit, by and with the advice of the Council of State, to issue this my Proclamation for laying an embargo on provisions, *viz.* on all beef, pork, bacon, wheat, Indian corn, pease or other grain, or flour or meal made of the same; to continue until the first of May next. And I do hereby strictly prohibit all mariners, masters, and commanders of vessels, and all other persons whatsoever in this state, from loading on board any vesel for exportation, and from exporting all or any of the above species of provisions by land or water...." [77]

The following month word reached Virginia through an express from General Washington that "the enemy meditate an invasion." On the eleventh of December Washington wrote Jefferson from his headquarters in Morristown, New Jersey: "I have received advice from New York that a very large embarkation has taken place... and that the fleet containing them was at the Hook on the point of sailing; their destination reported to be for Chesapeake Bay, on a combined operation in the first place against the French Squadron there, and afterwards to attempt to rescue the Convention Troops. Their naval force may consist of 5 sail of the line and 2 frigates of 44 (besides a 50-gun ship)...." [78]

On Christmas Day Washington again wrote Jefferson to say that his warning of an invasion had been "premature," but recommending "a continuation of the precaution which I then pointed out." [79] Before this second communication had had time to reach Virginia, Jefferson had addressed a letter to Benjamin Harrison, Speaker of the House of Delegates, laying the state of affairs before the House. Consciously or not, the letter draws a picture of the lamentable weakness of Virginia—weakness in regard to her defense, in regard to her financial situation, and in regard to the unfortunate limitations with which she had surrounded her executive. "It is our duty," Jefferson writes, "to provide against every event, and the executive are accordingly engaged in concerting proper measures of defense. Among others we think to call an immediate force from the militia to defend the post at York, and to take a proper port on the south side of the James River; but the expense, the difficulties which attend a general call of the militia into the field, the disgust it gives them, more especially when they find no enemy in place, and the extreme rigor of the season, induce us to refer to the decision of the General Assembly, whether we shall on the intelligence already received and now communicated to them, call a competent force of militia to oppose the numbers of the enemy spoken of; or whether we shall make ready all orders and prepare other circumstances, but omit actually issuing those orders till the enemy appear and we have further proof of their intentions. The Assembly will also please to determine whether, in case the enemy should make a lodgement in the country, it would be expedient to avail ourselves of the laudable zeal which may prevail on their first landing and enlist a sufficient number to oppose them and to continue in service during the invasion or for any other term. Perhaps it may not be amiss to suggest to the Assembly the tardiness of collecting even small numbers of men by divisions, that if any better method should occur to them they may prescribe it. The present state of the treasury in more points than one will no doubt be thought an obstacle to every military endeavor which may be unnecessary." [80]

It was a situation that would have dismayed any but the stoutest heart.

IV. The Conquest of the West

WHILE THE British menace was constantly growing more ominous on the eastern front, dramatic developments were transpiring in the west under the brilliant leadership of George Rogers Clark. The first overtures, to be sure, occurred under Patrick Henry. It was Jefferson, however, who shared Clark's vision and who became his most ardent and determined supporter. At the outbreak of the Revolution, the British, assuming the role of the red man's friend, had organized a series of expeditions against the common enemy. Particularly active in this field of endeavor, and with a fine appreciation of the more barbarous forms of savagery, was Henry Hamilton, lieutenant governor of Detroit, the first civil officer after the British took over that post. By enlisting the help of the Indians in raids aimed to destroy the newly settled western outposts in the territory which was subsequently to become Kentucky, Illinois, and Indiana, the British hoped to establish themselves as masters of the vast lands that lay to the west of the Alleghenies. It would be a nice blow to the "rebels" and enable them to be attacked from another side.

To the great good fortune of these settlers and to the glory of Virginia, a young native of Albemarle whose father's farm was near Jefferson's ancestral acres, took to heart the interest of these unorganized, lonely, and scattered people, and thus turned the course of the history of this country. This was the dauntless George Rogers Clark, a man described by Jefferson as of "enterprising and energetic genius," whom he was to recommend to the Indians as "our great, good, and trusty warrior."

Clark, an adventure-loving youth of twenty, made his first trip into the wilderness of the west in 1771. The following year saw him there again. He is described by one of his companions as "a young gentleman from Virginia, who with several others, inclined to make a tour in this new world." [1] So enamored did he become of the rich and beautiful country this new world revealed, that he determined to settle there. On April 1, 1775, he wrote his brother: "I have engaged as a deputy surveyor under Cap'n Hancock Lee, for to lay out lands on the Kentuck, for the Ohio company, at the rate of 80 £ per year, and the privilege of taking what land I want." [2] By the following year he had left Virginia and removed permanently to Kentucky.

At this period Kentucky was, of course, not an independent country, much less a state, but part of a vast, undefined territory to which Virginia laid claim under her charter of 1609. Originally this comprised all the land west of the Alleghenies and north of the North Carolina boundary, extending to the Pacific. The Cherokee Indians, the King of England, Spain, and the Indiana and Vandalia land companies likewise claimed these lands, all or in part. Certain states to the north of Virginia, fearing she would become too powerful, and at the same time eager for a share of the riches this new country promised, joined in urging Congress to decree the land west of the Alleghenies as being owned jointly by all the states. More recently Richard Henderson and his associates of North Carolina, claiming to have purchased large tracts of land from the Cherokees, had formed the powerful Transylvania Company and in 1775 were attempting to institute some form of government. The same year Lord Dunmore declared the Henderson claim void, and in 1776 the new government of Virginia did likewise. Finally a number of Kentuckians, uncertain of their own status and the titles to their property, petitioned the Virginia Convention to take them under its wing or, if it lacked that power, "in your goodness, recommend the same to your worthy delegates to espouse it as the cause of the colony." [3]

In the midst of this confusion, Clark appeared upon the scene, determined to take some action. "While in Virginia I found there were various opinions respecting Henderson's claim," he writes in his *Memoir*. "Many thought it was good; others doubted whether or not Virginia could, with propriety, have any pretensions to the country. This was what I wanted to know. I immediately fixed on my plans, that of assembling the people, get them to elect deputies, and send them to the assembly of Virginia and treat with them respecting the country. If valuable conditions were procured, to declare ourselves citizens of the state, otherwise establish an independent government.... To carry this scheme into effect, I appointed a general meeting at Harrods Town, on the 6th June, 1776." [4] At this meeting Clark and John Gabriel Jones were elected, not delegates to the Virginia legislature, but members of it, an entirely irregular proceeding.

It was a bold plan, and a brilliant one—one that succeeded largely because of the vigor and determination of Clark's own personality. As he remarked on a later occasion, "I knew my case was desperate, but the more I reflected on my weakness, the more I was pleased with the enterprise." [5] No words more truly describe his character. Similar sentiments guided him now.

Clark's long overland journey to Williamsburg, following this meeting, is one of the most dramatic in his astonishing career. It was one of incredible hardship, of which he himself says, "... we traveled in greater torment than I ever before or since experienced." On arriving in Virginia, he suffered the bitter disappointment of finding the Assembly no longer in session. His heroic efforts, however, were not to go unrewarded. Patrick Henry, then governor of Virginia, not only lent a sympathetic and attentive ear to Clark's account of the situation of the Kentuckians, but strongly recommended him and his request for assistance to the Council. That body, in the absence of the legislature, was much more cautious. On August 23, however, it ordered that "Mr. George Rogers Clark having represented to this board the defenseless state of the inhabitants of Kentucky, and having on their behalf requested that a quantity of ammunition may be supplied them, resolved that five hundred pounds of gunpowder be forthwith sent to Pittsburg and delivered to the commanding officer at that station, to be safely kept and delivered to Mr. Clark for the use of the inhabitants of Kentucky." [6]

The final consummation of Clark's plan took place on December 6, 1776. Over the violent opposition of the Henderson Company and of Colonel Arthur Campbell, who wanted this rich new land annexed to Washington County, which he represented, Kentucky was made an independent county. Clark had now achieved his dearest ambition. Kentucky had become an organized part of his "mother country," as he calls Virginia, sharing in the privileges and the obligations of the commonwealth.

Henceforth, Clark tells us, "the whole of my time when not thus employed in reflecting on things in general, particularly Kentucky, how it accorded with the interest of the United States, whether it was in their interest to support it [or] not, etc. This led me to a long train of thinking, the result of which was to lay aside every private view, engage seriously in the war, and have the interest and welfare of the public my only view until the fate of the fall of the continent should be known.... Those ideas caused me to view Kentucky in the most favorable point of view, as a place of the greatest consequence, and ought to meet with every encouragement, and that nothing I could engage in would be of more general utility than its defense...."[7]

As a result of his reflections Clark came to the conclusion that if the Kentucky settlements were to survive against the machinations of the British, a campaign would have to be undertaken in the country beyond the Ohio. Knowing, as he says, that "the commandants of the different towns of the Illinois and Wabash ... were busily engaged in exciting the Indians, their reduction became my first object."[8] To achieve this, Clark once more started on the long journey to Virginia. The blessing of the governor and of the Council were necessary for his enterprise, to say nothing of more substantial aid. "When I left Kentucky October 1, 1777," he writes, "I plainly saw that every eye was turned toward me as if expecting some stroke in their favor."

He arrived at Williamsburg on the fifth of November and spent two weeks in the capital, settling the accounts of the Kentucky militia and "making remarks on everything I saw or heard that would lead me to the knowledge of the disposition of those in power." On December 10 he presented his plan to Patrick Henry, a plan infinitely more ambitious and far-reaching than the one with which he had come the preceding year. "At first view," says Clark of Henry, "he appeared to be fond of it," but the daring and hazardous aspects of the enterprise gave the Governor pause. Unwilling to assume the entire responsibility himself, and unable to lay the matter before the legislature then in session, for fear "it would soon be known throughout the frontiers," he had, Clark continues, "several private councils composed of select gentlemen."

The men upon whom Henry called for counsel and advice were Thomas Jefferson, George Wythe, and George Mason. Thus Jefferson's name first becomes definitely linked with Clark's momentous undertaking. What was his contribution to the discussions with the Governor and with the Council is, unfortunately, not recorded. It is equally obscure whose idea it was to write into the instructions given Clark: "It is in contemplation to establish a post near the mouth of the Ohio," a move of the utmost importance. This would not only give the Americans a commanding position on both rivers, but establish the Mississippi rather than the Ohio or even, as might have been, the Allegheny Mountains as the western boundary. That Jefferson may have contributed more than his share to this proposal, and that he envisioned in Clark's scheme more than the annexation of another county and the protection of its inhabitants, is clear from a letter he wrote Clark shortly after the latter had left Williamsburg. "Much solicitude will be felt," he says, "for the result of your expedition to the Wabash; it will at least delay their expedition to the frontier settlement, and if successful, have an important bearing ultimately in establishing our northwestern boundary." [9] This fort was not built until 1780, when Jefferson was governor, and when he directed Joseph Martin, Indian agent at the time, to treat with the Cherokees for the land on the south side of the mouth of the Ohio.[10]

On the second of January 1778, according to the *Journal of the Council*, "the Governor informed the council that he had had some conversation with several gentlemen who were well acquainted with the western frontiers of Virginia and the situation of the post at Kaskasky held by the British King's forces, where there are many pieces of cannon and military stores to a considerable amount, and that he was informed that the place was at present held by a very weak garrison, which induced him to believe that an expedition against it might be carried on with success, but that he wished the advice of Council on the occasion."[11] "After making every inquiry into my proposed plan of operation," Clark says, "the expedition was resolved on ... and on the second day of January, 1778, [I] received my instructions and received 1200£ for the use of the expedition, and [an] order on Pittsburg for boats, ammunition, etc. ... On the fourth I set forward, clothed with all the authority I wished for."[12]

In the instructions Clark received from the Council there is a remarkable passage, rendered doubly striking by the events that were to follow. "It is earnestly desired," the instructions read, "that you show humanity to such British subjects, and other persons, as fall in your hands. If the white inhabitants at the post and the neighborhood will give undoubted evidence of their attachment to this state, ... let them be treated as fellow citizens, and their persons and property duly secured. ... But if those people will not accede to these reasonable demands, they must feel the miseries of war, under the direction of that humanity which has hitherto distinguished Americans."[13]

After receiving his instructions, Clark set off at once to recruit the seven companies of men authorized, a project in which he encountered no little difficulty and opposition. By May he had managed to gather a little band of 170 men. They proceeded down the Ohio and set up camp on Corn Island, opposite the present site of Louisville. On June 24 he and his men were ready to start "in search of new adventures," as he puts it. "I resolved to begin my career in the Illinois," he says, "where there were more inhabitants but scattered in different villages and less danger of being immediately overpowered by the Indians." On the evening of the fourth of July he surprised the important town of Kaskaskia and "before daylight had the whole town disarmed." Within a short time he had likewise received the surrender of Cahokia, a post on the Mississippi a few miles from where St. Louis now stands. Meanwhile Father Gibault, a priest at Kaskaskia, undertook to win for Clark the support of the French inhabitants of Vincennes. In a few weeks, says Clark, he "returned with intelligence agreeable to my wishes." The American flag was raised, and one of Clark's most trusted associates, Captain Helm, was dispatched to take charge of the militia there. "I now found myself in possession of the whole," Clark writes George Mason, "in a country where I found I could do more real service than I expected; which occasioned my situation to be more disagreeable as I wanted men." [14]

The disconcerting news of Clark's success reached Governor Hamilton in Detroit. Gathering a small force of British and a considerable one of Indians, he marched on Vincennes. He seized the post and adjoining Fort Sackville on December 16, 1778. Through spies Clark learned that no attempt was to be made by the British to recapture the Illinois country until the spring, as "the passage is too difficult at present." He learned, furthermore, as he wrote Governor Henry, "that Mr. Hamilton had weakened himself by sending his Indians against the frontiers and to block the Ohio." [15] Although Clark had received no reinforcements, and, as he wrote Henry, not "a scrape of a line from you for over twelve months, and had a right to feel disheartened," he determined to risk everything. "I know the case is desperate," he continued, "but, Sir, we must either quit the country or attack Mr. Hamilton.... Who knows what fortune will do for us? Great things have been effected by a few men well conducted." [16]

On February 5, 1779, Clark set out with an army of only about 170 men, partly American, partly French volunteers. An overland march of 240 miles, in the dead of winter, lay before them. Their hardships almost passed human endurance. In his remarkable letter to George Mason, giving a short sketch of his "enterprise and proceeding in the Illinois," Clark says: "If I was sensible that you would let no person see this relation, I would give you a detail of our suffering for four days in crossing those waters [the Wabash River] and the manner it was done; as I am sure that you would credit it. But it is too incredible for any person to believe except those that are well acquainted with me as you are." [17] Nevertheless, he observes, "I cannot account for it, but I still had an inward assurance of success; and never could, when weighing every circumstance, doubt it." [18]

Clark's premonition proved to be correct. On February 23, after a march of sixteen days, the party arrived within sight of the fort. Clark tells us that "a thousand ideas flashed through my head at that moment.... I resolved to be as daring as possible." Before anyone was aware of his presence, he attacked the town, which "immediately surrendered with joy, and assisted in the siege." The following day, despite his boast that "the garrison was not disposed to be awed into anything unbecoming British soldiers," Hamilton surrendered with his force of twenty-nine men. "All my past sufferings vanished," Clark exclaims. "Never was a man more happy." The news of Clark's success did not reach Virginia until the middle of May. The first messenger bearing letters with details of the event was murdered by a party of Indians as he passed through Kentucky on his way to Williamsburg. Nevertheless Patrick Henry was able to inform the Assembly: "... this enterprise has succeeded to the utmost of our wishes," and to jubilate: "... this is a most gallant action and I trust will secure our frontiers in a great measure." [19]

This was the state of the western campaign when Jefferson became governor. He was immediately to be caught up in a whirlpool of unpleasantness, charges and countercharges, resulting from it. On the seventh of March Clark had sent the infamous trio, Henry Hamilton, lieutenant governor, Philip Dejean, justice of the peace for Detroit, and William Lamothe, captain of volunteers, and other prisoners, under guard to Virginia. They arrived in the middle of June. The three were brought to Williamsburg "to be severely dealt with," as Jefferson wrote Richard Henry Lee. A long memorial, dated "In Council, June 18, 1779," signed by the clerk, Archibald Blair, but very likely written by Jefferson himself, describes the incredible brutality of the conduct of the three prisoners and concludes: "... this board has resolved to advise the Governor that the said Henry Hamilton, Philip Dejean, and William Lamothe, prisoners of war, be put in irons, confined in the dungeon of the public jail, debarred the use of pen, ink, and paper, and excluded all converse except with their keeper. And the Governor orders accordingly." [20]

To justify its action, Council summarized the situation in the following inexorable words which could have come only from the pen that wrote the indictment of George III in the Declaration of Independence: "They [i.e. the Council] have seen that the conduct of the British officers, civil and military, has in the whole course of this war been savage, and unprecedented among civilized nations; that our officers taken by them have been confined in crowded jails, loathsome dungeons and prisonships, loaded with irons, supplied often with no food, generally with too little for the sustenance of nature ... that captivity and death with them have been almost synonymous....

"Their prisoners with us have, on the other hand, been treated with humanity and moderation; they have been fed, on all occasions, with wholesome and plentiful food, suffered to go at large within extensive tracts of territory, treated with liberal hospitality, permitted to live in the families of our citizens, to labor for themselves, to acquire and enjoy profits, and finally to participate of the principal benefits of society, privileged from all burdens.

"Reviewing this contrast, which cannot be denied by our enemies themselves, in a single point ... called on by that justice we owe to those who are fighting the battles of our country, to deal out, at length miseries to their enemies, measure for measure, and to distress the feelings of mankind by exhibiting to them spectacles of severe retaliation," [21] the measures already mentioned were decided upon.

The Hamilton case immediately became a *cause célèbre*—partly because of the prominence of the chief prisoner, partly because of his arrogance, and partly because the extreme inhumanity of his conduct had led Virginia to take steps that had never before been taken in the war. Sir Guy Carlton, governor of Canada, whose deputy Hamilton was, and General William Phillips, commander of the British prisoners at Charlottesville and himself a prisoner of war, took it upon themselves to write Jefferson, taking exception to the action of the Council. Within a few weeks he found himself, as he says, charged with "violation of natural faith."

It was the first great problem to confront Jefferson in his career as governor. How conscientiously he tried to follow the right course, despite his indignation at Hamilton's conduct as expressed in his reply to Phillips, can be seen in the letter he wrote Washington at this time. As usual, he had turned to his books, but he ended by appealing to the superior wisdom of General Washington in military affairs.

Enclosing a copy of the order of Council, as well as of General Phillips's letter, Jefferson writes: "The General seems to suppose that a prisoner on capitulation cannot be put into close confinement, though his capitulation may not have provided against it. My idea was that all persons taken in war were to be deemed prisoners of war. That those who surrender in capitulation (or convention) are prisoners of war also, subject to the same treatment as those who surrender at discretion.... I have the highest idea of the sacredness of those contracts which take place between nation and nation at war, and would be the last on earth who would do anything in violation of them. I can find nothing in those books usually recurred to as testimonials of the laws and usages of nature and nations which convicts the opinions I have above expressed, of error. Yet there may be such an usage as General Phillips seems to suppose, though not taken notice of by these writers. I am obliged to trouble Your Excellency on this occasion, by asking of you information on this point. There is no other person whose decision will so authoritatively decide this point in the public mind, and none with which I am disposed so implicitly to comply. If you shall be of opinion that the bare existence of a capitulation in the case of Governor Hamilton privileges him from confinement, though there be no article to that effect in the capitulation, justice shall most assuredly be done him." [22]

Washington answered at length on August 6, saying he had consulted "with several intelligent general officers," who were of the opinion that "Mr. Hamilton could not according to the usages of war after his capitulation, even in the manner it was made, be subjected to any uncommon severity.... Whether it be expedient to confine him in his present confinement from motives of policy or to satisfy the people," Washington continues, "is a question I cannot determine.... I should not hesitate to withhold from him a thousand privileges I might allow to common prisoners...." [23]

A few weeks after this Washington received a letter from the British Commissary of Prisoners concerning the Hamilton case, stating that the enemy intended to retaliate. On September 13, Washington sent Jefferson a copy of the communication, saying, "By this Your Excellency will be able to judge how far it may be expedient to relax the present treatment of Mr. Hamilton. Col. Mathews, who will have the honor of delivering this, comes out at the request of the Virginia officers in captivity to solicit such indulgence for him and his companions, as will induce the enemy to relinquish the execution of their threats." [24]

On the twenty-ninth of September the Council, following the advice of Washington's letter of August 6 "to publish all the cruelties he [Hamilton] has committed or abetted ... that the world, holding his conduct in abhorrence, may feel and approve the justice of his fate," issued a statement along these lines which was printed in the *Virginia Gazette* on October 9. In conclusion it advised the Governor "to send Lieutenant Governor Hamilton, Captain Lamothe, and Phillip Dejean to Hanover Courthouse, there to suffer them to be at large within certain reasonable limits, taking their parole in the usual form." [25]

Hamilton and his associates refused the parole. "They objected to that part of it, which restrained them from saying anything to the prejudice of the United States, and insisted on 'freedom of speech,'" Jefferson wrote Washington. "They were, in consequence, remanded to their confinement in jail, which must be considered as a voluntary one, until they can determine with themselves to be inoffensive in word as well as in deed." [26]

There was still the question of British reprisals to be considered. Jefferson's reply to Washington's letter, delivered by Colonel Mathews on October 2, was as near to being hot-headed as he ever permitted himself to be. "Were I to speak from present impressions," he writes, "I should say it is happy for Governor Hamilton that a final determination of his fate was made before this new information.... It is impossible they can be serious in attempting to bully us in this manner. We have too many of their subjects in our power, and too much iron to clothe them with; and, I will add, too much resolution to avail ourselves of both, to fear their pretended retaliation." [27]

To Colonel Mathews, the officer of the 9th Virginia Infantry, then on parole, who had come to plead for himself and his fellow prisoners, Jefferson addressed a letter in which he reviewed the Hamilton case in detail, defending the position Virginia had taken. His concluding words must have brought solace as well as inspired courage and determination in the heart of every man who found himself one of those unfortunates, a prisoner of war. "I beg you to be assured," Jefferson wrote him, "there is nothing consistent with the honor of your country which we shall not at all times be ready to do for the relief of yourself and companions in captivity. We know that ardent spirit and hatred for tyranny which brought you into your present situation will enable you to bear up against it with the firmness which has distinguished you as a soldier, and to look forward with pleasure to the day when events shall take place against which the wounded spirits of your enemies will find no comfort even from reflections on the most refined of cruelties with which they have glutted themselves." [28]

Pressure continued to be brought on Jefferson for Hamilton's release, but he remained adamant. On September 5, 1780, Washington wrote him: "Now that I am on the subject of prisoners, I would wish to be informed in what light I am to consider Governor Hamilton, as I do not observe him included in the list. The gentleman has already been the subject of several propositions on the part of the enemy, and should others be made before I hear again from Your Excellency, I shall be embarrassed, as I shall not know on what footing to place him. Indeed, there will shortly be an interview on exchange at which it is more than probable he will be again mentioned." [29]

Jefferson replied on the twenty-sixth: "You are not unapprised of the influence of this officer with the Indians, his activity and embittered zeal against us; you also perhaps know how precarious is our tenure in the Illinois country, and how critical is the situation of the new counties on the Ohio. These circumstances determined us to detain Governor Hamilton and Major Hay within our power when we delivered up the other prisoners. On a late representation from the people of Kentucky by a person sent here from the county, and expressions of what they had reasons to apprehend from these two prisoners in the event of their liberation, we assured them they would not be parted with, though we were giving up our other prisoners. Lieutenant Colonel Dubuysson, aide to Baron de Kalb, lately came here on his parole with an offer from Lord Rawdon to exchange him for Hamilton.... These and other overtures do not lessen our opinion of the importance of retaining him; and they have been and will be uniformly rejected. Should the settlement indeed of a cartel become impracticable without the consent of the states to submit their separate prisoners to its obligation, we will give up these two prisoners, as we would anything rather than be an obstacle to a general good. But no other circumstances would, I believe, extract them from us." [30]

Closely allied with the organization of Kentucky and the conquest of the Illinois country was the dispute over the boundary line between Virginia and Pennsylvania. The dispute was an old one. The inhabitants of the uncertain area enthusiastically disliked each other and whichever state claimed sovereignty. Jefferson had early concerned himself with it. In July 1776, while a member of the Virginia delegation to the Continental Congress, he had written a letter at its behest to the Pennsylvania Convention discussing this troublesome matter. Aside from the question under review, the letter is interesting as showing that Jefferson, in the brief interval that had elapsed since the signing of the Declaration, had not yet become accustomed to think of Virginia as a state instead of a colony, and that the form of any union of the colonies was still very nebulous in his mind. "The honorable the Convention of Virginia," the letter reads, "attending to the inconveniences which may arise from unsettled jurisdiction in the neighborhood of Fort Pitt, have instructed us to propose to your honorable house to agree on some temporary boundary which may serve for preservation of the peace in that territory until an amicable and final determination may be had before arbiters mutually chosen. Such temporary settlement will from its nature do prejudice to neither party when at any future day a complete information of facts shall enable them to submit the doubt to a just and final decision. We can assure you that the Colony of Virginia does not entertain a wish that one inch should be added to theirs from the territory of a sister colony, and we have perfect confidence that the same just sentiments prevail in your house. Parties thus disposed can scarcely meet with difficulty in adjusting either a temporary or a final settlement. The decision, whatever it be, will not annihilate the lands. They will

GEORGE ROGERS CLARK. By Matthew Harris Jouett. (*Courtesy of the Filson Club*)

BENEDICT ARNOLD. From the engraving after Pierre Eugène du Simitière. (*Courtesy of the Library Company of Philadelphia*)

remain to be occupied by Americans," he proudly concludes, "and whether those be counted in the numbers of this or that of the United States will be thought a matter of little moment." [31]

Nothing seems to have come of the matter at this time. The minutes of the Convention show that the letter was read and that "it was ordered that further consideration thereof be deferred." Certain notes among Jefferson's papers from this period show how much he had it on his mind, however; and what he, or the Virginia delegates, were prepared to propose to Pennsylvania. "If the Monongahela is the line," they read in part, "it will throw 300 Virginia families into Pennsylvania ... not one-third of that number of Pennsylvanians would be thrown on the Virginia side. If the Laurel hill is the boundary, it will place on the Virginia side all the Virginia settlers and about 200 families of Pennsylvania settlers. A middle line is thought to be just." After discussing the route this middle line would follow, he concludes: "This would give tolerable satisfaction to Virginia, would throw about 150 Pennsylvanians into Virginia and about 20 or 30 Virginians into Pennsylvania. The 150 Pennsylvanians live in such manner dispersed ... that no line will throw them into Pennsylvania." [32]

Thus the matter simmered along until 1778, when George Rogers Clark began attempting to raise recruits for his first expedition. He writes: "I found also opposition to our interest in the Pittsburg country. As the whole was divided into violent parties between the Virginians and Pennsylvanians respecting territory, each trying to counteract the idea of men being for the State of Virginia affected the vulgar of the one party.... Many gentlemen of both parties conceived it to be injurious to the public interest to draw off men at so critical a moment for the defense of a few detached inhabitants." [33]

On May 23 Patrick Henry addressed a letter to the Speaker of the House of Delegates, stating that "the unsettled state of the boundary line between this commonwealth and Pennsylvania is likely to prove the source of much mischief. Consequences of the most alarming nature seem likely to follow if the legislature do not interpose, the executive not being competent to the business. The papers I send herewith relate to this subject which is become so interesting, and I beg you will please lay them before the General Assembly." [34] No action was taken. An identical letter, repeating the request, dated November 27, finally engaged the attention of the House. On the ninth of December, we learn from its *Journal,* a committee reported "that there are great disorders and frequent commotions prevailing on the northwestern frontier of this commonwealth adjoining the border of Pennsylvania, occasioned by part of the inhabitants' considering themselves inhabitants of the commonwealth of Pennsylvania, each reciprocally refusing obedience to the civil power, whereby the exertions of both are enfeebled, to the injury of the common cause." [35] The committee, for which Jefferson's friend, William Fleming, reported, was disposed to appoint another committee to "return an answer to the last proposals made to this Assembly by the Assembly of Pennsylvania, and to adjust and propose some temporary boundary, to be established and continued, until the true and proper boundaries between the two states can be finally ascertained and settled." [36] The Reverend James Madison, president of the College of William and Mary, and Robert Andrews, a professor there, were ultimately named commissioners for Virginia. They met with the Pennsylvania commissioners during the last days of August 1779. On the thirty-first a compact was signed whereby it was agreed "to extend Mason's and Dixon's line due west five degrees of longitude to be computed from the River Delaware for the southern boundary of Pennsylvania, and that a meridian drawn from the western extremity thereof to the northern limit of the said state be the western boundary of Pennsylvania forever." [37]

Although the commissioners were appointed and had come to an understanding, they were not immediately dispatched. "The novelty of the line proposed for the western boundary of Pennsylvania by the joint commissioners may well account for a hesitation to confirm it," Jefferson writes. Meanwhile feeling in Congress had been growing high, prodded by Pennsylvania interests, which feared the growing power and influence of Virginia. Every little occasion was used to stir up trouble. On December 15, 1779, alarmed at Clark's spectacular success in the west, President Reed of Pennsylvania blustered to the Pennsylvania delegates in Congress: "We have seen the state of Virginia in progressive encroachments advancing upon the old allowed territory of this state, taking possession and otherwise establishing themselves on lands ever deemed and considered the property of Pennsylvania, until Lord Dunmore in the extravagance of his views and designs set up claims which in their infancy were reprobated by those who now have thought proper to adopt them." [38]

The upshot of this was that on December 27 Congress passed a resolution "that it be recommended to the contending parties not to grant any part of the disputed land, or to disturb the possession of any persons living thereon, and to avoid every appearance of force until the dispute can be amicably settled by both states...." [39] On receipt of this, Jefferson, on February 9, 1781, took occasion to write one of his masterly letters clarifying the situation. He cites the torrent of immigration which had compelled Virginia to open a land office in May 1779 and to send commissioners "to settle, on the spot, without delay, those various claims, which being once cleared away, would leave the residuary country open to the acquisition of other adventurers.... I can say nothing," Jefferson concludes in a burst of disarming passion, "to whatever looks like menace on the part of our brethren.... To history, therefore, I must refer for answer, in which it would be an unhappy passage indeed, which should show by what fatal indulgence of subordinate views and passions, a contest for an atom had defeated well-founded prospects of giving liberty to half the globe. That no such blot shall wipe out the sequel of our glorious struggle, I trust as well in the approved zeal of the gentleman who adorns the administration of the other state, as in the resolutions of our own government to postpone to the great object of liberty every smaller motive and passion." [40]

Another year passed. On March 31, 1781, Jefferson wrote the two commissioners that, the principles on which the boundary between the two states was to be run having been fixed, President Reed proposed that execution of the work be begun. As "the extent of five degrees of longitude shall be determined by celestial observations," Jefferson remarks to Madison and Andrews, "of course it will require one set of astronomers to be at Philadelphia and another at Fort Pitt. We ask the favor of yourselves to undertake this business, the one to go to the one place, the other to the other.... I delay proposing to President Reed this mode of locating the boundary until I know whether we can get the execution of it undertaken by gentlemen who will do us credit and justice." [41]

It was a good deal to ask of the two reverend gentlemen, but they acquiesced. Detailed arrangements concerning horses, pay, and astronomical instruments were made; and on April 17 Jefferson addressed a letter to Reed concerning the details and saying: "... our commissioners will attend to their respective stations at any time which Your Excellency shall think proper to appoint." [42] The twelfth of June was fixed upon.

Meanwhile came the invasion of Virginia. "As Madison and Andrews unfortunately reside in Williamsburg, a place supposed to be an object with the enemy," Jefferson writes Reed on May 22, "I am not without fear this new circumstance will create difficulties in the time of their attendance." [43] On Reed's suggestion the whole matter was postponed another year. The last two official letters written by Jefferson during his governorship deal with this matter—one, dated June 3, to President Reed, acquiescing in his suggestions; and another, the same day, to the surveyor of the county of Monongalia, directing him to extend Mason's and Dixon's line for twenty-three miles "with a surveyor's compass only, in the usual manner marking the trees very slightly." Thus the dispute of the boundary passed forever out of Jefferson's hands, although the solution proposed in his administration was the one finally adopted.

Jefferson's Indian troubles were not confined to the far western frontier. The then-powerful Cherokee nation which inhabited the southern Appalachian region and thus bordered on the three great southern states, Virginia, North Carolina, and South Carolina, had long presented a problem. Early in his career as governor, Jefferson wrote to the governors of the two adjoining states making a proposal which reveals the humanity which always characterized his relations with the Indians and the beneficent spirit he sought to infuse. It was likewise the most practical solution of the frontier problem yet devised. "I have lately received messages and information from the Cherokee nation of Indians," he wrote Governor Caswell of North Carolina, "painting their nakedness and general distress for want of European goods so strongly as to call for pity and all possible relief. Their great numbers, however, and the extent of their settlements when taken into view by any one of our states, bear a discouraging proportion to the moderate aids we can singly furnish, and render a general distribution of them very troublesome.

"These considerations have induced me to take the liberty of submitting to your Excellency (as I do to Governor Rutledge also by a letter of today's date) to divide the trouble and task of supplying them among our three states. The division of those Indians into Southern, Middle, and Northern settlements renders the apportionment of them obvious. The protecting from intrusion the lands of the Southern Cherokees and furnishing them with goods seems most convenient to South Carolina, the same friendly offices to the Middle settlements seem most within your power, and the Northern settlements are most convenient to us. The attachment which each settlement will by these means acquire to that particular state which is its immediate patron and benefactor, will be a bond of peace and will lead to a separation of that powerful people." [44]

A similar letter was dispatched to Governor Rutledge by Major Martin, agent for Virginia with the Northern Cherokees. "Their present distresses are so great," Jefferson writes, "that we have bought up everything proper for them in our own country without regard to price. This, however, goes but a little way toward providing for them. Long accustomed to the use of European manufactures, they are as incapable of returning to their habits of skins and furs as we are, and find their wants the less tolerable as they are occasioned by a war the event of which is scarcely interesting to them." [45]

Although the letter to Rutledge is endorsed "recorded, November 2, 1779," no reply from him or from Caswell seems to have come to light. Before action could be taken in those slow-moving days of difficult communication, the Carolinas were to be swept up in the oncoming conflict from the south. Beneficence to the Indian, or amelioration of his situation, became a side issue in the onrush of war.

V. Jefferson's Second Term

JEFFERSON'S TERM AS governor of Virginia may well be described as a crescendo of misfortunes. Beginning with his inauguration in June 1779, when the war, however harassing, still hardly touched Virginia, it rose in a gradual and mighty swell to the disastrous climax of Arnold's invasion in January 1781 and Cornwallis's subsequent devastation of the state. That these misfortunes cannot justly be laid at Jefferson's door, that they were in no wise due to any defect in his natural abilities or to a lack of assiduous devotion to duty, but rather to the inherent difficulties and peculiarities of the situation in which he found himself, is something that has all too often been overlooked. A scapegoat being a human necessity, the wartime governor of an invaded state was a fitting victim. The governors of other states, to be sure, such as New York, Massachusetts, Pennsylvania, or South Carolina, have never been singled out for condemnation because their country and their cities were overrun by the British hordes. No one has demanded that they should have, in effect, mounted a charger and ridden dramatically at the head of their countrymen to victory or to death. It has been Jefferson's misfortune that, because a hot-headed and ill-advised member of the Virginia Assembly demanded an investigation of his conduct, in which he was vindicated, and because our history has, in the main, been written by those not too much in sympathy with him or his principles, a certain aura of incompetence has been attached to his administration, and the stigma of cowardice to his personal conduct.

The success of the British arms in Georgia and Carolina marks the turning point in Jefferson's governorship. With the fall of Charleston on May 12, 1780, the main scene of the war was transferred to Virginia and its borders, and there it remained until the final surrender of the enemy at Yorktown. The campaigns and battles which were to determine the future of the whole country were fought in this area. Clinton had by this time become convinced that the destruction of Virginia's resources would be "cutting up by the roots resistance in the south," as Henry Lee observed. Jefferson, struggling to do his utmost against overpowering odds, was to be carried along on the tide of seemingly endless adversity and disaster until the commonwealth was in disorganization, until he was on the verge of being discredited by his enemies, and until he left office a bitter and disillusioned man. Few men have had the ability subsequently to build a brilliant career upon a foundation once so shattered.

It must not be forgotten that throughout this period—as indeed throughout the war—Jefferson concurred in Washington's belief in the importance of placing the good of the whole union, however tenuous that union might as yet be, above the good of the individual state. Thus it came about that Virginia gave generously and unhesitatingly the best of her men and matériel to the "grand army," as Jefferson called it, while at home she was obliged to rely largely upon the slender resource of a poorly armed and unwilling militia. And thus it likewise came about that Jefferson was led to the brink of ruin by faithfully adhering to the policy and the judgment of his commander in chief.

Even the loss of a large number of Virginia troops in the surrender of Charleston did not shake Jefferson's determination to continue the same course. On June 7 he writes Samuel Huntington, president of the Continental Congress: "The enclosed intelligence from Governor Nash [of South Carolina] seems to indicate an intention [on the part of the British] to penetrate as far northwardly as they can. Whether under these appearances it may be expedient to send further aids to the southern states can only be decided by Congress on a view of the operations which they may have in contemplation elsewhere. I have no doubt such aids will be sent, unless greater good to the general union will be produced by employing them where they are. In either event, great supplies of military stores are immediately requisite here. North Carolina has none at all, those of South Carolina are in the hands of the enemy, and ours inadequate to the arming of our own militia. As far as they will go, they have been and will be cheerfully submitted to the common use.... No motives will induce us to let the general good labor even a moment for want of anything we have." [1]

News of the surrender of Charleston, an event so momentous for Virginia, had been slow to filter northward. A month after the disaster, on June 11, 1780, Jefferson wrote Washington: "Our intelligence from the southward is most lamentably defective. Though Charlestown has now been in the hands of the enemy a month, we hear nothing of their movements which can be relied on. Rumors are that they are penetrating northward.... There is nothing to oppose the progress of the enemy northward but the cautious principles of the military art." [2] On May 28 Jefferson had received a report from Major Hartshorne, who had been sent to Congress by Governor Rutledge of South Carolina, which he embodied in a paper, hitherto unpublished and here merely summarized, headed "State of things at Charlestown," as they stood on April 27. The force of the enemy is described as being "between 11,000 and 12,200 men, *viz.* 7,000 to 8,000 under Clinton in the lines before the town on the neck of land, and between 4,000 and 5,000 under Cornwallis on the north side of the Cooper River. Cornwallis has overrun the whole country south of the Santee River, which is the whole of what is valuable, except the district of Georgetown on the north side of Santee. Has burned all the grain and killed all the cattle which he could not carry off. His posts on Cooper River prevent all communication with the town and have rendered the blockade complete." [3] It was a bitter foretaste of the scorched-earth policy Cornwallis was to pursue so ruthlessly and so successfully in Virginia.

The surrender of Charleston had the added effect of at last arousing the legislature of Virginia to the seriousness of the situation in the southern theater of war. The members were stimulated, as we have seen, not only to provide for increased taxes at this time, and to issue still more money—measures which proved totally ineffective—they were likewise goaded to energetic action in other respects. Although in Collier's raid a year and a half before, Virginia had had a taste of what it meant to have the enemy upon its own soil, now, for the first time, the dangers and horrors of invasion loomed as an actuality. Now the legislature passed an act giving further powers to the governor and Council. "Whereas," it reads, "in this time of public danger, when a powerful and vindictive enemy are ravaging our southern sister states, and, encouraged by success, are making a rapid progress towards our own borders, it has become highly expedient, as well to oppose the common enemy in general, as to provide for the safety and defense of this state in particular, to vest the executive with extraordinary powers for a limited time." The governor, with the advice of Council, was given full power to "call into actual service from such counties as shall be judged most proper, any number of militia not to exceed 20,000 men, including those already ordered out by special act for the aid of South Carolina...." When regimented they might be marched either to the northern states or to the assistance of any of the southern United States.[4]

To supply the troops the governor, with the advice of Council, was authorized to obtain "so many live cattle, linen for tents (except so much as is necessary for the use of each particular family), horses, wagons, boats, or other vessels and their crews, and other necessaries as may be wanted to supplying the militia or other troops that are or may be ordered into actual service from this commonwealth ... provided always that not more than half of the bullocks and barren cows belonging to any person, fit for slaughter, shall be subject to such seizure."[5] It was further decreed that: "Whereas several well-disposed, spirited friends to their country have offered to collect and serve as volunteers in the horse, provided they can be armed, accoutered, and provided with forage and other provisions at the public expense," the governor be empowered "to call into the public service as many companies of volunteer cavalry as the public good may require."[6] To take care of the loyalists, who continued to be a serious menace in Virginia as elsewhere, authority was given to establish what today would be called a concentration camp, where the governor and Council were directed to "commit to close confinement any person or persons whatsoever, whom there may be just cause to suspect of disaffection to the independence of the United States, and of attachment to their enemies."[7]

During these months Virginia was thus girding herself for the struggle in every way that seemed possible or feasible. "We have been preparing, in the best manner we can, to meet the storm that is brewing against us in the south," Richard Henry Lee wrote Theoderick Bland, "but I fear that our exertions, unassisted by our northern friends, will not be sufficient to oppose the collected strength of our enemies. We want clothes, arms, ammunition, tents, and many other important stores. I cannot reckon much upon the ten millions of pounds, now issuing by order of this assembly; it will pass away like a vision in the first instance, and remain afterwards a poisonous medium, obstructing future operations."[8]

All measures proved to be inadequate, however. The bitter truth of Washington's statement that there is a material difference between voting battalions and raising them, was to be painfully brought home to the executive as well as to the legislature. The gentlemen who comprised that body might empower the governor to impress horses, wagons, cattle, and other supplies. They could not, however, create what did not exist. Cloth for shirts, uniforms, and tents was practically not to be had. The recruits would arrive at their rendezvous in a state of virtual nakedness, as was often observed, expecting the government to equip them. Thus in October 1780 General Gates wrote Jefferson from Hillsboro, North Carolina: "Forty of your 18-months men from Botetourt County arrived in camp yesterday. They are entirely unequipped and unprovided with everything that is necessary for the service they are intended to perform and for the term they are engaged to serve." He begs the governor to see that no more men are sent unless provided with clothes, shoes, blankets, and every necessity for immediate service. "I have not a single article to supply them with," he concludes.[9]

Jefferson's correspondence at this period is a heartbreaking commentary on the inadequacy of every phase of the military and economic scene in Virginia. There were not enough men, there were not enough arms, there was not enough ammunition, there was not enough food, clothing, tents, wagons, or horses. There was, in short, not enough of anything. A never-ending stream of letters from the distraught commanding officers of the various troops, beseeching the executive to send supplies, flooded Jefferson's desk day after day. One from General Edward Stevens, as late as March 1781, is expressive of the tone of all throughout these years. "My force," he writes, "has never been during any stage of the campaign equal to any decisive effort.... Every day has given me hopes of being stronger, but I have been as constantly disappointed. The militia indeed have flocked in from various quarters and seemed to promise me as much as I could wish, but they soon get tired with difficulties and go and come in such irregular bodies that I can make no calculations on the strength of my army, or direct any future operations that can insure me the means of success. At the present time I have not above 8 or 900 of them, 30 of whom only are Carolinians, notwithstanding there have been near 5,000 in motion within the course of a few weeks. A force fluctuating in this manner can only serve to destroy the wealth of our country without promising the most distant hope of success." [10]

Even Washington was moved to write his confidant, John Mathews of South Carolina: "Your Southern affairs wear a most disagreeable aspect and prove more and more the necessity of renouncing that feeble system which has brought this country to so perplexing a crisis. If there were any hope of our councils assuming that complexion which the exigency demands, the progress of the enemy at this period would seem to me an advantage rather than an evil.... You have your wish," he continued, "in the officer appointed to the Southern command; I think I am giving you a general; but what can a general do without men, without arms, without clothing, without stores, without provisions?" [11]

Jefferson faithfully acknowledged all letters, listened to complaints, and exerted himself to the utmost to arrange for and forward the supplies so urgently needed. Nowhere do we find a trace of the weariness, the discouragement, and the anguish that must have afflicted him during this trying period. On the contrary, his determination and energy never flagged. Although only a portion of his official correspondence as governor is preserved—the larger part having been carried away by the British during the invasion—it is enough to fill a stout volume of more than 500 pages, attesting to the care and consideration he gave the multiform problems that came to his attention. His personal papers likewise abound in notes and memoranda most varied and detailed in character. There are numerous lists of the "State of the Virginia forces in the Continental service, including the rank and file and noncommissioned officers." There are rolls of the officers of the state regiments, garrison regiments, and regiments of artillery, all neatly and meticulously charted in Jefferson's fine hand. There are "returns of military stores, harness, camp equipment, tools, etc."; list of "tents delivered to the army and militia during the last and present invasion, October 1780"; elaborate notes on the proposed removal of the Convention prisoners after the defeat at Camden; reports from various officers on "ammunition, cannon, small arms, wagons, horses, etc."; diagrams of the returns of old and new militia battalions, with the number of men, command officers, staff officers, etc.; elaborate notes on "an act to regulate the Navy during invasion"; to mention but a small number.[12]

A letter to General Gates is typical of the details with which Jefferson had to concern himself and the energy with which he did so. It may well be questioned whether such matters should have been repeatedly brought to the attention of the governor, or whether they might not have been handled in their entirety by the quartermaster or the Board of War. "Your several favors of July 19, 21, and 22 are now before me," he writes. "I have enquired into the state of the cartouche boxes which were sent for our magazines. The quartermaster assures me they were in very good order. I must therefore conclude that the 300 complained of by General Stevens were some sent from Petersburg by the Continental quartermaster or that they were pillaged of the leather on the way, to mend shoes, etc. We had hopes of getting 2000 from the Board of War, but got only about 600, and they are said to be unfit for use. We are engaged in making bayonet belts, which shall be forwarded. But it is extremely difficult to procure leather. . . . I have ordered the 500 axes you desired with some tomahawks to be made. They turn out about 20 a day. About 100 will go by the wagons General Stevens sent us, which are now loading at this place. These wagons will carry some ammunition and spirit. A vessel with about 3,000 stand of arms coming down the bay for the use of your army was driven by privateers into Wicomico. We are endeavoring to get them forward either by land or water. The want of wagons will greatly retard them. What is to be done for tents I know not. I am assured that very little duck can be got in this country.... I communicated your orders to Col. Finnie and to Col. Buford and have directed proper applications for the repairs of the bridges, etc., you mention...."[13] The letter concludes with a further report concerning such practical details as the purchase of horses, blankets, and beef.

This was the situation when Jefferson was elected to his second term as governor on June 2, 1780. He informed the Assembly that he "would cheerfully again encounter the anxieties and assiduities inseparable from the important office to which you are pleased a second time to call me and only wish to be able to call forth those effectual exertions of my country, which our friends expect, and the present emergency requires." He could not anticipate all this year was to hold in store for him or for his country. Virginia was in a grave situation. By midsummer the main British force, under the command of the able and ruthless Lord Cornwallis, was encamped near the North Carolina-Virginia border. Thoroughly alarmed at the turn of events, Congress was roused to action. As the greater part of the Continental soldiers in the southern department had been surrendered by General Lincoln at Charleston, a new army had to be formed, and General Horatio Gates, the hero of Saratoga, was appointed by Congress to take command. In April Washington had dispatched some 2,000 Continentals under the command of Baron de Kalb to the relief of Lincoln. On reaching Petersburg, Virginia, De Kalb learned of the disaster at Charleston but determined to continue. July found him encamped about fifty miles north of the British in South Carolina.

Meanwhile Jefferson and the legislature had again been using every possible means to spur recruiting. A detailed report to Washington, in April, on the state of recruiting in Virginia, declaring that "there are some draughted soldiers in different parts of the country, but they are so far so disposed and enlisted for so short a time that we have not thought them worth the expense of gathering up," makes clear the further efforts that were now being made.[14] In June Jefferson once more took up with the commander in chief the question of the armed forces, their needs and their numbers. "North Carolina is without arms," he writes. "We do not abound. Those we have are freely imparted to them, but such is the state of their resources that they have not yet been able to move a single musket from this state to theirs. All the wagons we can collect have been furnished to the Marquis de Kalb and are assembling for the march of 2,500 militia under General Stevens of Culpepper, who will move on the 19th inst. I have written to Congress to hasten supplies of arms and military stores for the southern states.... The want of money cramps every effort. This will be supplied by the most unpalatable of all substitutes, force. Your Excellency will readily conceive that after the loss of one army our eyes are turned towards the other, and that we comfort ourselves if any aids can be furnished by you without defeating operations more beneficial to the general union, they will be furnished.... Could arms be furnished, I think this state and North Carolina would embody from ten to fifteen thousand immediately, and more if necessary." The letter concludes with a statement "of the force in and about to be put in motion." It shows a total of 1,290 Virginia regulars, 1,900 Maryland and Delaware troops and artillery, making a total of 3,190, along with 2,500 Virginia militia, 400 North Carolina militia under General Caswell, and 4,000 "ditto embodying under Governor Caswell if they can be armed."[15]

This, including De Kalb's Continentals, said by Henry Lee to have numbered 1,500 men, was the force of which General Gates took command on his arrival in South Carolina on July 25. His reaction to it is described in a letter to Jefferson written from his camp on the west bank of the Pee Dee River on August 3, 1780, less than a fortnight before the battle that was to ruin his career and cast a lasting shadow on the valor of the Virginia militia. "Since I joined the army upon Deep River," he writes, "my distress has been unconceivable." After laying blame for the situation on both North Carolina and Virginia, he continues, "I will yet hope Your Excellency is doing all in your power to supply your half-starved fellow citizens. Flour, rum, and droves of bullocks should without delay be forwarded to this army, or the Southern Department will soon want one to defend it. It has rained furiously for several days, and your militia are still without tents. Therefore I expect desertion, and the hospital will speedily leave General Stevens without any to command. I wish I could present Your Excellency with a more pleasing account of the public affairs this way, but the duty I owe to the United States obliges me to represent things truly as they are." [16]

Despite these conditions, despite the incredible hardships, despite the lack of cavalry support, Gates determined to march his army towards Camden, the main British post about 120 miles distant. It was a desolate country of pine barrens and dismal swamps, incapable of supplying provisions or forage. The excessive, humid heat of August, alternating with the torrential rains of this season, added to the distress of the men. On this unfortunate terrain, early on the morning of August 16, the American and British troops met. One of the most disastrous battles of the Revolution was fought. It turned into a rout. The militia, half-starved, half-naked, less than half-trained, in terror and desperation threw their arms to the ground and "took to the woods in all directions," as Gates stated.

The officers were powerless. Although the Maryland and Delaware lines, likewise engaged, stood, it was of no avail. General Stevens summed up the situation subsequently by declaring that the defeat was "brought on by the damned cowardly behavior of the militia." From memoranda in Jefferson's papers we learn who the militia were and what forces were involved in the engagement. There are two lists in Jefferson's hand and a detailed report from Adam Hoops on the British strength. According to Jefferson there was the 23rd British Regiment, to the extent of 400 men; the 33rd with 300; the 71st with 300; "Lord Rawdon's corps, 350; Tarlton's legion, 420; reinforcements from Charleston under Lord Cornwallis of the 63rd Regiment of Hessian corps, 700; Bryant and Harrison's new levy, 600"—making a total of 3,070 men. In addition there were "Tories incorporated, number unknown, but did no damage having run away the first fire of artillery." The American forces are listed as the Maryland Division, 800; Armand's, Porterfield's, and Armstrong's corps, 200; Caswell's North Carolina militia, 1,000; and Steven's Virginia militia, 800—a total of 2,800.[17]

Four days after the battle Gates sent a report of it to the governor of Virginia and to Congress. He tells how he tried to rally the militia "but the enemy's cavalry continuing to harrass their rear, they ran like a torrent, and bore all before them." The lack of entrenching tools and ammunition contributed to his difficulties. All the small arms that the enemy did not take were carried off by the militia. "The distresses of the campaign previous thereto," he philosophizes, "almost exceed description. Famine, want of tents for the militia, and of every comfort necessary for the troops in this unwholesome climate has no doubt, in a degree, contributed to our ruin.... It is a considerable consolation to my mind," he concludes, "that I never made any movement of importance or took any considerable measure, without the consent and approbation of all the general officers." [18]

Although the battle of Camden was fought on the soil of South Carolina, it was essentially Virginia's battle. Not only was the breakdown of the militia a severe blow to the state, but the material losses were bitter. "Our two millions are all exhausted," writes Jefferson. "Large debts are contracted for the horses purchased for the cavalry and wagons, which were sent on with the Maryland troops and our militia. These wagons, which, with those belonging to North Carolina were 400 in number, being all lost, we are now obliged to get 200 more with team and gear.... The loss of every tent has been a circumstance of great distress. The loss of all the small arms not less so." [19] Even more important was the change in the attitude of the enemy. From the time of his overwhelming success at Camden, Lord Cornwallis became even more confident of himself, his prowess and his judgment. He believed, furthermore, as Edmund Randolph observes, "the British arms to be invincible in the southern states," [20] a conviction shared by Clinton. Disregarding Clinton's plans of campaign, Cornwallis became virtually his own commander in chief. His dream was a crushing defeat for the Americans in what had been one of His Majesty's most treasured colonies, the vigorously independent state of Virginia.

Shattering as was the blow at Camden, Jefferson reacted to it with fortitude. As he wrote General Stevens, who had commanded the Virginia militia on this unfortunate occasion, "instead of considering what is past, however, we are to look forward and prepare for the future." There is among Jefferson's papers a memorandum that has the breathless quality of having been made on the day the news reached him, when his mind was stung to violent and immediate activity. In it he outlines plans for the calling of troops, the number of militia each county should furnish, and those where men should not be called out. "Stop troops going to the southward," he snaps out commands, "call vessels and stores from shipyard. Provide batteaux at foundry. Order away conventioners. Beeves from Warm Springs to come to Barracks. Col. O. Wood [in charge of Convention troops] to impress wagons, provisions, stores, etc., at Williamsburg. Write to General Nelson, Gates, Congress." [21]

In a calmer mood he sat down on September 3 to write the defeated general, who was also his friend. There is no note of passion or reproach in the letter. The catastrophe could not be remedied. All Jefferson's thoughts were turned towards action and the future. "I am extremely mortified," he writes, "at the misfortune incurred in the south, and the more so as the militia of our state concurred so eminently in producing it." With this single reference to what must have been more than mortifying and humiliating to his correspondent, Jefferson turns to the steps that are being taken to replace the troops, and embodies much of his memorandum.[22]

The same day, and in much the same vein, he wrote to General Washington, to Stevens, to Governor Nash of North Carolina, and to the president of Congress. To each he submitted a report of the steps being taken to raise a new army. "Another army is collecting," he writes Washington. "This amounted on the 23rd ult. to between four and five thousand men, consisting of about 500 Maryland regulars, a few of Harrison's artillery and Porterfield's corps, Armand's legion, such of the fugitive militia as had been reclaimed, and about 3,000 N. Carolina militia newly embodied. We are told they will increase these to 8,000.... We are calling out 2,000 militia.... About 350 regulars marched from Chesterfield a week ago; 50 march tomorrow; and there will be 100 to 150 more from that post when they can be cleared of the hospital. This is as good a view as I can give you of the force we are endeavoring to collect. But they are unarmed. Almost the whole small arms seem to have been lost in the late rout. There are here on their way southward 3,000 stand of arms sent by Congress, and we have a few still remaining in our magazine. I have written pressingly, as the subject well deserves, to Congress, to send us immediate supplies, and to think of forming a magazine here that in case of another disaster we may not be left without all means of opposition." [23]

In his plea for arms, addressed to the president of Congress, Jefferson touches upon one of the fundamental reasons for the humiliating conduct of the Virginia troops at Camden. "Should any disaster, like the late one, befall that army which is now collecting," he writes, "and which will be so much weaker in regulars as that brave corps is lessened in the unequal conflict which was put upon them, the consequences will be really tremendous if we be found without arms. With a sufficiency of these, there can be no danger in the end. The losses of our brethren in the meantime may be great, the distresses of individuals in the neighborhood of the war will be cruel, but there can be no doubt of the ultimate recovery of the country. The scene of military operations has been hitherto so distant from these states, that their militia are strangers to the actual presence of danger. Habit alone will enable them to view this with familiarity, to face it without dismay; a habit which must be purchased by calamity, but cannot be purchased too dear." [24]

No matter how great the determination of the Governor, it proved no easy matter to raise the men he had promised. On September 4 letters were sent to the county lieutenants of the various counties informing them that "the late misfortune to the southward renders it necessary that we send a reinforcement of militia from this state to assist in stopping the progress of the enemy should they be able to do no more." Those counties which had just been called on to send men southward were required "to furnish now so many as failed to march there of the quota called on." The others were required to send substantial aid "in the proportion called for by the general assembly on the late occasion from the other counties." [25]

A number of these are described by Jefferson as "1,000 good western militia from the counties of Fauquier, Loudoun, Frederick, Berkeley, Hampshire, Shenandoah, Rockingham, Augusta, Rockbridge" [26]—in other words, men from the pioneer counties accustomed to encountering the Indians and other marauders, who took fighting as part of the day's work. "This," Jefferson contended, "will be a reinforcement of about 4,000 men besides the delinquents and fugitives whom I apprehend can never be got to fight." The fugitives had to be dealt with, however. On September 12 Jefferson wrote General Stevens, who was complaining of the large number of desertions: "I have sent expresses into all the counties from which those militia went, requiring the county lieutenants to exert themselves in taking them; and such is the detestation with which they have been received that I have heard from many counties they are going back of themselves. You will, of course, hold courts-martial on them and make them soldiers for eight months." [27]

At this same time there was a demand for men to arm the ships which were supposed to clear the bay. "One difficulty," writes Jefferson, "say impossibility, is to get men. The terms of the assembly were proposed. Not a single man could be engaged. We then calculated that the bounty (converted into a daily pay of three years), the clothing allowed by law converted into a daily sum, and both added to the daily pay, would do—these amounting to about 10 dollars a day. A few men were raised for the cruise and on these terms, aided by volunteers (mere landsmen) engaged for the special purpose of going up the bay. We have been able to send the brig and boats on these two small expeditions, but the Commodore assures me that with such a crew the brig is in danger of being taken by very inferior vessels." [28]

Virginia was now to suffer another blow, presaging an even more serious one a few months later. It was as though the enemy were staging a rehearsal in an effort to gauge the strength of the state's defenses and the temper of the resistance that would have to be met. Invasion had been feared and rumored on many occasions. It had, indeed, as we have seen, briefly taken place in May 1779, when Collier attacked Portsmouth and devastated the surrounding country.

In the late summer of 1780 reports were again going about that invasion was imminent. On September 11 Washington wrote Jefferson that another embarkation was forming in New York, and that "the prevailing opinion is that they are either bound to Virginia or Carolina." He advised the Governor to "direct the removal of any public stores which may be upon navigable waters, and to make arrangements for defense in case such an event should take place."[29]

Early in the morning of October 20, British sail appeared in Hampton Roads. On the twenty-fifth the *Virginia Gazette* electrified the state with the terrifying news that there had "arrived in Chesapeake Bay a British fleet of 54 ships, 25 of which are large, the residue small. On the twenty-third they landed 1,000 infantry and 100 horse at Newport News, who immediately proceeded to Hampton, of which they took possession. Part of them are gone into Elizabeth River, but whether they have effected any landing there is not certainly known. It is supposed the whole land force is 5,000 men commanded by General Leslie, and the fleet is said to be commanded by Commodore Rodney, son of the admiral of the same name. The people in the neighborhood of the invasion turn out with great alacrity and spirit and trust they will be immediately supported by their upper brethren."

A more vivid account was sent Theoderick Bland, then in Congress, by John Banister. "I wrote you yesterday," he says, "and after dispatching the letter was informed of the enemy's landing within the cape and that they had before sunrise next morning possessed themselves of the narrow pass, at the Great Bridge, securing by that means all the county of Princess Anne without opposition, by which means all the cattle our commander had collected for the public use fell into their hands. The same day they debarked some troops at Portsmouth, and it is highly probable will attempt to reduce this place and Richmond.... This stroke has been impending over our heads so long that it must be a matter of surprise to all the world that we should again be found in a defenseless state."[30]

The news reached Jefferson in Richmond on the morning of the twenty-second. He instantly sent an express to Washington and to the president of Congress in Philadelphia with the fateful tidings.

During the invasion he kept them informed every few days of the turn of events. These letters give us as vivid a picture of what was happening as if we had been on the spot. His words conjure before the mind's eye a picture of the fleet appearing in the wide, blue waters of the bay. We see the enemy disembarking and filing, unopposed, along the lonely Tidewater roads, their scarlet coats a flagrant note against the brown October plains. After "committing horrid depredations," we watch them retiring to their ships, which were ominously "strung along the road from New-ports-News to the mouth of Nansemond." It would be audacious to paraphrase or use any but Jefferson's words in describing these days, or to impose an artificial interpretation while we have a living one from Jefferson's own pen.

Jefferson faced the situation calmly, even though the task of defense was an almost hopeless one. "We are endeavoring to collect as large a body to oppose them as we can arm," he writes Washington. "This will be lamentably inadequate, if the enemy be in any force. It is mortifying to suppose that a people, able and zealous to contend with their enemy, should be reduced to fold their arms for want of the means of defense. Yet no resources that we know of, insure us against this event. It has become necessary to divert to this new object a considerable part of the aids we had destined for General Gates. We are still, however, sensible of the necessity of supporting him, and have left that part of the country nearest him uncalled on at present, that they may reinforce him as soon as arms can be received. We have called to the command of our forces Generals Weedon and Mühlenberg of the line, and Nelson and Stevens of the militia. You will be pleased to make to these such additions as you may think proper. As to the aids of men, I ask for none, knowing that if the late detachment of the enemy shall have left it safe for you to spare aids of that kind, you will not await my application." He concludes with the resigned and tragic statement: "Of the troops we shall raise, there is not a single man who ever saw the face of an enemy." [31]

No stone was left unturned, however. An appeal was sent to Congress for arms. "The want of arms prevents every hope of effectual opposition," Jefferson writes. "I have perfect confidence in Congress that this want will be suffered to fetter us not a moment after they can supply it."[32] Not content with addressing the president only, he laid the situation before the Virginia delegates in Congress: "Our whole arms are or will be in the hands of the force now assembling. Were any disaster to befall these, we have no other resource but a few scattered squirrel guns, rifles, etc., in the hands of the western people."[33] Letters were also at once dispatched to the various county lieutenants directing them to require "one-fourth of the militia of your county to repair immediately to Richmond, armed and accoutered in the best manner possible. Let every man bring his own blanket.... They are to be furnished with provisions by impressing it as directed by the provision law, giving to the persons from whom they take it a certificate of the article, price, and purpose, and transmitting to me a list of all such certificates. I am to request that you lose not a moment's time in the executing of these orders."[34]

The western counties, whose adventure-loving inhabitants were more accustomed to shouldering a rifle for defense than for sport, were likewise appealed to. "The necessity of vigorous exertions to repel the enemy to the seashores," Jefferson wrote William Preston, county lieutenant of Montgomery, in southwestern Virginia, "and thereby to prevent the necessity of disturbing the operations of husbandry in more interesting seasons, and the peculiar aptitude of the mode of warfare to which your people are habituated for effecting this desirable purpose, induce me to apply in the warmest terms to your well-known zeal for the American cause to use your most strenuous endeavors for promoting the object of the enclosed advice of Council, and thereby giving a decisive blow to the southern operations of our enemies."[35]

Nevertheless, despite every effort, Jefferson was to write General Stevens three weeks after the invasion: "The force called on to oppose the enemy is yet in a most chaotic state, consisting of a fragment of 3-months militia, 6-months men, 18-months men, volunteers, and new militia."[36] The men were stationed at two points. The main force, under General Mühlenberg, was at Stoner's Mills on Pagan Creek in Isle of Wight County; and a second body, commanded by General Nelson, had assembled on the north side of the James. Their function seems to have been interpreted as that of standing by and observing, rather than offering active resistance.

On the twenty-fifth the Governor again reported to Congress and to the commander in chief. "Since my last informing you of the appearance of an enemy's fleet," he writes Huntington, "they have landed 800 men in the neighborhood of Princess Anne County. On the twenty-third in the morning they landed 1,000 infantry and 100 cavalry at Newport News, who immediately took possession of Hampton. The horse were proceeding up the road at the time of our last intelligence. The residue of their force remains still on board. The unarmed state of our people leaves it not in our power to say precisely when one hundred horse will be stopped. The few who have arms have turned out with the greatest alacrity, but they are not of a nature to oppose horse. Such a corps as Major Lee's would now be of infinite value to us.... The spirit which has shown itself among the people on this occasion has given me the greatest pleasure, but I must notwithstanding assure you, Sir, that if great supplies of arms are not immediately sent on, there is no event which may not be expected." [37]

It was the irony of fate that in horse-loving Virginia the lack of cavalry was to prove as disastrous at this time as it had at Camden. On May 30, 1780, the House of Delegates in a moment of economy had resolved "that the Governor be desired, on account of the low state of the treasury, to suspend the purchase of horses to mount the cavalry at present." Nevertheless, at the time of the invasion there were three troops of cavalry, commanded by Major Nelson, in the Continental service,[38] and Jefferson was writing Washington: "Next to a naval force, horse seem to be most capable of protecting a country so intersected by waters." [39] Although the point was ultimately reached where one in every fourth horse was impressed in certain counties, William Constable, Lafayette's aide, wrote on May 26, 1781: "Our whole force in cavalry at present is about 60, and the enemy have 500 horse. The mounted militia have all gone home. Notwithstanding positive orders they have carried off their accouterments, which has incapacitated us from mounting others." [40]

By the third of November much of the mystery enveloping the

movements of the enemy had cleared away, and their plans were known to the Virginians. On this day, a most anxious one for Jefferson, as Mrs. Jefferson that night gave birth to their fifth child, Lucy Elizabeth, he wrote Huntington: "The enemy have withdrawn their force from the north side of James River, and have taken post at Portsmouth, which we learn they are fortifying; their highest post is Suffolk, where there is a very narrow and defensible pass between Nansemond River and the Dismal Swamp, which covers the country below from being entered by us. More accurate information of their force than we at first had, gives us reason to suppose them to be from 2,500 to 3,000, of which between 60 and 70 are cavalry. They are commanded by General Leslie and were convoyed by the *Romulus* of 40 guns, the *Blonde* of 32, the *Delight* sloop of 16, a 20-gun ship of Jno. Goodrichs, and two row galleys, commanded by Commodore Gayton. We are not as yet assured that they have landed their whole force.... Their movements here induced me to think they came in expectation of meeting with Lord Cornwallis in this country, that his precipitate retreat has left them without a concerted object, and that they were waiting further orders...."[41]

Jefferson's surmises proved correct. On November 10 he sent Washington a copy of an intercepted letter from General Leslie to Lord Cornwallis, who was languishing with a fever in Winnsboro at the time, "taken from a person endeavoring to pass through the country from Portsmouth towards Carolina." In the time-honored manner of his kind, this person attempted to "carry something towards his mouth, as if it were a quid of tobacco." It was found to be a letter "written on silk paper, rolled up in gold-beater's skin, and nicely tied at each end, so as not to be larger than a goose-quill." Jefferson describes it as "the first authentic disclosure of their purpose in coming here, and may serve to found, with somewhat more of certainty, conjectures respecting their future movements." The letter, dated November 4, reads: "My Lord—I have been here near a week, establishing a post. I wrote to you to Charleston, and by another messenger, by land. I cannot hear, for a certainty, where you are: I wait your orders. The bearer is to be handsomely rewarded, if he brings me any note or mark from your Lordship. A.L."[42]

The vessel which was presumed to have been sent to Charleston by Leslie for orders returned to Virginia on the twelfth, and, as Jefferson writes the President of Congress a week later, "the enemy began to embark soon after from Portsmouth, and in the night of the fifteenth completed the embarkation of their whole force. In the morning of the sixteenth, some of our people entered Portsmouth. They had left their works unfinished and undestroyed. Great numbers of Negroes who had gone over to them were left either for want of shiproom or from choice. They had not moved from Elizabeth River at eleven o'clock A.M. of the sixteenth. They gave out that they intended up James River, but the precipitate abandoning of works on receipt of some communication or other from Charlestown, was not likely to be for the purpose of coming up James River. I received this intelligence by express from General Mühlenberg yesterday morning. As the enemy's situation was such as to give reason to expect every moment a movement in some direction, I delayed sending off notice to you in hopes that the movement would point out their destination." [43]

On the twenty-first Jefferson received word from Nelson, who was at Suffolk, that "the fleet is not yet gone and I am of the opinion they will land again as they had yesterday as fine a wind as could blow, and did not make use of it." [44] By the twenty-fourth, however, Jefferson was able to report good news of the enemy's withdrawal to the House of Delegates. "I received yesterday evening," he writes, "a letter from General Nelson dated Rich Neck November 22, at half after five P.M., including a note by which we learn that the vessels of the enemy were all under way except one which was getting under way, and the whole standing out for the Capes." [45]

Jefferson now proceeds to sum up the military outlook, forecasting what was to come with a dreadful accuracy and adjuring a dazed and sluggish legislature to take adequate steps for the defense of the state. It is one of the most forceful letters of the many he was destined to pen in his career, and one which must forever exculpate him from any insinuation of neglect of duty, which some of his detractors have been fond of hinting.

"This event," he writes of the withdrawal, "though relieving us in a certain degree by opening again the door of our commerce and also by putting it in our power to avail ourselves of the whole resources of our country, seems yet to call for an increase rather than an abatement of military preparations. Should those now leaving us proceed to enforce the hostile army in the south, should the same be the object of a new embarkation said on good authority to be preparing in New York, we shall but too probably and speedily see our own retreating enemy treading back their footsteps and menacing this country with a force to which the southern states have yet seen nothing equal. South Carolina and Georgia we are to consider as weighing nothing *in our scale*. North Carolina has been exhausted by the ravages of two armies. On this state, therefore, rests the weight of the opposition, and it is infinitely important that our own efforts be such as to keep the war from our own country, nor does it seem that we have a moment to lose should the enemy be disposed to lose no time on their part.

"Men to form a permanent army," he continues, taking up the idea Washington had been advocating for some time, "clothing, covering, arms, subsistence, transportation, and money are to be provided. We have left no measures unessayed for procuring supplies of these different kinds as far as the circumstances of our country would admit. Of tents we have a tolerable prospect, and better hopes of supplies of arms than we some time ago entertained. We shall press them forward with unremitting endeavors.... Clothing, blankets, and transportation are objects of immense difficulty, and money is necessary to set every wheel in action.

"I thought it my duty," he concludes, "as soon as the motives of the enemy indicated the point to which our efforts would probably be called, to suggest to the General Assembly these several matters, not doubting but that they will give them all the attention they deserve, and adopt such measures as in their wisdom shall appear best calculated for making effective opposition wherever the enemy may think proper to show themselves." [46]

On the eleventh of December Jefferson again addressed a communication to the House of Delegates concerning the condition of the army. He enclosed a letter from William Lee on the general subject of the defense of the state, as well as one from Baron von Steuben, now in Virginia as temporary Continental commander charged with the reconstitution and equipment of the Virginia Continentals. Steuben's report was dismal indeed. The majority of the men in the levies recently raised were declared to be "old men, boys, or decrepit," and "for this reason he means to decline continuing them in Continental service and to return them to the state." With an appeal to the legislature to create a standing army, Jefferson brings his letter to a close. "The proposals herewith transmitted," he writes, "for raising a standing body of forces for the defense of this state, requiring conditions beyond the powers of the executive, I beg leave to submit them to the wisdom of the General Assembly." [47]

Still the legislature did not act on the question of a standing army. In spite of what had been happening to the states south of Virginia, in spite of the recent invasion of the state, the members appear to have been blind to the danger so inexorably approaching. It is difficult to believe that they were apathetic, it is kind to think they were optimistic and easy-going, it is, perhaps, true that they were recalcitrant—if we may believe what Theoderick Bland wrote his son: "I am now to inform you of the proceedings of our Assembly, a majority of whom, I fear, are enemies to America, or fools, or knaves, or all three. They have determined to raise as many men as will make up the quota of our Continental troops for three years only. No arguments could prevail on them to raise the men during the war; and if they can't be raised by voluntary enlistment, then an indiscriminate draught is to take place for eighteen months. In short, their proceedings have been such that God grant it may not bring about a revolution in this state, which I fear is the wish of a majority in the Assembly." [48]

Although the lawmakers may have dawdled, the Governor was in a state of great activity. If the legislature was not aware of what was in store for the state, Jefferson was. He was feverishly engaged in making every preparation within his power to meet the danger, which threatened not only from the sea and the east, but from the west as well. The British, past masters of stirring up trouble among the Indians, had no idea of leaving this weapon unexploited. More than any of his associates in the government, Jefferson realized the importance of a consolidated western frontier. Indeed, he went so far as to recommend that "we aim the first stroke in the western country and throw the enemy under the embarrassments of a defensive war rather than labor under them ourselves." [49]

As early as February 1780, Jefferson had written General Washington about a proposed expedition against Detroit under George Rogers Clark. Owing to "want of men, want of money, and difficulty of procuring provisions, with some other reasons, more cogent if possible, and which cannot be confided to a letter," the project had had to be abandoned even though "that nest is too troublesome not to render the relinquishment of the attempt to destroy it very mortifying to us." [50]

Washington replied on the tenth of March that "the reduction of this post would be a matter very interesting from its situation and consequent importance to the tranquility of the western country. I have long wished to effect it, but hitherto unhappily our force and means at the westward have not appeared sufficient to authorize an attempt." After reading over the letter, he added a postscript which must have been very heartening to Jefferson and, of course, to Clark: "If the expedition against Detroit is undertaken, and I am advised of the time, it may possibly be in my power to favor it in some degree, by directing a movement of part of the troops at Fort Pitt, by way of diversion." [51]

Six months later, on September 26, Jefferson once more addressed Washington on the subject. "The exposed and weak state of our western settlements and the danger to which they are subject from the northern Indians acting under the influence of the British fort at Detroit, render it necessary for us to keep from five to eight hundred men on duty for their defense. This is a great and perpetual expense. Could that post be reduced and retained, it would cover all the states to the southeast of it. We have long meditated the attempt under the direction of Colonel Clark, but the expense would be so great that whenever we have wished to take it up, the circumstance has obliged us to decline it. Two different estimates make it amount to two millions of pounds, present money. We could furnish the men, provisions, and, I believe, every necessary except powder had we the money, or could the demands from us be so far supplied from other quarters as to leave it in our power to apply such a sum to that purpose.... When I speak of furnishing the men, I mean they should be militia, such being the popularity of Col. Clark and the confidence of the western people in him that he could raise the requisite number at any time." Jefferson concludes by asking Washington to determine whether "such an enterprise would not be for the general good, and if you think so, to authorize it at the general expense." [52]

Washington, already sufficiently harassed, his attention and efforts focused primarily on the war being conducted on the eastern seaboard, adroitly shifted responsibility for a decision. Reaffirming his belief in the desirability of such an undertaking, he concludes by saying if "Your Excellency should determine to attempt the reduction of the post either at the expense of the state or at that of the United States with the consent of Congress, it is possible the quantity [of powder] you may have occasion for, may be spared, if it is not too great and the means of transportation can be procured." [53]

Before this letter reached Jefferson and before he had chance to appeal to Congress, the British fleet with General Leslie appeared in the bay, and the proposed war in the west had temporarily to be abandoned. It was not for long, however. Towards the end of the year—the exact date does not appear to be certain—George Rogers Clark arrived in Richmond to advocate the cause of his people, to picture their distressed situation—plagued by the enemy, robbed of their corn and stock, and deserted by the soldiers sent to protect them.

Inflamed by Clark's representations, and thoroughly aroused by the recent invasion, the Governor determined upon immediate action. It was obvious that the war could not be fought on one front only. On December 15 he wrote Washington a letter at once energetic and realistic, outlining his ideas for the conduct of the war in both departments. "Since the date of my letter," he says, "the face of things has so far changed as to leave it no longer optional in us to attempt or decline the expedition, but compels us to decide in the affirmative and to begin our preparations immediately. The army the enemy at present have in the south, the reinforcements still expected there, and their determination to direct their future exertions to that quarter, are not unknown to you. The regular force proposed on our part to counteract those exertions, is such, either from the real or supposed inability of this state, as by no means to allow a hope that it may be effectual. It is therefore to be expected that the scene of war will either be within our country or very nearly advanced to it, and that our principal dependence is to be on militia, for which reason it becomes incumbent to keep as great a proportion of our people as possible free to act in that quarter.

"In the meantime," he continues, "a combination is forming in the westward which, if not diverted, will call thither a principal and most valuable part of our militia. From intelligence received, we have reason to expect that a confederacy of British and Indians, to the amount of 2,000 men, is formed for the purpose of spreading destruction and dismay through the whole extent of our frontier in the ensuing spring. Should this take place, we shall certainly lose in the south all aids of militia beyond the Blue Ridge, besides the inhabitants who must fall a sacrifice in the course of the savage irruptions. There seems to be but one method of preventing this, which is to give the western enemy employment in their own country." After stating that Colonel Clark is ready to undertake this task, he goes on: "We have therefore determined to undertake it and commit it to his direction. Whether the expense of the enterprise shall be at Continent or state expense we will leave to be decided hereafter by Congress, in whose justice we can confide as to the determination." In a final plea for help he concludes, not without a little justifiable pride in the contributions Virginia had already made: "Independent of the favorable effects which a successful enterprise against Detroit must produce to the United States in general by keeping in quiet the frontier of the northern ones, and leaving our western militia at liberty to aid those of the south, we think the like friendly offer performed by us to the states whenever desired, and almost to the absolute exhausture of our own magazines, give well-founded hope that we may be accommodated on this occasion." [54]

Without waiting for Washington's reply, on December 24 Jefferson dispatched letters to the county lieutenants of the various outlying counties—Berkeley, Hampshire, Greenbrier, Frederick, Fayette, Lincoln and Jefferson, Monongalia and Ohio—saying that "a powerful army forming by our enemies in the south and an extensive combination of savages in the west, will probably render the ensuing campaign exceedingly active, and particularly call forth all the exertions of this state. It is our duty to look forward in time and to make a proper division of our force between these two objects. There seems to be but one method of preventing the savages from spreading slaughter and desolation over our whole frontier, and that is by carrying the war into their own country.... Your county is alloted to the western defense. You will therefore be pleased to send of your militia under proper officers by the way of Pittsburgh to the falls of Ohio to join under Colonel Clark in an expedition over that river and to continue in service during the expedition as to which Colonel Clark is instructed from hence...." [55] Details follow as to the number of men, accouterments, provisions, and so on.

There was welcome news for Jefferson in Washington's letter of December 28, although it did not, of course, reach Virginia until after Arnold's invasion. "I am so well convinced of the general public utility with which this expedition, if successful, will be attended," Washington wrote, "that I do not hesitate a moment in giving directions to the commandant at Fort Pitt [Colonel David Broadhead] to deliver to Colonel Clark the articles which you request, or so many of them as he may be able to furnish. I have also directed him to form such a detachment of Continental troops as he can safely spare.... There is also a Continental company of artillery at Fort Pitt, which I have likewise ordered upon the expedition, should it be prosecuted." [56]

Jefferson spent Christmas Day, 1780, writing out Clark's instructions. The long letter is a model of clarity, of foresight, of anticipation of every need and eventuality, insofar as they could be envisioned. Jefferson's critics have only to read this letter to realize with what competence and with what infinite pains he entered into every detail of the problem and laid out the general scheme of campaign. The purpose of the expedition is stated to be "the reduction of the

British post at Detroit, and incidental to it the acquiring possession of Lake Erie." Clark is informed exactly what troops he may expect, "Colonel Crockett's battalion, Major Slaughter's corps, with detachments of militia from the counties of Fayette, Lincoln, Jefferson, Ohio, Monongalia, Hampshire, Berkeley, Frederick, and Greenbrier, making in the whole 2,000 men." Rowland Madison, quartermaster of the expedition, has been directed to buy given amounts of ammunition, powder, lead, 300 pack horses and subsistence for them. Tents, medicine, and clothing are to go forward from Richmond, 1,000 pounds of rifle powder from Staunton, and 400 camp kettles from Fredericksburg; an agent is sent to Baltimore to purchase four tons of cannon powder. John Francis Moore, deputy commissary general, is instructed to secure 200,000 rations of beef and flour and to procure 100 light barges fit for transporting men and stores either up or down stream. The date of rendezvous is set for the fifteenth of March at the falls of the Ohio.

"All the preceding order," Jefferson continues, describing Clark's large discretionary powers, "except for the numbers of men from each county, are submitted to any alterations you may think necessary, and you are authorized to supply any deficiencies in them. Staff officers are submitted absolutely to you, and on removal of any of them by death, resignation, or declining to act, you are to appoint others.... What numbers of men, and whether regulars or militia, you shall leave to garrison the posts at the falls and mouth of the Ohio, is left to yourself.... You will then, with such part of your force as you shall not leave in garrison, proceed down the Ohio and up the Wabash or along such other route as you shall think best against Detroit. By the construction of a fort or forts for retreat at such place or places as you shall think best, and by such other cautions as you find necessary, you will provide for the ultimate safety of your men in case of a repulse.... Should you succeed in the reduction of the post, you are to promise protection to the persons and property of the French and American inhabitants, or of such at least as shall not on tender refuse to take the oath of fidelity to this commonwealth.... To the Indian neighbors you will hold out either fear or friendship as their disposition and your actual situation may render most expedient.

"Finally," he concludes in a peroration worthy of his best efforts, "our distance from the scene of action, the impossibility of foreseeing the many circumstances which may render proper a change of plan or dereliction of object, and, above all, our full confidence in your bravery, discretion, and abilities, induce us to submit the whole of our instructions to your judgment, to be altered or abandoned whenever any event shall turn up which may appear to you to render such alteration or abandonment necessary, remembering that we confide to you the persons of our troops and citizens which we think it a duty to risk as long and no longer than the object and prospect of attaining it may seem worthy of risk. If that post be reduced, we shall be quiet in future on our frontiers, and thereby immense treasures of blood and money be saved; we shall be at leisure to turn our whole force to the rescue of our eastern country from subjugation ... and in the event of peace on terms which have been contemplated by some powers, we shall form to the American Union a barrier against the dangerous extension of the British Province of Canada, and add to the empire of liberty an extensive and fertile country, thereby converting dangerous enemies into valuable friends." [57]

It was on January 18, when the distress and excitement of Arnold's foray up the James was beginning to subside, and after Clark had done his part in repelling the invaders there, that he acknowledged Jefferson's letter. Its tone leaves us in no doubt that Jefferson alone was the author of the instructions, and that the military advisers with which certain writers have liked to surround Jefferson were nonexistent in this case, as well as in most others. "I have examined your proposed instructions," Clark writes. "I don't recollect of anything more except the mode of paying the expenses of the garrison at Detroit, in case of success...." [58] This offhand statement is certainly not the mode of speech of a man who has dictated his own terms.

The expedition authorized by this letter was the culmination of all Clark's hopes and ambitions. The stage seemed set for the realization of his dearest desires. But despite this, despite the strong support of both Washington and Jefferson, he was not to succeed. He could not know that at the very moment Jefferson was engaged in writing this letter, a British fleet was approaching the shores of Virginia, and that the ensuing invasion would change the course not only of the war, but of his own destiny. This was undoubtedly the basis for the defeat of his plans. Despite his enormous personal popularity, despite the "unbounded confidence which I am told the western people repose in him," as Washington observed, he found it quite impossible to raise the necessary men. No one wanted to fight on the western frontier, certainly not the men from eastern Virginia, who felt they were needed nearer home. Even the western men were obstinate about undertaking a campaign at such a distance. All were blind to the importance of it. As Colonel John Smith of Frederick County, who was supposed to furnish 285 men by the first of March, wrote in mid-February, "the difficulty will be to compel these men to march, owing to their aversion to this expedition. Even should this be accomplished, we cannot procure twenty guns in the country, and without arms they could do nothing." [59] Colonel Joseph Crockett of Shepardstown added a last discouraging word: "I must beg leave once more to mention to Your Excellency the great distress the regiment is in for want of clothing, the soldiers being almost naked for want of linen and entirely without shoes. Colonel Clark informs me he expects a considerable quantity of linen at Winchester, of which we shall have a part. As for shoes, I know not where to turn." [60]

Once again there was too little of everything. Once again the legislature and the governor might authorize the purchase of equipment, of clothing, of food, of horses, but these things were not to be had.

VI. The Parricide Arnold

THE LAST DAY of the year 1780 fell on a Sunday. When, as was his habit, Jefferson rose with the sun, there was nothing to distinguish this from any other winter day in the dreary little hamlet of Richmond. By eight o'clock in the morning, however, before the family had sat down to breakfast, the whole picture had changed. A messenger arrived with news of the most alarming character. Curiously enough, the letter he carried was not addressed to the governor, but to General Nelson. It was from Jacob Wray, a well-known merchant of Hampton, saying that twenty-seven sail of vessels had been seen the day before just below Willoughby's Point, the lonely tip of land directly opposite Old Point Comfort. Their purpose and destination were unknown. It was equally uncertain whether they were friend or foe. Their appearance was ominous.

It has never been explained why this news was not sent directly to the governor, nor why this first word was not followed more immediately with further details. Two weeks later, when the damage had been done, Jefferson wrote Wray: "To want of intelligence may be ascribed a great part, if not the whole, of the enemy's late successful incursion to this place. Though they appeared in the Bay on Saturday, no notification of it addressed to the Executive came to hand till 10 o'clock A.M. on Tuesday.... I mention these circumstances to show you the necessity of our being better furnished with intelligence of the enemy's movements, and to apologize for my troubling you with the task of communicating everything interesting through the line of expresses stationed at every 15 miles from hence to Hampton.... I hope you will be so good as to undertake this trouble and to continue it so long as it may be necessary to keep up the line."[1]

In any case, on receipt of the letter to Nelson, Jefferson, in his role of commander in chief of the militia, at once dispatched General Nelson, as he says, "into the lower country, to take such measures as exigencies may require for the instant, until further information is received here." [2] He likewise sent word to Captain James Maxwell, commissioner of the navy, and to the county lieutenant of Charles City, "requiring several necessary measures to be taken," and gave orders for establishing a series of expresses from the Bay to Richmond "for obtaining proper intelligence." [3] Most important of all, he instantly wrote Baron von Steuben that his "aid and counsel would be deemed valuable in the present emergency." Steuben, a major general in the Continental Army, had come to Virginia with General Greene the previous November and had remained as temporary commander in charge of raising troops for the Continental service. He and Jefferson had already been in daily contact, and Jefferson had developed a keen appreciation of the Baron's abilities. He was now to become the Governor's trusted adviser and to direct the military policy of the state during the invasion. On the fourth, the day before the British, in their swift race, actually reached Richmond, Jefferson wrote him: "I beg you will be so good as to consider the militia of every place as under your command from the moment of their being embodied, and to direct their motions and stations as you please." [4]

In turning over the command of the militia to Steuben, Jefferson was not avoiding responsibility. He was asking a trained military expert to take charge of a situation requiring the services of just such a man. As he observed in eloquent defense of his conduct to Henry Lee: "I was not with the army! True. First, where was it? Second, I was engaged in the more important function of taking measures to collect an army; and, without military education myself, instead of jeopardizing the public safety by pretending to take its command, of which I knew nothing, I had committed it to persons of the art, men who knew how to make the best use of it, to Steuben, for instance, to Nelson and others, possessing that military skill and experience of which I had none." [5]

Meanwhile, Jefferson, retaining general oversight, continued to act in conjunction with Steuben, as the exchange of letters between them at this period testifies. That neither man was able to give a more brilliant account of himself on this occasion was due not to lack of abilities, but to forces that were beyond their control.

No further word came on the thirty-first. Although tortured with doubt and, as he says, "in great suspense as to the destination of this fleet, whether it be up the bay or up our river," Jefferson engaged in the usual business of the day. His account book, often so revealing, merely shows that he "paid a midwife £30," and "rec'd of the Treasurer, £3,870." He did, however, write Benjamin Harrison, Speaker of the House, that a fleet had appeared in the bay and "that its size has given suspicions that it may be hostile, more especially as we have been lately informed that an embarkation was taking place in New York. I have thought it my duty to communicate it to the General Assembly before their rising, as they might perhaps wish to give some advice to the executive on this subject." [6]

On the second of January, confirmation of the dreaded news finally arrived in a letter from Nathaniel Burwell, county lieutenant of James City. "Sir," he writes from Burwell's Ferry at 10 o'clock in the morning, "the enemy's fleet have just now come to off this place. They consist of twenty-three sail, including two men-of-war. A number of flat-bottomed boats are astern of the ships full of men. We have near two hundred men under the command of Colonel Innes and myself, a number very insufficient for the [illegible] purpose. However, nothing shall be wanting as far as we're able to oppose the enemy if they attempt to land. A small party of foot and horse are now engaged with a boat detached from the fleet." [7]

This letter, preserved among the Steuben Papers, was apparently sent to the Baron by Jefferson with his own hurried note of the second, the very appearance of which betrays his distraction, delegating the direction of the militia to this competent and thoroughly experienced officer. On receipt of this news from Burwell, and on the basis of some further information, Jefferson wrote the Speaker of the House of Delegates the same day: "I have this moment received a confirmation of the arrival of a hostile fleet.... The advance of a fleet were yesterday morning in Warrasqueak Bay and just getting into motion up the river with a favorable wind and tide. Their destination, from the intelligence of deserters and some captured mariners whom they put on shore, is up James River. I beg the favor of you to communicate this to the General Assembly." [8] "The wind being fair and strong," Jefferson observes in a subsequent letter, "the enemy ascended the river as rapidly as the expresses could ride, who were dispatched to us from time to time to notify their progress." [9]

With this news the Council leaped into action. Their *Journal* for this day is one of the very few still preserved from this period. We learn that in addition to the Governor, there were five members present: David Jameson, William Fleming, Andrew Lewis, George Webb, and Jacquelin Ambler. They advised "that there be called into immediate service" half the militia of Henrico, Hanover, and Goochland counties, and one-fourth of the more distant counties of Fluvanna, Albemarle, and Amherst. These men were to rendezvous at Richmond. Half the militia of Chesterfield, Powhatan, and surrounding counties were to assemble at Petersburg, along with a fourth from the numerous counties in the southern and southwestern parts of the state. Even sparsely settled Shenandoah, Rockbridge, Rockingham, and Augusta were to furnish a stipulated number of men "to bring good rifles and to be under their own field officers." The arms and other stores from Petersburg were ordered "brought towards Richmond"; the powder from the powder mills was to be carried to Westham; canoes were to be prepared to carry the stores farther up the river should it prove necessary.[10] Colonel Nelson was made a brigadier general during the invasion and empowered to draw out the militia of certain counties. "I pray you," Jefferson beseeches him in sending him his commission that day, "to send us as frequent intelligence as possible, expresses being ready for the purpose at Williamsburg and New Kent Courthouse." [11]

Jefferson likewise dispatched a circular letter on this day to the various county lieutenants, giving detailed directions and advising them that "the arrival of a hostile fleet within our state being confirmed and their movements indicating an intention to come immediately into the heart of the country, renders it necessary to call for ——— of your militia under proper captains and subaltern officers to rendezvous ———.

"That there may not be a moment's delay, let them come in detached parties as they can be collected. Every man who has arms bring them. The good of the service requires that the field officers at least should be experienced in the service; for this reason these will be provided for at the rendezvous. I beg that this may not be considered by the militia field officers as proceeding from want of respect for them. We know and confide in their zeal; but it cannot be disreputable to them to be supposed less knowing in the art of war than those who have had greater experience in it; and being less knowing, I am sure that true spirit of patriotism with which they are animated will lead them to wish the measure to be adopted which will most promote the public safety, however it may tend to keep them from the post in which they would wish to appear in defense of their country." [12]

This change of policy, revolutionary to Virginia, of not having the militia officered by the men who usually commanded them, undoubtedly reflects Steuben's point of view and was the result of conversations between him and Jefferson. Among the Steuben Papers is a memorandum dated only January 1781, endorsed by Jefferson: "The above is a copy of the letter I mean to send to the officers to be called into service. I take the liberty of sending it to Baron Steuben as an explanation of our idea of arranging them." The letter reads: "The readiness with which the gentlemen who had formerly borne commissions in the regular line made a tender of their services on the late invasion of their country, induced me to rely on their aid in repelling the present enemy, headed by the blackest traitor who has ever disgraced American history. With those gentlemen who have continued in service it is not within my powers to give you the priority of rank which you may have formerly held. I must therefore only undertake to preserve it in respect to those who, having been out of commission, shall again come into service on the present occasion. A large body of militia being called into the field, and likely to be all in by the 20th instant, I take the liberty of asking the favor of you to accept of a command over them in the rank you formerly held, and that for this purpose you will be pleased to repair within that space of time to Major General Baron Steuben's headquarters, to arrange for commands in the principles before laid down." [13]

To Colonel James Innes, who for a time took over Nelson's command during an illness, Jefferson subsequently wrote: "On the present invasion the favor was asked of Baron Steuben to arrange the commands on principles laid down by the executive, being the same determined on Leslie's invasion." [14]

At the meeting of Council on this January 2 it was likewise resolved "that Colonel Taylor be directed to take measure instantly for the removal of the residue of the Convention troops to Fort Frederick in Maryland or Fredericktown, as shall be ordered." [15] These troops had been a constant source of worry to the executive for some months, ever since an invasion of the state threatened. On September 14, 1780, Jefferson had written the president of Congress enquiring where to send them should such an event occur.[16] When Leslie actually did invade, Jefferson again addressed Huntington urging their removal, saying it would be "utterly impractical as long as they remain with us to prevent the hostile army now in this state from being reinforced by numerous desertions from this corps.... Should, moreover, a rescue of them be attempted, the extensive disaffection which has been lately discovered [in Washington, Montgomery, Bedford, and Henry counties, where many hundred had enlisted in the British service], and almost total want of arms in the hands of our good people, render the success of such an enterprise by no means desperate." [17]

Eight hundred British prisoners were removed. Shortly after this, "the Germans, 1,400 in number, being thought less dangerous, were permitted to remain until accommodations could be provided for them in Maryland." Subsequently Congress decreed that the Germans should remain permanently where they were. Now, with Arnold sailing up the James, the Assembly resolved that they should be sent out of the state. "The executive are placed in a very disagreeable situation," Jefferson wrote Benjamin Harrison on January 29. "We can order them to the banks of the Potomac, but our authority will not land them on the opposite shore." [18] Before this delicate legal question could be settled, Lord Cornwallis was approaching, and the prisoners were marched to "our northern boundary, while Congress could be consulted as to what should be done with them." [19] On March 12 a letter finally arrived from the president of Congress directing that they should "be moved northwardly by way of Noland's ferry [about forty miles above the present city of Washington]," and from that point Virginia's heavy responsibility ceased.

Having completed its immediate business, the Assembly voted to rise on this same January 2. It was resolved that "when this House adjourns, it will adjourn until the last day of March next" and ordered "that Mr. Edmonds do acquaint the Senate therewith." Fully aware of the gravity of the situation, the Delegates took the precaution of resolving that "in the case of the next meeting of the General Assembly at this place be rendered inconvenient by the operations of an invading enemy, that the next meeting of the Assembly be at such proper place as the Governor, with the advice of Council, shall appoint by proclamation." [20] The House of Delegates had already determined the preceding November "that during an invasion of the state by British troops, fifty members of this House be a sufficient number to proceed to business." [21]

In a memorandum concerning the invasion, obviously intended to make clear that the responsibility for such action as was taken rested not solely on him, and in explanation of the rising of the Assembly, Jefferson states that "the legislature was sitting when the entrance of the enemy into James River was made known. They were informed, without reserve, of the measures adopted. Every suggestion from the members was welcomed and weighed, and their adjournment on the second of January furnished the most immediate and confidential means of calling for the militia of their several counties. They accordingly became the bearers of those calls, and they were witnesses themselves, that every preparation was making which the exhausted and harassed state of the country admitted." [22]

The following day, the third of January, was a day of great anxiety. No further information was forthcoming. Finally, late in the afternoon, news arrived that the night before, the enemy had sailed defiantly up the broad and unresisting James and anchored off Jamestown. Williamsburg was believed to be their goal. At five o'clock on the morning of the fourth, Jefferson's brother-in-law, Francis Eppes, arrived with his family and servants from Eppington, which was feared to be in the path of the invader. He brought word from Benjamin Harrison that, owing to a shift in the wind, the British had continued up the James and cast anchor off Kennons, a settlement opposite Brandon.

This was no time to think of the militia in terms of a half or a quarter of the men available. Jefferson immediately called every eligible male from the adjacent counties. At five o'clock in the evening Captain de Ponthière, Baron Steuben's aide, reached Richmond with the devastating intelligence that the enemy, still favored by nature, had taken advantage of the incoming tide and the continued favorable wind to proceed as far as Westover, where they had debarked. On the way they had passed through the narrow strait at Hood's, where a battery of two small guns and a howitzer had been set up and garrisoned with some fifty men. A few shots were fired at the leading ships. A landing party, however, promptly drove off the garrison and took possession of the works, thus leaving the upper river undefended and giving the British an unopposed opportunity to advance as far as they would.

At three o'clock in the afternoon of the fourth, Nelson sent a letter from a point twelve miles above Williamsburg with the latest news. "I have just received the enclosed letter from Williamsburg," he writes, "which gives the best account of the enemy's force that I have yet obtained. Their intentions are higher up the river, either to Petersburg or Richmond, which they will make a bold push for, if not checked on their landing. If they discover a determination of the inhabitants to oppose them, they will work with caution, and perhaps return to Hampton with disgrace. They will proceed as high up the river as they can for fear of desertion among their troops, to which they are much disposed.

"I remain still very weak, having received no reinforcements from the neighboring counties yet. Our expresses behave most infamously, and in what manner to act with them I know not. Unless some vigorous measures are taken with them we shall have no regularity." [23]

Jefferson, who, he says, had been "anxious to know whether they would pass Westover or not, as that would show the side they would land," on learning that they had done so, "ordered arms and stores, etc. (which till then had been carrying to Westham), to be thrown across the river at Richmond," to the south side. To a trusted aide, whose name is not appended to the letter but which bears a subsequent endorsement, "taken from papers of War Office, A.D. 1781," he wrote a hasty and harried note saying, "Baron Steuben asks the favor of you to appoint some confidential officer or gentleman to go immediately to Chesterfield Court House to take charge of the wagons which are there loaded with arms, conduct them up into the country under such orders as the Baron will give him, for which reason he must call on the Baron immediately. I think some such person necessary at Westham." [24]

There are preserved among the Steuben Papers two letters, almost identical, from General Nelson dated January 4 and written at Byrd's Tavern, sixteen miles from Williamsburg. There is no superscription, but it is obvious that one was intended for the Governor and the other for Steuben, now acting as commanding general. Unaware that Nelson had also written the Baron, Jefferson seems to have sent his letter to him. "On my way here this evening," Nelson writes, "I received information that the enemy had landed their whole force at Westover and were marching for Richmond. I have ordered the whole strength of King William, King and Queen, and Gloucester to rendezvous at Bacon's ordinary five miles above New Kent, whence I shall march them as will appear best for the service. The whole militia of New Kent are now turning out." The letter, apparently intended for Steuben and endorsed by him, is identical, except that after saying where the militia will rendezvous he adds, "I shall tomorrow march what force I can collect by the route of Holt's forge and thence as the movements of the enemy shall direct. I expect my force will by tomorrow noon be about 350. It will give me pleasure to receive from you as frequently as possible such advice as you shall think proper to communicate." [25]

At half-past seven that same evening Jefferson "set out to the foundry at Westham [some six miles above Richmond] and set Captain Brush, Captain Irish, and Mr. Hylton to see everything wagoned from the magazine and laboratory to Westham, and there thrown over—to work all night." [26] Meanwhile he had sent his wife and three little daughters, along with the Eppes's and their small son—who was one day to marry his Polly—to the greater safety of their cousins at Tuckahoe. He himself joined them there at one o'clock in the morning of the fifth, "having attended late at Westham, to have the public stores and papers thrown over." Early the same day he carried the family across the river and sent the little party along to Fine Creek, the plantation some twenty miles above Richmond where his father had been born and which had come to him.

Jefferson himself now crossed back over the river and at the bridge at Tuckahoe joined Colonel John Nicholas, who was in charge of the local militia. Together they rode to Britton's, opposite Westham, "to see about the further safety of the arms and other property." In the brief and breathless diary he kept during the invasion, "often written on horseback, and on scraps of paper taken out of my pocket at the moment," Jefferson says he now "gave orders for withdrawing ammunition and arms (which lay exposed on the bank to the effect of artillery from opposite shore), behind a point. Then went to Manchester [on the south side of the James opposite Richmond]; had a view of the enemy. My horse sunk under me with fatigue." Leaving the animal lying on the public road and carrying the saddle and bridle on his own shoulders, Jefferson walked to the nearest farm, where he borrowed an unbroken colt. Mounting it, he rode "to Chetwoods, appointed by Baron Steuben as a rendezvous and headquarters, but finding him not there and understanding he would go to Colonel Henry's, I proceeded there for quarters." [27]

The enemy meanwhile, Jefferson recounts in his report of the affray to Washington and the president of Congress—a vignette of characteristic clarity and economy of words—had "marched from Westover at 2 o'clock in the afternoon of the fourth and entered Richmond at 1 o'clock of the afternoon of the fifth. A regiment of infantry and about 30 horse continued on without halting to the foundry. They burnt that, the boring mill, the magazine, and two other houses, and proceeded to Westham. But nothing being in their power, they retired to Richmond. The next morning they burnt some buildings of public, and some of private, property, with what stores remained in them, destroyed a great quantity of private stores, and about 12 o'clock retired towards Westover, where they encamped within the neck the next day.

"The loss sustained is not yet accurately known," Jefferson continues his report, which was written on January 10. He apologizes for the seeming tardiness by saying of the recent events that "such has been their extraordinary rapidity, and such the unremitted exertions they have required from all concerned in government, that I do not recollect the portion of time which I could have taken to commit them to paper." As far as had been so far ascertained, he continues, the losses "consisted at this place in about 300 muskets, some soldiers' clothing to a small amount, some quartermaster's stores, of which 120 sides of leather is the principal articles, part of the artificers' tools and wagons. Besides which, five brass 4-pounders we had sunk in the river were discovered by them, raised, and carried off. At the foundry we lost the greater part of the papers belonging to the auditor's office, and of the books and papers of the council office. About 5 or 6 tons of powder, as we conjecture, was thrown into the canal, of which there will be a considerable saving by remanufacturing it. The roof of the foundry was burnt, but the stacks and chimneys and furnaces not at all injured. The boring mill was consumed."

Thus, "within less than 48 hours from the time of their landing," Jefferson sums up the situation, "19 from their destination being known, they had penetrated 33 miles, done the whole injury, and retired. Their numbers, from the best intelligence I have had, are about 1,500 infantry, and as to their cavalry, accounts vary from 50 to 120, the whole commanded by the parricide, Arnold.

"Our militia," he continues, in defense and explanation of the meager resistance encountered by the enemy, "dispersed over a large tract of country, can be called in but slowly. On the day the enemy advanced to this place, 200 only were embodied. They were of this town and its neighborhood, and were too few to do anything effectual. At this time [five days later] they are assembled in pretty considerable numbers on the south side of James River, but are not yet all brought to a point. On the north side are two or three small bodies, amounting in the whole to about 900 men. The enemy were at 4 o'clock yesterday evening still remaining in their encampment at Westover and Berkeley Neck.

"In the meanwhile," he concludes, outlining the plans for present defense, "Baron Steuben, a zealous friend, has descended from the dignity of his proper command to direct our smallest movements. His vigilance has in a great measure supplied the want of force in preventing the enemy from crossing the river, which might have been very fatal. He has been assiduously employed in preparing equipments for the militia as they should assemble, pointing them to a proper object and other offices of a good commander. Should they [the enemy] loiter a little longer, and we be able to have a sufficient force, I still flatter myself they will not escape with total impunity. To what place they will point their next exertions, we cannot even conjecture. The whole country on the tidewaters, and some distance from them, is equally open to similar insults." [28]

In his *Military Journal* Lieutenant Colonel Simcoe of the Queen's Rangers gives a detailed and scarcely flattering account of the operations at Richmond, one on which most writers have hitherto depended. Claiming that Arnold's force did not amount to eight hundred men, he goes on to say that "within seven miles of Richmond a patrol of the enemy appeared, who, on being discovered, fled at full speed.... On approaching the town Arnold ordered the troops to march as open and to make as great an appearance as possible; and the ground was so favorable that a more skillful enemy than those who were now reconnoitering would have imagined the numbers to be double. The enemy at Richmond appeared drawn up on the heights, to the number of two or three hundred men. The road passed through a wood at the bottom of these heights and then ran between them and the river into the lower town. Lieutenant Colonel Simcoe was ordered to dislodge them. He mounted the hill in small bodies, stretching away to the right, so as to threaten the enemy with a design to outflank them; and as they filed off, in appearance to secure their flank, he directly ascended with his cavalry.... Luckily the enemy made no resistance, nor did they fire, but on the cavalry's arrival on the summit, retreated to the woods in great confusion." [29]

Another contemporary report is preserved in the Jefferson Papers.

It is a copy of a letter, in Jefferson's hand, from Colonel William Tatham to William A. Burwell, dated June 13. Tatham was an Englishman who had come to the colony in 1769, interested himself in the American cause, and become an auxiliary officer on Nelson's staff during the invasion. It is particularly significant for the informal picture of Jefferson it presents; likewise as a contemporary defense of his conduct, at this time already under criticism. "Being in Richmond at the time of Arnold's invasion in 1781," he writes, "and hearing that the express was arrived at the Governor's with intelligence of the approach of an invading enemy, I immediately rode to his house and met Governor Jefferson walking out. He told me he had received such an express, but that as other intelligence led him to suppose they were nothing more than a foraging party, unless he had further information to justify the measure, he should not disturb the country by calling out the militia. He would thank me nevertheless if I would go down to the late Major General Baron Steuben who was at Wilton [6 miles below Richmond] and receive his orders if needful. The Baron dispatched me to General Nelson at Williamsburg, where I found the town in confusion, expecting an immediate attack, the enemy being at anchor and having a boat then actually taking the soundings towards the shore at King's Mill [3 miles below Williamsburg]. They proceeded, however, up the river, and I remained in the suite of General Nelson some days, when I was desired by him to be the bearer of some dispatches to the Governor, of such importance that I must avoid all risk of being taken. Knowing the country well, I ventured in among the plantations till I got to that of Daniel Trueheart near the Meadow bridge in Chickahominy. Here I learned that the enemy's picket was first called in and returned from the bridges towards the main body at Richmond.

"I followed the piquet carefully, entered Mr. Duval's house at Mount Comfort while the floor was flowing with the liquors spilled by the British soldiers, and pushed into Richmond, from whence the army had just retreated. Here one of our well-affected citizens (I think old Richard Crouch) referred me to Moses Tredway in Manchester, who conducted me to Mr. Jefferson at a house then occupied by Dr. Evans, and here I delivered my dispatches and spent part of the evening. I understood the enemy encamped that night about Four Mile Creek, perhaps about 10 to 12 miles in a direct course, and were then on their retreat.

"On another occasion," he continues, referring to Phillips's invasion in April 1781, "when the British Army marched from Petersburg up to Manchester, being at an advanced post near Osborne's, commanded by Col. Goode, and his videts coming in successively with intelligence that the enemy were advancing in force, I covered Col. Goode's retreat with a small party of volunteer cavalry. We came off slowly before them till we gained the heights above Osborne's; and afterwards alarming the intermediate route along the road, I was with Mr. Jefferson several times in the course of the night, conversing with him in his bed, where he seemed to be without any apprehensions, although within about 4 to 7 miles of the enemy's encampment, which was, I believe, that night about Ampthill and Warwick. The following morning I joined Baron Steuben, near the coal pits [10 or 12 miles above Manchester] and, by his order passed in between the enemy's main body and flanking parties, being so near the flair of their drums that my horse erected his ears at them, in getting off through a thicket. This was less than two miles from where Mr. Jefferson slept, and I afterwards delivered Baron Steuben's orders to Major Call, who commanded the cavalry hanging on their rear." [30]

During the period of Arnold's invasion Richmond was in a state of chaos. The letters of various officials who had occasion to write the Governor or Steuben at this time give a picture of complete disorder. Thus Major Richard Claiborne, deputy quartermaster general, writes on the eighth: "There is no commander here, nor will anybody be commanded. This leaves what public stores a few of the virtuous inhabitants have collected, exposed to every passenger, and the property of the individuals to the ravages of the Negroes. Both public and private property have been discovered to a considerable quantity, that was secreted clandestinely in and about town; and I am sorry to say that there is a stigma which rests upon the conduct of some of our own men with respect to the pillaging of public and private goods, that does not upon the British troops." [31]

To Steuben he reported that "the Negroes of Richmond have

created great ravages and burnt one house here in the night. The public stores were plundered by them, and the goods are secreted in and about town. ... I had a party of the militia given me by Colonel Haskins and patrolled the streets of Richmond during the night. I am sorry that the militia differ so much from the Continental soldiers, but by constant watch I kept them alert and constantly at their duty." [32]

Colonel William Davies, who was shortly to succeed the ineffective Colonel Muter as commissioner of war, wrote Jefferson the same day that he was informed "a considerable number of public papers, brimstone, and other articles are lying round the works at Westham, many of them very little damaged. I cannot well spare anyone on this side to collect them, but think it my duty to give Your Excellency the information." [33] On the twelfth he reported that he had taken his "quarters in the Senate House and find in one of the rooms below a great variety of public papers scattered about and open to everybody. I am told this is the case with the papers of the General Court at the lower end of town." [34] A week later, when he was about to leave town, there were still "lying open in the Senate House a number of valuable books that may be carried off by anybody that chooses." [35]

This circumstance was forthwith seized upon as an example of the Governor's laxity and neglect of duty. The story spread and grew until ultimately, some years later, Jefferson felt obliged to solicit a statement regarding it from Dr. James Currie, a leading citizen of Richmond. "On application made to me if I recollect anything of the circumstances which led to the loss of the public papers in the year 1781," he writes, "during the invasion of the British Army, when Mr. Jefferson was governor—do well remember that he appeared expressly anxious and very active in having them removed from Richmond and deposited in a place of safety, and if possible entirely out of the reach of the enemy, and for that and the duties of his office as chief magistrate did remain in town fully as long as was either proper or prudent for him to do so without manifest danger of becoming the prisoner of the invading army, who were fast approaching the seat of government without any [adequate] force that could at that time be brought against them, to stop their march, and that his conduct was then perfectly proper and that of a real patriot and friend of his country will be very fully evinced by the concurrent voice of the gentlemen who then acted with him in Council as well as the unanimous approving voice of the Virginia Legislature at the subsequent meeting of the assembly of the state." [36]

The British, on this January 6, exhausted by their efforts, many of their men drunk and beyond control, left Richmond at twelve o'clock and encamped at Four Mile Creek. Jefferson, as he tells us, "went to Westham, ordered books and papers from the magazine.... In the evening I went up to Fine Creek," to his family. The following morning he "returned to Westham, and then came down to Manchester, where I lodged. The enemy encamped at Westover and Berkeley. It had rained excessively the preceding night and continued to do so till about noon." From Westham Jefferson wrote Steuben at two o'clock in the afternoon: "I have thought myself very unfortunate in missing of you for two days, though riding over the same ground as you were. On my arrival here I was informed you were at Ampthill and was setting out from there when a gentleman came who assured me you were at Osborne's and, having rode thirty miles through the rain, I have not resolution enough to undertake to go to Osborne's this evening.... I mean to continue here or at Richmond to see whether I can collect the several staff officers of the state, and have the benefit of their services on the present occasion.... While at either of these places I shall be able to communicate both with yourself and General Nelson, and do everything you will be pleased to suggest for the service. I fear the want of arms fit for service will be a most distressing circumstance. Are there no Continental arms which can be used in the present occasion? I mean to endeavor to collect hands and tools immediately to repair arms. Tools will be the most difficult to be procured." [37]

At half-past seven o'clock on the morning of the eighth, after paying expenses at Treadway's of £51, Jefferson returned to Richmond. "The wind gets, about this time, to northwest, a good gale," he writes, "in the afternoon becomes easterly. The enemy remain in their last encampment. General Nelson at Charles City Court House, Colonel Nicholas with three hundred men at The Forest [Mrs. Jefferson's

BARON VON STEUBEN. By Ralph Earl. (*Courtesy of the Gallery of the New York State Historical Association*)

LORD CORNWALLIS. By Thomas Gainsborough. (*Reproduced from* The Pageant of America. *Copyright, Yale University Press*)

girlhood home]." There is little for Jefferson to report on the ninth except that the wind was "almost nothing. The enemy remain in their last encampment, except embarking their horse." On the tenth the British finally embarked their infantry and fell "down the river, the wind having shifted a little north of west, and pretty fresh." [38]

During this period Baron Steuben was on the south side of the James, directing operations there. On receipt of Jefferson's letter of January 2 stating that "we shall be very glad of the aid of your counsel in determining on the force to be collected and other circumstances to be attended to, for the purpose of opposition, if it be convenient for you to call on the Council immediately," [39] he "directly waited on the Governor and Council, requesting four thousand militia might be called out, estimating the enemy's force at twenty-five hundred. The distressed situation of the Continental troops at Chesterfield Court House would permit only one hundred and fifty of them to be ordered out." [40] Steuben, an Old World soldier accustomed to the strict discipline of the Prussian Army, could not quite grasp that to request four thousand troops was no guarantee he would receive them—certainly not very promptly. It was equally impossible for him to understand what he describes as "the nakedness of the troops," to say nothing of the lack of arms. "The greatest distress we now feel," he writes General Greene, "is the want of arms; great part of those belonging to the state were damaged by the late invasion [Leslie's], or were scattered at different places and never collected or repaired. Those at Richmond were, at the enemy's approach, sent off in such disorder that part of them are not yet found. The militia are coming in and no arms to put in their hands, while on the other side General Nelson has fifteen hundred stand and only five hundred men. . . . The troops have neither tents nor camp kettles. It is impossible to describe the situation I am in—in want of everything; and nothing can be got from the state, rather for want of arrangement than anything else." [41]

So different, indeed, were conditions in Virginia from those he knew, and so many the lessons he had to learn, that he finally appealed to Jefferson for relief. The Governor wrote his old friend, John Walker: "Baron Steuben, who commands the military force in this state on the present invasion, being very much unacquainted with its laws, customs, resources, and organization, while he has hourly cause to apply them, has desired we will prevail on some gentleman acquainted with these to be of his family, to point his applications to the proper persons and places, and to enable him to avail himself of our strength and resources. Searching about for such a person, we cast our eyes on you, and hope you will undertake the office." [42] Walker's reply has not come to light, but we know he accepted the post and smoothed Steuben's way so ably that General Greene was shortly writing the Baron: "Colonel Lee tells me that you are on exceeding good terms with the governor and legislature of Virginia, and that they respect and venerate you in the highest degree. I fear when you leave it nothing will be done. The state is lifeless and inactive unless they are often electriced." [43]

While Steuben was on the south side of the James, hopefully waiting for the militia and overseeing the salvage of stores and supplies, General Nelson was on the north side. It proved impossible for him to form any connection with Steuben. He wrote the Baron from "Holt's Forge on the Chickahominy river seven miles from Charles City Court House," at ten o'clock on the morning of the sixth. The letter reads: "It has given me the greatest concern that I could not afford you the assistance necessary to disappoint the enemy in their attempt on Richmond, but the situation of the country and other causes which your knowledge of our affairs will readily suggest to you, have defeated my utmost exertions. I shall take post today with the troops I have collected at the long bridge eight miles higher up the river than this station. There I expect considerable reinforcements from neighboring counties, the whole of whose militia I have called for and which I understand are in motion. The long bridge is an advantageous post, both for attacking the enemy on their retreat, and our own security. It will afford me the greatest satisfaction to hear from you and receive any instructions you may be pleased to give." [44]

On the eighth, in response to two letters from Jefferson which do not seem to have been preserved, Nelson reported his situation in a letter betraying deep feeling. "I am pained to the very soul," he writes, "that we have not been able to prevent the return of the enemy, but even the elements have conspired to favor them. On Saturday night I intended to blow at their rear, when the gates of heaven were opened and such a flood of rain poured down as to render my plan abortive by almost drowning the troops, who were in bush tents, and by injuring their arms and ammunition so much that they were quite unfit for service. That they may not go off without some injury, I have ordered two pieces of cannon to be planted at Kennons, where am told we may do them mischief. These cannon I propose to defend by infantry as long as I can. Should they overpower us, it is better to lose the guns than not to attack them somewhere...." [45]

Nelson and his men were in the same situation as Steuben in regard to ammunition and other supplies. Indeed, he is said to have been so destitute of them that he did not even have a telescope. "I am now with the troops under my command at this place by order of General Nelson," Colonel Charles Fleming wrote Jefferson on the seventh. "I have to inform Your Excellency that there is not a fourth part of the regiment supplied with ammunition, and as I am ordered by the General to join the Baron and begin my march early tomorrow, unless ammunition is sent me, or ordered to follow me, I shall find myself in rather an awkward situation." [46]

On the seventh of January Steuben informed Jefferson that he had "ordered the militia of Chesterfield, Powhatan, and Amelia to march with all possible expedition to Petersburg. Tomorrow I march there myself with 400 men I have here. My intention is that at the same time I cover Petersburg, to endeavor something at Hoods, if any cannon can be got and a force sufficient collected to prevent their landing. General Smallwood is arrived at Petersburg and will give me his assistance." [47]

It was at Hood's, on the tenth, that the first real affray of the invasion took place. The previous day Jefferson had written Steuben: "Colonel Clark of Kaskaskia, having heard of the situation of things, has come to me this morning. I send him to you, supposing you must be in want of officers." [48] Clark was the very man Steuben needed, but, although he was in charge of the detachment involved, it cannot be described as a glorious occasion. Even Clark could not cope with the Virginia militia. "It had been found impractical to remount the cannon at Hood's," Steuben says in a dramatic account, "or to prepare any obstruction to their passing that place. Of this, however, the enemy were ignorant; and thinking it very probable they would land a party to examine these works before they attempted to pass, I ordered three hundred infantry and about thirty horse, under Colonel Clark, to lie in ambush to receive them. About twelve o'clock the fleet got under way, and at four o'clock I saw them, from Hood's, come to within cannon shot. At dark they landed troops from eighteen boats—deserters say five hundred—who immediately attacked a small picket we had, and pursued them to within forty paces of the ambuscade, when our troops gave them a fire; but on their returning it, and charging bayonets, the militia immediately fled. After throwing their cannon into the river, the enemy returned to their ships." [49]

Following this, Steuben marched with seven hundred of the militia to Cabin Point in Surry County. "On the fourteenth the enemy landed at Hardy's Ferry, twenty-two miles below Cabin Point," he tells us, "and began their march toward Smithfield. Supposing Colonel Parker, with the militia of the lower counties, would oppose them in front, I detailed Major Willis with three hundred infantry and fifty horses to harass their rear. My orders were badly executed, and the enemy entered Smithfield on the fifteenth without opposition. Having that day received a reinforcement of four hundred men, I immediately detached them under General Lawson with orders to march towards Smithfield.... On General Lawson's approach, the enemy crossed Nansemond River at Sleepy Hole and encamped on the opposite bank; and General Lawson, being joined by the troops under Colonel Parker, occupied Smithfield. The nineteenth the enemy marched to Portsmouth, where Arnold established himself, and their vessels fell down to Hampton Roads." [50]

Nelson likewise sent an account of these days to the Governor. After observing that the enemy "land on the south side wherever they have a prospect of getting valuable plunder," [51] he wrote from Williamsburg on the sixteenth, "In my letter of yesterday I informed Your Excellency that the enemy's fleet had fallen down to Hardy's Ferry. This afternoon I have intelligence that it was on its way again, and standing for Newport News. Yesterday about twelve o'clock the enemy were seen from this shore to land a number of men on a point below the mouth of Pagan Creek, and soon afterwards a heavy firing commenced, the issue of which has not yet reached me. Very few men have joined me from those counties, whose militias, according to yours of the fifteenth, were to compose the armament for our defense on this occasion; for which reason it will not be immediately in my power to comply with your instructions. So soon as it can be done I shall pay them due attention. The Louisa militia I have ordered to file off for the defense of Fredericksburg. The number of effective men now at this port and York is about one thousand, some of whom are not yet arrived, and as it appears to be impracticable such shall be discharged. I shall be careful to have communicated to you everything of moment." [52]

In a graphic letter written on the eighteenth, Jefferson reported the events of these last days to the Virginia delegates in Congress, waiting breathlessly in Philadelphia for further word from home. "The occurrences since my last to the President," he writes, "are not of any magnitude. Three little rencounters have happened with the enemy. In the first, General Smallwood led on a party of two or three hundred militia and obliged some armed vessels of the enemy to retire from a prize they had taken at Broadway [on the Appomattox in Prince George] and, renewing his attack the next day with a 4-pound or two (for in the first day he had only muskets), he obliged some of their vessels to fall down from City Point to their main fleet at Westover. The enemy's loss is not known. Our men was four men wounded.

"During their encampment at Westover and Berkeley, their light horse surprised a party of about 100 to 150 militia at Charles City Court House, killed and wounded 4, and took, as has generally been said, about 7 or 8. On Baron Steuben's approach towards Hood's, they embarked at Westover. The wind, which till then had set directly up the river from the time of their leaving Jamestown, shifted in the moment to the opposite point. Baron Steuben had not reached Hood's by 8 or 10 miles, when they arrived there. They landed their whole army there, Arnold attending in person.

"Colonel Clark of Kaskaskies had been sent on with 240 by Baron

Steuben, and, having properly disposed of them in ambuscade, gave them a deliberate fire which killed 17 on the spot and wounded 17. They returned it in confusion, by which we had 3 or 4 wounded, and, our party being so small and without bayonets, were obliged to retire on the enemy's charging with bayonets. They fell down to Cobham, from whence they carried all the tobacco there (about 60 hhds.), and the last intelligence was that on the sixteenth they were standing for Newport News. Baron Steuben is of the opinion they are proceeding to fix a post in some of the lower counties.

"Later information has given us reason to believe their force more considerable than we at first supposed. I think since the arrival of the three transports which had been separated in a storm, they may be considered as between 2,000 and 2,500 strong." After giving a list of the enemy's naval force, "according to the best intelligence," Jefferson concludes with the information that "we have about 3,700 militia embodied, but at present they are divided into three distinct encampments—one under General Weedon, at Fredericksburg, for the protection of the important works there; another under General Nelson at and near Williamsburg; and a third under Baron Steuben at Cabin Point. As soon as the enemy fix themselves, these will be brought to a point."[53]

The question naturally arises as to where was the Virginia navy during Arnold's invasion. The answer is that, between the losses during Collier's raid in 1779 and the action of the Virginia Assembly since then, it had to all intents and purposes become nonexistent. We have seen the effort made by the legislature in the fall of 1779 to reduce the number of ships as well as the personnel. In August of the following year Jefferson had directed Captain James Maxwell, who had been appointed commissioner of the navy on the abolition of the boards of trade and war in May 1780, to defer advertising for sale the ship *Tartar*, as well as the galley *Safeguard*. The Council likewise decided "to suspend the sale of the *Lewis* galley till the Assembly shall declare their sense in the matter."[54] This same month the Governor was informed of the serious situation of the galleys *Accomac* and *Diligence*. Deserted by both officers and men, they were "left open to be plundered of their guns and furniture." Orders were given

James Barron, commodore of the armed vessels of Virginia, to arrest the officers, seize the men, bring one of the vessels to the "bayside of the eastern shore," the other to the "western shore," for repair. The presence of numerous privateers in the bay, as well as the subsequent British invasions, "prevented the immediate execution of the orders," as Jefferson says, so that by spring the vessels had "been much plundered and their hulls so injured as to render it doubtful whether worth repairing." [55]

The difficulty of getting men to arm such ships as there were is described by Jefferson as an impossibility. The Assembly used every means at its command. The pay of able seamen was raised to two shillings a day, of ordinary seamen or landsmen to one shilling sixpence, of boys to one shilling. It was further decreed that officers and seamen should be entitled to the whole of any prize taken. The captains of armed vessels were to issue clothing and slops to the seamen and mariners of their ships. Even the officers received some consideration. A commodore was henceforth to be paid fourteen shillings a day, a captain eight shillings sixpence, a lieutenant six shillings. Finally a resolution was passed that "officers and seamen of the navy shall be entitled to the same advantages as officers belonging to this state in the land service, agreeable to their several stations." But it was of no avail. Nothing could make the navy popular.[56]

Following Leslie's invasion, the Assembly had become panic-stricken. An "act for the defense of the eastern frontier of this commonwealth" was passed. The brig *Jefferson* and the armed boats *Liberty* and *Patriot* were "to be forthwith manned and fitted out for the purpose of suppressing the cruisers belonging to the enemy, and affording protection and safety of the good citizens inhabiting the shores of the bay and rivers exposed to the ravages of the cruisers." The galleys *Thetis* and *Lewis* were immediately to be "made ready and completed for the same purpose." The impressment of seamen was authorized under certain circumstances, duties on various imported goods were earmarked to support the navy, and, finally, "for the future protection of Chesapeake Bay, the Commissioner of the Navy shall acquire true and exact plans for the galleys built by order of Congress in 1776 and have two built of the same construction."

The arms they were to carry were likewise specified. In order that the navy might not be utterly destitute of personnel, the courts were ordered "to bind out at least half their male orphans to the sea." [57]

It was further decreed that "proper attention shall be paid to the defense of the commerce and the shores of Chesapeake bay and its dependencies, for which purpose there shall be constantly kept cruising one armed vessel carrying at least 14 guns, none less than 4-pounders, with a competent number of men, and a small armed tender for the said vessel." [58]

Unfortunately for Virginia, the few weeks that intervened between Leslie's and Arnold's invasions did not suffice for the results of these measures to become apparent. In the leisurely south, time is not measured in such short spans. January 1781 found Richard Henry Lee lamenting to Theoderick Bland: "The want of a small marine aid, secretly and judiciously applied, is inconceivably injurious to us. This motley band of Arnold's is sufficient to employ (by its quick transition from place to place) a number of men more than ten times enough to ruin them, if they could be brought to action at any one point, with that tenth part. And the next consequence resulting from this great number of militia being then necessarily employed is, that they eat up our resources, starve thereby the regular army, and thus the enemy may destroy the concert by playing interludes. For Heaven's sake, for the preservation of the sacred cause of liberty, press every motive and strain every nerve to procure an adequate naval aid...." [59]

It was, alas, too late for prayers or exhortations—or even for appeals to the Continental Congress.

When the enemy finally invaded, Captain Maxwell, in response to Jefferson's warning of the day before, wrote the Governor on January 1: "Yours of yesterday's date I received this morning by Mr. Webb, and am to inform Your Excellency that in consequence of the news I heard of the enemy's arrival, have fitted out the *Lewis* galley and sent her down the river under the command of the lieutenant of the *Jefferson*, with twenty volunteers from the same vessel, who have agreed to serve for the present invasion. The brig has been totally dismantled of everything she had on her for heaving down, having been aground and in want of repair. But from the above news have got her guns on board, and are putting in the best posture of defense we are able. I have also sent off the letter you were pleased to send me for the aid of the militia which am afeared we shall want much, as all the peoples' time, belonging to the Brig, is expired, and cannot get any of them to agree to continue any longer in the service. Shall therefore be under the disagreeable necessity of detaining them against their will." [60]

Captain Maxwell's gesture may have been a brave one, but a single galley was a pathetically inadequate force to be sent out against the British fleet.

Such was the contempt for the "parricide Arnold," and so great was the humiliation as well as the indignation caused by his activities, that various patriotic citizens undertook schemes, all unfortunately abortive, to attempt his capture. The Governor was, of course, taken into their confidence. The most energetic of these gentlemen was a lusty Captain or Major—he is called by both titles—B. Edgar Joel. Jefferson wrote General Nelson on January 16 that "he proposes to engage two others to undertake with himself an enterprise on the enemy's fleet wherever it shall be collected in harbor. As he requires only an old vessel of the most worthless kind, and proper preparations for her, I think the object will justify the risk.... I cannot do better than give a general sanction to it and ask the favor of yourself to have everything provided he may think necessary to ensure success...." [61]

On the ninth of February Joel informed Jefferson that after infinite trouble he had found a vessel, the *Dragon*, which had lain under water many months. Undeterred, he had raised her, and in five days she was ready for service. He next secured a pilot and started on his venture. The pilot subsequently ran the ship on a bar, where she lay for three days. Joel remained undaunted. When this difficulty had at last been overcome, he was thwarted by a much greater one—General Nelson's conviction that the plans had "become so universally known as to leave little doubt of the enemy's being apprised of it and of course prepared against it." [62]

A letter of complaint to Jefferson brought the reply: "I am sorry that any circumstances have arisen to occasion the laying aside the enterprise which you had undertaken, bold in itself, and, if successful, advantageous. As it was, however, pretty certain that the enemy had received notice of it, there seemed little hope of its success for the present, with however bold a hand it might have been conducted. Attempts of this kind have been generally deemed to depend for their issue on surprise, a little notice enables the enemy to withdraw from their pen or parry their approach. To prosecute them after such notice is to sacrifice the lives of the brave men whose conduct would be better reserved for other occasions; of these circumstances General Nelson, to whom we referred the directions altogether, was better able to judge than we were at this distance. Some time hence perhaps the enemy may again be taken napping, and the vessel, being reserved in her present condition, will give an opportunity of effecting whatever may be undertaken." [63]

Jefferson, meanwhile, had a scheme of his own. It seems strangely out of character to think of him engaged in anything with so much a tinge of the melodramatic as plotting and planning the capture of Arnold, yet the affront to his own position and to his country warranted extreme measures. He decided to confide in General Mühlenburg. "Acquainted as you are with the treasons of Arnold," Jefferson writes him on January 31, "I need say nothing for your information, or to give you a proper sentiment of them. You will readily suppose that it is above all things desirable to drag him from those under whose wing he is now sheltered. On his march to and from this place I am certain it might have been done with facility by men of enterprise and firmness. I think it may still be done, though perhaps not quite so easily. Having peculiar confidence in the men from the western side of the mountains, I meant as soon as they should come down, to get an enterprise proposed to a chosen number of them, such whose courage and fidelity would be above all doubt. Your perfect knowledge of those men personally, and my confidence in your discretion, induce me to ask you to pick from among them proper characters, in such number as you think best, to reveal to them our desire, and engage them to undertake to seize and bring off this greatest of all traitors. . . .

"Whether this may be better effected by their going in as friends and awaiting their opportunity," he continues, "or otherwise, is left to themselves. The smaller the number, the better, so that they be sufficient to manage him. Every caution must be used on their part to prevent a discovery of their design by the enemy.... I will undertake, if they are successful in bringing him off alive, that they shall receive five thousand guineas' reward among them. And to men formed for such an enterprise, it must be a great incitement to know that their names will be recorded with glory in history...." [64]

Before any plans of this sort could be carried out, they became merged with a more general one to capture all the British forces under Arnold at Portsmouth. To this end Washington dispatched Lafayette to Virginia on February 20, and a new chapter in the history of the war began.

VII. The Burdens of State

To be quick to criticize a man's efforts in a difficult situation, and tardy in appreciating them, is doubtless a human trait. Certain it is that, in the case of Jefferson's governorship, and especially in regard to Arnold's invasion, emphasis has been primarily on the former. Few have taken the trouble to investigate his exertions on behalf of the state, which were supreme. A casual observation that he was an industrious, if inefficient, governor has usually sufficed. There is no better evidence of the way Jefferson developed and grew with his governorship, as the difficulties and problems multiplied, than a comparison of the letters he wrote at the time of the threatened invasion of December 1779 with those a year later, when Arnold actually sailed up the James. The former still have a certain vagueness, an aura of theory about them. "It is our duty to provide against every event," he writes on that occasion, "and the executive are accordingly engaged in concerting proper measures of defense. Among others we think to call in an immediate force from the militia to defend the post at York," [1] and so on.

By January 1781 he had ceased to recommend or advise. He was snapping orders. "It is necessary for us instantly to build proper shops and magazines at Westham," he writes Colonel Senf, "and first of all things a plan is to be laid. I will beg the favor of you to come to this place and lend us your assistance in forming the plans." [2] Or, to Major Claiborne: "It being necessary to collect at Hood's as large a number of boats as possible to transport men and horses across the river as occasion may require, you are hereby authorized to impress the boats on this and the Chickahominy River, except only one to be left at each ferry." [3] Or, again, to Colonel James Callaway: "The invasion of this state calling for an immediate and large supply of lead, be pleased to send us immediately all the lead you have on hand, notwithstanding my former direction to let one-half go to the southward army."[4] To Colonel John Nicholas he wrote with determination: "I am not fond of encouraging an intercourse with the enemy for the recovery of property; however, I shall not forbid it while conducted on principles which are fair and general. If the British commander chooses to discriminate between the several species of property taken from the people, if he chooses to say he will restore all of one kind, and retain all of another, I am content that individuals shall avail themselves of this discrimination; but no distinction of persons must be admitted. The moment it is proposed that the same species of property shall be restored to one which is refused to another, let every application to him for restitution be prohibited. The principles by which his discrimination would be governed are but too obvious, and they are the reverse of what we should approve."[5]

During the trying days of the invasion, Jefferson in effect filled the multiple offices of secretary of state, quartermaster general, intelligence officer, and general factotum. He was likewise, as we have seen, commander in chief of the Virginia militia. He conveyed this title to Steuben[6] when invoking his aid, but he retained the power of making ultimate decisions in certain cases. Although not signed by him, yet identifiable through its wording, the description of the invasion appearing in the *Virginia Gazette* for January 13, 1781, is nothing less than a communiqué issued by the Governor, acting as public-relations officer. Deserted even by the Council—the advisers provided by law—deprived of the advice and wisdom, such as it may have been, of members of the Assembly, every decision made, every action taken fell to the lot of this young man of thirty-seven. There was no meeting of the Council from the fourth of January, "when the executive having been obliged to remove on account of the enemy's taking possession of the town of Richmond," until the nineteenth, "there not having been since a sufficient number of members attending to constitute a board until this day."[7] Jefferson had written Dudley Digges, the lieutenant governor, requesting his presence so that there might be a quorum. Digges had replied on the seventeenth, with the utmost urbanity: "It gives me pain that some days must elapse before I shall be able to attend where my duty and inclination would certainly induce me to go. I am thus far on my way to Williamsburg to collect the scattered remains of my property, which was hastily distributed in such places as were deemed the most secure. When this business is effected, I shall without delay wait upon you at Richmond, and in the meantime, I have to hope that sufficient number of members may be found to prevent any inconsequences." [8]

The only persons upon whose assistance Jefferson could rely, and whose help he could invoke, were General Steuben and a few lesser officers.[9] It is true that General Nelson was also in the field, but he was in the lower country, with communication very difficult. He conceived of his function, one gathers from his letters, rather to be that of carrying out orders. Jefferson's daily, and often more frequent, letters to Steuben not only indicate how closely the two men worked together, but reveal the thought and care the Governor gave to every detail, from forwarding supplies to sending the latest intelligence to his generals in the field. Several letters, hitherto unpublished, serve to illustrate this. On January 9, at eleven o'clock in the morning, Jefferson writes: "The state commissary having come to me yesterday, I sent him on to your headquarters to provide subsistence for the troops and observe your orders in everything. A wagonload of fixed ammunition passed this place for General Nelson. The residue (I believe about two wagonloads) was ordered on to you yesterday. I am very happy to hear you have General Smallwood's assistance, though the means with which you are furnished are not likely to add to your reputation, except that, by undertaking to make the most of them, your zeal will be still more fully displayed. A battalion of Hanover militia which were at Westham were ordered to you.

"Your favor of yesterday was put in my hands this morning," he continues. "The enemy encamped at Westover the night before last, and had not moved at midnight last night. They keep very close. General Nelson was last night at Charles City Court House. Colonel Nicholas with 300 militia was at The Forest, six miles above Westover. Colonel Harrison is exerting every endeavor to get a couple of 18-pounders over to you. Those who sunk the boats here did them such injury that it is difficult to repair them. I really fear they will be much too late for you. However, a possibility of their getting to you in time is worth every exertion we can use. I have desired Colonel Nicholas to communicate to me every movement of the enemy, which I will forward to you immediately." [10]

The following day, in answer to another communication from Steuben concerning the peril to Hunter's iron foundry and arms factory at Fredericksburg, he wrote: "I shall immediately dispatch an express to General Weedon and recommend to him to attend the measures necessary for the preservation of Mr. Hunter's works. I have heard that he has with difficulty armed some four or five hundred men, and means with them to join General Nelson. I am really at a loss what to advise him. If he comes away with that force, it may leave the neighborhood unable to protect Hunter's works; and if he does not come, General Nelson will not have a force sufficient to cover the country below him.

"I think therefore," he continues, "to leave him to act according to his discretion, recommending to him to send on his force if, from a knowledge of circumstances, he thinks a sufficient number can be armed and embodied to protect Hunter's works; otherwise to remain there. Will it be in your power, if the enemy should point towards Williamsburg, to have boats enough to throw hastily over a body of men to support General Nelson? If you think of anything better than what I have above proposed to write to General Weedon, be so good as to communicate it, and I will by another express correct what is amiss.

"I was misinformed," he concludes, "as to the situation of General Nelson. Colonel Nicholas, who had given me the information, corrected it in his next letter. General Nelson had been stationary at Holt's Forge on Chickahominy, but proposed to move yesterday to the Shipyard. I am not certainly informed of his force. Colonel Nicholas is with 300 militia at Malvern Hills. A party of 140 militia at Charles City Court House were surprised by the enemy's horse the night of the eighth. One killed, 3 or 4 badly wounded, and some (I know not how many) taken. Colonel Fleming with 500 militia of Hanover and Goochland leave Manchester this morning to join you. They are armed. I saw one 18-pounder set out from there at sunrise this morning. The carry [illegible] for the other is not quite ready. The enemy remained at three o'clock P.M. yesterday at Westover and Barclay [Berkeley], their former encampment. I cannot conceive what has kept them there so long." [11]

Without waiting for Steuben's answer, Jefferson wrote General Weedon the same day along the lines he had outlined to the Baron.[12] Weedon replied on the twelfth: "I . . . should have stood fast today had I not heard from General Nelson. That gentleman recommends our return immediately and thinks the enemy will make only sudden descents on the lower counties, if they disembark again at all. I have in consequence set the troops in motion this morning and shall proceed up to Fredericksburg with all dispatch, keeping them embodied until the further designs of Mr. Arnold are known. . . . I have sent off an express to the lower counties in the Northward Neck warning them of what may happen, and shall have the earliest intelligence should the enemy approach Potomac." [13]

An anonymous letter dated Petersburg, January 9, addressed to Jefferson, increased his determination to take no chances in losing the Fredericksburg works, as had happened with the foundry at Westham. "I would suggest to you the defenseless condition of Hunter's works at Fredericksburg," his correspondent writes, "full as great or greater object than any were at Richmond. The people in that part of the country are as destitute of arms as they are in this. The distance the works are from Potomac River about half as far as from Westover to Richmond. I would recommend it to Your Excellency to order some fortification erected to protect those works and some militia from the neighboring counties sent them to defend them." [14]

As a result, Jefferson sent a letter to James Hunter on the same day. "The importance of your works," he says, "to the operations of war will doubtless point them out as a proper object of destruction to the desolating enemy now in our country. They are at this time at Westover, and will possibly embark there. Their next expedition we cannot foresee; lest it should be to demolish your works, I write to General Weedon to take measure for protecting them. In the meantime I would advise you to move directly off into the country everything movable. Should you not be able to effect this by your own and

THE BURDENS OF STATE

hired wagons, I hereby authorize you to impress wagons, teams, and drivers for that purpose, only placing yourself instead of the public in point of responsibility to the owners." [15]

To afford further protection to these valuable works, on the twelfth Jefferson ordered Colonel Sampson Mathews, county lieutenant of Augusta, who "was on the road with the militia from beyond the Ridge ... to turn off immediately to Fredericksburg, and to proceed with all possible dispatch. There General Weedon will be ready to direct your operations. It is apprehended the enemy (if they aim at that place) will land on Potomac, through which they will have some miles to march through woods and defiles. The distance is short, but the ground very favorable for rifle service." [16]

By the eighteenth, when it was obvious that the threat to Fredericksburg would not eventuate, Jefferson was able to send Steuben a letter from General Weedon "which, I suppose, will inform you as it did me, that he has between six and seven hundred men embodied and expects five hundred more in the course of this week from the western side of the Blue Ridge. By a letter of the sixteenth from General Nelson he informs me he has ordered the Louisa militia (about 150) to turn off to Fredericksburg. They were not called on at all, so that they may either be discharged at Fredericksburg, or brought on to Williamsburg, as you think best. Orders shall immediately be given for sending to Hoods all the boats from this river which can be found fit for that place. In discharging the militia," he concludes, "I must beg the favor of you to let none be discharged who do not produce proper vouchers for the delivery of whatever public arms or accouterments shall have been put in their hands." [17]

Meanwhile the inhabitants of Fredericksburg had been giving very tangible evidence of their patriotism. "I have just time to acquaint you," Major Charles Dick writes the Governor on January 4, "that the gentlemen of this town and even the ladies have very spiritedly attended at the gunnery and assisted to make up already above 20,000 cartridges with bullets, from which the Spotsylvania militia and from Caroline have been supplied." [18]

During this period Steuben proved as hard a taskmaster for the Governor as for the timid and inexperienced militia he was trying to conjure into an army. Jefferson was bombarded with letters and memoranda, not once a day but several times. There is preserved among the Steuben Papers a series of questions the Baron propounded, with answers noted in Jefferson's hand in the margin. The document is significant chiefly as indicating once more the infinite attention Jefferson found time to give to each detail in these harrowing days. It was accompanied by a letter of January fourteenth in which Jefferson writes: "Your letters of the twelfth and thirteenth are now before me. They are in some measure answered by some marginal notes on the several articles in a paper delivered to me by Major Walker...." [19] The paper, endorsed "Questions asked the Governor," is in the form initiated by Louvois, the great war minister of Louis XIV, thenceforth adopted in European military practice. It reads, in part:

"1. To know if all the state arms are already distributed—if not, where are the remainder."

"[Governor:] All are delivered."

"2. To fix on a plan where all the arms, ammunition, and camp equipage may be collected—and appoint some officer to collect and distribute them. If the Governor thinks proper, Capt. Pryor may be appointed to distribute them after they are collected."

"[Governor:] Richmond and Westham. They shall be delivered to Capt. Pryor."

"3. The arms out of repair should immediately be put in order and as fast as they are repaired, delivered to the person appointed to distribute them."

"[Governor:] We are endeavoring to do this."

"4. The ammunition already made up should be delivered to the same person. At least 60,000 must be immediately prepared."

"[Governor:] Colonel Harrison says he will see to this."

"5. Tents and camp kettles sufficient for the troops now in the field must be immediately sent to them, besides which a sufficiency of these articles must be collected for the troops coming in, always reckoning on the 4,000 ordered out. The 2nd must be determined immediately that I may acquaint Generals Weedon and Nelson to whom to apply."

"[Governor:] There are no tents. All the camp kettles we had have been delivered, and we shall send to Fredericksburg immediately for more."

"6. If it would not be proper to have with me some officer of government who, being better acquainted with the resources of the state—I would confer with him on any emergency— This officer to keep a constant correspondence with the executive power."

"[Governor:] If I can find such a person who will be of real utility, I will send him to the Baron."

"7. To put in order immediately 6 or 8 of the 10-pounders at Richmond. A blockhouse and battery to be built at Hoods to defend the river. This I insist on in the name of the United States. Colonel Senf is already making the plans of the work. I wish to have men there."

"[Governor:] This shall be done. It is proper to inform Baron Steuben that among the cannon at South Quay there are 10 twenty-four pounders Swedish, and there were two at Suffolk some time ago. Whether destroyed or carried away by the enemy at the former invasion, I know not." [20]

The question of the fortifications at Hood's, mentioned in this document, was the reef upon which the friendly relations between Steuben and Jefferson were almost wrecked. On February 11 Steuben sent a letter to the Governor, hitherto unpublished except for a brief excerpt, in which he reviewed the situation. "Immediately after my arrival in this state," he writes, "Colonel Senf [21] represented to me the necessity of establishing a battery at Hoods and some other [illegible] works at Hoods in the vicinity of the James River. His opinion appeared to me to be well founded. I did not hesitate to submit it to Your Excellency, and I am informed you laid it before the Assembly, but that it was not taken into consideration.

"The last invasion and a more perfect knowledge of the ground convinces me still further of the necessity of putting a battery at the above place, covered by a redoubt with a blockhouse, the whole to contain about 60 men and to cost about 12 or 1500 dollars. When I accordingly laid before Your Excellency and the Council a plan of the work proposed with an estimation of the expense of the articles necessary to finish it in five weeks, I was happy in finding it approved.

The most important article required was 40 Negroes and 20 artisans, and if I understood Your Excellency correctly, these were to be furnished by the nearest counties and to be at the spot the 7th inst. I therefore ordered Captain Senf to Hoods on that day to receive the workmen and tools and to begin the work.

"At my return from Cabin Point I was much surprised at Colonel Senf informing me that he had not been furnished with any workmen and that government had declared they had it not in their power to furnish any, and in consequence I ordered him to return to Richmond.

"Three weeks are now elapsed since the enemy went down the river. In this time the work could have been half finished. If government think the work unnecessary, I have only to beg they would for my own information give me their opinion in writing.

"I must beg Your Excellency to consider that the unsuccessful opposition made to the last invasion of the enemy falls in some measure on me as the commanding officer in the state, and I cannot but reckon it among my misfortunes to have been here at the time, and my wish is to prevent a repetition of the disgrace; but as I can do nothing without the assistance of the government, I must beg Your Excellency to give me answer to this that I may have it in my power to justify my own conduct." [22]

The following day Jefferson sent a somewhat sharp reply to this letter. He takes issue with Steuben's recollection that 40 Negroes and 20 artificers were to have been supplied by the nearest counties, stating that "the Executive have not by the laws of this state any power to call a freeman to labor, even for the public, without his consent, nor a slave without that of his master." He recalls in complete detail the conversation that took place between himself and the Baron on the evening before the latter last went to Cabin Point and concludes: "The Executive are far from thinking this work unnecessary; nor yet that it will be out of their power to furnish the necessaries for erecting it. ... Sensible that a necessary work is not to be abandoned because their means are not so energetic as they could wish them ... they propose to pursue this work, and if they cannot accomplish it in a shorter, they will in a longer time." [23]

THE BURDENS OF STATE 161

Despite his statement that "we stand discharged of having failed to fulfill such an agreement," Jefferson seems to have been stung into action. On the fifteenth he addressed a letter to "several prominent men" of Henrico, Chesterfield, Dinwiddie, Prince George, and Charles City counties stating that "for the future protection of the stores and country on James River, it has been thought necessary to erect a defensive work at Hood's. Among other requisites 40 laboring slaves are wanting for two months. After trying the exertions of the ordinary officers to procure them, we have been able to procure 13 only, who are to be at the place on Monday next. I must therefore resort to the aid of the zealous citizens in the counties round about that part to endeavor to prevail on the people for spare laborers. Give me leave to beg your assistance in this way and to rely on you for procuring on the best terms you can within your county 6 able, laboring slaves to be at Hood's immediately and to continue there for two months." [24]

The next day, the sixteenth, Jefferson asks a certain Captain Allen to oversee the work at Hood's, according to Colonel Senf's instructions, and informs him that carpenters have been sent from Richmond. Smiths are already at Hood's, and one of Mr. Ryland Randolph's slaves is a bricklayer. Three or four other bricklayers are to be sent, and Captain Allen is directed to hire or impress vessels to transport the bricks and lime necessary.[25]

No matter how energetic the steps proposed by the Governor, it seemed impossible to overcome the lethargy he met at every turn. Two months later nothing had yet been accomplished at Hood's. On the twelfth of April Jefferson wrote Colonel William Call of Prince George, "The whole work projected required from the first but little labor. I endeavored by calling on five counties to furnish or hire six hands apiece for a moderate time to effect its completion, but in this we failed in a great measure. Every day bringing in new proof of the necessity of still pressing this work, I am induced to make to you on behalf of your county the following proposition, that every man of your county who will go or send an able laborer to work at Hood's eight days between this time and the last of the month, carrying with him an axe and a spade, if he has it, otherwise a hoe, shall be exempted from military duty out of his county for two months from this date." [26]

Such were the lengths to which the governor of Virginia was obliged to go to induce the citizens to act for the defense of their state. But it was not enough. A counter-proposition was made by Colonel Call, more agreeable to the gentlemen of his county. A substitute might be sent. On April 20 Steuben received from Colonel Senf a letter saying: "Since Saturday last I have been at Hood's and done as much as possible. Yesterday morning I received an express from the Governor.... He has now ordered the whole county of Prince George for each man to send a hand to Hood's to work for twelve days, and his twelve days should exempt them from six weeks' military duty." [27]

By the time the citizens of Prince George had given this consideration, it was once more too late. The British were again able to sail unopposed up the James. In his report to the House of Delegates of this last catastrophe, Jefferson says: "A battery on each river, at a proper position ... would, in the opinion of the most respectable characters among us, protect our vessels and, in a favorable position, would stop the passage of an enemy.... These small works are certainly within the compass of our finances. Yet we have in vain attempted to have such erected on each river. It has been found that money will not procure laborers; a militia of free men cannot easily be induced to labor in works of this kind. Slaves are by law excluded from the militia.... But whether male slaves might not under proper regulations be subjected to routines of duty as pioneers and to other military labors, can only be determined by the wisdom of the legislature." [28]

It was not only questions such as have just been discussed that filled Jefferson's days. There was no detail, apparently, that escaped his attention. Constant complaints concerning the destitute condition of the troops and the lack of supplies of every sort kept pouring in daily —before Arnold's invasion, during and after it. "It is needless to repeat to you," Colonel Henry Lee, Jr., wrote Steuben on his arrival in Virginia, "our nakedness and wants ... shoes, boots, overalls, shirts, blankets, vests, and coats comprise the essential part of our distress. We want axes and horseshoes exceedingly, being entirely destitute of these articles."[29] "Use every argument you can," General Greene felt obliged to urge Steuben, "to convince the Assembly of the necessity of clothing their troops. If they mean they shall render any service, or do not wish them to fall a sacrifice to death, desertion, and disease, I beg them to give their men good covering, for without it, this will be their portion."[30]

Jefferson was deaf to none of these grievances, whether directed to him or to Steuben. Many, if not most, should doubtless have been handled by the quartermaster's office, but that department was scarcely functioning. Indeed, in the midst of the invasion, on January 7, Steuben complained to Jefferson that aside from his want of arms, of ammunition, and of all the materials of war, he was much distressed to provide food for the troops. There was not a single quartermaster or commissary.[31] After begging Jefferson to send someone for this purpose, he adds, "The method of suffering corps to provide for themselves is exceedingly distressing to individuals and ruinous to the state."[32]

On the fourth Jefferson had, indeed, written Lieutenant Colonel Richard Meade, one of Washington's aides-de-camp, on this point. "The present invasion having rendered it necessary," he says, "to call into the field a large body of militia, the providing them with subsistence and the means of transportation becomes an arduous task in the unorganized state of our military system. To effect this we are obliged to vest the heads of the commissary's and quartermaster's department with such powers as, if abused, will be most afflicting to the people. Major General Baron Steuben, taught by experience on similar occasions, has pressed upon us the necessity of calling to the superintendence of these two offices some gentleman of distinguished character and abilities who, while he prescribes to them such rules as will effectually produce the object of their appointment, will yet stand between them and the people as a guard from oppression. Such a gentleman he would propose to consider as of his family; under this exigency we have taken the liberty of casting our eyes on yourself as most likely to fulfill our wishes, and therefore solicit your undertaking this charge."[33]

No action having been taken by those presumably responsible, Jefferson himself, on January 3, ordered the tailors and shoemakers of Warwick to repair to Chesterfield Court House,[34] where Steuben's troops had been directed to assemble. Even in these times, that American bugaboo, labor trouble, developed. On the seventeenth Captain John Peyton wrote Colonel Davies: "Have this morning set the tailors to work on the soldiers' coats. I am afraid it will not be in my power to prevail on the women in the neighborhood of this place to undertake the making of the shirts, as in the first place they object to the price being allowed, only fifteen dollars per shirt—their second objection is taking certificates for payment." [35]

After the sack of Richmond we find Jefferson appealing to all patriotic citizens and addressing a letter to "the person employed to collect workmen," saying: "The destruction of the public storehouses, magazines, laboratories, shops, and other works at this place and Westham by the enemy having left our arms, powder, and other stores exposed in open houses to plunder, and our artificers unfurnished with houses to proceed in the repair of arms and other necessary works, obliges me, as the only resource for a hasty collection of sawyers, carpenters, and wheelwrights, to apply to the public spirit of the gentlemen of this country who possess workmen of that kind. You will therefore go out for this purpose and address yourself to them, apprising them fully of the necessity of throwing up hasty works for these purposes. Whatever workmen they have we hope they will spare and send in immediately with their saws and tools. They will not be long wanted, and their hire shall be fixed by some impartial and judicious person according to the rates in hard money formerly allowed, with a proper attention to the late advance in wages." [36]

Again, in response to desperate pleas for clothing, he writes Colonel Davies: "As for the outer clothing for the soldiers, there is no early prospect but from the 1,495 yards of cloth sent you some time ago. We purchased 100 or 150 blankets and 400 pairs of stockings of Mr. Ross.... There are some blankets (perhaps 100) included in a purchase from Mr. Braxton.... Mr. Armistead will deliver to your order as much linen as will shirt all your men if you can have it made up. Four hundred shirts have lately been provided by Mr. Duncan Rose.

... Mr. Armistead has about 100 pairs of shoes here which he will deliver to you and, being offered 100 pairs at Petersburg, is sending an agent.... We expect a couple of wagons from Charlottesville with leather.... Mr. Armistead has now some sole leather which he will deliver you. I should suppose the shreds which might be saved by the tailors would go far towards mending clothes.... Oznaburgs and thread for the same purpose shall be furnished you...."[37]

There was, indeed, no detail that escaped him, no effort too great to make.

Yet from the very moment the British set sail up the James, vilification has been hurled at Jefferson. It has taken every form, from insinuation to direct and furious attacks. He has been accused of almost every blunder, of every failing, every gaucherie that could possibly be connected with the event. The most generous of his critics have been content to brand him as lackadaisical, bewildered, and inefficient. His enemies have not hesitated to call him a coward. He has been held personally responsible for Virginia's mistakes and misfortunes.

Only Washington, ever wise and looking beyond momentary irritation and pettiness, saw in the event not a major catastrophe, but an incident in the whole picture of the war. Replying to Jefferson's report of January 10, he wrote on February 6: "I am much obliged to Your Excellency for your letter of the tenth of January, giving me an account of the enemy's incursion into your state. Baron de Steuben has informed me of their successive operations to five miles below Hood's. It is mortifying to see so inconsiderable a party committing such extensive depredations with impunity, but considering the situation of your state, it is to be wondered you have hitherto suffered so little molestation. I am apprehensive you will experience more in future: nor should I be surprised if the enemy were to establish a post in Virginia till the season for opening the campaign here. But as the evils you have to apprehend from these predatory incursions are not to be compared with the injury to the common cause and with the danger to your state in particular, from the conquest of those states southward of you, I am persuaded the attention to your immediate safety will not divert you from the measures intended to reinforce the southern army and put it in a condition to stop the progress of the enemy in that quarter." [38]

Girardin has probably stated the case as succinctly and as fairly as anyone. Says he: "With an empty treasury, with scarcely any arms, with a formidable combination to oppose in the west, an advancing foe to meet in the south, and continual demands on her resources to answer in the north, it is no matter of surprise that she should not be fully prepared to repel this new invader from the east." [39] To Baron Steuben, on his arrival in Virginia, the scene had appeared equally ominous. "The derangement of the finances is more sensibly felt here than in any part of the continent," he had written Washington and the Board of War. "All the wheels of the administration are stopped; the late invasion of the enemy [Leslie's] has completed the confusion.... The Quartermaster's Department, and indeed almost all the departments, have no head. The executive part of the administration is carried on only by expedients, while the legislature cannot agree on any system whatsoever.... I find it impossible to give you an exact account of the troops of this state.... All these men I have found naked and as ill-armed as possible." [40]

The discipline of the army, at the same time, was practically nonexistent. "This state," Steuben writes, seeing conditions with a fresh eye on his arrival, "having only a handful of regulars in the field, is continually ransacked by bands of officers and soldiers, who have always a pretext for not joining their regiments, and who are drawing pay and rations for doing no service at all, while they are committing excesses everywhere.... The officers do not care for their soldiers, and they scarcely know the officers who have to command them." [41]

All these circumstances were conditions of long standing. They were evils that had grown up during the course of the war—before Jefferson came into power. It was impossible to remedy them in a few months, after it was realized how definitely the scene of the war was henceforth to be laid in the south. That steps at reformation should have been taken long ago, that the system of the Virginia militia was ill-adapted to the type of warfare going on at that time, cannot be laid at Jefferson's door.

Jefferson has been criticized for many things—particularly, by certain writers, for countenancing the rising of the Assembly. As one puts it, for saving "the cost of courier service by asking the legislators to carry the militia call back to their counties with them."[42] To anyone familiar with rural Virginia, the idea of "courier service" is nothing short of fantastic. It is a conception that can only be entertained in connection with the closely settled northern states. As recently as twenty-five years ago, before the advent of hard-surfaced roads in Virginia, any communication with outlying counties and settlements, particularly in the winter months, was extremely difficult. January rains and thaws converted the roads, many scarcely more than cart tracks, into an apparently bottomless morass of sticky red mud. In January of 1781 these unpleasant circumstances were undoubtedly vastly superior even to January a century and a half later. A legislator was fortunate to reach home himself. To entrust important business to the uncertain mercies of a messenger would have been foolhardy.

These critics, furthermore, fail to realize that Jefferson had no voice in the rising of the Assembly. He might, to be sure, call it together "before the time to which they stand adjourned"—which he did by a proclamation of January 23, 1781, when he appointed the first day of the following March, "at which time their attendance is required at the Capitol in the town of Richmond."[43] Adjournment, however, was a matter for the Assembly itself—indeed, the constitution specifically forbade the governor to prorogue it.

That the members of the legislature were impatient to get home, there is no doubt. It had been a particularly unhappy session. Called for October 16, there were not enough members present at that time to hold a session. On the twenty-fourth those who were there began ordering the sergeant-at-arms to take the absent members into custody. Leslie's invasion intervened, and it was not until the sixth of November that committees were finally appointed and business transacted. But the hearts and the thoughts of the legislators remained with their families. There was trouble in the air. On December 15 Richard Henry Lee wrote Theoderick Bland, who was in Philadelphia: "There is much business before the House, but as Christmas approaches, so does the anxiety of getting home, and it remains a doubt whether the House can be kept together when the holidays come on." [44]

They were kept together in form but not in actuality. On Saturday, December 23, a shocking number of absences were noted. The names of the members who failed to appear were listed, and the sergeant-at-arms was again ordered to take them into custody. The House, further, resolved that it would "with all the severity of censure, publish the names of those who shall in future absent themselves from their duty in the House at this critical juncture, without leave; that the calamities which will probably ensue upon leaving our affairs deranged, may be attributed to the authors of them." [45]

When the Assembly met on the morning of January 1, "the Speaker laid before the House a letter containing intelligence of the arrival of an enemy fleet, which was read and ordered to lie on the table." [46] Immediately the news was on every tongue. There was no power on earth that could have kept the members of the Assembly at their post after this, and they rose, on the second, as we have seen. They did not adjourn, however, before having passed a resolution yielding more than half of the western territory claimed by Virginia under her charter—a resolution which, in its magnanimity and its far-reaching effects on the welfare and the history of this country, was never equaled by any other state. "The General Assembly of Virginia being well satisfied that the happiness, strength, and safety of the United States depend, under Providence, upon the ratification of the articles for a Federal Union..." it reads, "Resolved, that this Commonwealth yield to the Congress of the United States for the benefit of the said United States all right, title, and claim that the said Commonwealth hath to the lands northwest of the river Ohio, upon the following conditions, to wit: That the territory so ceded shall be laid out and formed into states containing a suitable extent of territory, and shall not be less than one hundred or more than one hundred and fifty miles square, or as near thereto as circumstances will admit; that the states so formed shall be distinct republican states and be admitted members of the Federal Union, having the same rights of sovereignty, freedom, and independence as the other states." [47]

In a brief note transmitting the resolution to the president of Congress, Jefferson wrote, "I shall be rendered very happy if the other states of the Union, equally impressed with the necessity of that important convention [confederation] shall be willing to sacrifice to its completion. This single event, could it take place shortly, would overweigh every success which the enemy have hitherto obtained and render desperate the hopes to which those successes have given birth." [48] How patriotic Virginians reacted to the cession of his country which, as Richard Henry Lee observed, "is greater in extent than that which remains to us between the ocean and the Ohio, and in point of climate and in soil is far preferable," is well expressed by that gentleman in the words he addressed to Samuel Adams. "It will be a means of perfecting our union by closing the confederation—and thus our independency will be secured in a great measure." [49]

Jefferson has likewise frequently been criticized for not paying more heed to Washington's warning of a possible invasion. This is a criticism that seems dictated largely by hindsight. The governors of the seaboard states had received frequent notifications of threatened attack by the British fleet during the course of the war. Some were true; mostly they were false. Thus on December 11, 1779, Washington had sent Jefferson word of an embarkation at New York said to be destined for the south. Jefferson had communicated this to the Assembly, with recommendations for various measures for defense. Before these could become effective, another letter arrived, written on the twenty-fifth, saying the previous information had been a mistake. The fleet of 100 ships, with no troops, had sailed apparently for England.[50]

Although on July 1, 1780, Jefferson laid before the Council a letter from Colonel Mallory of Elizabeth City reporting the appearance of a fleet supposedly hostile, and the Council directed the Governor to inaugurate certain defense plans, there is no further suggestion of invasion in the letters that passed between Washington and Jefferson until September 11, 1780. At this time Washington again wrote that an embarkation was forming in New York, bound either for Virginia or Carolina. "I think it would be prudent," he adds, "to direct the removal of any public stores which may be upon navigable waters, and to make the arrangements necessary for defense in case such an event should take place." [51] The warning was repeated in a letter of October 10.

On November 8 Washington once more wrote: "Another embarkation is said to be preparing in New York, and I think it a very probable circumstance considering the situation of the enemy's affairs in South Carolina, and ours in this.... Should the enemy continue in the lower parts of Virginia, they will have every advantage by being able to move up and down the river in small parties, while it will be out of our power to molest them for want of the means of suddenly transporting ourselves across those rivers to come at them." [52] He concludes his letter with a recommendation for building a certain type of flatboat which would solve this problem—and which Jefferson eventually ordered built on January 16, 1781.[53]

One last warning, if information concerning supposed embarkations can be called that, was contained in the postscript to a letter Washington sent Jefferson from New Windsor on December 9. "I am this moment informed from New York," he writes, "another embarkation is taking place consisting of 1 batall. grenadiers, 1 battal. lt. infantry, 1 batt. Hessian grenadiers, Knyphausen's regiment, 42nd British, a draft of 5 men from each company in the line, and two troops of light dragoons under Generals Knyphausen and Phillips, supposed to be destined southward." [54]

Jefferson's critics fail to realize that it would have been entirely impossible to have kept the militia steadily under arms during this long and uncertain period. It would have been equally impossible to call them out as frequently as these alarms, unfounded on many occasions, would have necessitated. Common sense, as well as his knowledge of the organization of the militia, kept Jefferson from crying "wolf!" once too often.

Contemporary criticism was quite as persistent and quite as virulent as that of later years. James Madison and Theoderick Bland, Jr., Virginia delegates to Congress, united in addressing a letter to the Governor on January 1, 1781, on the subject of the proposed defense of the state. After speaking of Washington's letter with the news of the threatened British embarkation, they say: "*Our* conjecture is that they are destined to the southward, and, indeed, all the enemy's political and military maneuvers seem to indicate their intention of making a vigorous effort against the southern states this winter.

"We are sorry to inform Your Excellency that we receive very little authentic intelligence of the steps which are taking to counteract these vigorous operations," they continue, "that we are in a great measure uninformed of the progress that has been made in raising the new army, and on what terms; of what has been, and will be, done in establishing magazines for its support; and, above all, to the measures pursuing to cancel the old money and give effectual support to the new, by providing for its punctual and final redemption with specie. This is a crisis at which we conceive a most assiduous application to these great objects to be necessary, and next to the completion of the Confederacy (which is the basis of the whole) of the first importance to America, therefore highly importing us to know, as the measures of so large a state as ours cannot but have considerable effects on the other states in this union." [55]

When the news of the feared invasion finally reached them, they were led to write Jefferson again, on January 25. This letter is not so much one of reproach as one which tends to overlook past misfortunes and to build toward the future. "It is with much concern," they write, "that we have learned from Your Excellency's and Baron de Steuben's letters to Congress, the misfortunes our country has suffered from the invasion under the command of the detestable Arnold, and that he has ventured with impunity even to our Capitol."

After discussing Arnold's probable strategy, which they believe will be to remain in the bay, harass "our military, increase our expense, waste our resources, destroy our magazines and stores," they continue: "This, Sir, is a game we are open to at every period of our short enlistments, and in a great measure exposed to, for want of a militia organized to take the field, a few gunboats or galleys, and some good fortifications in the most advantageous situations on our rivers, for defense. But this late event has rendered this so obvious that we are fully persuaded our country will now see the necessity of adopting arrangements very different from what have been of late trusted to." [56]

To John Page, until recently lieutenant governor, and, as we know,

Jefferson's stanchest friend and admirer, the events of January 1781 were nothing short of catastrophic. He became enveloped in a gloom inspired and fed by a fanatical patriotism. "The repeated disgrace that our country has suffered," he wrote Theoderick Bland on the twenty-first, "and that with which she is at present overshadowed, have sunk her so low in the eyes of the world that no illustrious foreigner can ever visit her, or any historian mention her but with contempt and derision.... Arnold, the traitor, with about 1,300 men, has disgraced our country, my dear friend, so much that I am ashamed and ever shall be, to call myself a Virginian.... To our eternal disgrace, so unarmed and undisciplined after a five years' war are our militia, that nothing like this has been done." [57]

Jefferson was stung by the criticism of his conduct during Arnold's invasion as by nothing else in his whole career. Even Cornwallis's depredations and Tarleton's penetration of Albemarle County to his very doorstep were as nothing compared to the reproach of having permitted the capital of the state to be invaded and burned by the enemy. The unjust imputation of incompetence and failure to do his duty were something he could neither forgive nor forget. Years after it had occurred, the memory still rankled. From Daniel Hylton, who had assisted him in the removal of the public stores at that time, Jefferson secured a statement in 1796 intended to exonerate him.

"I, the subscriber," the document reads, "an inhabitant of the county of Henrico, do hereby certify that in January 1781, when Arnold invaded this place, I was living very near the Foundry at West Ham: That I was going out to join the militia to oppose said Arnold, when I was stopped by Mr. Jefferson, the governor of the state, and requested by him to attend to the removal of the powder, ammunition, arms, and other property belonging to the public then in the magazine near West Ham; that his orders were to have everything removed with all possible expedition across the River. That on the night preceding the day of Arnold's arrival at the foundry, Mr. Jefferson was at the subscriber's house as late as eleven or twelve o'clock at night, attending and giving directions about the public property. That he then said he should go up the river, about 8 or 10 miles, cross the next morning, and come down to Brittain's opposite

Westham and that carriages, etc., should be provided to take off the said property; that this was done; that a very considerable quantity (I suppose about fifteen tons) of gunpowder and ammunition, with a number of arms, stores, etc., were transported as directed and thereby saved to the public; that the enemy were so close upon us that I was obliged to have about three hundred stand of arms thrown into the river, the greater part of which were afterward recovered; that in the night preceding the day of invasion, the wagons (driven by white men) employed to bring the records, etc., from Richmond, by mistake attempted to get to the magazine, instead of the landing on the river and near the magazine, overset and broke some arms, etc.; that in consequence of this accident, the packages, which I found afterwards contained records, were lodged at the magazine, and carriages could not be procured in time for their removal, as the alarm was so great and sudden; that almost every person in the neighborhood was endeavoring to put some of his property in a state of safety by removing it. That it then and ever since has appeared to the subscriber that the said Mr. Jefferson did everything which the nature of the case and his situation would admit, for the public interest." [58]

Nothing, however, seemed able to erase the memory of these days from Jefferson's mind. As late as May 15, 1826, less than two months before his death, he sent Henry Lee a spirited defense of his conduct in the emergency while he was governor, in which the events nearly half a century past stand out with the vividness of yesterday's happenings. "Is the surprise of an open and unarmed place, although called a city, and even a capital, so unprecedented as to be a matter of indelible reproach?" he cries. "Which of our capitals during the same war was not in possession of the same enemy, not merely by surprise and for a day but permanently? That of Georgia? Of South Carolina? North Carolina? Pennsylvania? New York? Connecticut? Rhode Island? Massachusetts? ... Is it then just that Richmond and its authorities alone should be placed under the reproach of history because, in a moment of peculiar denudation of resources, by the *coup de main* of an enemy, led on by the hand of fortune directing the winds and weather to their wishes, it was surprised and held for twenty-four hours? Or strange that that enemy with such advantages should be enabled then to get off, without risking the honors he had achieved by burnings and destructions of property peculiar to his principles of warfare? We, at least, may leave these glories to their own trumpet." [59]

VIII. Between Invasions

ARNOLD'S WITHDRAWAL to Portsmouth and his efforts to establish a post there provided a brief and uneasy breathing spell for Jefferson. He wrote General Nelson on the fifteenth that he had "never heard a tittle of the enemy since your information that they were at Sandy Point the day after they left Westover; nor is anything known at this place as to their movements."[1] It was as though an evil phantom had swept up the James and back, vanishing into nothingness, leaving as the only token of its reality the burned and broken buildings of Richmond and Westham.

Jefferson used this interval to return to the never-ending problems of raising men and securing provisions for the Continental Army. The halt in this procedure caused by the invasion was very grave, and he applied himself to remedying the situation with the utmost vigor and determination. To the president of Congress and the president of the Board of War he sent a long communication on the inequality of Continental requisitions in regard to provisions, and on the larger question of who was to supply the southern army. This had come to the foreground in a requisition from Congress that Virginia furnish one-half the supplies for the Convention troops which had been moved to Maryland. "You cannot be unapprised of the powerful armies of our enemies at this time in this and the southern states," he writes, "and that their future plan is to push their successes in the same quarter by still larger reinforcements. The forces to be opposed to these must be proportionately great, and these forces must be fed. But by whom are they to be fed? Georgia and South Carolina are annihilated, at least as to us. By the requisition to us to send provisions into Maryland it is supposed that none are to come for the Southern Army from any state north of this. . . . Upon North Carolina, then, already exhausted by the ravages of two armies, and on this state are to depend for subsistence those bodies of men who are to oppose the greater part of the enemy's force in the United States, the subsistence of the German, and of half the British Conventioners. ... I am far from wishing to count or measure our contributions by the requisitions of Congress. Were they ever so much beyond these, I should readily strain them in aid of any of our sister states. But while they are so far short of those calls to which they must be pointed in the first instance, it would be great misapplication to divert them to any other purpose; and I am persuaded you will think me perfectly within the line of duty when I ask for a revisal of this requisition." [2]

By the nineteenth of January conditions had so far returned to normal that it was possible to hold a meeting of the Council, the first in over two weeks. Present, aside from the Governor, were David Jameson, Joseph Prentis, George Webb, and Jacquelin Ambler. A matter-of-fact notation in the *Journal of the Council* reads: "His Excellency communicated his proceedings during the recess, together with the copies of the letters which have passed between him and certain persons, which being read and approved, the board directs to be registered." [3] This is the only reflection of those swift and devastating days, with their heartbreaking experiences, that had marked Jefferson's activities since the board last came together.

The most important business to come before the Council this day was Jefferson's proclamation on so-called paroles. From the developments that followed, there is little doubt but that this was Jefferson's own idea, to which the Council subscribed. This vicious custom, immobilizing large numbers of the population, the British had already put into practice in other invaded states. As Jefferson very truly observed, it was an attempt to disarm "a whole country which they cannot otherwise subdue. They have conquered South Carolina by paroles alone. They will conquer us also if we admit their validity." [4] This practice was destined to cause more ill feeling in Virginia than almost any of the high-handed methods employed by the enemy. In his proclamation concerning it, issued the same day, Jefferson describes the procedure as a practice that "hath been introduced by them unauthorized by the law of nations and unattempted in any other age or by other enemy, of seizing peaceable citizens while in their beds or employed in domestic occupations, and extorting from them paroles, 'that they will not on pain of life and fortune be aiding or assisting in any respect to the enemies of Great Britain,' which paroles such citizens have given sometimes through ignorance, and at other times with the wicked design, while they enjoy all the benefits of government, to shift from themselves their first share of its burdens." [5]

The proclamation provided that "citizens taken or yielding themselves in the manner before described are incapable by law of contracting engagements which may cancel or supersede the duties they owe to their country while remaining in it, and that notwithstanding such paroles or engagements, they will be held to the performance of every service required by the laws in like manner, as if no such parole or engagement had been entered into.... All citizens ... who conceive themselves under such conscientious obligation to refuse obedience to the laws of their country, are hereby authorized and required ... forthwith to repair to some of the posts, encampments, or vessels of the forces of His Britannic Majesty and by surrender of their persons to cancel such engagements, and thereafter to do as to themselves and those in whose power they shall be, shall seem good, save only that they shall not rejoin this Commonwealth but in a state of perfect emancipation from its enemies, and of freedom to act as becomes good and zealous citizens." [6]

This proclamation was a blow not only to the British, but to their sympathizers, of whom there were many in Virginia. Its stern words, summoning such individuals to abandon their comfortable circumstances and surrender their persons to the forces of the enemy, were anything but palatable to them. Although Jefferson wrote Steuben on February 15, "I am glad my proclamation has offended Arnold. It proves it to be right," [7] the British were undeterred by his action. They continued to molest peaceable citizens and to flout the proclamation. The matter was taken up by the legislature in its March session, and on the twenty-first it came to the following resolution: "Whereas the enemy have lately introduced a practice of paroling citizens not taken in arms, but found pursuing their domestic employments, which practice is not warranted by the usage of nations and is destructive of those duties which every citizen owes his country, Resolved that such paroles are hereby declared null and absolutely void. And that if the enemy shall on pretense of such void paroles treat any citizen of this Commonwealth ill who shall be found in arms, called into the field by legal authority, that prompt and just retaliation shall be inflicted on such persons of the enemy as have fallen, or may fall, under the power of this state. Resolved that the Governor be requested to cause this resolve to be communicated by flag to the commander of the enemies troops at Portsmouth." [8]

The commanding officer at the moment happened to be Benedict Arnold. In a covering letter to Lafayette, enclosing the resolution, Jefferson asks him if possible to deliver the message to the naval commander instead, "as nothing can be so disagreeable to me as to be compelled to a correspondence with the other." [9] As fate would have it, Phillips succeeded to the command on March 20, thus Jefferson's letter was doubtless handed to him.

The letter reads: "Some of the citizens of this state taken prisoners when not in arms and enlarged on parole, have reported the commanding officer as affirming to them they should be punished with death if found in arms. This has given occasion to the enclosed resolution of the General Assembly of this state. It suffices to observe at present, that by the law of nations, a breach of parole (even where the validity of parole is unquestioned) can only be punished by stricter confinement.

"No usage has permitted the putting to death a prisoner for this cause. I would willingly suppose that no British officer had ever expressed a contrary purpose. It has, however, become my duty to declare that, should such a threat be carried into execution, it will be deemed as putting prisoners to death in cold blood, and shall be followed by the execution of so many British prisoners in our possession. I trust, however, that this horrid necessity will not be introduced by you, and that you will, on the contrary, concur with us in endeavoring as far as possible to alleviate the inevitable miseries of war by treating captives as humanity and natural honor requires...." [10]

The letter was handed to Phillips by Samuel H. Radford, aide to

General Weedon. The British general, a man of high temper and exaggerated ideas concerning the superiority of his country, was infuriated. He did not deign to reply to the Governor, but, after waiting some days, informed Radford: "I mean to pursue during my stay in Virginia a conduct of the strictest liberality and humanity, and I do assure you that nothing shall turn me aside from such benevolent principles but the rash and violent conduct I have reason to fear may be taken up by your Governor, Council, and House of Delegates. I have received on my arrival here a letter signed by Mr. Jefferson, of so barbarous—excuse me for saying, Sir, insolent—a nature, that it would be unbecoming my rank and situation to give any answer to it. I will, however, declare to you, Sir, that should any part of the savage threats contained in that letter, and the resolution of your House of Delegates, be put into execution, I shall consider Virginia as intending to carry on a peculiar war, abstracted from the general unhappy one, and I will treat the colony accordingly." [11]

A second proclamation similar to that of November 30, 1780, laying an embargo on the exportation of provisions was issued the same January 19. John Brown, commissioner of the provision law, was instructed to "give orders to his deputies in the several senatorial districts to call on the owners of all wagons, teams, and drivers, and all vessels for river tranportation, with their navigators within the same, to register with them their said wagons, teams, and drivers, vessels and crews, to divide the said wagons into brigades of ten each and the vessels as may be most expedient, appointing some trusty person to act as master of the brigade when called into service" [12] at such time as it should become necessary to impress these articles.

On the nineteenth Jefferson likewise dispatched a circular letter to the various county lieutenants, informing them of "those acts of the Assembly which required immediate execution. The principal of these, the law for recruiting the army, having been framed on the idea that the militia of the several counties would be quiet at home, has been peculiarly retarded by the necessity we were under of calling militia from almost every county." After explaining the provisions of the law in detail, he continues in a manner almost paternal: "Such is the present aspect of the enemy towards this country, that no foresight can predict the moment at which your militia will be called to active duty. Let me exhort you, therefore, and through you your officers and men, to consider that moment as if now come, that every man who has or can procure a gun, have it instantly put into the best order, a bayonet fitted to it, a bayonet belt, cartouche box, canteen with its strap, tomahawk, blanket, and knapsack. Some of these articles are necessary for his own safety, and some for his health and comfort. ... Let me again entreat you, Sir, not only to give out general orders to your captains that these preparations be instantly made, but see yourself, as far as possible, that your orders be carried into execution. The soldiers themselves will thank you when, separated from domestic accommodation, they find through your attention to their happiness provided with conveniences which will administer to their first wants." [13]

Virginia was, indeed, making every preparation possible.

It was obvious that the war could not be successfully carried on unless the Assembly were in session and Jefferson resolved to call it, no matter how unpopular such a step would be with the members. His determination was strengthened by a letter from General Nelson, dated Williamsburg, January 22. "I am just favored with yours of the 20th instant," he writes, "inclosing your proclamation respecting those who have been paroled, which shall be strictly adhered to.... I would also take the liberty of suggesting another matter to you, that is the necessity of calling the Assembly. From disagreeable experience I am convinced that the defense of this country must not rest on the militia under its present establishment. They have been so much harassed lately that they would give nearly half they possess to raise regulars, rather than be subject to the distresses they feel at leaving their plantations and families. We have been obliged to call out the whole of the militia from several counties, some of whom I have not been able to discharge for want of men to relieve them. I am ordered by Baron Steuben to keep in this neck 1,000 or 1,200 men, and were I to discharge the men who were on duty in the last invasion, which I confess they have a right to claim, I should not have one-third of that number. Many of the paroled men of Elizabeth City have taken up arms, and others will do so if they can be supported. This I am about to do with a light corps. There are many things which the service requires to be done, which cannot be effected for want of money. If the state of the treasury will admit of it, I must therefore request that the quartermaster be furnished with same." [14]

Thus stimulated, and realizing as he had all along that the legislature must remain in session to act on the increasing calls for money, men, and supplies, Jefferson issued a proclamation on the twenty-third, setting the first day of the following March for its meeting. He was human and wise enough, knowing how loath the members would be to leave their families at such a perilous time, to send a circular letter to each man in the Assembly on this occasion. "I am sorry after so long and laborious a session of the Assembly," he writes, "the public exigencies should be such as to call for an earlier meeting of the members than was intended. A proclamation has been this day issued for convening you on the first of March, and though that alone was necessary in point of formality, I could not deny myself the apprising you by letter of those circumstances which have rendered the measure necessary, and which could not with propriety have been explained in the public proclamation. Such is the load of public debt contracted by certificates, and such the preparations necessary for the summer to enable us to meet our enemies in the North, South, East, and West, that before any considerable progress was made in paying the past and providing for the future, the whole sums allowed to be emitted were engaged. It became a matter of certainty that in a few days we should be unable to move an express or repair an arm, or do any other the smallest thing, though the existence of the state should depend on it, for want of money. It was impossible to think of hazarding the state in this condition through the months of February, March, April, and probably May, while we have an enemy within our country and others approaching it on every side. Information also from the general officers brought us assurance that our defense could not be rested on militia.... Men and money will therefore be the subject of your deliberations. I have no doubt but some legislative aid may also be rendered necessary for securing the executions of the acts for recruiting men and procuring beef, clothing, and wagons...."

After discussing the delay in informing the militia of the recent act of the Assembly, he concludes philosophically: "The zealous citizen unable to do his duty so soon as was prescribed, will do it as soon as he can, but the unwilling will find much room for objection which the authority of the legislative alone will be able to remove...." [15] Well might he have echoed Washington's words about the New Englanders, in regard to his fellow Virginians: "It is among the most difficult tasks I ever undertook in my life to induce these people to believe that there is, or can be, danger till the bayonet is pushed at their breasts." [16]

Meanwhile, on January 30, Benjamin Harrison, Speaker of the House of Delegates, started for Philadelphia on a special mission. As he says in his letter of February 16 to Washington, he was "sent by our Assembly to make application to Congress for immediate assistance in men, arms, ammunition, and clothing, and was also directed to wait on you on the same subject." Harrison minced no words. "Our Assembly," he continues, "on taking a full and accurate view of the southern war and of our own situation, on whom very much of its success depends, are justly alarmed. They find the country greatly exhausted in the articles of provisions, arms, and military stores of all kinds, and that there is but little prospect of assistance in these particulars from the adjoining states.... The greatest part of the ammunition sent to the south went from Virginia, by which means we are left with about 47,000 wt. of powder of all kinds.... Several thousand stand of arms have also gone, but very few of them have been returned.... From this summary state of the matter you may easily conclude that our own safety forbids us to disfurnish ourselves any farther, as from the foregoing invasions of late, we conclude that the enemy mean to overrun us whenever an opportunity shall offer." [17]

Harrison carried with him a letter of instruction from the Governor, as well as a detailed statement, in the form of an elaborate and minute table, of Virginia's situation in regard to arms, ammunition, and military stores of all kinds.[18] It is another testimonial to the painstaking Jefferson and to how thoroughly he had mastered every detail of the complicated military affairs involving state and Continental troops and supplies. He takes up topics such as "how many arms have we in the state fit for service, bayonets, etc.?" to which the pitiful answer is that in the magazines there are exactly 68 muskets in good repair, 2,273 out of repair, 159 bayonets fitted, 161 cartouche boxes. "Dispersed in counties much exposed" were 3,315 muskets. He likewise goes into the question of the number of arms lent North Carolina since the war and since the invasion of South Carolina, the stock of munitions and military stores in hand, the number of arms furnished by Congress, "how many tents or tent-cloth and other camp necessaries have we?" and "what prospects have we of supplies of the above? Also blankets and cloth for soldier's clothes?" The answer is inevitably too little, too few, or none at all.

This document was laid before Congress. On the strength of it and of Harrison's representations, that body proceeded on February 20, to vote elaborate and extensive commitments—the southern army was henceforth to be "composed of all the regular troops from Pennsylvania to Georgia, inclusive," with certain exceptions, 400 wagons were to be bought, "10,000 suits of clothes, complete," were to be supplied, 860 tents, 700 camp kettles, and so on.[19] Virginia had never hoped for such success or dreamed of such riches. Harrison, blunt realist that he was, and veteran statesman, had seen gentlemen vote before. Although he wrote Washington on February 28, "I am extremely glad to hear you are sending us assistance and hope you can with convenience spare it; if the French fleet had come on with about 2,500 men, a very few days would have put the traitor, his army, and fleet into our hands, as Baron Steuben is on one side of him with at least 3,000 men, and those being on the other, he could not have escaped,"[20] his report to the Governor was more realistic. He allowed that he had been treated with the greatest politeness and had "every reason to expect they will grant me full as much as I asked, but I foresee very great difficulty in their carrying their resolutions into effect, they being extremely poor and their credit but low."[21]

Whether Jefferson's statement came to Washington's attention is questionable. He was in Newport at the time and thus did not even see Harrison personally. It was not until March 27 that Washington answered Harrison's letter. Then it was not to hold out any hope for relief but to reprove the state for its shortcomings. "I very early saw the difficulties and dangers to which the southern states would be exposed," he writes, "for want of resources of clothing, arms, and ammunition, and recommended magazines to be established as ample as their circumstances would admit. It is true they are not so full of men as the northern states, but they ought, for that reason, to have been more assiduous in raising a permanent force, to have been always ready, because they cannot draw a head of men together as suddenly as their exigencies may require. That policy has, unhappily, not been pursued either here or there, and we are now suffering from a remnant of the British Army what they could not in the beginning accomplish with their force at the highest."

After rehearsing in detail the lamentable situation of the Continental Army in regard to men, ammunition, and clothing, he continues: "You will readily perceive from the foregoing state that there is little probability of adding to the force already ordered to the southward." He then makes a statement clearly indicating that he had not yet grasped the full ominousness of the British designs on Virginia. "You may be assured," he writes, "that the most powerful diversion that can be made in favor of the southern states will be a respectable force in the neighborhood of New York.... Nothing which is within the compass of my power," he concludes, "shall be wanting to give support to the southern states, but you may readily conceive how irksome a thing it must be to me, to be called on for assistance when I have not the means of affording it." [22]

Before Harrison had even reached Philadelphia with his plea, Jefferson was sending Washington and the president of Congress news of a most disconcerting character and again calling to their attention the distressed situation of the state. "I have just received intelligence," he writes on February 8, "that a fleet of the enemy's ships have entered Cape Fear River, that eight of them had got over the bar, and many others were laying off; that it was supposed to be a reinforcement to Lord Cornwallis.... I thought it of sufficient importance to be communicated to Your Excellency by the stationed expresses. The fatal want of arms puts it out of our power to bring a greater force into the field than will barely suffice to restrain the adventures of the pitiful body of men they have at Portsmouth.

Should any other be added to them, this country will be perfectly open to them by land as well as by water." [23]

To General Greene, in North Carolina, he wrote the following day: "Every moment brings us new proofs that we must be aided by your northern brethren. Perhaps they are aiding us, and we are uninformed of it. I think near half the enemy's force are now in Virginia and the states south of that. Is half the burden of opposition to rest on Virginia and North Carolina? I trust you concur with us in crying aloud on this head." There was one note of hope, however, heralding what was eventually to mean salvation: "I have the pleasure to inform you that we have every reason to expect, during the two ensuing months, very full supplies of all necessaries for our army from France, on a contract we had made last spring. I hope, too, that their escort is such as not only to render their entrance secure, but to promise something further." [24]

News of the operations even then going forward in North Carolina was slow to reach Virginia. Lord Cornwallis's "plan for the winter's campaign," as he tells us, "was to penetrate into North Carolina, leaving South Carolina in security against any probable attack." [25] It was not until February 12 that letters arrived from General Greene and Governor Nash with accounts of the battle of Cowpens, described by Cornwallis as "the unfortunate affair of the seventeenth of January . . . a very unexpected and severe blow; for besides reputation, our loss did not fall below 600 men." Convinced, as he says, "that defensive measures would be certain to ruin the affairs of Britain in the southern colonies, this event did not deter me from prosecuting the original plan," [26] and he boldly started in pursuit of the Americans. For Greene the victory became a Pyrrhic one. "Almost fatigued to death" and with "many hundreds of the soldiers marking the ground with their bloody feet," [27] he was obliged to retire for more than 200 miles until he and his men ultimately reached safety on the Virginia shore of the broad and swollen waters of the River Dan.

As soon as Jefferson had learned the news from Carolina, but before he had become aware of the success of Greene's retreat, he sent a brief report to Washington and the president of Congress. With it he enclosed a letter from Greene to Baron Steuben "by which you will learn the events which have taken place in that quarter since the defeat of Colonel Tarlton by General Morgan." It is impossible not to detect a note of resigned discouragement and despondency in the words with which he concludes this letter. "These events speak for themselves," he says, "and no doubt will suggest what is necessary to be done to prevent the successive losses of state after state, to which want of arms and a regular soldiery seem more especially to expose those in the south." [28]

On the night of the fourteenth, a messenger arrived with another letter from Greene which dispelled any gloom and inspired Jefferson once more to do his utmost, no matter what the outlook. In immediate and determined action on his part and that of the Virginia militia, he saw an opportunity to bring the war in the south to a speedy close by the defeat or capture of Cornwallis's army. The following morning he sent a letter to the county lieutenant of each county, using all his powers of eloquence and persuasion to rouse them from what all too often seemed to be a congenital lethargy, and to exhort them to action.

"I have just received intelligence from General Greene," he writes, "that Lord Cornwallis, maddened by his losses at the Cowpens and Georgetown, has burnt his own wagons to enable himself to move with facility, and is pressing forward towards the Virginia line, General Greene being obliged to retire before him with an inferior force. The necessity of saving General Greene's army and, in doing that, the probability of environing and destroying the army of the enemy, induce me to press you in the most earnest terms, in the instant of receiving this, to collect one [one-fourth, or whatever the case might be in a given county] of your milita, and to send them forward well armed and accoutered under proper officers to repair to the orders of General Greene, wherever he shall be. By this movement of our enemy he has ventured his all on one stake. Our stroke is sure if the force turns out which I have ordered and without delay; in such a crisis expedition decides the event of the contest. Reflecting that it depends in a great measure on your personal exertions in effecting a rapid juncture of your men and General Greene, whether the southern war be terminated by the capture of the hostile army or entailed on us by permitting them to fix in our bowels, I cannot believe you will rest a moment after receiving this till you see your men under march." [29]

Two days later the Governor learned that Lord Cornwallis had already advanced to the Roanoke. He issued orders "to embody every man between this and that for whom a firelock can be procured" to march to the aid of General Greene. The same day he sent a lengthy résumé of the situation to General Washington and to the president of Congress. To General Gates, then living in retirement in Berkeley County, he dispatched a brief and dramatic kaleidoscope of recent events. "The situation here and in Carolina is such as must shortly turn up important events one way or the other," he writes. After giving a sentence to Cornwallis's burning of his wagons and baggage, he continues: "The prisoners taken at the Cowpens were saved by a hair's-breadth accident and Greene was retreating. His force 2,000 regulars and no militia, Cornwallis's 3,000. Davidson [brigadier general of the North Carolina militia] was killed in a skirmish. Arnold lies still at Portsmouth with 1,500 men. A French 64-gun ship and 2 frigates of 36 each arrived in our bay three days ago. They would suffice to destroy the British shipping here (a 40., 4 frigates, and a 20) could they get at them. But these are withdrawn up Elizabeth River, which the 64 cannot enter. . . .

"I have been knocking at the door of Congress for aids of all kinds," he concludes, "but especially of arms, ever since the middle of summer. The Speaker Harrison has gone to be heard on that subject. Justice indeed requires that we should be aided powerfully. Yet if they would repay us the arms we have lent them, we should give the enemy trouble, though abandoned to ourselves." [30]

The situation on the Virginia border was becoming so acute that Jefferson, anticipating more recent custom, determined to send a personal representative to Greene's headquarters to observe and to report directly to him. On the eighteenth of February he wrote Major Charles Magill, a major in a Virginia state regiment: "The situation of southern affairs having become very interesting to this state, I am to desire the favor of you to proceed without delay to the headquarters of General Greene, to remain there or at any other place from which you shall think the best intelligence may be obtained. You will be pleased to communicate with me the interesting movements of both armies, the calls which may be made on our counties for supplies of men, provisions, and other things, how these calls are complied with, what shall appear to be the spirit of the people, what is doing in the rear of Lord Cornwallis, and such other facts as you shall think important." [31]

To Greene he wrote the same day: "The very interesting situation of southern affairs with respect to our state at this crisis, and the multiplication of your business which alone must forbid me to hope for a very frequent communication from you, have induced me to send on the bearer, Major Magill, to give us from time to time notice of the movements of the two armies and other important occurrences that we may be able to adapt to them the measures to be taken by them. The zeal, discretion, and good sense which have recommended Major Magill to us for the execution of this office, will render him worthy of any countenance and civilities you shall think proper to show him. Give me leave to hope also that you will trust him with any communications which you may think not improper to be made to us, of which we shall endeavor to make the best use for the common good." [32]

Jefferson's polite introduction failed to smooth the way for Magill. On March 2 he reported that, "agreeable to the directions received from Your Excellency, I proceeded with utmost expedition to the headquarters of the Southern Army. On my arrival I found that the policy of the army would not permit me to penetrate into the secret reasons that had actuated General Greene in his difficult movements, that nothing had unfolded itself worthy of communication." [33]

Despite the cool reception, Magill was able to accomplish his purpose. In a series of seven letters, from the second to the nineteenth of March after the battle of Guilford Court House, after which he felt his services were no longer necessary, he sent Jefferson information of the utmost importance. He reported on Cornwallis's movements and plans, Greene's policy, Tarleton's activity, the condition and behavior of the troops, the inhuman brutality of the British and Tories, and related questions. These letters contain details which

BANASTRE TARLETON. From the mezzotint after Sir Joshua Reynolds. (*Courtesy of the Philadelphia Museum of Art*)

JEFFERSON'S BUST OF LAFAYETTE. By Houdon. (*Courtesy of the Boston Athenaeum*)

Jefferson would otherwise scarcely have learned so promptly, certainly not in time to be of value to those to whom he communicated them—Washington and the Speaker of the House of Delegates.[34]

The meeting of the House of Delegates had been called for the morning of the first of March, but, as usual, a quorum was not present until the next day. It was an occasion of the utmost importance. Knowing the hesitance with which the members had left their families and property in these perilous times, Jefferson took occasion, through the Speaker, to address a long communication to them. "It is with great reluctance that after so long and laborious a session as the last," he says, "I have been again obliged to give you the trouble of convening in General Assembly within so short a time and in so inclement a season. But such was the situation of public affairs as to render it indispensable." He proceeds to outline the work that lies before them. "One army of our enemies lodged within our country, another pointing towards it, and since in fact entered into it, without a shilling in the public coffers, was a situation in which it was impossible to rest the safety of the state.... The invasion which took place on the close of the last session of Assembly having necessarily called for the attendance of a number of militia in the field, interrupted, of course, the execution of the act for recruiting our quota of troops for the Continental Army.... Accidents derived from the same movements of the enemy delayed the promulgation of the act for supplying our army with clothes, provisions, and wagons until it became evident that the times of execution would be elapsed before the laws could be received in many counties. I undertook, notwithstanding, to recommend their execution at as early a day as possible, not doubting but that the General Assembly, influenced by the necessity which induced them to pass the act, would give their sanction to a literal departure from it, when its substance was complied with. I have reason to believe that the zeal of the several counties has led them to a compliance with my recommendations, and I am therefore to pray a legal ratification of their proceedings"[35]—which was given, as the *Journal* of the House shows.[36]

"These were the subjects which led immediately to the calling of the General Assembly," Jefferson continues. "Others, though of less moment, it is my duty also [to] lay before you being now convened." After discussing these, he concludes his message with a résumé, succinct and masterly, of the events of the recent invasion and the various measures adopted to repel the enemy. There was not a man present who could have failed to be moved by this recital.

Meanwhile, Jefferson had not been knocking at the door of Congress in vain. His pleas to that body, which were always likewise addressed to Washington, had not fallen on deaf ears. On February 28, when the outlook was dark indeed and when cries of distress were reaching him from every quarter, he received a letter from Washington containing the first good news for Virginia in many a day. That it heralded ultimate victory, he could, of course, not know. "From an apprehension that the enemy may take such a position as will enable them to defend themselves and their shipping without a land operation," Washington writes, "and knowing that militia cannot be depended on for the vigorous measures that it may be necessary to pursue, I have put a respectable detachment from this army in motion. It is commanded by Major General the Marquis de la Fayette. It will proceed by land to the head of Elk, at which I calculate it will arrive by the sixth of March at farthest, and will fall down the Chesapeake in transports." [37]

Washington was at last tacitly acknowledging that the major scene of the war was being shifted to Virginia. The hope of capturing Arnold and his force at Portsmouth was proving a tempting bait. On the same day Lafayette wrote Jefferson of his coming, saying the expedition seemed "to promise an opportunity to gratify the high sense I have of my personal obligation to the state of Virginia," and expressing "the most ardent zeal to do anything in my power which may promote the wishes of Your Excellency." [38]

Lafayette was as certain of his needs and of what he expected Virginia to do and to furnish as Steuben had been shortly before. He wrote Jefferson on the third of March asking for a substantial number of militia to join his men and requesting that sufficient horses should be furnished for the artillery, that boats should be provided for landing the troops and cannon, and that all possible vessels, both public and private, should be assembled to escort his expedition to its destination on the James.

Jefferson was overjoyed. The atmosphere seemed transformed. Jubilantly he described to Lafayette, on the second of March, the preparations in train, adding: "I think the prospect flattering of lopping off this branch of the British and of relieving the southern operations by pointing all their efforts to one object only. The relief of this state being the most immediate effect of the enterprise, it gives me great pleasure that we shall be so far indebted to a nobleman who has already endeared himself to the citizens of these states by his past exertions and the very effectual aids he has been the means of procuring them." [39]

An even warmer and more cordial letter was written by the Governor a week later. At the same time he prepared the way for Lafayette to understand that conditions might not be what he had expected. A close association of several months with Baron Steuben had convinced Jefferson of the radical difference in the European and American points of view. "Intending that this shall await your arrival in this state," he writes, "I with great joy welcome you on that event. I am induced to it from the very great esteem I bear your personal character, and the hopes I entertain of your relieving us from our enemy within this state.... Mild laws, a people not used to war and prompt obedience, a want of the provisions of war and means of procuring them, render our orders often ineffectual, oblige us to temporize, and when we cannot accomplish an object in one way, we attempt it in another.... I still hope you will find our preparations not far short of the information I took the liberty of giving you in my letter of the 8th instant." [40]

Jefferson indited this letter in a spirit of optimism bred by the imminence of substantial help, as he believed. Baron Steuben likewise wrote the Marquis by the same express, explaining the operations he had in mind. The Governor had left no stone unturned in trying to meet Lafayette's demands and in seeking to insure the success of the enterprise. Never had he given a more dazzling exhibition of his abilities as an administrator. "The number of militia desired by the Baron will be provided," he writes, "though not quite so early as had been proposed.... Arnold's retreat is at this time cut off by land. Provisions and arms for the troops are in readiness, and the quartermasters are exerting themselves to get horses. Their success is slow and doubtful. Oxen, I apprehend, must be used in some measure for the artillery. We have no heavy field artillery mounted. Four battering cannon (French 18-pounders) with two 12-inch mortars fall down from this place this evening. Scows I am afraid cannot be used for the transportation of your cannon on the wide waters where your operations will be carried on. We shall endeavor to procure other vessels the best we can. The total destruction of our trade by the enemy has put it out of our power to make any great collection of boats. Some armed vessels of public and some of private property are held in readiness to co-operate.

"Baron Steuben," he continues, "is provided with the most accurate drawings we have of the vicinities of Portsmouth. They are from actual surveys of the land; and as to information of the navigation, the most authentic will be obtained from the pilots in that neighborhood, ten of the best of which are provided. I shall continue to exert my best endeavors to have in readiness what yet remains to be done," he concludes, "and shall with great pleasure meet your desires on this important business, and see that they be complied with as far as our condition will render practicable." [41]

In anticipation of the long-heralded aid from the French fleet, which had been confirmed by Theoderick Bland's letter from Congress on February 9,[42] and spurred, in part, by the news of Lafayette's expected arrival, Jefferson determined once more to attempt to reanimate the nearly defunct Virginia navy. This time the force was to consist not only of public but also of impressed private vessels. On February 16, two days after Commodore de Tilly, commander of the French squadron sent from Rhode Island at this time, had entered the Chesapeake, Jefferson had written Captain James Maxwell, commissioner of the navy: "The arrival of a French naval force will render it necessary for us to put into immediate order for service and to man every vessel we have capable of rendering any service. You will therefore be pleased to have this done, and to have the vessels kept in readiness to move at a moment's warning. You are also desired, having left this matter in a proper train, to proceed yourself and examine the different armed vessels in James River which, in your opinion, might be of service in an enterprise on the British fleet in Elizabeth River, to report to us their condition and to endeavor to engage them to enter into that service." [43]

The same day Jefferson communicated an outline of his plans to General Nelson. "I am very anxious to prepare for co-operating with our allies," he writes, "and for providing for their support. For the former purpose measures are taking as agreed on this moment in a conference with Baron Steuben. For the latter we suppose Yorktown the most effectual to prepare as an asylum for their vessels. Colonel Senf comes down with instructions to point out what may be done there in a short time; the Baron will send Colonel Harrison or some other artillery officer to superintend the execution of what he shall plan; and I must resort to your influence to take such measures as may call in a sufficient number of laborers with their tools to execute the work. Whatever you do for this purpose shall be approved by us." [44]

The twenty-eighth found Jefferson directing Maxwell "to proceed immediately to Hampton to procure a number of the best and most trusty river and bay pilots. If you cannot otherwise get them, you must force them into the service. Immediately on your arrival at Hampton, wait on the commanding officer of His Most Christian Majesty's Fleet to know the number of pilots wanting, and to receive and forward by express to me any communications he may think necessary. I have reason to believe that his squadron had on board some stores and small arms for this state. You will be pleased to receive them and forward them to this place.... I should be glad that you would take measures for rendering the armed vessels of this state subservient to the general service, and particularly to the performing necessary offices for the French fleet." [45]

Jefferson's plan for impressing private vessels was curtailed by the Council. He wrote Steuben on February 16: "I make no doubt from what passed in Council in your presence you were led to believe, as I was, that I should be advised to impress immediately all armed vessels in James River to co-operate with the French force. The board, however, decide against an impress, so that I am only able to endeavor to engage the willing. I mention this to you that nothing more may be expected than is likely to be obtained from this measure." [46] Nevertheless, "on supposition that the armed vessels of private property may some of them be usefully employed against the enemy for two or three weeks to come," Jefferson ordered all those in the James and Appomattox rivers impressed. "As yet," he wrote Commodore Tilly on the fourth of March, "I have a report of four only. As it is possible there may be others in these as well as the other rivers of this state, and that they may be endeavoring to pass out, I would take the liberty of authorizing you to detain any such as you shall think may be useful against the enemy." [47]

A week later Jefferson received the discouraging news, in a confidential report from Lafayette, that the French squadron was returning to Newport. Maxwell was in Hampton, looking for pilots and trying to find means to deliver certain dispatches to the French commander. Jefferson at once sent him this intelligence, saying it would be hopeless to search for De Tilly outside the Capes, and that "no attempt must be made to carry my letter out till a French naval force is actually known to be in the Bay.

"I wish you immediately to come up to the Shipyard," he continues, "there see that the *Jefferson* and such other public vessels as can be in readiness, be prepared, and either proceed to Hood's or to such other place as you shall think best to carry into execution such orders as shall be given by the Continental commanding officer or myself. Men must be impressed. You will also be pleased to proceed to Hood's or wherever else in James River you shall find the private armed vessels which are taken into the public service, and are under the direction of Captain Mitchell and Captain Lewis, and take such measures as may still be necessary to have them in readiness for cooperation." After giving certain further directions, he orders lookout boats for Lafayette, one to lie in the Piankatank, one in the Rappahannock. "This you can effect by proper agents," he concludes, "and use force when the consent of the owner cannot be obtained." [48]

In view of Maxwell's absence, Jefferson likewise wrote the superintendent of the Shipyard to make all possible haste in getting the vessels ready, and on the fourteenth of March informed Maxwell's subordinates, Captains Robert Mitchell and William Lewis, that Lafayette had arrived at York. "Whether a naval force is come yet or not," he says, "I have not heard. I hope this will find you at Hood's with your little fleet. Should it not, I must request you to fall down there immediately with all the vessels...." [49] That he was ordering the fleet assembled for convenient destruction by the British within a few weeks, Jefferson could, of course, not know.

Reassuring news arrived the next day from both officers. They had reached Hood's. "I set off from Richmond on the 12th inst. with twenty militia in a scow," Mitchell writes. "On the way down, I put five men on board of a brig lying at Warwick, called the *Marrs*, and gave the Captain orders to make all the dispatch in his power down to this place, to form the fleet. Then proceeded down the river in the scow. The wind proving fowl and blowing very hard, could not get her any further. The vessels lying here, is the ship *Renown*, 16 guns, the *Willing-Lass* brig, 10 guns, the brig *Wilkes*, 12 ditto, and sundry small vessels fitting to carry troops. Likewise the two crafts with the cannon and mortars safe here. There are two more armed vessels expected down here this evening to join the fleet. The field pieces that came from the northward will be put on board today." [50] Lewis sent a similar report but added the human note that "we have never had a drop of spirits on board the fleet since we have taken in states service, and seamen are creatures that must have it, especially when an expedition of this kind is on foot." [51]

From a letter of Maxwell to Jefferson on the twenty-sixth of April, as well as from a "list of armed vessels at Coxendale with their force and present complement of men," drawn up by Maxwell just before the encounter with the British, we learn what ships made up the navy at this time. There was the ship *Tempest* with 16 six-pounders; the brig *Jefferson* with 12 four-pounders; the *Renown*, 16 six-pounders; the *Apollo*, 18 six-pounders; *Willing-Lass*, 12 four-pounders; *Wilkes*, 12 four-pounders; *Marrs*, 8 four- and six-pounders. In addition there were the *Patriot*, boat; *Lewis*, galley; *Thetis*, *Tartar*, and *Dragon*, ships.[52] It is shocking to realize that the first group of ships mentioned was manned by only 78 men. According to Maxwell's report, 512 were wanted. Jefferson had directed they be "manned by impress or enlistment, either general or special," [53] but the navy proved no popular service, and small wonder. According to Captain Travis of the brig *Jefferson*, who had "several young officers of honor and courage" under him, "these injured gentlemen have not clothes sufficient of any kind to defend them from the inclemency of the weather, and to my knowledge frequently shun company, not having been able to appear as an officer." [54] The last Assembly had, furthermore, reduced their pay by one-fifth. When Lafayette, whose main concern was certainly not the navy, appealed to the Governor to procure seamen for the armed vessels, Jefferson could only reply: "I know of no method of effecting this but by draughting from the lower militia such men are are used to the water." [55]

It was in a vein of real discouragement, after the British had again invaded the state in April, that Jefferson submitted the problem of naval defense to "the wise discussion of the General Assembly" at its session in May. "A country so intersected by navigable waters can be defended by a naval force alone," he writes; "and where the resources of a nation are not equal to the equipment of a respectable navy, perhaps nothing better can be devised than galleys constructed on plans approved by experience. But an asylum for these galleys seems as necessary as the galleys themselves.... A battery on each river, at a proper position, protected by such works as would require a garrison of a single company only, would, in the opinion of the most respectable military characters among us, protect our vessels and in a favorable position would stop the passage of an enemy so long as to give time for the assembling of militia.... These small works are certainly within the compass of our finances. Yet we have in vain attempted to have such erected on each river. It has been found that money will not procure laborers; a militia of freemen cannot easily be induced to labor in works of this kind." [56]

On the evening of March 21 a messenger brought Jefferson a letter from James Barron, commodore of the armed vessels of the commonwealth of Virginia, a post to which he had been appointed in July 1780. He was at Hampton. His letter had been written the previous day. The news it contained was becoming a familiar refrain.

"Yesterday morning," it read, "twelve large ships came within the capes and anchored. Sent up one frigate this morning under English colors, which proves them to be a British fleet. The frigate lies now in Hampton Road with Arnold's ships—the other ships are still in the bay at anchor. I take them all to be men of war, and no transports among them." [57]

Jefferson laid the letter before the Council at their meeting the following morning, and they advised him "to order two good boats to go from the eastern shore, and keep a constant lookout for the French fleet and give them this information. The Board also advise that the vessels, stores, and public property be removed from the Shipyard, and that fifty men be ordered from the County of Charles City to assist in this important work." [58] The following day, in a further attempt to muster all possible vessels, they appointed a committee to see whether the galleys *Accomac* and *Diligence*, which had been damaged by robbery and plunder, were worth salvaging.[59] On the twenty-second the Governor informed the Speaker of the House of the arrival of a British fleet and added: "Should this be confirmed beyond all doubt, I shall think it proper to discharge the armed vessels of private property which had been impressed into public service. In the meantime they are coming up to a safer part of the river, and a valuation of them is making, so that if any future events should be thought to make the state liable for them, their work may be precisely established." [60]

When the news of the appearance of the British fleet reached him, Jefferson was not yet aware that it had already been in contact with a second French squadron sent from Newport on March 16. As a result, Des Touches, the French commander, had been obliged to retire, leaving the British in undisturbed control of Chesapeake Bay. The Governor had, of course, not yet learned that on March 21, Sir Henry Clinton was dispatching from New York a large and strong detachment under General Phillips to join Arnold at Portsmouth, with the purpose of reinforcing him. The news was not long in reaching him, however. At eight o'clock in the evening of the twenty-sixth, Steuben dispatched an express from Williamsburg. "I am this moment informed," he writes, "of the return of the English fleet into Lynhaven Bay, in the night of the twenty-fourth, and that this morning 18 more sail arrived and joined them. It is very possible the last are transports with the reinforcements expected from New York." [61] Letters poured in. Richard Barron, brother of James, wrote on the same day: "This morning came into our Bay 15 or 16 sail more vessels, which made 30 some odd, which I suppose to be all British.... We have no account of what they are, but conjecture them to be some from New York." [62]

General Weedon wrote twice to the Governor and to Steuben. In his letter of the twenty-ninth to the latter he said: "I wrote you yesterday, since which have received intelligence from below informing that the reinforcement lately arrived is commanded by General Phillips. They are convoyed by the *Chatham* of 50 guns, the *Rainbow*, 44, *Roebuck*, 44, *Hancock*, 32, and some other frigates. Arbuthnot still lays in Lyndhaven Bay. I got my information from Captain Ross.... Captain Ross informs the troops were in 23 transports carrying 150 to 200 men each. Eight square-rigged vessels he says are freighted with horse. With regard to their destination, he is utterly unacquainted. Their object appears clearly to me to be that of reinforcing Lord Cornwallis by penetrating North Carolina.... If we do anything in the matter we talked of, it must be suddenly, as not a moment can be lost. Nelson," he concludes, "is still very ill." [63]

The long-dreaded invasion had suddenly become a reality. Immediately the whole picture changed. Virginia was now put on the defensive. There was no longer any question of contemplating operations against Portsmouth. At a meeting of the Council that day, the board decided against Steuben's proposal to send a detachment of 2,000 militia, embodied on the south side of the James, to Greene's relief in North Carolina. "Although the proposition seems to them to be founded on very probable principles," the *Journal* states, "yet the number of arms that such a detachment would necessarily carry with them bearing a very great proportion to what will afterwards remain in the state, it will be a measure unjustifiable in the present circumstances of affairs." [64] Captain Mitchell was directed by the Governor to discharge all the armed vessels that had been impressed except those having on board military stores and provisions, [65] "the arrival of the British fleet and reinforcement having occasioned a discontinuance of those purposes for which the armed vessels were impressed," and the Council already having decided "they are a heavy and daily expense to the public."[66] "The operations against Portsmouth being discontinued, economy and respect for the rights of our citizens require that the horses impressed for that purpose be returned to their owners. This will be a troublesome and expensive undertaking,"[67] Jefferson observed, but it was bound to be a popular one, for the taking of their horses had been resented by the citizens even more than militia duty.

The strength of the new troops under Phillips was undetermined. The lurking danger was not fully suspected. This is readily seen by the discussions reflected in the *Journal of the Council*. How troubled Jefferson was, we may gather from his letter to the president of Congress on March 31. "The amount of reinforcement to the enemy arrived at Portsmouth is not yet known with certainty," he writes. "Accounts differ, from 1,500 to much larger numbers. We are informed they have a considerable number of horse. The affliction of the people for want of arms is great. That of ammunition is not yet known to them. An apprehension is added that, the enterprise on Portsmouth being laid aside, the troops under the Marquis Lafayette will not come on. An enemy 3,000 strong, not a regular in the state, nor arms to put in the hands of the militia, are indeed discouraging circumstances."[68] To the Virginia delegates in Congress, to whom he wrote in a similar vein on April 6, he added, "Should this army from Portsmouth come forth and become active (and as we have no reason to believe they came here to sleep), our affairs will assume a very disagreeable aspect.... To what a deplorable state shall we be reduced if the Bay continues blocked up. Commerce, both public and private, is already taking its turn to Philadelphia, our Continental money is all gone, or going off, in that channel, and no other resources for remittances to that place."[69] It was indeed not a pretty picture.

The Chevalier de la Luzerne, the French minister, had meanwhile written Jefferson on March 23, once more promising help to Virginia. In his reply of April 12, Jefferson took occasion to unburden himself as he had not to Washington, to the Virginia delegates in Congress, or to anyone else. The obliviousness to Virginia's situation, the injustice of the demands on the state, the lack of support from the north, all of which had been rankling for many months, burst out in a cry of anguish. But it was the cry of a brave man determined that his people should not perish. "I shall with great pleasure," he writes, "communicate to the citizens our prospect of aid from His Most Christian Majesty, to whom we are already so infinitely indebted. I assure you, Sir, that these prospects are necessary to inspirit them under the present aspect of their affairs. We suppose one-half of the enemy's force in the United States to be to the southward. Georgia and Carolina have long been theirs.... I believe it may ... with truth be said that the opposition to the two hostile armies in North Carolina and Virginia falls at present on Virginia only, aided with about 500 men from Maryland, while our northern brethren, infinitely superior in numbers, in compactness, in strength of situation, in access to foreign supplies, of necessaries, possessed of all the arms and military stores of the continent, opposed by an enemy not superior to ours, have the protection of almost the whole of the Continental Army, with the very important addition of the army and fleet of our allies.

"A powerful enterprise meditated by the northwestern savages," he continues the indictment, "has obliged this state to have an army of between two and three thousand men collected at this time on the Ohio.... To support General Greene and prevent the enemy entering our country on the south, we are obliged to send the whole of our regulars and continual reliefs of militia, and on our seaboard an enemy three thousand strong is posted.... Notwithstanding all this, I believe from what I have lately seen that we should be substantially safe were our citizens armed, but we have not as many arms as we have enemies in the state.

"Under such circumstances it is not easy to foretell events, and it is natural for our people to ask if they are to have no help from others.... The northern states are safe; their independence has been established by the joint efforts of the whole. It is proved, as far as testimony can prove anything, that our enemies have transferred every expectation from that quarter and mean nothing further there than a diversion in favor of their southern arms. It would be unfortunate indeed should it be again proposed to lose a campaign in New York, and to exhaust on that the efforts of the confederacy, to give up provinces in the south for towns in the north." [70]

On the seventh of April Jefferson had written the president of Congress that the enemy had "made no movement yet. Their preparation of boats is considerable; whether they mean to go southward or up the river, no leading circumstance has yet decided." [71] A week later he enclosed to the Virginia delegates in Congress a copy of an intercepted letter from a British captain giving "a display of the present plan of the enemy as to Chesapeake Bay and its waters," as well as "copies of letters from Captain Reade and Colonel Richard Henry Lee showing that the plan is now in a course of execution. I trouble you with them," he observes with what in anyone else would be suspected as sarcasm, "as it may enable you to avail us of any opportunity which may occur of getting the Bay secured." [72]

At this moment the British were chiefly engaged in what might be called nuisance raids. A letter from Richard Henry Lee written to the Governor on April 13, soliciting ammunition, describes how "Robert Carter, late of the Council, has had 25 Negroes taken off a few nights ago from a quarter close by the riverside, and from Cedar Point warehouse in Maryland they have lately taken a considerable quantity of tobacco in open day, besides burning a house or two, and plundering largely." He concludes from "the number of vessels that are now here, and by the concurring accounts of deserters, and of our own people who have come from the enemy, it appears that Potomac River will be much the scene of their predatory war this summer." [73] In reply Jefferson laments that it is "out of our power to furnish you with cartridge paper and lead, the former has been entirely exhausted from our magazines by the southern and eastern armies." Answering his request for news, he adds: "Our last news from the south was of the 6th instant, when Lord Cornwallis was near Wilmington and General Greene setting out on his march from Deep River for South Carolina. Phillips commands in Portsmouth, his whole force is 2,500. I think you may rely from the intelligence we have had," he concludes, with what is intended to be words of encouragement, "that no land force from thence [is] in the vessels which are distressing the Potomac." [74]

Complaints continued to pour in from Westmoreland, King George, Stafford, and the other counties adjacent to the Potomac. The county lieutenants were insatiable, and remained unsatisfied, in their demand for arms. Spiritual comfort was about all the Governor had to offer. To one of them he wrote: "I am exceedingly sorry to learn that the enemy are committing such cruel depredations in your part of the country; however, it may tend to produce immoveable hatred against so detestable a nation and thereby strengthen our union." As to arms, he could only offer 200 stand which had recently been purchased for the state by Sir John Peyton in Baltimore. "Were you to send a person in quest of these," he adds, "he would probably be able to meet with or find them out and have them forwarded to you." [75]

Meanwhile Steuben, suspecting the worst, was taking such measures as he saw fit. On the sixteenth we find him writing Claiborne: "It has become necessary immediately to move every species of public stores from Petersburg, Chesterfield, Richmond, and any other places contiguous to navigation. You will therefore take such measures as are necessary to procure wagons for this purpose. The stores at Richmond must be moved to Goosland [Goochland] Court House. Stores at Chesterfield and Petersburg to Powhatan Court House." [76] Experienced soldier that he was, he permitted himself no illusions. In the words of the Governor, he was confident that "the British had not come here to sleep."

IX. Phillips and Cornwallis

THE BLOW FELL on April 18. It was a sunny spring day, with the daffodils and paper-white narcissi for which the Tidewater even then was famous, nodding in the breeze. At four o'clock that afternoon, Colonel James Innes, who had taken command of Nelson's troops when that gentleman fell ill of a violent pleurisy the end of February, sent word to the Governor from Williamsburg that he had just received a message informing him eleven vessels of the enemy had plowed through the wide blue waters of Hampton Roads and had passed Newport News Point at ten o'clock that morning. As the wind was fair from the southeast, they would be able to reach Burwell's Ferry by evening. At the same time he dispatched a note to Baron Steuben, telling him he was making the best disposition he could to receive the enemy, the van of whose fleet had been sighted by the officers at Burwell's Ferry. At midnight Innes sent another express saying: "I have received further intelligence of the enemy's vessels—two of which carry cavalry, are ascending the James River, and are this evening several miles advanced up. At the stern of the vessels are a number of flat-bottomed boats. I have ordered all the public stores at this place to be packed up and in readiness to move on a moment's warning. I wish my present force was adequate to the opposition I wish to make. However, weak as I am, nothing shall be left unassayed that can with propriety be attempted." [1]

When the Council met at ten o'clock the next morning, Jefferson laid Innes's letter before it. This time that body adopted no halfway measures. It advised that "the county lieutenants of Henrico, Prince George, Dinwiddie, Goochland, Hanover, Powhatan, and Chesterfield be immediately called upon for every man in their county able to bear arms, with proper officers and the best arms he has—that the county lieutenants of Cumberland and Amelia be called upon for one half of their militia ... to rendezvous at this place, Petersburg, Manchester, or Manakintown Ferry as the Governor shall direct—that the treasurer, register, auditors, commissioners of the navy, and clerks of the Assembly, general court, and chancery be notified of the movements of the enemy and assured that such assistance as can, shall be afforded them to remove their papers and records, which the board recommend be done as speedily as possible." [2]

These letters were dispatched the same morning. As far as those to the various state officers were concerned, results were achieved.[3] On the thirtieth, Bolling Starke wrote the Governor from Fairfield, on Carter's Creek in Gloucester County: "It is probable Your Excellency may have heard that I reached Cumberland Old Court House [fifty miles above Richmond] on Wednesday last with the books and papers belonging to yours and the other public boards, where I judged they would be perfectly secure from the enemy; but on Saturday we were alarmed with the account of their having penetrated the country as far as Chesterfield Court House; at which place they had destroyed every house, etc.—that General Mühlenberg, conscious of his inferiority, was retreating before them—this disagreeable piece of intelligence determined me to recross James River, and, thinking the papers would be more secure at a *private* than a *public house*, I have taken the liberty of throwing myself and them upon the hands of my old acquaintance and relation, Colonel John Bolling, where they will remain until it becomes safe to return them to Richmond—unless Your Excellency thinks it necessary to remove them to some other place." [4]

The militia, however, lagged as usual. Jefferson wrote Innes on the twenty-first that "not a man is yet assembled here. I am told the Powhatan militia will be in today. Certainly those in this county will be as early. This fatal tardiness will, I fear, be as unfortunate for Williamsburg on this occasion as formerly it was for Richmond." [5] The following day he told Steuben he had "no return of the numbers of militia here; indeed, it is changing every hour by the arrival of others. Report makes them three or four hundred at this place and Manchester." [6] By this time Steuben was growing philosophical. He had learned not to expect much. "Everything is in the same confusion as when Arnold came up the river," he informed Washington on the twenty-first. "There is not a single company of regular troops in the state, and the militia are too inexperienced to hope for the least resistance from them."[7]

Further news of impending disaster arrived on the twentieth. James Barron sent word from Blunt's Point, halfway between Newport News and Mulberry Island, to the commanding officer at Williamsburg that "the vessels which were bound up James River are now at anchor off the mouth of Peggen [Pagan] Creek [across the river from Blunt's Point] consisten of five ships, two brigs, two schooners and three sloopes, with thirty flatt-bottomed boats astearn. The *Fowcy* 24-gun ship in Burwell's Bay and a brig at anchor. What their intentions are I know not, but it may be proble they intend up in the night to supprise Williamsburg—Was their intention to land at Smithfield, should have thought they would done it some hours past, as they anchored ther at one o'clock today. Two sloops and a schooner are horsemen."

Innes relayed this to the Governor and to Steuben, adding that "fourteen flat-bottomed boats, a ship, two brigs, two sloops, and one schooner heavily manned" had already arrived at Burwell's Ferry, less than three miles below Williamsburg. "From every appearance I think they mean to land," he writes, "as they have halted with a favorable tide. I believe they wait for nothing but the arrival of two schooners which have their cavalry on board. These vessels, I am this moment informed, have just turned Mulberry Island point."[8] In a second message that day Innes announced that he would "immediately march the troops up the New Kent road and take up such a position as to enable me to operate vigorously without exposing my rear and flanks." He concludes that he has just learned that "16 flat-bottomed boats are above Jamestown."[9]

Jefferson could no longer complain that he did not hear "a tittle" of the enemy. "I must entreat you to let us hear from you daily while the scene is so interesting," he wrote Innes, and the Colonel complied. He sent reports to the Governor and to Steuben every day, often twice. In a third letter on the twentieth, written from Allen's

Ordinary on the New Kent road, six miles to the northwest of Williamsburg, he informed Jefferson that the enemy had "made good their landing" at two o'clock in the afternoon. "At the same time," he continues, "several armed vessels and sixteen flat-bottomed boats proceeded up to Jamestown, where I have been informed they since landed. As soon as I found the designs of the enemy, I moved the troops to this place, which is the nearest position to town that can be taken with safety while the enemy are masters of the water. There was some slight skirmishing between the advance of the enemy and our guards of observation at Burwell's Ferry. We have sustained no loss." [10]

Simcoe, the British officer in command of the landing party, gives a more detailed account, with his usual emphasis on the readiness of the "rebels" to flee. "The enemy had thrown up entrenchments to secure the landing," he writes, "and these appeared to be fully manned.... Near a mile below the ferry was a small creek which ran a little way into the land from James River, and at the point formed by this separation, it was determined to land.... The boats, preceded by the gunboat, moved directly toward Burrel's ferry. On a signal given, they all, except the gunboat, turned and rowed rapidly towards the point where the landing was to take place, assisted by the wind and tide.... The troops disembarked as intended.... Lieutenant Colonel Simcoe met no opposition on his march to Burrel's Ferry, from whence the enemy fled with percipitation, and where General Phillips with the army immediately landed." [11]

On the twenty-first, Innes withdrew eight miles further, to Hickory Neck Church, still standing beside the rush of a modern motor highway, a lonely sentinel of the past. Here, he wrote Steuben: "Yesterday about five o'clock a detachment of the British Army landed at Burwell's Ferry under Generals Arnold and Phillips. On their landing some slight skirmishing with my guards posted at that place. Observing, however, by the movement of the sixteen flat-bottomed boats and several ships of war up towards Jamestown that opposition could not be made with safety below Williamsburg, I ordered out my guards to join my main body and retreated last night six miles.... I am this moment informed that sixteen flat-bottomed boats are advancing up

Chickahominy River towards the shipyard from whence there leads a road that will effectually circumvent me. I shall therefore immediately put the troops in motion and advance up New Kent road towards Richmond." [12]

The twenty-first was a day of furious excitement. Richmond was tense with rumors, aghast at the news brought in by express riders stationed only fifteen miles apart. The designs of the enemy could only be conjectured. The worst was feared. On this day Jefferson wrote Steuben no less than three times—at seven o'clock in the morning, again at eleven, and once more at seven in the evening. Steuben was at Chesterfield Court House, directing the formation of a cavalry corps and the moving of military stores from Powhatan Court House to points farther up the river. These brief and hasty bulletins, hitherto unpublished, at once giving directions and sending the most recent intelligence, reflect the existing turmoil. The first, enclosing a letter from Colonel Innes, suggests that "the circumstances of their halting under a favorable tide seems to show their destination to be Williamsburg and that their putting their men into boats is not merely a feint. I am told the Powhatan militia will be at Manchester today; also that a part of Captain Moseby's new-raised cavalry will be there. It is the desire and expectation of the Executive that the militia, after receiving from them their call into the field, shall be subject to your orders altogether, for which reason we issue none to them."

The second letter informs Steuben that "the public stores at this place are almost wholly removed, and by this evening will be at Manakintown Ferry. The heavy cannon are still here. I understand the Henrico militia will be in today." He repeats his remarks of earlier in the day on the Powhatan militia. "I was informed by a reputable man this afternoon," he writes in the evening, "that he saw about three hundred of the enemy land this morning at Sandy Point [some ten miles above Jamestown Island]. He said that twenty-five of our guard had crossed the river there last night and carried their boats up a creek on the opposite side, and that the twenty-five which remained on this side retreated. Since then the enclosed has come to hand. This account and Colonel Innes's cannot both be right. They seem, however, to prove that the enemy's object is on the north side of James River. I fear that our boats at Sandy Point are lost to us. I hope that by tomorrow there will be a respectable body of militia here and at Manchester." [13]

These hopes were once more to be dashed. At eight o'clock the next evening Jefferson wrote Innes that, on the fourth day after the call had been issued, only about four hundred men were gathered at Richmond and Manchester. Meanwhile the outlook had become darker. That body of the enemy which had landed at Burwell's Ferry had been ordered to proceed to Yorktown. Williamsburg, lying on the way, was the first object of their attention. "As the night was uncommonly dark and tempestuous," Simcoe deferred his visit until morning. Supported by forty cavalry, "he gallopped into town, surprised and secured a few of the artillerymen. The others made off in a boat. He directed the guns of the batteries, already loaded, to be fired, as a signal to the *Bonetta Sloop*, which sailed up and anchored off the town; and he burnt a range of the rebel barracks.... The army marched to Barret's Ferry, near Chickahominy, and embarked immediately." [14]

Their next operation was the seizure of the Shipyard on the Chickahominy. This spot, on the low, marshy banks of that peaceful and neglected stream, is today still marked on the navigator's chart as Shipyard Landing, from which Shipyard Creek curls lazily into the river. "By the most unaccountable inattention," Jefferson observes, "the *Lewis* and *Safeguard* galleys have withdrawn up Chickahominy instead of James River," and provided fair prey for the enemy. Three days later he had not yet been informed of the damage done. "I take for granted they have burnt an unfinished 20-gun ship we had there," he reported to the president of Congress and to Washington. "Such of the stores belonging to the yard as were movable had been carried some miles higher up the river. Two small galleys also retired up the river. Whether by this either the stores or the galleys were saved, is yet unknown. I am just informed from a private hand that they left Williamsburg early yesterday morning. If this sudden departure was not in consequence of some circumstance of alarm unknown to us, their expedition to Williamsburg has been unaccountable. There were no public stores there but those which were necessary for the daily use of the men stationed there. Where they mean to descend next, the event alone can determine. Beside harassing our militia with this kind of war, their being taken from their farms at the interesting season of planting their corn will have an unfortunate effect on the crop of the ensuing year." [15]

The twenty-second found Innes and his troops twenty-four miles beyond Willamsburg. From Frances [?] Tavern, which can probably be identified as the old whitewashed brick building still standing in sleepy New Kent Courthouse, he sent the Governor and Steuben the latest information at seven o'clock in the morning. To the Baron he wrote that "the movement of the enemy on western side of Chickahominy ... has rendered it expedient for me to take my present position, which I think a very defensible one, from which I can file off towards Richmond without exposing my flanks or rear to anyone. They possessed themselves of the Shipyard about 4 o'clock yesterday, and I am apprehensive from the fire discovered in that quarter last night they have totally destroyed it." After complaining that his troops are worn down, that he is without horse or aid from neighboring counties, he concludes: "If I had the power of impressment, I should be able to form a very useful corps of observation. I am in want of wagons, provisions, and almost every necessary." [16]

By the twenty-third, reports were even more alarming. Innes, now encamped at Ruffin's Ferry on the Pamunkey River in King William County, reported that "General Phillips marched his troops from Williamsburg to Jamestown, where he embarked them yesterday evening. The fleet is now standing up James River. A detachment of the British Army, consisting, it is said, of 1,000 men, are marching rapidly by the Charles City road for Richmond. I shall put the troops under my command in motion immediately and march to Richmond by the way of Roger's [?] Warehouses." [17]

The same day he sent the Governor a long letter in defense and explanation of his continued retreat. "Having received intelligence last evening that the enemy were moving up Chickahominy River road with an intent to attempt a stroke at the party under my command, and had actually advanced so far as to be able to compel me to give them action on the most disadvantageous terms, should I endeavor to retreat by the way of New Kent Court House," he goes on to explain that his troops were exhausted, that he had over one hundred sick men, and that he was burdened with twenty wagons of provisions, whereas the enemy had the advantage of fresh troops and of cavalry. Under these circumstances, and on the advice of all the field officers, he determined to take no risk, but proceeded to Ruffin's Ferry, where he "passed all the stores and troops over Pamunkey River." He was now in a position to dispose of the invalids, refresh his troops, and prepare to march to Richmond. "Last night," he concludes, "they destroyed the vessels and buildings at the Shipyard and some naval stores at Diascon Bridge. I am also informed, though not officially, that the party which moved up the Chickahominy road have burnt Holt's Forge [the present Providence Forge] and are moving in three columns towards New Kent Court House." [18]

These letters were crossed by one from Steuben written from Petersburg. "I have this moment received intelligence that the enemy have left your side and come in at Hood's," he says. "This being the case, it would be necessary that you should approach James River. Should they land on your side, a more excellent position cannot be found to oppose the enemy than at Turkey Island." [19] The Virginians, however, were not to choose their own battle ground. Early on the morning of the twenty-fourth word came from Captain Maxwell that he had, with his own eyes, seen the enemy land at Westover the preceding evening. "If it be impossible that he should have been deceived," Jefferson wrote Steuben, "it is equally unaccountable that we are uninformed of it from the videts sent.... There are here about 200 militia armed, and 300 unarmed. At Manchester there is, I am told, a larger number armed, but of this I have no proper information.... Can the object of the enemy be our vessels at Osborne's?" he concludes. "There are no public stores *here*, and they have showed that private depredation is not within their views." [20]

By evening the design of the enemy was clear. There was no longer any doubt but that Petersburg was their destination. Nearing Westover with "13 topsail vessels and 23 flat-bottomed boats full of men," they sailed up the river to City Point, which lies on the southern side of the confluence of the James and Appomattox rivers. Here they landed. Colonel John Banister, Jefferson's lifelong friend, for whom he early designed Battersea, that beautiful house reminiscent of Brandon, which Simcoe used as headquarters, has left us the most lively account of the action that ensued. "On Wednesday the twenty-fourth," he says in a letter to Theoderick Bland, "they approached Petersburg by the way of my Whitehall plantation, where they halted in the heat of the day and refreshed; then proceeded at about 2 o'clock to advance in two columns, one by the old road leading to the church, the other along the lane and across the ravine at Miller's old mill. Here they received a fire from Captain House, of Brunswick County, at the head of 40 militia which was supposed to do execution, but only a Jäger was known by us to have been killed. Captain House continued to retreat and fire until he came to Taylor's mill, where he joined Colonel Dick at the head of 300 picked militia, who kept up a constant fire and prevented their taking the heights for upward of half an hour, but attaining these, they, with cannon and three times the force, dislodged Dick from his ground, but notwithstanding he made a regular and steady retreat through Blandford and formed behind a battalion posted at Bollingbrook warehouse....

"This was our last resistance. The enemy advanced, in front their infantry and German riflemen. Against these our battalion kept up a steady and constant fire, until they were ordered to retreat, which was not until four pieces of cannon, from the hill between Dr. Black's and Mr. Bolling's, flanked them effectually. Then they retreated in order along the causeway to Pocahontas Bridge, which they took up, but ascending the hill to gain the heights of T. Shore's house, the enemy played their cannon with such skill that they killed and wounded ten of our men; all the wounded are since dead. Our cannon was served well from Baker's, but the enemy's extreme caution has prevented our getting an account of their killed and wounded.... [Their] gunboats are of infinite use to the enemy, bringing them up in force to the shallowest landing. They carry from 50 to 80 men.

"After our militia had gained the hill, they retreated towards Chesterfield Court House, where they halted the next day. This little affair shows plainly the militia will fight, and proves that if we had force to occupy the heights, they would not with that force have entered the town. In consequence of this I was obliged to abandon my house, leaving all to the mercy of the enemy. The enemy the next day ordered the inhabitants to move out the tobacco, or the warehouses should be consumed with it. By the exertions of the people the tobacco was removed and by the soldiery burnt, and the houses spared, except Cedar Point." [21]

The official reports of the engagement are more terse. In his statement to Washington and the president of Congress, Jefferson merely says the enemy "were received by Major General Baron Steuben with a body of militia somewhat under 1,000, who, though the enemy were 2,300 strong, disputed the ground very handsomely two hours, during which time the enemy gained one mile only, and that by inches. ... Our loss was between sixty and seventy killed, wounded, and taken." [22] Steuben, who gives a more graphic account, says that he selected "Blandford as the place of defense and the bridge of Pocahontas as our retreat." Blandford lies on the heights at the outskirts of Petersburg. In the ancient graveyard surrounding the old, vine-covered church, lies the body of General Phillips, who was to die within a few weeks of this encounter. "Towards noon," writes Steuben, "the enemy came in sight, formed themselves, and displayed to their left; but it was near three o'clock before the firing commenced, which continued from post to post till past five o'clock, when the superior number of the enemy and a want of ammunition obliged me to order the retreat, and the bridge to be taken up, which was executed in the greatest order, notwithstanding the fire of the enemy's cannon and musketry. The troops, with the same good order, retreated to this place, where they are just encamped." [23]

Although heavy rains had succeeded the fair weather of the preceding weeks, and thus "rendered the Continental's arms unfit for fire," according to Lafayette's aide, it was this time not the militia, but the enemy, who "broke twice and ran like sheep till supported by fresh troops," as Jefferson described it. He must have experienced a moment of satisfaction, rare in these days, for he wrote Steuben on receiving his report, "I cannot but congratulate you on the initiation of our militia into the business of war. General actions, I dare say, you will think should not be risked but with great advantages.

But the more the militia are employed in the small way, the more contentedly they will remain, and they will improve the more." [24]

The British subsequently continued their plundering. They burned all the tobacco in the warehouses, both public and private, in Petersburg and the vicinity, to the extent of four thousand hogsheads, according to Arnold. Gloatingly he wrote: "A considerable magazine of flour and bread has fallen into our hands near this place, and the country abounds in cattle." They likewise "destroyed one ship and a number of small vessels on the stocks and in the river." As Madison wrote Mazzei: "No description can give you an adequate idea of the barbarity with which the enemy have conducted the war in the southern states. Every outrage which humanity could suffer has been committed by them. Desolation rather than conquest seems to have been their object. They have acted more like desperate bands of robbers or buccaneers than like a nation making war for dominion. Negroes, horses, tobacco, etc., not the standards and arms of their antagonist, are the trophies which display their seekers. Rapes, murders, and the whole catalogue of individual cruelties, not protection and the distribution of justice, are the acts which characterize the sphere of their usurped jurisdiction." [25]

On the twenty-seventh the whole army crossed the Appomattox, burned the bridge, and marched in the direction of Osborne's, the region on the south shore of the James near Dutch Gap connected with the earliest Jeffersons in Virginia. One division, under Phillips, marched to Chesterfield Court House, about ten miles to the west, on their mission of destruction; another, under Arnold, went on to Osborne's, where a number of vessels were anchored in the river. "Finding the enemy had a very considerable force of ships four miles above Osborne's, drawn up in a line to oppose us, I sent a flag to the commodore, proposing to treat with him for the surrender of his fleet, which he refused, with this answer, 'that he was determined to defend it to the last extremity.' I immediately ordered down 2 six- and 2 three-pounders, brass field pieces, to a bank of the river, nearly level with the water, and within one hundred yards of the *Tempest*, a 20-gun state ship, which began immediately to fire upon us, as did the *Renown*, of 26 guns, the *Jefferson*, a state brigantine of 14 guns, and several other armed ships and brigantines. About two or three hundred militia on the opposite shore at the same time kept up a heavy fire of musquetry upon us; notwithstanding which, the fire of the artillery, under the direction of Captain Fage and Lieutenant Rogers, took such effect that the ships were soon obliged to strike their colors, and the militia drove from the opposite shore. Want of boats, and the wind blowing hard, prevented our capturing many of the seamen, who took to their boats and escaped on shore; but not without first scuttling and setting fire to some of their ships, which could not be saved.

"Two ships, three brigantines, five sloops, and two schooners, loaded with tobacco, cordage, flour, etc., fell into our hands. Four ships, five brigantines, and a number of small vessels were sunk and burnt. On board the whole fleet (none of which escaped) were taken and destroyed about two thousand hogsheads of tobacco, etc., and very fortunately we had not a man killed or wounded this day: but have reason to believe the enemy suffered considerably. About five o'clock P.M. we were joined by Major General Phillips with the light infantry." [26]

Two days later the British, after establishing camp near Ampthill, the seat of Archibald Cary in Chesterfield County, three or four miles south of Richmond, reached the heights of Manchester, where they burned twelve hundred hogsheads of tobacco.

The only note of hope in this dismal situation was the coming of Lafayette, so long anticipated. On April 17 he had written Jefferson from Baltimore that he and the detachment under his command were hurrying by forced marches to Richmond, where he hoped to receive orders from Greene. "From the intelligence I get of the number General Phillips's army consists of," he adds, "I apprehend that the state of Virginia must need an immediate support." Jefferson acknowledged this letter on the twenty-third, the day he learned that the Virginia forces had been obliged to retire beyond the Pamunkey. However devastating this news, however heavy his heart, he had the vision and the wisdom to realize that this event was but a minor diversion, that the fate of his country was not sealed by the burning of some crops and the destruction of a few ships, but was interwoven with broader operations even then going forward. In this vein he wrote Lafayette. After welcoming him, he continues: "I have heard nothing certain of General Greene since the 6th instant, except that his headquarters were on Little River the eleventh. We still consider his as the interesting scene of action. As long as we can keep him superior to his antagonist, we have little to fear in this country. Whenever he shall be obliged to retire before Lord Cornwallis and bring him also into this state, our situation will become dangerous. North as well as South Carolina, being once in the hands of the enemy, may become the instruments of our subjugation and effect what the enemy themselves cannot. The British force may harass and distress us greatly, but the Carolinas alone can subdue us. ... We therefore think it our first interest to keep them under in that quarter, considering the war in our own country but as a secondary object. For this reason we mean to send our new levies for the regular army to General Greene as fast as they shall be raised, acting with our militia on the defensive only in this state." [27]

Lafayette's dramatic arrival in Richmond, which coincided in such a spectacular manner with that of the British at Manchester, had a sobering effect upon the enemy. A sizable body of militia had at last gathered. This, in addition to the sight of nine hundred regulars under Lafayette, discouraged the British in their attempt to take the capital. The two belligerents drew up on opposite sides of the river and, apparently, glared at each other. The British, according to Simcoe, had a fine "view of M. Fayette's army." The Americans, for their part, with a superior force, were content to remain "quiet spectators of the destruction of all the warehouses and tobacco, with several dwellings adjoining," [28] as John Banister observed. Lafayette, in his report to Greene, says that after burning the warehouses at Manchester, "six hundred men ventured on this side, but were timely recalled, and, being charged by a few dragoons of Major Nelson, flew into their boats with precipitation. Knowing General Phillips's intention against Richmond (orders for attack had already been given), I directed Baron de Steuben to join us, and collected our force to receive the enemy, but the same night they retreated to Osborne's, from thence to the neck of land formed by James River and Appomattox, where they have re-embarked." [29]

Jefferson gives a more dramatic account of the incident in his report to Congress. After mentioning the destruction of the warehouses at Manchester and Warwick, he continues: "Ill-armed and untried militia who never before saw the face of an enemy, have at times during this war given occasion for exultation to our enemies; but they afforded us while at Warwick a little satisfaction in the same way. Six or eight hundred of their picked men of the light infantry, with General Arnold at their head, having crossed the river from Warwick, fled from a patrol of sixteen horse, every man to his boat as he could, some pushing north, some south, as their fears drove them." [30]

Whether Jefferson was one of those who "had a view of the enemy," as he had done on the occasion of Arnold's invasion, we have no way of knowing. It is scarcely to be doubted, however. He remained in Richmond throughout, once more the sole representative of government. Each morning he repaired to the council chamber, only to find no quorum. There was no meeting of the Council from April 25 to May 7. Once more the gentlemen of that body, with the exception of George Webb and David Jameson, had felt the obligation to their families and their homes to be greater than that to their country. Dudley Digges and Joseph Prentis resigned on the thirteenth, after not having attended for nearly two months.

The members of the Council were not the only men whose sense of duty lagged during this period. Jefferson had already observed that it had been "found by experience that the men of those counties where the enemy are, cannot be kept in the field. They desert and carry off their arms." [31] Steuben had likewise lamented to Greene: "I despair, my dear General, of ever seeing a Virginia line exist. Everything seems to oppose it; with all the trouble I can take, I find it impossible to assemble either officers or men. And even when a few are got together, I hear of nothing but of furloughs for the officers, and of the desertion of the men." [32] And Greene had complained: "All the way through the country I passed I found the people engaged in matters of interest, and in pursuit of pleasure, almost regardless of their danger. Public credit totally lost, and every man excusing himself from giving the least aid to Government, from the apprehension that they would get no return for any advances." [33]

Now, with the enemy knocking at the door, indeed with the door nearly forced open, a wave of resentment against military duty swept the state. It was not only in the back country, where danger from invasion was remote, that men were loath to comply with orders for Continental or militia service, but even in a county so likely to be immediately affected as Gloucester. The backwoodsmen were vocal. Thus Colonel James Callaway of Bedford regretted that, instead of the 384 militia requested, he was able to furnish only 130. The busy season of the year among the common people, he commented, outweighed any necessity of turning out unless the enemy threatened them. [34] Major Posey of Augusta wrote that the number of men he had "collected in this place (in deserters and others) amount to twenty-one." People were particularly opposed to the eighteen-months duty required for the Continental Army. A considerable number had met and in a very bold and daring manner had "seased the papers and destroyed them. I don't know where this may stop," he concludes, "if there is not a timeous check in hanging a few for examples to the rest." [35] James Barbour wrote in a similar vein from Culpeper. Captain James Reid, obviously a philosopher, declared that since his arrival in New London he had had "a very easy time of it. Not more than seven soldiers has been delivered to me, and two of them deserters." Showing that he was reasonably familiar with the last developments of the war, he continued: "They tell me Arnold and his crew has burnt all the Hutts at Chesterfield C. H., and I am afraid has took my portmantew and cloaths I left at Mr. Ball's. If they are gone, I wish the first man that puts any of them on may brake his neck." [36]

It was time for determined action—and the Governor took it. Colonel Garret Van Meter of Hampshire informed him on April 14 that he had issued orders for the full number of men for the draught but feared they would not be complied with in view of the disaffection among the inhabitants of the county. "A certain John Claypole," he writes, "said that if all the men were of his mind, they would not make up any cloathes, beef, or men, and all that would join him should turn out." On being joined by those of his sentiments he "got liquor and drank King George Third's health and damnation to Congress, upon which complaint was made to three magistrates."[37] Rioters had assembled in other parts of the county "determined to stand in opposition to every measure of government.... Their principal object is to be clear of taxes and draughts."

Jefferson replied to this a fortnight later. "I am sorry such a spirit of disobedience has shown itself in your county," he writes. "It must be subdued. Laws made by common consent must not be trampled on by individuals. It is very much the interest of the good to force the unworthy into their due share of contributions to the public support.... Their [the county lieutenants] best way, too, perhaps, is not to go against the mutineers when embodied, which would bring on perhaps an open rebellion or bloodshed most certainly, but when they shall have dispersed, to go and take them out of their beds singly and without noise, or if they be not found the first time, to go again and again, so that they may never be able to remain quiet at home."[38]

Colonel Abraham Penn of Henry County, who had used every influence to have the militia of that county relieved of being sent for a tour of duty with Greene, was informed on May 4: "I am exceedingly sorry that the public situation should be such as to render it necessary to call our citizens from their farms, at this interesting season of the year. But the enemy will not suspend their operations till we can sow or reap, so that we must have an army on foot as well at these as the other seasons of the year.... I am confident that if the reinforcement of the militia now under orders to General Greene is marched, and serves the two months with him which is intended, that by that time he will be so reinforced by regulars as to retain possession of the North and the greatest part of South Carolina, and thus to keep the war at a distance from us.

"Of the eleven counties called on," Jefferson concludes, "seven have applied to be excused. You will immediately see, Sir, what would be the consequence of complying with their request. The executive have therefore been obliged to insist on their requisition. Mr. [Patrick] Henry has written on the same subject, as to your county, but the grounds on which a relaxation of the order is proposed, being such that every other county has, or as would go to, a perpetual exemption from military duty, we cannot withdraw the call." [39]

Even so, the response was lamentable. Jefferson was obliged to say to Lafayette, in sending him a list of the counties which had been called on to furnish men to "perform a full tour of duty, and others to make or present opposition to the junction of the two hostile armies," that "the delay and deficiencies of the first are beyond all expectation, and if the calls on the latter do not produce sufficient reinforcements to you, I shall candidly acknowledge that it is not in my power to do anything more than to represent to the General Assembly that, unless they can provide more effectually for the execution of the laws, it will be vain to call on the militia." [40]

These were strong words, but no stronger than were demanded by the situation. When the legislature met in Charlottesville on the morning of Monday, May 28, Jefferson called upon that body to take some action. "Further experience together with recent information from the commanding officer in this state," he observes in his message to the Speaker, "convince me that something is necessary to be done to enforce the calls of the executive for militia to attend in the field. Whether the deficiencies of which we have had reason to complain proceeded from any backwardness in the militia themselves, or from a want of activity in their principal officers, I do not undertake to decide. The laws, also, to which they are subject while in the field seem scarcely coercive enough for a state of war." [41]

The following day the Assembly ordered that "leave be given to bring in a bill to amend and reduce into one the several acts 'for regulating and disciplining the militia'; and that Messrs. Nicholas, Henry, Page, Cabell, Taylor of Caroline, Strother, Tabot, Syme, Lomax, Morgan, and Rucker, do prepare and bring in the same." [42] No further action was taken before the Assembly was obliged to adjourn to Staunton on the fourth of June, and by that time Jefferson was no longer the Governor.

An additional indication of the sluggishness of the people, indeed of disregard of their own interests, until it became a problem demanding action by the Governor as well as by the Assembly, was their careless practice in regard to their horses. In view of the store set upon horses in an agricultural community, above all on a horse-loving and horse-racing one such as Virginia, it is incomprehensible. When the Assembly met in May 1781, one of the main problems before them was to deal with this situation. "Very great misfortunes are likely to be brought on us," Jefferson told that body, "by the tardiness of our citizens in driving off their stocks and cattle, and still more their horses, on the approach of an enemy. This negligence has enabled the enemy to take possession of some of the most valuable horses in the commonwealth and to establish a corps of horses which, from their numbers and quality, may become very formidable to this state." [43] With the desperate need for cavalry and the consciousness of the great disadvantage in which the state was placed owing to this lack, it must have been bitter, indeed, to view such indifference with equanimity.

In his letter to the county lieutenants on May 8, Jefferson had already ordered "all horses fit for cavalry which shall be at any time within twenty miles of the enemy, and all other horses which shall be directly in their front, be removed by their owners; or if they shall refuse or delay to do it, then that you have them taken up ... and carried to our camp, giving the owners a receipt and description of them." [44] On the twelfth Captain William Langhorne, aide-de-camp to Lafayette, brought Jefferson a message from the Marquis urging that all horses that could possibly fall into the hands of the enemy be brought in. He had been informed that the country exposed to the enemy on the south side of the Appomattox "abounds in the best horses of this country." Should the enemy seize these, they would have a cavalry "almost equal to our little army." [45]

As a result the Governor directed a circular letter to "the persons appointed by the Marquis Fayette to remove horses out of the route of the enemy," rehearsing his instructions to the county lieutenants and saying, "Time having now been given for the execution of this business, lest there be any failure in the people or in the county lieutenants, you are hereby authorized to proceed and take such horses. ... And moreover to proceed along the whole route from Petersburg to Halifax, as far as it lies within this Commonwealth, and to require a removal of all such horses within twenty miles of that route, and on failure of the owner to comply with your requisition within a short and reasonable time, to take such horses and retain them either for public service or to be returned to the owners, as shall hereafter be directed."[46] The county lieutenants of those counties adjacent to the activities of the enemy were instructed "to carry such horses and cattle to the Marquis Fayette's headquarters for the use of our army, having them only appraised."[47]

Meanwhile, after having destroyed the fine mills of Colonel Cary at Ampthill on the thirtieth of April, following the depredations at Manchester, the British had again retired to Osborne's, thence to Bermuda Hundred, where they embarked on the second of May. On the third they proceeded as far as Westover, then fell down the river to Hog Island. Here, "on the arrival of a boat from Portsmouth and a signal given," Jefferson continues his report of the ninth, "the whole crowded sail up the river again with a fair wind and tide, and came to anchor at Brandon. There six days' provision were dealt out to every man; they landed and had orders to march an hour before day the next morning. We have not yet heard which way they went or whether they are gone."[48]

It had been feared, and expected by Lafayette, that Phillips would round the points and proceed to Fredericksburg with the intention of destroying Hunter's works there. The apparent change of plan was due to a letter from Lord Cornwallis, received on the seventh, in which Phillips was directed to return up the river again with the object of joining forces with Cornwallis at Petersburg. Phillips meanwhile became very ill, and the troops were delayed a day at Brandon while a post chaise was secured for him. On the ninth part of the British force proceeded to City Point and landed there. The rest marched the thirty miles towards Petersburg, where Phillips died on the thirteenth.

The news of Cornwallis's letter reached Jefferson and Lafayette almost as soon as it did Phillips. Having "received authentic information that Lord Cornwallis had on the 1st instant advanced from Wilmington halfway to Halifax," Jefferson wrote Congress and Washington, "we have no doubt, putting all circumstances together, but that these two bodies are forming a junction. We are strengthening our hands with militia as far as arms, either public or private, can be collected, but cannot arm a force which may face the combined armies of the enemy. It will therefore be of very great importance that General Wayne's forces be pressed on with the utmost dispatch; arms and a naval force, however, are what ultimately must save us. This movement of our enemies," he concludes, bringing home the full gravity of the situation, "we consider as most perilous." [49]

At its meeting on Tuesday, May 8, the Council was informed of these latest developments. The members present, Dudley Digges, David Jameson, and George Webb, "on consulting with the Marquis Fayette, advise the Governor to order out immediately to join the Marquis as many men as can find arms" from twenty-three counties. Jefferson accordingly once more addressed a letter to the various county lieutenants, informing them that "the British Army under Major General Phillips having landed at Brandon and meaning to press southwardly; and Lord Cornwallis being now advanced northwardly with a design probably of uniting their force, it behooves us immediately to turn out from every county as many men as there are arms to be found in the county in order to oppose these forces in their separate state if possible, and if not, to do it when combined. You will therefore be pleased, with the assistance of the captains and subalterns, to collect immediately every firearm in your county in any wise fit for military service, and to march so many men with these arms in their hands to Prince Edward Courthouse or to Taylor's Ferry on Roanoke, as shall be most convenient, having respect for what you hear of the movements of the hostile armies and of our army under Major General Marquis Fayette. The object of your detachment being to join the latter, and keep clear of the former...."

"It is fixed that no tour shall exceed two months in the field," he continues, "but our expectation is that the present crisis will be over in a much shorter time.... Cavalry, in due proportion, being as necessary as infantry, you will be pleased to permit, and even to encourage, one-tenth part of those who are come into duty, as above required, to mount and equip themselves as cavalry. They must not be received, however, unless their horses are good and fit for service. A short sword can be furnished them by the state.... I need not urge to you," he concludes, "that the greatest events hang on the dispatch which is used in getting the militia into the field." [50]

Lafayette had, in the meantime, "moved towards Williamsburgh, and, by forced marches, had crossed the Chickahominy at Long bridge" when the British fleet returned to Brandon, according to Arnold's report to Clinton. This "retrograde motion of ours occasioned him to return as rapidly by forced marches to Osborne's, where he arrived the eighth, and was preparing to cross the river to Petersburg when we arrived there...." [51] From Osborne's, Lafayette wrote the French minister, Luzerne, with the engaging frankness that marks all his letters:

Ma situation, monsieur le chevalier, ne laisse pas que d'être un peu gênante; quand je regarde à gauche voilà le general Phillips avec son armée et le commandant absolu de James River; en tournant à droite l'armeé de lord Cornwallis s'avance à toutes jambes pour m'avaler, et le pis de l'affaire est qu'en regardant derrière moi je ne vois que 900 hommes des troupes continentals et quelques miliciens, tantôt plus tantôt moins, mais jamais assez pour n'être pas completement rossé par la plus petite des deux armées qui me font l'honneur de leur visite....

Me voici dans l'ancien camp des enemis, possesseur du quartier et du lit du général Phillips [he continues lightheartedly] *mais trop poli pour ne pas le lui rendre aussitôt qu'il en aura besoin; quelque milices sont sur le côte de nord de James River, et j'ai tant bien que mal établi ma communication sur la protection de Richmond ... nous n'avons point de batteaux et ce n'est pas le premier sujet de plainte dans un pais où il n'y a point d'armes. Le peu de milices que nous aurions est inutile faute de fusils, et c'est avec grand peine que nous pouvons avoir des cartouches.*

..... Quoique ma situation ne soit par merveilleuse, je ne puis m'empêcher de sourire à la ridicule figure que nous ferons contre ces deux messieurs réunis, et de la mine qu'auront nos dragons de milice sans pistolet, sans epée, sans selle, sans bride, et sans botte contre les Simcoes et les Tarletons....

Pour l'amour de dieu envoyez nous les Hussards de Lauzun.[52]

Two days later, "the Marquis made his appearance on the opposite side of the river with a strong escort," according to Arnold, "and, having stayed some time to reconnoiter our army, returned to his camp at Osborne's; and we are this day (the twelfth) informed he is marched to Richmond." [53] The Marquis, by no means strong enough to dislodge the British, now established himself at Wilton, the home of William Randolph on the north bank of the James, some eight miles below Richmond. His men were encamped in the surrounding woods. There was nothing to do but await the arrival of General Wayne and his Pennsylvanians, long overdue. Although the situation must have been a blow to his pride, he took it philosophically. To Wayne he wrote, in urging speed, that the enemy "have an absolute command of the water, and every movement I can make upon their left leaves this shore, the capital upon which it stands, and the country the north side of James River entirely exposed. Lord Cornwallis was at Halifax and is probably by this time on his way to Petersburg. There is hardly a man, or at least hardly a gun, to oppose him.... You will know my regular force when I tell you it is 300 men less than when I was with you at Philadelphia. We have some militia but are in such a want of arms that I dare not venture them into action, for fear of an irreparable loss." [54] To Steuben he stated that "the enemy are now at Petersburg and we have no communication over Appomattox. A general engagement is now in the enemy's power, and it is not in ours. This disadvantage and my inferiority forces me to cross the river.... I request everything that can do for crossing a river, boats, canoes, scows." [55] No sooner had this been communicated to Jefferson than he wrote the county lieutenants of Hanover and New Kent: "Whenever the Honorable Major General Marquis la Fayette shall think it necessary and shall so inform you, you will be pleased to have collected all the boats and other small vessels, whether public or private, on Pamunkey, either on or opposite to the shore of your county, and to have them carried to such places as he shall direct." [56]

In writing Lafayette, Jefferson was as philosophical as the Marquis, indeed, he may have believed the young man needed a few words of encouragement in his plight. "I sincerely and anxiously wish," he says, "you may be enabled to prevent Lord Cornwallis from engaging you till you shall be sufficiently reinforced to engage him on your terms. This may be the case when your superiority in cavalry shall become decided, which I have the most sanguine hopes the Assembly will immediately provide for. In the meantime the upper country will afford you a secure retreat, presenting hills inaccessible to horse and approaching them to their most dangerous enemies, the riflemen." [57]

Raising the desperately needed cavalry was the main concern of Jefferson and Lafayette at this moment. "By seizing the fine horses on James River," Richard Henry Lee wrote Washington, the enemy "have mounted a gallant and most mischievous cavalry of 5 or 600 in number. We have plenty of horses left, to be sure, but we are deficient in proper accouterments, though I understand the Marquis is endeavoring to mount a thousand men as quickly as possible to control the boundless ravages of the enemy's horse." [58] At the meeting of the Assembly on the twenty-eighth, the Governor presented a letter from Colonel John Walker, who acted as liaison officer, disclosing Lafayette's eagerness to have the power to impress horses. The House promptly resolved that the Governor issue warrants to the Marquis for that purpose in the counties contiguous to the invasion. The following day Jefferson wrote Lafayette, who had retired to Colonel Dandridge's on the South Anna River, "I have now the pleasure to inclose to you eight impress warrants, accompanied with resolutions of the House of Delegates, which I obtained yesterday, and to inform you that as soon as the other branch of the legislature is convened, I believe they are disposed to strengthen you with cavalry to any amount you think proper, and with as good horses as you shall think economy should induce us to take. Stud horses and brood mares will be always exempted, because to take them would be to rip up the hen which laid the golden eggs.

"I will take the liberty of recommending to you," he concludes, "that officers of mild and condescending tempers and manners be employed, and particularly instructed while they prosecute their object steadily, to use every soothing art possible. A high tone of conduct will, as it did in a former instance, revolt the people against the measure altogether, and produce a suppression of it." [59]

Once again, and as one of the final acts of his administration, Jefferson addressed the county lieutenants of Powhatan, Chesterfield, Henrico, and a dozen other counties. "It having become essentially necessary to raise immediately a large body of cavalry," he writes, "and having no means of providing accouterments, we are obliged to attempt the recovery of all the public arms and accouterments for cavalry dispersed in private hands through the state, which, if they can be secured, will arm and equip a very respectable force. I am therefore to press you instantly and diligently to search for any such in your county, not in the hands of men in actual service, and send them to such place as Colonel White shall appoint, and if collected before such appointment is known to you, then send them to the headquarters of the Marquis Fayette." [60]

Despite every effort, the results were once more not merely disappointing but disheartening. Lafayette wrote General Morgan on the twenty-first that the enemy "have much cavalry, we have forty." [61] It is not surprising that Greene, on learning of the pitiful inadequacy of this force, should have written Jefferson: "I feel for the sufferings of Virginia, and if I had been supported here in time, I should have been there before this, with a great part of our cavalry.... The importance of cavalry, and the consequences that might follow the want of it, Your Excellency will do me the justice to say, I early and earnestly endeavored to impress upon your legislature, and they must blame themselves if they experience any extraordinary calamities. You would have been in a tolerable situation had your cavalry been sufficiently augmented, and the last reinforcement from New York not arrived." [62]

When Greene learned that Cornwallis "was moving northerly," he "gave orders for the Marquis to halt and take the command in Virginia." [63] The news reached Lafayette by the seventeenth, when he was still at Wilton. This young man of twenty-four now found himself in an extremely precarious position. To meet the vastly superior British forces it had only been possible to assemble, in addition to his nine hundred-odd Continentals, some twelve to fifteen hundred militia, the forty cavalry, and six pieces of artillery. "Our militia are not numerous," he wrote Alexander Hamilton with some discouragement, "come without arms, and are not used to war. Government wants energy, and there is nothing to enforce the laws." [64] Realizing that it would be impossible to prevent the junction of Cornwallis and Arnold, much less give battle, he retired to Richmond on the twentieth of May, the very day the two forces joined. Here, he observed, "I have so many arrangements to make, so many difficulties to combat, so many enemies to deal with, that I am just that much of a general as will make me an historian of misfortunes and nail my name upon the ruins of what good folks are pleased to call the army of Virginia." [65]

With the insouciance of youth he gaily remarked to Luzerne on the twenty-second: "*Nous sommes encore en vie, monsieur le chevalier, et notre petit corps n'a pas jusqu'à ce moment reçu la terrible visite.*" Turning more serious, he continued: "*Lord Cornwallis est à Petersburg, et a tranquillement passé à travers la Caroline du Nord; il paiera bien un droit de péage pour traverser la Virginie, mais nous ne pouvons pas espérer de faire grande résistance, la proportion en infanterie regulière est en quatre et cinq contre un, en cavalrie dix contre un; il y a quelques torys dont je ne m'embarrasse guères; notre milice n'est pas nombreuse sur le papier, l'est bien moins encore* in the field. *Nous manquons d'armes, nous n'avons pas cent* riflemen, *et si nous sommes battus, c'est à dire si l'on nous attrappe, tout se dispersera.*" [66]

Watchful waiting was not a policy that appealed to the Virginians. So much had been expected, so much promised from French help, and so much hoped for, that it was heart-rending for them to watch the unopposed advance of the enemy. Cornwallis, described by Captain Young "as a suttle fellow and I fear will be too many for the Marquis," lost no time. Well might Jefferson say: "The whole country lies open to a most powerful army, headed by the most active, enterprising, and vindictive officer who has ever appeared in arms against us." [67] Immediately, "his lordship proceeded to learn the state of the enemy and the country, and to form arrangements, previous to his entering upon active operations. The light troops and spies were directed to find out the situation and strength of the Marquis de la Fayette." [68] On the twenty-third, according to William Constable, aide to Lafayette, "Colonel Tarleton with three hundred horse of his legion, profiting by the very heavy rains which rendered the Continental arms unfit for fire, and having intercepted the videtts, surprised a party of militia at Chesterfield, about two miles southwest of Colonel Cary's mill. They killed six and took about forty prisoners. [On the] twenty-fourth the British evacuated Petersburg and destroyed the bridge they had constructed on the Appomattox. They marched to Maycox [69] and crossed about 1,000 men that evening for Westover. The next day they were employed in crossing the rest of their army." [70] Somewhat smugly Tarleton observes that "the passage of the river at that place afforded an easy entrance into a fertile quarter of Virginia, and enabled the British to prosecute such operations against the Americans as future circumstances should render eligible." [71]

From "Byrd's plantation north of James river," Cornwallis reported confidently to Clinton on the twenty-sixth, "I shall now proceed to dislodge LaFayette from Richmond, and with my light troops to destroy any magazines or stores in the neighborhood which may have been collected either for his use or for General Greene's army. I purpose to move to the neck at Williamsburg, which is represented as healthy, and where some subsistence may be secured, and keep myself unengaged from operations which might interfere with your plan for the campaign until I have the satisfaction of hearing from you." [72]

In pursuit of these aims, Cornwallis marched his men to Turkey Island, on one of the great bends of the river some thirteen miles from Richmond, and encamped near by on White Oak Swamp, on the twenty-seventh. Learning that Lafayette had abandoned Richmond and crossed the Chickahominy, "the royal army pointed their course towards Bottom's Bridge, on that river, and the Americans moved with celerity across the South and North Anna." [73] It was indeed true, as Tarleton observed, that "at this period, the superiority of the army, and the great superiority of the light troops, were such as to have enabled the British to traverse the country without apprehension or difficulty, either to destroy stores in the neighborhood of the rivers, or to undertake more important expeditions." [74]

Lafayette suffered enormously in prestige during these days. The Virginians, humanly enough, could not see that they were themselves largely to blame for their situation. As General Greene wrote General Lawson of the militia, "I have done all in my power to give protection in every quarter, but the efforts of the states have been by no means equal to the emergency; and therefore they must patiently submit to the misfortunes which their own tardiness has brought upon them. My utmost exertions shall be continued, and I am ready and willing to encounter every danger and hardship to afford relief to this distressed country. But without support, what is to be done?" [75]

Rather than put on the coat, it was a much simpler matter to lay the blame on the "foreigners who had come to help them. The people of this country don't like people that they can't understand so well as they used to," wrote forthright Captain Young at this time. "I fear the Marquis may lose his credit—deserters, British, cringing Dutchmen and busy little Frenchmen swarm about headquarters. The people do not like Frenchmen. Every person they can't understand, they take for a Frenchman." [76]

The feeling against the French was no new thing. As early as April, John Banister had written Theoderick Bland: "The French did not, as you suppose, bring a single article of military store for us; nor render us the smallest service by their battle with the English fleet, not having attempted to throw in any succors of land forces, but after their action at sea, went safely into port at Rhode Island and, I suppose, there remain, as spectators of very affecting tragedies in these states. The Marquis, too, we are told is ordered back to the American Army, where there is no war, and we are abandoned by our northern friends, as they are called, and left with unarmed militia to encounter a great proportion of the British army here, and Lord Cornwallis's in North Carolina." [77]

Lafayette was not unaware of the dangerous policy he was pursuing, however obligatory, or of the criticism being leveled against him. "I ardently wish my conduct may meet with your approbation," he wrote Washington in extenuation on May 24. "Had I followed the first impulse of my temper, I should have risked something more; but I have been guarding against my own warmth, and this consideration, that a general defeat which, with such a proportion of militia, must be expected, would involve this state and our affairs in ruin, has rendered me extremely cautious in my movements.... I am wavering between two inconveniences. Was I to fight a battle, I'll be cut to pieces, the militia dispersed, and the arms lost. Was I to decline fighting, the country would think itself given up. I am therefore determined to skirmish, but not engage too far, and particularly to take care against their immense and excellent body of horse, whom the militia fear as they would so many wild beasts.... Was I anyways equal to the enemy," he concludes in his engaging way, "I should be extremely happy in my present command. But I am not strong enough even to get beaten. Government in this state has no energy, and laws have no force." [78] To Hamilton he confessed: "To speak the truth, I was afraid of myself as much as of the enemy. Independence has rendered me more cautious, as I know my own warmth." [79]

The French soldiers themselves, whether disheartened or whether convinced that even in war-torn Virginia they had found an El Dorado, now began to desert. On May 29, Jefferson issued the following orders to the county lieutenants of those counties adjacent to the great waterways of Virginia: "Information having been given me that a considerable number of men have deserted from the French army and navy in America, which the commanding officers are very anxious to have apprehended, I must desire you to give orders at the several ferries in your county that all foreigners offering to cross at them, and having the appearance of soldiers or seamen, be examined with great strictness, and if there be good reason to believe them to be deserters, that they then be delivered to such persons as you shall appoint to guard them till you can have all opportunity by militia or otherwise, to send them with a state of the circumstances of suspicion to the headquarters of Major General the Marquis la Fayette." [80]

We can only surmise how these shattering events affected Jefferson. To see his country overrun by a brutal and ruthless enemy must indeed have been bitter. To feel that the mighty efforts of the past two years, to which he had devoted every resource of his mind and to which he had given, in lavish measure, every vestige of his physical strength, were apparently in vain, must have been doubly so. Yet, as always in crises in his life, Jefferson has left no slightest trace of his thoughts or his emotions. In eight days there is but one entry in the voluble account book, when he notes that on May 26, "my wagon was this day impressed by ——— Carr to attend Albm. militia."

Four days before his term as Governor came to an end, Jefferson sent Washington a résumé of events since the arrival of Lord Cornwallis at Petersburg. Between the lines of his restrained account it is not difficult to observe that he was fully aware of the prevalent anxiety and discontent, not to say the spirit of hopelessness that animated large numbers of his contemporaries. "The whole force of the enemy within this state," he writes, "from the best intelligence I have been able to get, I think is about 7,000 men, infantry and cavalry." The Marquis Lafayette commanded "3,000 men, regulars and militia, that being the whole number we could arm till the arrival of 1,100 arms from Rhode Island.... A number of privateers and small vessels which are constantly ravaging the shores of our rivers, prevent us from receiving any aid from the counties lying on navigable waters.

"The powerful operations meditated against our western frontier by a joint force of British and Indian savages," he continues, broaching the subject of the onslaughts of the enemy from the east and south, "have, as Your Excellency knew before, obliged us to embody between two and three thousand men in that quarter. Your Excellency will judge from this state of things, and from what you know of our country, what it may probably suffer during the present campaign. Should the enemy be able to produce no opportunity of annihilating the Marquis's army, a small proportion of their force may yet restrain his movements effectually while the greater part is employed in detachment to waste an unarmed country and to lead the minds of the people to acquiescence under those events which they see no human power prepared to ward off." [81]

Loyal patriot that he was, George Mason was among the many who shared these sentiments, and he did not hesitate to give them expression. "Our affairs have been for some time going from bad to worse," he wrote his son, who was in France at this time. "The enemy's fleet commands our rivers and puts it in their power to remove their troops from place to place, when and where they please, without opposition, so that we no sooner collect a force sufficient to counteract them in one part of the country, but they shift to another, ravaging, plundering, and destroying everything before them. Our militia turn out with great spirit and have in several actions behaved bravely, but they are badly armed and appointed.... The enemy's capital object, at this time, seems to be Virginia....

"You know from your own acquaintance in this part of Virginia that the bulk of the people here are stanch Whigs, strongly attached to the American cause and well affected to the French alliance; yet they begin to think that our allies are spinning out the war in order to weaken America, as well as Great Britain, and thereby leave us at the end of it as dependent as possible upon themselves....

"However unjust this opinion may be, it is natural enough for the planters and farmers, burdened with heavy taxes and frequently dragged from their families upon military duty, by the continual alarms occasioned by the superiority of the British fleet. They see their property daily exposed to destruction, they see with what facility the British troops are removed from one part of the continent to another, and with what infinite charge and fatigue ours are too late obliged to follow, and they see, too, very plainly that a strong French fleet would have prevented all this. If our allies had a superior fleet here," he concludes gloomily, "I should have no doubt of a favorable issue to the war, but without it I fear we are deceiving both them and ourselves." [82]

In concluding his letter to Washington, Jefferson gave voice to a sentiment that was firing the minds and sustaining the hearts of large numbers of Virginians—a cry for the presence of the commander in chief. His military genius, his singular judgment, his solid common sense were proverbial. Was he not a Virginian? Had he not before transformed disaster into victory?

"We are too far removed from the other scenes of war," Jefferson writes in introducing this idea, "to say whether the main force of the enemy be within this state; but I suppose they cannot anywhere spare so great an army for the operations of the field. Were it possible for this circumstance to justify in Your Excellency a determination to lend us your personal aid, it is evident from the universal voice that the presence of their beloved countryman, whose talents have so long been successfully employed in establishing the freedom of kindred states, to whose person they have still flattered themselves they retained some rights, and have even looked upon as their *dernier resort* in distress, that your appearance among them, I say, would restore full confidence of salvation and would render them equal to whatever is not impossible.

"I cannot undertake to foresee and obviate the difficulties which stand in the way of such a resolution," he concludes, aware of the boldness of the suggestion. "The whole subject is before you, of which I see only detached parts, and your judgment will be formed on view of the whole. Should the dangers of this state and its consequences to the union be such as to render it best for the whole that you should repair to its assistance, the difficulty would be but to keep men out of the field. I have undertaken to hint this matter to Your Excellency not only on my own sense of its importance to us, but at the solicitation of many members of weight in our legislature which has not yet assembled to speak their own desires." [83]

This letter undoubtedly reflects the informal conversations Jefferson may have had with members of the legislature who had even then assembled in Charlottesville. The meeting had originally been called for early May. On the first Jefferson addressed a letter to the members saying that he had "deferred changing the place of calling the Assembly in hopes that every day would give us a prospect of getting rid of the enemy in the neighborhood of Richmond.... Nevertheless, as we know that rumors have gone abroad very generally that the enemy are in possession of Richmond, and the time of meeting of Assembly is too near to admit these to be corrected." He therefore particularly solicited "so many members of the nearer counties as will suffice to make a House" to attend, so that it would not be brought into dissolution and the state left without one until the "next regular period of election." [84]

There was no quorum on the seventh of May, neither on the eighth or ninth. On the tenth, "information being given the House of the approach of an hostile army of the enemy towards this place," it was "resolved to adjourn to Thursday, May the twenty-fourth, and meet at Charlottesville." [85] There was no quorum on the appointed day, but on the twenty-eighth a brief meeting was held. Meanwhile Jefferson had repaired to Charlottesville on the fifteenth, as he wrote Lafayette, to "see that provision be made for the reception of the public boards and bodies," [86] although, as he observed to the Virginia delegates in Congress, "I rather expect that the want of accommodations there will oblige them to adjourn again to some other place." [87] The hospitable doors of Monticello were opened to as many members of the legislature as could be accommodated, and there is no doubt that the unusual signs of life and activity going forward in a house dark for the greater part of two years, led one of his neighbors to wonder "would His Excellency's magnificent building be illuminated if the enemy should come?" [88]

Meanwhile, Richard Henry Lee, who on occasion could rival Jefferson as a master of the pen, was moved to make an even more eloquent and impassioned appeal to Washington. "The enemy's army is in the heart of the country," he writes, "employing with exquisite industry every engine that force and fraud can move to effect a conquest of the whole or far greater part immediately. I think, Sir, that they will succeed if adequate prevention be not presently applied. ... It would be a thing for angels to weep over if the goodly fabric of human freedom which you have so well labored to rear, should in one unlucky moment be leveled with the dust. There is nothing I think more certain than that your personal call would bring into immediate exertion the force and the resource of this state and its neighboring ones, which, directed as it would be, will effectually disappoint and baffle the deep-laid schemes of the enemy. Our country is truly, Sir, in a deplorable way," he concludes, "and if relief comes not from you, it will probably come not at all." [89]

Washington did not permit these letters to disturb his Olympian calm. Although conceding that "the progress which the enemy are making in Virginia is very alarming," he wrote Lee that "the plan you have suggested as a relief for it, in my judgment, is a greater proof of your unbounded confidence in me than it is that the means proposed would be found adequate to the end in view, were it practicable to make the experiment, which at present it is not." [90] He then proceeded to give his reasons, in words almost identical to those in which he addressed the Governor on June 8.

After acknowledging Jefferson's letters of the ninth and twenty-eighth of May, Washington reaffirms his faith in the plan to which he had so long clung and which, as things turned out, was not the one that proved the determining factor either in the relief of Virginia or in bringing the war to a successful conclusion. "Were it prudent to commit a detail of our plans and expectations to paper," he writes, "I would convince Your Excellency by a variety of reasons that my presence is essential to the operations which have lately been concerted by the French Commanders and myself and which are to open this quarter provided the British keep possession of New York.... Should I be supported by the neighboring states in the manner which I expect, the enemy will, I hope, be reduced to the necessity of recalling part of their force from the southward to support New York.... The prospect of giving relief to the southern states by an operation in this quarter, was the principal inducement for undertaking it. Indeed, we found upon a full consideration of our affairs from every point of view that, without the command of the water, it would be next to impossible for us to transport the artillery, baggage, and stores of the army so great a distance, and besides that we should lose at least one-third of our force by desertion, sickness, and the heats of the approaching season, even if it could be done...." [91]

Jefferson's appeal to Washington was one of the last acts in his career as Governor. The day it was written, the twenty-eighth, he had sent a short message to the Speaker of the House announcing the resignation from the Council of Dudley Digges, lieutenant governor, and calling for a remedy for the "great evils and dangers [which] are to be apprehended from the total want of authority of the military power over citizens within the vicinities of his [the commanding general's] and the enemy's encampments." [92] He had likewise called on the county lieutenants of certain counties for additional militia, and had sent a report of the military situation to the president of Congress.

In closing his letter to Washington, Jefferson had remarked: "A few days will bring to me that period of relief which the constitution has prepared for those oppressed with the labors of my office, and a long-declared resolution of relinquishing it to abler hands has prepared my way for retirement to a private station."[93] Washington, in his reply, took occasion to pay tribute to the most important contribution of Jefferson's governorship—his complete loyalty to the larger aims of the war, even at the sacrifice of his own reputation. He had had the sagacity to see it was not only the independence and the soil of Virginia that were at stake, but the successful union of the several states to form a great and united nation. This insight was not shared by many of his countrymen, who could not see beyond the limits of their plantations and the immediate welfare of their families, or who failed to realize that a country overrun is not a country conquered. It must have been infinitely gratifying to read the words of his commander in chief: "Give me leave before I take leave of Your Excellency in your public capacity, to express the obligations I am under for the readiness and zeal with which you have always forwarded and supported every measure which I have had occasion to recommend through you, and to assure you that I shall esteem myself honored by a continuation of your friendship and correspondence should your country permit you to remain in the private walk of life."[94]

X. Retirement and Vindication

THE DETERMINATION to retire was not a new idea with Jefferson. Indeed, it was an ideal that haunted him throughout life, no matter what public office he held. As early as May 1779, before he had assumed the governorship, he had expressed this desire, and his mentor, Edmund Pendleton, had been led to write him: "You are too young to ask that happy quietness from the public, and should at least postpone it till you have taught the rising generation the forms as well as the substantial principles of legislation." [1]

Jefferson's was essentially a domestic temperament, as is testified by the long and happy years from 1809 to 1826, when at last he reached the goal towards which he had been striving a lifetime. As he wrote Maria Cosway in 1795, during a brief period of retirement: "Your letter found me returned to my home in the full enjoyment of my farm, my family, and my books, having bidden an eternal adieu to public life, which I always hated, and was drawn into and kept in by one of those great events which happened only once in a millenium, I thought." [2] Similarly, in the heyday of his years in Paris, he remarked to a friend of his early youth: "I had rather be shut up in a very modest cottage with my books, my family, and a few old friends, dining on simple bacon and letting the world roll on as it liked, than occupy the most splendid post that any human power can give.... There are minds which can be pleased by honors and preferments; but I see nothing in them but envy and enmity. It is only necessary to possess them, to know how little they contribute to happiness, or rather, how hostile they are to it." [3]

This, however, was not to be his fate. Conscious that "there is a debt of service due from every man to his country, proportioned to the bounties which nature and fortune have measured to him," [4] Jefferson each time obeyed the call of those who, as he said, had "brought forward his name." Thus he was reluctantly kept in the service of the people throughout the greater part of his life. All the disillusionment which public office, and particularly his governorship, had brought to him is reflected in the words with which he speculated on his first candidacy for the presidency. "On principles of public interest I should not have refused," he exclaimed, "but I protest before my God that I shall from the bottom of my heart rejoice at escaping. I know well that no man will ever bring out of that office the reputation which carries him into it. The honeymoon would be as short in that case as in any other, and its moment of ecstasy would be ransomed by years of torment and hatred." [5]

During the turbulent years of his governorship there was little chance for the quiet pleasures of domesticity or indulgence in intellectual pursuits. Jefferson has left scarcely a trace of his private life during this period. There are no letters to friends or close associates to give us a glimpse. He remained, of necessity, close in Richmond. His account book is an endless, matter-of-fact recital of routine payments of minor household expenses in the fantastically inflated currency of those months. There is an almost daily "pd. for milk £ 4, pd. for beef and fowls, £ 254, pd. Wiley for eggs, £ 15, pd. Houghton for beer in full £ 835, pd. for oysters £ 9." On March 16 he received from James Cocke of Malvern Hills "a horse mule, Dr. Slop, and a mare mule, Capt. Molly, both three years old, for which I am to pay 3,000 lb. tobo." The only reference to his beloved Monticello, then still building, is on April 3, when he "sent David Watson, a British deserter, housejoiner by trade, to work at Monticello." [6] The only concession to his intellectual interests are the purchase of Hutchen's map, for which he sent James Madison in Philadelphia £ 150 on April 7, and a letter from John Fitzgerald of Alexandria advising the Governor that he has made the purchase of an encyclopedia as desired.

His domestic life was clouded by tragedy during this period when, on the fifteenth of April, his little daughter, Lucy Elizabeth, died at ten o'clock in the morning. She had been born on the third of the previous November, during the troubled days following Leslie's invasion. Ten years had not yet passed since the marriage of Jefferson and Martha Wayles. Five children had been born to them and three had died, along with the infant John Skelton, issue of Mrs. Jefferson's first marriage. The loss of Lucy Elizabeth seemed more than this stricken woman could bear. In one of the few times during his career Jefferson put personal concerns before public affairs. He wrote to David Jameson, a member of the Council: "The day is so very bad that I hardly expect a Council, and there being nothing that I know of pressing, and Mrs. Jefferson in a situation in which I would not wish to leave her, I shall not attend today." [7] The records of the Council show that the meeting was held, and a resolution recommended in the last part of his letter, adopted. His Excellency, however, was not present. The business of state was carried on by William Fleming, George Webb, David Jameson, and Jacquelin Ambler.[8]

The news of Phillips's invasion arrived only three days after this. From now on, life in the Jefferson family was largely a matter of refugeeing, as the Virginians say. As soon as Mrs. Jefferson was able to collect herself, her husband sent her and their two little daughters to safety at Elk Hill, their plantation near the Point of Fork. The family set out on the twenty-fourth, in the care of Jupiter, who so often acted the trusted courier. On the thirtieth, when Bolling Starke wrote the Governor that the public papers had been safely concealed, he added a personal note saying: "Mrs. Jefferson and your little family were very well yesterday at Elk Hill, and were endeavoring to procure a vessel to cross over the river to Mr. C. Harrison's, but I doubt they would find it difficult, for the quartermasters had the day before collected all the canoes in the neighborhood and sent them down the river loaded with grain for the use of the army." [9]

Jefferson went to fetch his family on the tenth of May, after writing the long letters to the Speaker of the House, to the Virginia delegates in Congress, and to General Washington, already discussed. There was a meeting of the Council at ten o'clock that morning, at which considerable business was dispatched. No meeting was called for Friday or Saturday, not until Monday, the fourteenth. William Langhorne, Lafayette's aide-de-camp, writes on the twelfth from Tuckahoe: "I arrived here last evening in hopes of having the honor of seeing Your Excellency," [10] but his bird had flown—apparently to

Elk Hill. On the thirteenth the pocket account book notes that Jefferson "paid ferriage at Goochland Court House," and on the fourteenth he "gave Zack at Tuckahoe £ 4-10." The same day he wrote Lafayette from Richmond: "I am sorry the situation of my family had occasioned my absence from this place when you were pleased to send Captain Langhorne to me." [11] The Council records show that he was in Richmond by ten o'clock on the morning of that day, and that on the fifteenth that body adjourned to meet again in Charlottesville on the twenty-fourth. In concluding his letter to Lafayette Jefferson observed: "Lest anything should suffer which it is in my power to prevent, I have concluded to stay here this evening and to do myself the pleasure of calling on you at your quarters tomorrow morning."[12] After this he seems to have gone to Tuckahoe, where he paid £30 for "mending chair," and then to Charlottesville to prepare for the reception of the Council and legislature.

At this time—if, indeed, not earlier—Jefferson had arranged to send all his books and papers away from Monticello. They had still not been returned on March 22, 1782, when he wrote Madison, à propos of some "designs against the territorial rights of Virginia": "I had thought to have seized the first leisure on my return from the last Assembly to have considered and stated our rights," he says, "and ... to have derived some assistance from ancient manuscripts which I have been able to collect. These, with my other papers and books, however, had been removed to Augusta to be out of danger of the enemy, and have not yet been brought back." [13]

That a life of this sort was not to Jefferson's taste, is obvious. Indeed, he had soon found the governorship an irksome office. He expressed his feeling very clearly when he wrote an unknown correspondent as early as September 3, 1780: "... the application to the duties of the office I hold so excessive, and the execution of them after all so imperfect, that I have determined to retire from it at the close of the present campaign. I wish a successor to be thought of in time who, to sound Whiggism, can join perseverance in business and an extensive knowledge of the various subjects he must superintend." [14]

"I have no ambition to govern men," Jefferson was to write some years later, "no passion which would lead me to delight to ride in a storm." Similar sentiments must have been expressed in letters to John Page during that fall. These do not seem to have been preserved, but Page's replies are still among Jefferson's papers. They constitute a chorus of supplication, repeated in letter after letter during the course of three months in the fall of 1780. Page, who had been lieutenant governor under Patrick Henry and a member of the Council since Jefferson's election, expressed a desire to resign. Jefferson seems to have made the counter-proposal that Page stand for governor in the next election, which would occur on the first of June, 1781. In writing from Rosewell on September 22, 1780, Page says: "I shall only venture to say that should you resign, you will give me great uneasiness and will greatly distress your country. As to my succeeding you, if my abilities were ten times greater than my [illegible] vanity can ever prompt me to suppose them, I could not think of it in the present situation of my affairs." [15]

Jefferson was not persuaded on either point and must again have written Page urging him to accept the governorship, which could doubtless have been his in view of his previous record. On the twentieth Page begs Jefferson "not to think of proposing it to me again." He then continues: "Consider how inconsistently we should act if you should leave the helm when it required such vigilance, spirit, dextrous skill to steer through the storm, and if I, who had quitted the ship confessedly, because worn down with fatigue and unable to hand a rope or keep the deck even in a calm, should presume to take a helm out of your hands! It will never do indeed." [16]

The two old friends had again fallen into the relationship of early days, writing each other when separated, sending each other riddles, corresponding about meteorological observations and similar topics. "I shall be very happy if you will make good your threats," Page writes on December 9, referring to a proposed correspondence on scientific subjects. "I mean of being very troublesome to me in this way. But it gives me no small uneasiness to find, by reports and those confirmed by some passages in one of your letters, that I am not likely to receive those agreeable tasks from you unless your country loses the benefit of your services in the office you now hold. I know your love of study and retirement must most strongly solicit you to leave the hurry, bustle, and nonsense your station daily exposes you to. I know, too, the many mortifications you must meet with; but eighteen months will pass away. Deny yourself your darling pleasures for this space of time, and despise not only now, but forever, the impertinence of the silly world. All who know how eminently qualified you are to fill the si[tuation] you hold, and that circumstances may happen within the compass of the time above alluded to, which may require the exertion of greater abilities than can be found in any other person within this state; I know not who, besides yourself, we have, and R. H. Lee, I suppose, is too unpopular to be thought of, can possibly with tolerance (?) [illegible] reputation to the state, manage the important [illegible] which may occur. This I can tell you with [illegible] is the opinion of others as well as myself. Let me [illegible], Jefferson, conjure you not to think of resigning. Go on, serve out the time allowed by the constitution." [17]

George Gilmer, one of Jefferson's closest friends in Albemarle, likewise added his plea. Writing from Charlottesville on April 13, he says: "I long to behold the period when you may with propriety retreat to Montchello, but for your country's sake I hope you'll persevere to labor for its salvation in your present station so long as your country shall have virtue enough to continue you. The envious only hate that excellence they can not reach. Heavens inspire everyone with that laudable ambition of serving their country as you have done." [18]

As the second year of his governorship drew to a close Jefferson, as we have seen, looked forward with obvious eagerness to being relieved from office. There can be no doubt that he had made clear to his associates in the Council and the legislature his intention of not being a candidate for a third term, as the constitution permitted. To be sure, there were no outstanding aspirants. Dudley Digges, the lieutenant governor, had resigned. William Fleming of Botetourt, the senior member of the Council, who ultimately acted as governor until the election of Nelson, seems not to have been considered. There can likewise be no doubt that, since Arnold's raid, and increasingly so since Phillips, and now Cornwallis, had overrun the country, Virginia was in a state bordering on demoralization. The independence of spirit which had led the Virginians to take a leading part in breaking away from the mother country, manifested itself at this time in a manner not so fortunate for the state. Their own government may, perhaps, have been too new for them to feel a proper sense of obligation towards it. In any case, it was frequently impossible to obtain a meeting of either the Council or the legislature for days and even for weeks. Thus, although the Assembly was called to meet on October 1, 1781, it was not until November 19 that a quorum was obtained, and that not until the sergeant-at-arms had been ordered to take into custody the majority of the members. Very humanly, no doubt, the personal affairs of these gentlemen loomed larger in their minds than those of the commonwealth.

As early as March 1781 Davies had complained to Steuben: "The affairs of the state are strangely confused, and, I am sure, will continue so, unless a speedy reformation should take place. My best endeavors," he continues, "shall never cease to restore matters, if possible, and make them less absurd than they have hitherto been in their arrangements." [19] But things were destined to go from bad to worse. "I fear, my dear Sir," writes Colonel Josiah Parker to the Speaker of the House on June 9, while the governorship was still vacant and the legislature postponed action, "the spring of our government is rotten, and I dread the consequence.... I am foolishly fond of my country, and cannot bear to see her neglected." [20] Even after the election of the enormously popular Nelson, conditions failed to improve. David Jameson, a most conscientious member of Council, informed him three months later: "In my letter of the thirteenth I mention to you that we had not exceeded four members [of Council] since you left us. That evening General Lewis and Mr. Webb left us, so that there now remains only Mr. Ambler and myself, and when there will be more is very uncertain. The executive, my dear Sir, were held in small repute before, must they not become quite contemptible? Certain it is I cannot consent to stay here to hear the daily complaints and reproaches of the people, without the power of doing anything." [21]

The House of Delegates, as we have seen, met in Charlottesville on the twenty-eighth of May. On Wednesday, the thirtieth, they "resolved that this House will on Saturday next, proceed by joint ballot with the Senate to the choice of a governor or chief magistrate of the Commonwealth for the ensuing year." [22] On Saturday so great was the confusion, so alarming the reports of the approach of the enemy, that it was "ordered that the same be put off to Monday next." By Monday, June 4, there was chaos. On that day Jefferson notes in his account book, which often served as diary, "British horse came to Monticello." The legislature, seemingly, forgot all about the choice of a chief magistrate. They resolved "that during the present invasion forty members be a sufficient number to comprise a House to proceed on business," and agreed "that this House be adjourned until Thursday next, then to meet in the town of Staunton, in the county of Augusta." [23] When they met that Thursday, the choice of a governor was once more postponed, until the twelfth of June. The election of Jefferson's successor, Thomas Nelson, Jr., took place on that day.

Jefferson considered that his term as governor came to an end on the second of June, as indeed it did, for on June 2, 1780, he had been appointed "governor or chief magistrate of the commonwealth for one year." [24] There was no question of his resigning or of his having laid down his office, as has been intimated. He says in his "Memorandum relative to the Invasion," in speaking of the removal of the government to Charlottesville, "his [the governor's] office was now near expiring, the country under invasion by a powerful army, no services but military of any avail, unprepared by his line of life and education for the command of armies, he believed it right not to stand in the way of talents better fitted than his own to the circumstances under which the country was placed. He therefore himself proposed to his friends in the legislature that General Nelson, who commanded the militia of the state, should be appointed governor, as he was sensible that the union of the civil and military power in the same hands at this time, would greatly facilitate military measures. This appointment accordingly took place on the twelfth of June, 1781." [25]

Immediately following the election of the new governor, a resolution was introduced into the House that "at the next session of the Assembly an enquiry be made into the conduct of the Executive of this state for the last twelve months." [26] This was sponsored by George

RETIREMENT AND VINDICATION 245

Nicholas, eldest son of Robert Carter Nicholas, the treasurer of Virginia when it had been a colony, and one of Jefferson's earliest admirers. George Nicholas, a young man of twenty-eight, had only this very year moved from Hanover to Albemarle and now represented that county in the House. Like many young men with hot blood in their veins, he seemed of the opinion that to get ahead in this world it is advisable to do something spectacular. On the seventh of June, according to that excellent informant, Captain Henry Young, "he gave notice that he should this day [the 9th] move to have a dictator appointed—General Washington and General Greene are talked of. I dare say your knowledge of these worthy gentlemen will be sufficient to convince you that neither of them will or ought to accept such an appointment." Now Nicholas boldly brought charges against the retiring governor. In this maneuver, according to Edmund Randolph and others, he was associated with Patrick Henry.[27]

It was a stunning blow to Jefferson. Indeed, it was more than that, for the accusation, however subtly and vaguely worded, however disproved and discredited, was to haunt him throughout his political career. It was brought up again by Charles Symes of Alexandria, a violent Federalist, in 1796, when Jefferson was a candidate for the presidency, and again in the republican revolution following the election of 1800, more particularly by Thomas Turner, in his virulent attacks on the President in 1805. That Nicholas's charges, such as they were, were not directed personally at Jefferson, but at the executive, which included the Council, has largely been overlooked. As we have seen, it was impossible for the governor to take any action, to write any report or letter, without the advice of the Council. Although Jefferson may have been the inspiring force, and although the acquiescence of Council may have been a mere formality, that body legally and actually constituted part of the executive. That they realized this and were prepared to share the responsibility is readily seen from their statement of July 16, on which day the resolution of the House of Delegates concerning the executive was received by them. "The underwritten members," it reads, "who till now were strangers to such a resolution having passed, think it their bounden duty to declare that, conscious of the rectitude of their intentions through the course of the most arduous and expensive attendance on public business, however unsuccessful their honest endeavors may have been, they are ever ready and willing to have their public conduct enquired into with the most scrupulous exactness. That, as they cannot but feel most sensibly this implied censure on them, so they should not, from motives of delicacy alone, if there were no other, continue their attendance at the Board, at least till the result of the intended enquiry shall have convinced their fellow citizens that their honest and best endeavors have not been wanting to serve their country, but that a secession of the members, to whom the fore-mentioned resolution was addressed, would leave the state without a legal Executive at a time when the want of one may be productive of the most fatal consequences." It was signed by David Jameson, Andrew Lewis, and Jacquelin Ambler.[28]

On June 14, John Beckley, clerk of the House, wrote Jefferson: "I am directed by the House of Delegates to convey to you information respecting a resolution of their House of this date, for an enquiry into the conduct of the Executive for the last twelve months; I therefore, Sir, do myself the honor to inclose a copy of that resolution, and remain with great regards...."[29] The letter is endorsed by Jefferson as having been received on August 7.

Of course it did not take that length of time for the news to reach him. On July 8 he addressed a letter to Nicholas, the tone and even the handwriting of which betrays his deep emotion. "Sir," he writes, "I am informed that a resolution on your motion passed the House of Delegates requiring me to render account of some part of my administration, without specifying the act to be accounted for. As I suppose that this was done under the impression of some particular instance or instances of ill conduct, and that it could not be intended first, to stab a reputation by a general suggestion under a bare expectation that facts might be afterwards hunted up to bolster it, I hope you will not think me improper in asking the favor of you to specify to me the unfortunate passages in my conduct which you mean to adduce against me, that I may be enabled to prepare to yield obedience to the House while facts are fresh in my memory and witnesses and documents are in existence."[30]

Nicholas, whom Jefferson describes as "a very young man, but always a very honest one," replied on the thirty-first. His letter, which, like Jefferson's, strangely enough appears scarcely to be known, is one of considerable dignity. "By resolution of the House of Delegates," he writes, "an enquiry is to be made into the conduct of the Executive for the last twelve months. No particular instance of misconduct was specified. They seemed to think, and I am still of opinion, that the persons entrusted with the administration ought to be ready to give an account of the whole and every part of it.

"You consider me in a wrong point of view when you speak of me as an accuser. As a freeman, and the representative of freemen, I consider it as both my right and duty to call upon the Executive to account for our numberless miscarriages and losses so far as they were concerned in or might have prevented them. In doing this I had no private pique to gratify, and if (as I hope it may) it shall appear that they have done everything in their power to prevent our misfortunes, I will most readily retract any opinion that I may have formed to their prejudice.

"I shall exhibit no charges, but only join in an enquiry.

"At your request I will mention such things as strike me at present as wanting explanation, and if anything shall hereafter occur I will inform you by letter.

"The total want of opposition to Arnold on his first expedition.

"The dissolution of a considerable body of militia on our southern frontier at the time of Greene's retreat for want of orders from the Executive.

"The want of timely orders to the counties of Amherst, Augusta, etc., after the adjournment of the Assembly from Richmond.

"The great loss that the country has sustained in arms, etc., exclusive of those destroyed by the enemy.

"The rejection of an offer made by Cols. Campbell, Christian, and McDowell to raise regiments for the southern service." [31]

In his "Memorandum relative to the Invasion of Virginia," Jefferson states that "the heads of these [specific charges] were communicated through a mutual friend to Mr. Jefferson, who committed to writing also the heads of justification on each of them." [32] These charges, somewhat more specific than those given in Nicholas's letter, were:

"1st Objection—That General Washington's information was, that an embarkation was taking place, destined for this state.

"Answer—His information was, that it was destined for the southward, as was given out at New York. Had similar informations from General Washington and Congress been considered as sufficient ground at all times for calling the militia into the field, there would have been a standing army of militia kept up; because there has never been a time, since the invasion expected in December 1777, but what we have had those intimations hanging over our heads. The truth is, that General Washington always considered as his duty to convey every rumor of an embarkation; but we (for some time past, at least) never thought anything but actual invasion should induce us to the expense and harassment of calling the militia into the field; except in the case of December 1779, when it was thought proper to do this in order to convince the French of our disposition to protect their ships. Inattention to this necessary economy, in the beginning, went far towards that ruin of our finances which followed.

"2d Objection—Where were the post-riders established last summer?

"Answer—They were established at Continental expense, to convey speedy information to Congress of the arrival of the French fleet, then expected here. When that arrived at Rhode Island, these expenses were discontinued. They were again established on the invasion in October, and discontinued when that ceased. And again on the first intimation of the invasion of December. But it will be asked, why were they not established on General Washington's letters? Because those letters were no more than we had received upon many former occasions, and would have led to a perpetual establishment of post-riders.

"3d Objection—If a proper number of men had been put into motion on Monday, for the relief of the lower country, and ordered to march to Williamsburg, that they would at least have been in the neighborhood of Richmond on Thursday.

"Answer—The order could not be till Tuesday, because we then received our first certain information. Half the militia of the counties round about Richmond were then ordered out, and the whole of them on the fourth, and ordered not to wait to come in a body, but in detachments as they could assemble. Yet were there not on Friday more than two hundred collected, and they were principally of the town of Richmond.

"4th Objection—That we had not signals.

"Answer—This, though a favorite plan of some gentlemen, and perhaps a practicable one, has hitherto been thought too difficult.

"5th Objection—That we had not look-outs.

"Answer—There had been no cause to order look-outs more than has been ever existing. This is only in fact asking why we do not always keep look-outs.

"6th Objection—That we had not heavy artillery on traveling carriages.

"Answer—The gentlemen who acted as members of the Board of War a twelve-month can answer this question, by giving the character of the artificers whom, during that time, they could never get to mount the heavy artillery. The same reason prevented their being mounted from May 1780 to December. We have even been unable to get those heavy cannon moved from Cumberland by the whole energy of government. A like difficulty which occurred in the removal of those at South Quay, in their day, will convince them of the possibility of this.

"7th Objection—That there was not a body of militia thrown into Portsmouth, the Great Bridge, and Suffolk.

"Answer—In the summer of 1780, we asked the favor of General Nelson, to call together the county lieutenants of the lower counties, and concert the general measures which should be taken for instant opposition, on any invasion, until aid could be ordered by the Executive; and the county lieutenants were ordered to obey his call; he did so the first moment, to wit, on Saturday, December the 31, at eight o'clock, A.M., of our receiving information of the appearance of a fleet in the bay. We asked the favor of General Nelson to go down, which he did, with full powers to call together the militia of any counties he thought proper, to call on the keepers of any public arms or stores, and to adopt for the instant such measures as exigencies required, till we could be better informed.

"Query—Why were not General Nelson, and the brave officers with him, particularly mentioned?

"Answer—What should have been said of them? The enemy did not land, nor give them an opportunity of doing what nobody doubts they would have done; that is, something worthy of being minutely recited.

"Query—Why publish Arnold's letter without General Nelson's answer?

"Answer—Ask the printer. He got neither from the Executive.

"Objection—As to the calling out a few militia, and that late.

"Answer—It is denied that they were few or late. Four thousand and seven hundred men (the number required by Baron Steuben) were called out the moment an invasion was known to have taken place, that is on Tuesday, January 2.

"Objection—The abandonment of York and Portsmouth fortifications.

"Answer—How can they be kept without regulars, on the large scale on which they were formed? Would it be approved of to harass the militia with garrisoning them?" [33]

Meanwhile, as Jefferson says, "to place me on an equal ground for meeting the enquiry, one of the representatives of my county resigned his seat, and I was unanimously elected in his place." [34] James Marks and Isaac Davis were the representatives of Albemarle when the Assembly met in November. On the twenty-first the House resolved that "the said Isaac Davis, by accepting the office of deputy commissary of provisions hath vacated his seat in the House of Delegates as a member from Albemarle." [35] A writ was issued for the election of a new member, and Jefferson was appointed in the place of Davis, "who hath accepted an office for profit." He had written Edmund Randolph, however: "As I go with a single object, I shall withdraw when that is accomplished." [36]

Before the resolution proposing to investigate the conduct of the executive had been introduced into the House, an event had occurred which seemingly gave particular point to this proposal, and which undoubtedly had its influence on Nicholas. This was the famous "raid" on Monticello by Tarleton's troops. No incident in Jefferson's life has given rise to more legends, or more vilification, than this. For not remaining quietly at home and permitting himself to be captured by the enemy, he has, for a century and a half, been accused of cowardice. For taking his family to the safety of his plantation in Bedford and remaining with them after he had been incapacitated by a fall from his horse, he has been doubly condemned. That Edmund Randolph sent his family to Colle [37] when the British approached Williamsburg, that James Monroe wrote "from a small estate of mine in King George, whither I had retired to avoid the enemy, from the one I lately disposed of on the Patommack river," [38] that many members of the legislature had withdrawn with their families to plantations they owned in the back country, is not regarded as reprehensible.

The whisperings started within a few days of Tarleton's enterprise when Eliza Ambler, daughter of Jefferson's successful rival for the hand of Rebecca Burwell, maliciously wrote a friend: "This is not more laughable than the account we have of our illustrious Governor, who, they say, took neither rest nor food, for man or horse, till he reached Carter's Mountain" [39]—adjoining Monticello. Tarleton, who had been dispatched by Lord Cornwallis for the particular purpose of taking the Governor into custody, sought to divert attention from the failure of his mission by observing contemptuously that "the attempt to secure Mr. Jefferson was ineffectual. He discovered the British dragoons from his house, which stands on the point of a mountain, before they could approach him, and he provided for his personal liberty by a precipitate retreat." [40]

Jefferson has left two accounts of this event, one written from notes made at the time, another in answer to the questions of a friend a few years later. There is a third which, although not actually from his pen, is essentially his. This is by Girardin, in the fourth volume of Burk's *History of Virginia*. It was written, as Jefferson says, while Girardin was at "Milton, in this neighborhood, had free access to my papers while composing it, and has given as faithful an account of it as I could myself." [41] It can only be that curious perversion of the human mind which leads it to lend a willing and eager ear to whatever is least creditable that can account for the persistence of the canards and their triumph, even to this day, over the less dramatic actuality.

Jefferson, as we have seen, was at Monticello at this time with his family. John Tyler, the Speaker of the House, the Speaker of the Senate, and certain members of the legislature were staying with him. All were unaware that Lord Cornwallis had detached Tarleton with 180 dragoons and 70 mounted infantry with orders to proceed to Charlottesville, "to charge into town, to continue the confusion of the Americans, and to apprehend, if possible, the Governor and Assembly." [42] About sunrise a certain Captain Jouett, described as an eccentric citizen of Charlottesville, who happened to be in the Cuckoo Tavern at Louisa Court House when the British arrived, reached Monticello by way of the back roads, bringing the news of the enemy's designs. Jefferson put his wife and children in a carriage and sent them to Blenheim, the Carter plantation a few miles distant, where he and his new wife had stopped on their snowy wedding journey to Monticello nearly ten years before. He then turned to packing up such of his papers as had not already been sent to Augusta.[43] Meanwhile he ordered his horse, which was being shod, to be taken to the gate opening on the road leading to Blenheim. He was "still at Monticello making arrangements for his own departure, when a Lieutenant Hudson arrived there at half-speed and informed him that the enemy were then ascending the hill of Monticello. He departed immediately, and, knowing that he would be pursued if he took the high road, he plunged into the woods of the adjoining mountain, where, being at once safe, he proceeded to overtake his family. This is the famous adventure of Carter's Mountain," Jefferson concludes, "which has been so often resounded through the scandalous chronicles of federalism. But they have taken care never to detail the facts, lest they should show that this favorite charge amounted to nothing more than that he did not remain in his house, and there singly fight a whole troop of horse, or suffer himself to be taken prisoner." [44]

Tarleton himself did not go to Monticello but sent a Captain McLeod, who distinguished himself by a decency of conduct quite at variance with that of Cornwallis at Elk Hill. "You ask... details of my sufferings by Colonel Tarleton," Jefferson wrote a friend. "I did not suffer by him. On the contrary, he behaved very genteelly with me. On his approach to Charlottesville, which lay within three miles of my house at Monticello, he dispatched a troop of his horse under Captain McLeod.... He gave strict orders to Captain McLeod to suffer nothing to be impaired," and he "preserved everything with sacred care, during the eighteen hours he remained there." [45]

Jefferson accompanied his family "one day's journey," as he said, then returned to Monticello, where he found Tarleton had retired from Charlottesville after destroying many stores. He then "rejoined his family and proceeded with them to Poplar Forest, his plantation in Bedford, about eighty miles southwest." [46] It would appear that the journey to Poplar Forest took place from June 12-14, for on these days Jefferson notes paying for "entertainment at Amherst Court House £30," paying "Colonel H. Rose [of Amherst] for corn, etc., £150," and paying "at Lynch's Ferry [now Lynchburg] on acc't of ferriage £120." [47] Whether he passed by Elk Hill at this time, which seems most improbable, or whether he had gone there after the seventeenth of May—there are no entries in his account book from May 18-26—he had, as he says in his account of Cornwallis's depredations, "had time to remove most of the effects out of the house." [48]

After leaving Charlottesville, Tarleton and his troops converged on Point of Fork. Here he joined Cornwallis's army, which was gathered on the north shore of the James. According to custom, Cornwallis had taken as his headquarters the handsomest place in the neighborhood. This was Elk Hill, that lordly estate on an eminence above the James, overlooking the broad and fertile valley. He used the ten days of his stay to plunder and ravage the plantation and the neighborhood with a thoroughness remarkable even for the British. "He destroyed all my growing crops of corn and tobacco," Jefferson writes, "he burned all my barns, containing the same articles of the last year, having first taken what corn he wanted; he used, as was to be expected, all my stock of cattle, sheep, and hogs for the sustenance of his army, and carried off all the horses capable of service; of those too young for service, he cut the throats; and he burned all the fences on the plantation so as to leave it an absolute waste. He carried off, also, about thirty slaves. Had this been to give their freedom, he would have done right; but it was to consign them to inevitable death from the smallpox and putrid fever then raging in his camp. This I knew afterwards to be the fate of twenty-seven of them." [49]

In his Farm Book, containing the records of his various plantations, there is a concise and dispassionate table of his "Other Losses by the British." It forms an imposing monument to the ruthlessness and brutality of the British commander. Included, in part, are 9 blooded mares, colts, and plow horses; 59 cattle; 60 hogs; 200 barrels of corn in the house, 500 growing and destroyed; 250 pounds of hemp in the house and an equal quantity destroyed; 29 hogsheads of tobacco, 230 pounds of cotton; and 1,000 panels of fence destroyed. The number of slaves lost from his several plantations, some of whom fled to the enemy and died, others who returned and then died, number 32.[50] It was no inconsiderable loss even for a wealthy man.

"When I say that Lord Cornwallis did all this," Jefferson observes, "I do not mean that he carried about the torch in his own hands, but that it was done under his eye, the situation of the house in which he was, commanding a view of every part of the plantation, so that he must have seen every fire. I relate these things on my own knowledge, in a great degree, as I was on the ground soon after he left it. He treated the rest of the neighborhood somewhat in the same style, but not with that spirit of total extermination with which he seemed to rage over my possessions." [51]

Following these events, Jefferson devoted part of the summer to the defense of his conduct as governor which he would present to the Assembly. The charge of lack of timely orders to the specified counties calling the militia seems to have stung Jefferson to the quick, to judge by the evidence he has left us. A letter was sent by the faithful Jupiter to Hugh Rose, county lieutenant of Amherst, asking for a statement of the facts. Rose replied on September 26: "Herewith you will receive my affidavit with my certificate agreeable to your request in your favor by Jupiter. If either of them, from my aversion to prolixity, should not contain a due portion of the facts which came within my knowledge, I hope you will not scruple to require my attendance upon the Assembly, for be assured that no person will more readily step forth in exculpation of injured virtue, as far as integrity and honor will permit, than your affectionate friend and servant." [52] The affidavit reads: "On Tuesday evening, the second of last January (being in Richmond), I received a letter from the Governor earnestly requesting me to take charge of and to convey by some safe hand, the dispatches therein enclosed; they were for the commanding officers of Albemarle, Amherst, Fluvanna, and Goochland, requiring them immediately to send forth certain proportions of their militia in order to oppose Arnold, whose movements indicated an intention of penetrating into the country.

"After having received the said dispatches, and having dismissed the messenger, reflecting upon my situation (my horses not having arrived and that period being uncertain), I was very uneasy and resolved to deliver them to His Excellency the next morning; but fortunately, as I conceived, shortly after daylight on Wednesday morning I met with Colonel Wall of Rockingham on his passage home, to whom (as his route was through the counties of Goochland and Albemarle) I delivered the dispatches of those counties with the Governor's pressing injunctions for the speedy and safe delivery of them. I waited upon the county lieutenant of Goochland the next day with other dispatches, and he informed me that he had received those sent by Colonel Wall on the preceding evening." [53]

Rose likewise enclosed a second statement designed to settle the matter completely: "I do hereby certify that on the twenty-second of March last, the Executive granted a suspension from the draft of the militia of this county until further orders, which suspension was taken off by an order of Council dated April the twelfth, which order I received about the eighteenth of the same month and drafted the militia on the eighteenth day of May." [54]

The Assembly was due to meet in Richmond on the first of October. As no quorum could be obtained, it was not until the twenty-sixth of November that the matter of the investigation was finally taken up. It was "Resolved that the House will, on Wednesday the twelfth of December next, proceed, agreeable to a resolution of the twelfth of

June last, to enquire into the conduct of the Executive of this state for the last twelve months next preceding the resolution; and that, as well the information against the said Executive, as their defense, be received and heard on that day. Ordered that a committee be appointed to state any charges, and receive such information as may be offered, respecting the administration of the Executive. . . . And a committee was appointed of Messrs. Banister, Tyler, Nicholas, Southall, and Morgan." Jefferson's ordeal was, apparently, to be long drawn out.

On November 30 the Assembly expressed its confidence in the former governor, whom his enemies have pictured as being under a dark cloud, by conferring another distinction, as well as obligation, upon him. On that day "the House proceeded in the same manner, to the choice of a delegate to represent this Commonwealth in Congress until the first Monday in November next in the room of John Blair, Esq., who hath resigned." [55] John Page, Banister, and Alexander were appointed a committee to act with the Senate. It did no harm that Page was Jefferson's oldest friend and that Banister had sat with him in the House of Burgesses from 1769 to 1771, in the Virginia Convention of 1776, and in the Continental Congress. Jefferson was duly elected, and publicly vindicated by this show of confidence, but he resigned the appointment on December 19—the day he was cleared of Nicholas's charges and received the thanks of the legislature for his services.[56]

Again his friends shook their heads, and the cronies, Pendleton and Madison, exchanged opinions. "Mr. Jefferson, I am told," the former writes, "declines coming to Congress, nor do I learn that they purpose choosing another in his room." [57] In his reply of January 8, 1782, Madison regrets "the refusal of Mr. Jefferson to become a member of the Virginia delegation, not only as it deprives his country of that particular service, but I fear it proceeds from a fixed disinclination to all public employments." [58]

Meanwhile, on December 12, "Mr. Banister reported from the committee appointed to state any charges and receive such information as might be offered respecting the administration of the late Executive, that the committee did, according to order, convene for that

RETIREMENT AND VINDICATION 257

purpose...that the committee had come to a resolution thereupon. ...Resolved, that in the opinion of the committee, that the said rumors were groundless." [59]

The *Journal* of the House gives no further clue as to who spoke, what was said, or who was present. Neither does Jefferson elaborate on the event. From Edmund Randolph's account, however, it is not difficult to reconstruct the scene. The tall, spare figure of the accused rises before us as he stood in his seat, challenging his peers to condemn him. The certainty of his rightness, of his unselfish devotion to duty and to his country, fills us who relive it, as it did those who sat before him. "He appeared at that session," says Randolph, "as a delegate from Albemarle, and at the appointed day called for some accusation." Silence seems to have fallen over the House. George Nicholas, who "before that day became better satisfied as to what had been done," was not present "to bring forward the enquiry." [60] "Neither of those gentlemen [Nicholas and Henry] having pledged themselves to become prosecutors," Randolph continues, "they did not feel it a personal duty on either to appear as such. But Mr. Jefferson did not affect to be ignorant of the general imputation, which had been circulated, but was destitute of any precise shape. In an address to the House which amounted to a challenge of impeachment, he reviewed his administration so as to draw forth votes of eulogism.... He ought to have been satisfied, because they were the individual voice of his country, which had been prejudiced against him." [61]

Immediately Jefferson was seated—and we can be sure the room resounded with applause—the House resolved "that the sincere thanks of the General Assembly be given to our former governor, Thomas Jefferson, Esquire, for his impartial, upright, and attentive administration while in office. The Assembly wish, in the strongest manner, to declare the high opinion which they entertain of Mr. Jefferson's ability, rectitude, and integrity, as Chief Magistrate of this Commonwealth, and mean, by thus publicly avowing their opinion, to obviate and remove all unmerited censure." [62]

The news spread rapidly. Christmas Day found Madison writing Pendleton: "It gives me great pleasure to hear of the honorable acquittal of Mr. Jefferson. I know his abilities, and I think I know his fidelity and zeal for his country so well, that I am persuaded it was a just one. We are impatient to know whether he will undertake the new service to which he is called." [63] To this Pendleton replied on the thirty-first: "Since my last Mr. Jefferson's honorable acquittal of the loose censure thrown out at random on his character hath come to my hand, which I doubt not you'll have published in one of the Philadelphia papers, that this stain may be wiped out wherever it may have reached." [64]

Never was a man more completely vindicated, or more gloriously.

MARQUIS DE MARBOIS. From the engraving after the portrait at Versailles. (*Courtesy of the Frick Art Reference Library*)

THE NATURAL BRIDGE. From the engraving in the *Columbian Magazine*, September, 1787

XI. The Notes on Virginia

JEFFERSON SPENT the weeks immediately following his retirement from the governorship with his family at Poplar Forest, as we have seen. It was a period of complete seclusion—so complete that it is almost impossible to penetrate it. No letters which might give a clue to his thoughts and activities seem to have been written during this June, and there are only a scant dozen entries in his account book—none at all for the ten days from the eighteenth to the twenty-eighth of the month.

He had not been forgotten by the world, however. On June 14 Congress had resolved "that four persons be joined to Mr. Adams in negotiating a peace between these United States and Great Britain." One of these was Thomas Jefferson. The following day Samuel Huntington, president of Congress, wrote him that "a negotiation for peace between the belligerent powers may probably take place through the mediation of the Empress of Russia and the Emperor of Germany,"[1] and informed him of his appointment. The letter was transmitted to Jefferson through Lafayette and reached him on July 9. It was not until August 4, however, that he brought himself to reply. A much interlined draught, concealing the bitterness that filled his heart, yet showing how difficult a decision it was to make, is preserved among his papers.[2] "I fully feel," he writes, "how honorable is the confidence which Congress has been pleased to repose in me by their appointment to the high and arduous duty of assisting in the negotiations for peace, and do sincerely lament the existence of circumstances which take from me the right of accepting so desirable an office."

The accompanying letter to Lafayette reveals his true feelings as no official document could. He thanks the Marquis for his "kind sentiments and friendly offers on the occasion, which, that I cannot avail myself of, has given me more mortification than almost any occurrence of my life. I lose an opportunity, the only one I ever had, and perhaps ever shall have, of combining public service with private gratification; of seeing countries whose improvements in science, in arts and civilization it has been my fortune to admire at a distance but never to see, and at the same time of lending further aid to a cause which has been handed on from its first organization to its present stage by every effort of which my poor faculties were capable. These, however, have not been such as to give satisfaction to some of my countrymen, and it has become necessary for me to remain in the state till a later period in the present year than is consistent with an acceptance of what has been offered me." [3]

Meriwether Smith of Essex, one of the Virginia delegates to Congress at this time, sensing the state of mind of the late governor, thought it wise to add a few words of persuasion—as well as to point out to whom credit for the appointment was due. "Congress having received some important communications from the Minister Plenipotentiary of France respecting the intentions of the courts of Petersburgh and Vienna," he writes on June 21, "have come to some determinations thereupon which are not only interesting to the United States in general but to the state of Virginia in particular. I took the liberty therefore to insist that you should be added to the ministers of these states already in Europe, that the state of Virginia particularly and the United States in general might have the benefit of your abilities in a negotiation that may probably take place. I am not at liberty to communicate to you briefly by a letter the objects that will require your attention, or the nature of the restrictions by which you will be bound. You will therefore not be able to determine whether the Embassy will be agreeable and honorable, but I am confident that you cannot fail of rendering very essential services to the state by your intimate knowledge of its interests, and I am persuaded that it can only be requisite to suggest to you that the business will be very important and your usefulness in negotiating it very great, to induce you to accept the appointment." [4]

Jefferson's declination, which was read in Congress on August 27, came as a shock to some of his co-workers in the cause of freedom. Edmund Randolph, another delegate, refused to accept a negative answer. In a letter of September 7, referring to an earlier one from Jefferson, seemingly not preserved, he assures his friend that European affairs will "probably bear greater delay than you apprehended. What you call your temporary disability will be removed early enough to allow you to reach France by January.... These considerations fully answer your objection, and give me an opportunity of wishing for authority to say that you will embark upon the Embassy." [5]

In his reply, dated the sixteenth, Jefferson, after rehearsing the reasons given Lafayette for declining, continues: "Were it possible for me to determine again to enter into public business, there is no appointment whatever which would have been so agreeable to me. But I have taken my final leave of everything of that nature. I have retired to my farm, my family, and my books, from which I think nothing will evermore separate me." [6] He might well have added the sentiment he had expressed to Lafayette in the preceding letter: "The independence of private life under the protection of republican laws will, I hope, yield me that happiness from which no slave is so remote as the minister of a commonwealth." [7]

To Randolph was left the last word, and a rather bitter one it was. He writes on October 9: "I was much distressed on the receipt of your late favor by Mrs. Randolph, to find your irrevocable purpose of sequestering yourself to public life. If you can justify this resolution to yourself, I am confident that you cannot to the world. There remains now no alternative but either to consign southern interests wholly to the management of our present ministers, or to interdict them for the exercise of all discretionary power." [8]

Even Madison, his disciple and great admirer, was constrained to observe: "Great as is my partiality to Mr. Jefferson, the mode in which he seems determined to revenge the wrong received from his country does not appear to me to be dictated either by philosophy or patriotism. It argues, indeed, a keen sensibility and strong consciousness of rectitude. But this sensibility ought to be as great towards the relentings of the misdoings of the legislature, not to mention the injustice of visiting the faults of this body on their innocent constituents." [9]

Meanwhile, during the latter half of June—the exact date is not known—Jefferson was thrown from his horse and suffered injuries which kept him at home for some time. The first record we have of his going abroad again is on July 15, when he notes that he "gave guide on the way to Johnson's Mountains £15." Joseph Jones likewise speaks of having received a letter from him saying that he was at Bowling Green on the sixteenth, on his way home, "where I hope you will in future continue in safety, undisturbed by his lordship's plundering parties." [10]

Jefferson used this period of enforced inactivity to start writing his celebrated *Notes on Virginia*. They were inspired almost by an accident. Early in 1781 Joseph Jones of King George County, at that time a member of the Continental Congress, put in Jefferson's hands, as he says, "a paper containing sundry inquiries into the present state of Virginia." They had been formulated by the Marquis François de Barbé-Marbois, secretary of the French legation in Philadelphia, who is described by John Sullivan, in transmitting similar inquiries from that gentleman to the president of New Hampshire, as "one of those useful geniuses who is constantly in search of knowledge." [11] Arriving, as they did, in the turmoil following Arnold's invasion, the queries seem to have been momentarily laid aside. On the fifth of February Marbois wrote the Governor a letter recalling them. This Jefferson acknowledged on March 4, saying that he had intended answering some of the queries, but that he was not in the position to do so at once. "Hitherto," he writes, "it has been in my power to collect a few materials only, which my present occupations disable me from completing. I mean, however, shortly to be in a condition which will leave me quite at leisure to take them up, when it shall be one of my first undertakings to give you as full information as I shall be able to do on such of the subjects as are within the sphere of my acquaintance." [12]

True to his word, Jefferson now devoted his first leisure to this task. He had always, as he says, "made it a practice, whenever opportunity occurred, of obtaining any information of our country, which might be of use to me in any station, public or private, to commit it to writing. These memoranda were on loose papers, bundled up without order, and difficult of recurrence, when I had occasion for a particular one. I thought this a good occasion," he continues, "to embody their substance, which I did in the order of Mr. Marbois's queries, so as to answer his wish and to arrange them for my own use." [13] Characteristically, the result was not a series of hasty or cut-and-dried observations, but a learned treatise on his country, one in which he took under consideration its topography, its resources, and its natural history, as well as the inhabitants, their laws, and their customs. Everything that could be said or known about Virginia in the last quarter of the eighteenth century is embraced in this slender but compact little volume.

Marbois's request was the stimulus that was needed for Jefferson to set in order his thoughts on scientific subjects, particularly as applied to Virginia. As early as June 8, 1778, he had written Giovanni Fabbroni, the young Tuscan of whom we have already spoken: "Though much of my time is employed in the councils of America, I have yet a little leisure to indulge my fondness for philosophical studies. I could wish to correspond with you on subjects of that kind. It might not be unacceptable to you to be informed, for instance, of the true power of our climate, discoverable from the thermometer, from the force and direction of the winds, the quantity of rain, the plants which grow without shelter in winter, etc. I wish I could gratify your botanical taste," he adds, "but I am acquainted with nothing more than the first principles of that science; yet myself and my friends may furnish you with any botanical subjects which this country affords, and are not to be had with you." [14] The seeds of the *Notes on Virginia* are implanted in this letter.

The work on the *Notes* was interrupted during the summer of 1781 by Jefferson's preparation for his appearance before the House of Delegates to answer the charges against the executive. It was not until December 20 that he was able to write Marbois: "I now do myself the honor of enclosing you answers to the queries which Mr. Jones put in my hands. I fear your patience has been exhausted in attending them, but I beg you to be assured there has been no avoidable delay on my part. I retired from the public service in June only, and after that the general confusion of our state put it out of my power to procure the informations necessary until lately. Even now you will find them very imperfect and not worth offering but as proof of my respect for your wishes. I have taken the liberty of referring you to my friend, Mr. Charles Thomson, for a perusal of them when convenient to you. Particular reasons subsisting between him and myself induced me to give you this trouble." [15]

Jefferson wrote the same day to Thomson, *à propos* of his own election to the Council of the American Philosophical Society: "I received notice from the secretary of the American Philosophical Society some time ago that they had done me the honor of appointing me a counselor of that body.[16] The particular duties of that office I am quite a stranger to, and indeed know too little the nature of their institution to judge what objects it comprehends. In framing answers to some queries which M. Marbois sent me, it occurred to me that some of the subjects which I had then occasion to take up might, if more fully handled, be a proper tribute to the Philosophical Society, and the aversion I have of being counted as a drone in any society induced me to determine to recur to you, as my ancient friend, to ask the favor of you to peruse those answers and to take the trouble of communicating to me whether any and which of the subjects there treated would come within the scope of that learned institution, and to what degree of minuteness one should descend in treating it. Perhaps also you would be so friendly as to give me some idea of the subjects which would at any time be admissible into their transactions. Had I known nothing but the load of business under which you labor, I should not have ventured on the application, but, knowing your friendly disposition also, I thought you would take some spare half hour to satisfy a friend....

"P.S. I have mentioned to M. Marbois my request to you to ask of him the perusal of the paper I sent him without, however, communicating the purpose of that request." [17]

It was not until March 9, 1782, that the busy Thomson, who was secretary of the Continental Congress, replied. He had waited on Marbois and learned that the answers to the queries had not yet arrived. After expounding the purposes and interests of the Philosophical Society he goes on to say: "I am well persuaded that your answers to M. Marbois's queries would be a very acceptable present to the Society. This country affords to philosophic view an extensive, rich, and unexplored field. The history, manners, and customs of the aborigines is little known. It abounds in roots, plants, trees, and minerals to the virtues and uses of which we are yet stranger. What the soil is capable of can only be guessed at, and found by experiment.... The mind of man," he sagely adds, "is just awakening from a long stupor of many ages to the discovery of useful arts and inventions. Our governments are yet unformed and capable of great improvements. The history, manners, and customs of the aborigines are but little known. These and a thousand other subjects which will readily suggest themselves, open an inexhaustible mine to men of a contemplative and philosophical turn. And I therefore, though I regret your retiring from the busy, anxious scenes of politics, yet I congratulate posterity on the advantage they may derive from your philosophical researches." [18]

In writing his *Notes on Virginia* Jefferson was following in the footsteps of several worthy predecessors. Curiosity about this golden land had tormented the adventurous minded of the Old World from the time of its settlement. In 1588 Thomas Harriot, a member of the colony founded on Roanoke Island three years before, published the first account: *A Briefe and True Report of the New Found Land of Virginia, of Its Commodities, and of the Nature and Manner of the Naturall Inhabitants.* It was divided into three parts: "Of Marchantable Commodities," "Of Suche Commodities as Virginia is Known to Yielde for Victual and Sustenance of Man," and "Of such other Things as is be Hoofull for Those which shall Plant and Inhabit to Know of." [19] A glowing account, designed to foster colonization, it is not an insignificant antecedent of Jefferson's *Notes*, both in subject matter and treatment.

In 1684 the Reverend John Clayton, rector of Croften at Wakefield in Yorkshire, undertook a voyage to the New World. He was a man of keen intelligence, well abreast of the best scientific knowledge of his time. He carried with him his scientific apparatus, but it was lost at sea, and thus he was not able to make as careful a study as he had intended. In Virginia he made the acquaintance of John Banister, "a gentleman pretty curious in these things, [who] showed me likewise the joint of a whale's back-bone and several teeth, some whereof, he said, were found in hills beyond the fall of James River." [20] The result of his two years' stay in the colony was contained in a report to the Royal Society of London, *An Account of Several Observables in Virginia*, wherein he discourses "Of the Aire," "Of the Waters," "Of the Earth and Soyle," and "Of the Birds."

A less well-known book was written by a certain Frenchman named Durand, who describes himself as *"exilé pour la religion."* He made a trip to America at about the same time, which he described in his *Voyage d'un Français—avec une description de Virginie*, published in the Hague in 1687. It is remarkably sophisticated for the period, much more so than the two works just mentioned. The climate, the topography, the rivers—in which the James becomes the *"Gemerive"*—and the towns—of which he says *"il n'y a ni ville ni village qu'un seul nommé Jemeston"*—are described in detail, as well as the civil and military organization of the counties, the Indians, the Negroes, the domestic and wild animals, and *"les arbres de la Virginie."*

The most glowing of all these early descriptions is undoubtedly that of a Swiss gentleman whose account of the wonders of Virginia was published by the Helvatische Societät in 1737, under the well-chosen title *Neu gefundenes Eden*. He was taken under the wing of William Byrd (described as Wilhelm Vogel) and conducted by that gentleman in a gold-painted barge up the James and the Appomattox to the wilds of the Roanoke, where Byrd sold him a plot of land 26 miles long by 3/7 miles wide for £3,000 sterling. Despite this, Virginia was to this stranger "a new-found Eden," and there is no phase of it, its vegetation, animals, minerals, its life, customs, government, and religion, that does not come under his observation. He concludes, with modesty: *"Man kann mit Wahrheit sagen dass Virginien die schönste und fruchtbarste Provinz welche die Krone von England in Amerika hat, ist."* [21]

Two other works which preceded Jefferson's, although not dealing with Virginia, were the extraordinary *Nord-Amerikanischer Weg-*

weiser in Sonderheit von Carolina, by J. N. Ochs, published in Bern in 1711, giving unusually detailed descriptions of the weather, the natural resources, the rivers, the coast, the animals, birds, and vegetation. John Brickell's *Natural History of North Carolina* appeared in London in 1737 and attempted the same sort of thing, but it is much more archaic in character than the *Wegweiser*, to say nothing of the *Notes on Virginia*.

It is difficult, if not impossible, to ascertain with how many of these early books Jefferson was acquainted. His catalogue of 1783, on which we must largely depend for what we know of the books he owned before that period, does not show that he had any of them. Neither does he mention them in the footnotes to his *Notes*. This, however, can by no means be considered conclusive evidence.

One work, however, with which we know Jefferson was familiar is Thomas Hutchins's *Topographical Description of Virginia, Pennsylvania, Maryland, and North Carolina, Comprehending the rivers Ohio, Kenhawa... Illinois, Mississippi*, etc. published in 1778. This remarkable book by a remarkable man, who was first a professional soldier, subsequently geographer of the United States, is one on which Jefferson leaned heavily in his discussion of the character of the western lands and rivers. Hutchins had first traveled to this country in July 1760. In 1766 he made a trip down the Ohio River, and his map *The Courses of the Ohio River* was the result of this expedition. *A New Map of the Western parts of Virginia, Pennsylvania, Maryland and North Carolina* accompanied his *Topographical Description*,[22] and Jefferson makes acknowledgment to this in speaking of the drawing of his own map for the *Notes on Virginia*. There is likewise, among the Jefferson Papers, a letter from Hutchins dated February 11, 1784, discussing the times of flood of the great rivers, the distances from various points, and the length of time consumed in making a voyage from one to the other, which gives us a clue as to the period these observations were embodied in the *Notes*.

In the field of botany, to which large sections of the *Notes* are devoted, Jefferson had likewise had some distinguished predecessors. John Banister, who had come to Virginia before 1668, published in 1686 his *Catalogus Plantarum in Virginia Observatarum*, the earliest contribution on this subject in America. Dr. John Mitchell, settled on the Rappahannock early in the eighteenth century, had likewise added to the knowledge of this science; as did another John Clayton, of Gloucester County, Virginia. He was a correspondent of Linnaeus, Gronovius, and Collinson, and is described by the latter in 1764 as "the greatest botanist in America." Jefferson says of him in the *Notes:* "This accurate observer was a native and resident of this state, passed a long life in exploring and describing its plants, and is supposed to have enlarged the botanical catalogue as much as almost any man who has lived." [23] His *Flora Virginica,* completed by Gronovius, the famous Dutch botanist, from specimens collected by Clayton, appeared in 1739.[24] There was also Peter Kalm, often mentioned in the *Notes,* who came to America in 1748 "on Linnaeus's recommendation," and spent three years studying the flowers and plants of North America. Nor must one forget Jefferson's own grandfather, Isham Randolph, friend of Peter Collinson, the distinguished naturalist, who undoubtedly did much to arouse his grandson's interest in botany and the natural sciences.

Jefferson's early life coincided with that period of intense interest in natural phenomena which characterized the first part of the eighteenth century—and America was a virgin field. As he wrote Joseph Willard, president of Harvard College: "What a field have we at our doors to signalize ourselves in! The botany of America is far from being exhausted, its mineralogy is untouched, and its natural history or zoology totally mistaken and misrepresented." [25] In 1749 Buffon, the French naturalist, had electrified the world with the first three volumes of his *Histoire Naturelle* and earned for himself the distinction of being the first scientist to present in a popular and easily understood manner what had hitherto seemed to be the mysteries of natural science. Jefferson early acquired the edition of 1752 and continued his subscription to the work until the final volumes had appeared. Indeed, he subsequently owned other editions, including one presented by the author. There is no doubt that Buffon, however indirectly, had considerable influence upon Jefferson's *Notes.* On the appearance of the latter he was to take issue with Buffon in certain important respects and to engage in a spirited controversy with the Frenchman and his partisans.

It is unfortunate that we cannot entirely reconstruct the circle of friends and correspondents who shared these interests with Jefferson, and that the philosophical speculations in which they were fond of indulging are lost to us. Attendance at the Continental Congress in Philadelphia gave him the opportunity of meeting men whose thoughts and interests coincided with his own—notably David Rittenhouse and Charles Thomson, whose observations on the *Notes*, which he ultimately saw in manuscript, Jefferson considered as having "too much merit not to be communicated." He thus printed them as an appendix to the original edition. There were also General John Sullivan and General William Whipple, both of New Hampshire, with whom he was later to be in correspondence concerning the moose, elk, and caribou. Francis Hopkinson's ingenious turn of mind led to a voluminous interchange of letters on scientific subjects. "I shall be happy in corresponding with you," Hopkinson wrote his new friend, "if you give me any encouragement. My fancy suggests a thousand whims which die for want of communication—nor would I communicate them, but to one who has discernment to conceive my humors and candor with respect to my faults and peculiarities—such a friend I believe you to be." [26] A man "with a thousand whims" was born to be a delight to Jefferson.

From the few letters of this period that are preserved, we know that Jefferson was likewise in correspondence on scientific subjects with certain old friends who had long shared his interests. One of these was George Rogers Clark. In a letter of November 26, 1782, printed in all the editions of Jefferson's works as addressed to James Steptoe, but in fact written to Clark, as a comparison with the manuscript proves, Jefferson says: "I received in August your favor wherein you give me hopes of being able to procure for me some of the big bones. I should be unfaithful to my own feeling, were I not to express to you how much I am obliged to your attentions to the requests I made on that subject. A specimen of each of the several species of bones now to be found is to me the most desirable objects in natural history, and there is no expense of package or safe transportation which I will not gladly reimburse, to procure them safely. Elk horns of very extraordinary size, or anything else uncommon, would be very acceptable. New London in Bedford, Staunton in Augusta, or Fredericksburg are places whence I can surely get them. Mr. Steptoe in the first place, Colonel Matthews in the second, Mr. Dick in the third, will take care of them for me.[27] Any observations of your own on the subject of the big bones, or their history, or anything else in the western country, will come acceptably to me, because I know you see the works of nature in the great and not merely in detail. Descriptions of animals, vegetables, minerals, or other curious things; notes as to the Indians, information of the country between the Mississippi, and waters of the South Sea, etc., will strike your mind as worthy of being communicated." [28]

A further indication of the painstaking study Jefferson gave these scientific topics is to be found in a folder of miscellaneous papers containing well over a hundred pages of memoranda used in the preparation of the *Notes*, preserved in the Coolidge Collection at the Massachusetts Historical Society. Aside from various tables, notes to himself, corrigenda, addenda, and so on, these papers are particularly interesting as disclosing the names of some of the persons from whom he secured certain information described in the *Notes* as "reliable." Not all are in his hand, and not all the handwriting is readily identifiable, except that of Charles Thomson, whose observations, which became an appendix, are here included. Thus we learn, although no letter is preserved to tell us so, that Dr. Thomas Walker informed Jefferson he had known of a buffalo weighing 1,800 pounds, and John Bolling, a relative-in-law, "acknowledges" a deer of 230 pounds, whereas Jefferson had considered 175 pounds a maximum weight. A hog raised by one Millar in Augusta weighed 1,100 pounds, and a beef killed by Colonel Ingles tipped the scales at 1,500. His friend, Isaac Zane, had a horse 5 feet 8 inches, weighing 1,366 pounds, and Colonel Cary knew of a bear weighing 410 pounds.

A note from an unidentified writer informs Jefferson that catalpa trees, the name of which comes from the Indians of Carolina, "begin to appear about the north limit of the 37°'" (i.e. about Halifax County). He likewise sends notes on various birds, such as the night hawk, redbird, woodcock, and others, and says that he has "seen certificates in the hands of several respectable officers that a buck was killed near Presque Isle weighing 273 stones. Observed deer near Pittsburg are much larger than they are here, and further south much less." There is also information on the turtles of the Ohio, snakes, and lizards. This same correspondent contributes "a table of American animals that I am acquainted with, of the weights now ascertained or different from my experience or opinion," subsequently included in Jefferson's table of quadrupeds.

Much of this material in regard to plant and bird life as related to climate, is embodied in the seventh query, "A notice of all what can increase the progress of Human Knowledge." Jefferson uses this broad heading to embark upon a detailed account of the climate of Virginia in which he includes the country as far west as the Mississippi. Again he proved himself a pioneer and a leader. No such extensive observations had hitherto been made by any writer on Virginia. From early manhood Jefferson had been interested in the weather and had made it a practice to "make two observations a day, the one as early as possible in the morning, the other from 3 to 4 o'clock, because I have found 4 o'clock the hottest and daylight the coldest point of the 24 hours." [29] It was his custom to exchange data on the weather with various friends and correspondents, and he thus built up an unequaled knowledge of all phases of it, heat, cold, frost, winds, and the change of climate he believed was "taking place very sensibly."

Also included among these memoranda is a letter dated Tuckahoe, October 12, 1783. It is not in the hand of Colonel Thomas Mann Randolph, as we might have expected from the address. The writer had the advantage of having been in Europe, however, and was thus able to compare various American animals with European. His spelling and construction may have been bizarre, but his knowledge was valuable. It was likewise incorporated in Jefferson's table. His letter reads, in part, "I am sorry I have not been more attentive to the waights of many wild anamals for except a bear, an elk and several bucks, I never waighed any. I saw in England a panther said to be from the coast Gunia and a wolf said to be from Germany, both full grown, and I can assure you I have seen of both kinds much larger in Virginia. I killed a bear, not fat, which weighed 410 lb. after he was quartered, and have seen much larger but had no opportunity of trying their waight. My largest elk, a doe of 4 years old, waighed 83 per quarter. The largest buck, say bear, I ever killed waighed 42 per quarter. It was in August. They are not full fatt before November and it was thought had he lived to be so he would have reached 48 or 50. He was the largest I ever saw killed. But I have been told by Colonel Gist he has killed them about Pittsburg that have waighed upwards of 200, I think one 220.

"The same gentleman peforms me, for I let him see your letter this last week, he has seen elks which he judged to be 14½ hands high, and one that waighed nigh 600. He waighed a bull buffalo far from being fat, 1150; has killed much larger but no opportunity of finding their waight. Our foxes are not so large as the European, nor do I think [page torn] the same animal, as I am sure our hair [hare] is very [page torn]. More than once in the summer when pursued like the rabbit, of whose kindred she is, takes the first hole she can find for shelter. She is less than the English hare and the same size of their wild rabbit.

"Raccoons and Possums I never heard they had of either, for Europe. The former is about the size of their badger and not much unlike him. I killed in England a mink. Ours are in size and shape the same. Our ratts and mice do not so difference from the European.... I once saw what is called a hedge hog. It was killed by one of my overseers. It resembled in part the English hedge hog but much larger. I am told they are frequently seen in the mountains. We have a small anamal at about the size of our fox called a moonack. I have killed several but believe they have none in England. They burrow in the earth are rather darker than a raccoon and fight very fierce. You must have seen the polecat.

"As to domestic anamals I am fully sattisfied we have as large as any to be found, but as to the horse and ox I wish you to apply to the northward where, being better farmers, they are larger than with us. ... I have seen as large dogs and catts as I have ever seen in England and have raised hounds much larger than I ever saw there. The heaviest hog I ever saw reached 900 but Col. Tucker killed one the net weight above 2000. I have seen several mules nigh 15 hands. Sons of Midas. I have a pack two years old of his getting which is upwards of 13 hands and will be larger than his father. They have in Kent and about the fens in Linconshire very large sheep, much larger than in Virginia. The heaviest I ever saw here was 103 fit for market. I have frequently killed them above 90. . . .

"You observe that our elk is taken for the fallow dear. They are almost as unlike as the monkey and fox. Their horns are totally dissimilar. . . . I have seen a pair of elks horns 12 points on a beam, the extreme points of which measured 4 feet from one point to the other and were very nigh five feet in length. I have heard of larger.

"I think I have mensioned all the anamals I am acquainted with and have given as just an account of them as is in my power," he concludes. He cannot refrain, however, from uttering the philosophical observation that he believes it "proceeds from vanity in the European gentlemen who not only think our anamals less than theirs but assume as great a superiority to their minds as they do to the size of their anamals. Would to heaven we had the same opportunity of cultivating the mind as they have, and I verily believe we should exceed them as much as the people of Attaca did those of Beotia."

Although the *Notes* were sent to Marbois in December 1781, Jefferson considered them, as he many times repeated, very imperfect and far from complete. He continued to work on them, and the following winter he "somewhat corrected and enlarged them." He seems to have made one or more copies,[30] and these he handed to various friends for comment and criticism. One of them was Van Hogendorp, the gifted young Dutchman whose acquaintance Jefferson had made in Annapolis. "The condition in which you first saw them," he wrote after sending Hogendorp a printed copy, "would prove to you how hastily they had been originally written, as you may remember the numerous insertions I had made in them from time to time, when I could find a moment for turning to them from other occupations."[31] Another was the Marquis of Chastellux, whom Jefferson had first met in the spring of 1782 and whose "'worth and abilities," he says, "had impressed me with an affection for him which, under the then prospect of never seeing him again, was perhaps imprudent." The Marquis had a passion for natural history second only to Jefferson's own, some of which found expression in his *Voyages dans l'Amérique septentrionale dans les années 1780-81-82.* When Chastellux was preparing to return to Europe in December 1782, Jefferson, who at that time expected to go abroad as one of the ministers to negotiate peace, planned to travel with Chastellux, "fondly measuring your affections by my own," as he wrote, "and presuming your consent.... This will give me full leisure to learn the result of your observation on the Natural Bridge, to communicate to you my answers to the queries of M. Marbois, to receive edification from you on these and other subjects of science, considering chess too as a matter of science."[32] The proposed journey failed to take place, but Jefferson found another opportunity of securing the Marquis's opinion of his work.

Word of Jefferson's *Notes* gradually got about among the inner circle of intellectuals and demands to see them became constantly more pressing and incessant. Interest in natural history was as keen among the cultivated men of that day as it was in music during the peace of the nineteenth century, and as it is in economics in the chaos of today. When Jefferson returned to the Continental Congress in Philadelphia in the winter of 1783, he contemplated having a few copies printed there for distribution among his friends. Unfortunately he encountered a problem familiar to most promoters of such an enterprise—a rise in the cost of printing. As he wrote Thomson in May 1784, a few weeks before sailing for Europe: "My matter in the printing way is dropped. Aitken had formerly told me that he would print it for £ 4 a sheet. He now asks £5/10s, which raises the price from £ 48 to £ 66; but what was a more effectual and insuperable bar was that he could not complete it under three weeks, a time I could not wait for it. Dunlap happened to be out of town, so I relinquished the plan. Perhaps I may have a few copies struck off in Paris if there be an English printer."[33] Thus it happened that Jefferson carried the *Notes* with him to Paris, where they were printed in the spring of 1785 and where the matter of their publication, as we shall see, became an infinitely complicated and involved affair.

The Marquis de Marbois had submitted twenty-three queries, designed to give his government a complete picture of the state of Virginia—its history, its activities, its physical aspect and resources. They ranged from questions concerning the boundaries, rivers, seaports, mountains, climate, military and marine forces, to its laws, its constitution, its counties, towns, colleges, religion, manners, manufacture, and commerce, to mention only some of them. Similar questions were sent to persons in several of the other states then forming the union but, except for General Sullivan's observations on New Hampshire, Jefferson's replies are the only ones that seem to have survived.[34] Instead of setting down numbers and statistics in a detached official document, he illumined his observations with the richness of his own mind, his unparalleled education, and his gift for philosophical speculation. They were not the remarks of a small man looking at a piece of territory called a state, but of a great man regarding the world. By considering all of the country that was originally Virginia, including the part subsequently ceded to the union, he was able to extend his observations and to give a survey of the whole eastern part of the United States. As Charles Thomson wrote him, before he had seen the printed book and when he was familiar only with the unrevised manuscript: "I consider it a most excellent natural history, not merely of Virginia, but of North America, and possibly equal, if not superior, to that of any country yet published." Earlier in the letter he had "begged leave to submit to your consideration whether you do not owe it to your reputation to revise your work and publish it under a more dignified title.... I think it may deserve the title of *A Natural History of Virginia*."[35] The modest author, however, was not to be moved.

The first of the queries deals with "an exact description of the limits and boundaries of the state of Virginia," which at that time embraced what was subsequently to become West Virginia and Kentucky. Jefferson concludes his remarks with an enumeration of the seven acts which determined the extent of the state at the time he wrote, including the Treaty of Paris of 1763, by which Virginia lost considerable territory, and the recent cession. From this he passes to "a notice of its rivers, rivulets, and how far they are navigable." After discussing the important rivers of Virginia which played so great a role in its life—

the James, the Elizabeth, the York, the Potomac and certain others—he considers the great waterways of the west, the Mississippi, Missouri, Ohio, and Illinois, which he pictures as opening up the wonderland of the Mississippi Valley and the Great Lakes. It was, of course, inevitable that at the period at which he wrote, Jefferson should consider these rivers from the point of view of their adaptability to trade and commerce. No man's wildest dreams at that time could envisage the long, lumbering freight trains that within less than a century were to traverse the continent, robbing the rivers of their natural functions —to say nothing of the airplane, which now seems almost to have annihilated space. Thus he believed that "the Mississippi will be one of the principal channels of future commerce for the country westward of the Allegheny." [36] The distance to which it, and all other rivers, are navigable, the obstacles to navigation and how readily they may be removed, are of primary importance to him.

Notwithstanding that the larger part of this section of the *Notes* deals with the great western rivers, Jefferson justifies their inclusion by observing that, although "the Missouri, since the Treaty of Paris, the Illinois and northern branches of the Ohio since the cession to Congress, are no longer within our limits," yet "having been so heretofore, and still opening to us channels of extensive communication with the western and northwestern country, they shall be noted in their order." [37] He describes these rivers as though he had seen them, as though he, rather than his emissaries, had been the one who had charted their currents, sounded their depths, and observed the times of their floods and return to their banks. We feel it was he who had studied the fish and the reptiles they yielded, who had watched the herons in their meditation, and the ducks and geese in their flight over these vast waters and spaces. The eagerness with which he gathered information of the great western empire from such explorers as George Rogers Clark, or the Indians, whose country the white man had never yet penetrated, or with which he learned the length of the great Ohio River, "as measured according to its meanders by Captain Hutchins," shines through every word.

Thus he knows that "the Mississippi below the mouth of the Missouri is always muddy, and abounding with sandbars, which frequently change their places.... Its current is so rapid that it never can be stemmed by the force of the wind alone, acting on the sails. Any vessel, however, navigated with oars, may come up at any time and receive much aid from the wind. A batteau passes from the mouth of the Ohio to the mouth of the Mississippi in three weeks and is from two to three months getting up again." [38] In describing the Ohio, which lives for him as no other river, largely, no doubt, through Clark's enthusiasm, Jefferson grows almost lyrical. To him it is "the most beautiful river on earth. Its current gentle, waters clear, and bosom smooth and unbroken by rocks and rapids, a single instance only excepted." [39]

The Missouri he considers "the principal river, contributing more to the common stream than does the Mississippi, even after its junction with the Illinois. It is remarkably cold, rapid, and muddy. Its overflowings are considerable. They happen during the months of June and July.... The Spanish merchants at Pancore, or St. Louis, say they go two thousand miles up it. It heads far westward of the Rio Norte, or North River. There is, in the villages of Kaskaskia, Cohoes, and St. Vincennes, no inconsiderable quantity of plate, said to have been plundered during the last war by the Indians from the churches and private houses of Santa Fé, on the North River, and brought to these villages for sale. From the mouth of the Ohio to Santa Fé are forty days' journey or about 1,000 miles. What is the shortest distance between the navigable waters of the Missouri, and those of the North River, or how far this is navigable above Santa Fé, I could never learn," [40] is his regretful conclusion.

Jefferson brings the section on rivers to a close by observing: "Before we quit the subject of western waters, we will take a view of their principal connections with the Atlantic. These are three, the Hudson's river, the Potomac, and the Mississippi itself." His conclusions as to the part these rivers would play in commerce with Europe and "of all the country westward of Lake Erie, on the waters of the lakes, of the Ohio, and upper parts of the Mississippi" have now only an historical interest, in view of developments since his time.

The poet and the scientist in Jefferson struggle for supremacy in the fourth and fifth queries—which concern the mountains and caverns of Virginia. It was no whim that had led him to establish himself on a mountaintop, but rather a passion, and this strong feeling breaks through the bounds of matter-of-fact description when he speaks of the junction of the Potomac and Shenandoah rivers at Harper's Ferry. "The passage of the Potomac through the Blue Ridge," he exclaims, "is perhaps one of the most stupendous scenes in nature. You stand on a very high point of land. On your right comes up the Shenandoah, having ranged along the foot of the mountain a hundred miles to seek a vent. On your left approaches the Potowmac, in quest of a passage also. In the moment of their junction they rush together against the mountain, rend it asunder, and pass off to the sea. . . . But the distinct finishing which nature has given to the picture, is of a very different character. It is a true contrast to the foreground. It is as placid and delightful as that is wild and tremendous. For, the mountain being cloven asunder, she presents to your eye through the cleft, a small catch of smooth blue horizon, at an infinite distance in the plain country, inviting you, as it were, from the riot and tumult roaring around, to pass through the breach and participate in the calm below. Here the eye ultimately composes itself. . . . This scene is worth a voyage across the Atlantic." [41]

Although the Natural Bridge does not come strictly in the categories under discussion in these queries, Jefferson cannot resist giving a few words to it, considering it, as he did, "the most sublime of nature's works." After a detailed description he observes that, "though the sides of this bridge are provided in some parts with a parapet of fixed rocks, yet few men have resolution to walk to them and look over into the abyss. You involuntarily fall on your hands and feet, creep to the parapet, and peep over it. Looking down from this height about a minute gave me a violent headache.[42] If the view from the top be painful and intolerable, that from below is delightful in an equal extreme. It is impossible for the emotions arising from the sublime to be felt beyond what they are here; so beautiful an arch, so elevated, so light, and springing as it were up to heaven, the rapture of the spectator is really indescribable!" [43]

The sixth query Jefferson obviously considered of the utmost importance, for he devoted more space to it than to any other. Nowhere does he give a more dazzling display of his vast learning or the thoroughness with which he had mastered each of the subjects under discussion. These were "the mines and other subterranean riches" of the state, "its trees, plants, fruits, etc." This modest "etc." includes likewise a lengthy discussion of the quadrupeds of Europe and America, of the slave and slavery, as well as of the American Indian. After discussing the deposits of lead, copper, iron, coal, marble, and other minerals, Jefferson turns to consideration of the trees, plants, and fruits of Virginia. He does not attempt to be comprehensive but confines himself "to those which would principally attract notice." These he divides into the medicinal, edible, ornamental, and useful for fabrication, giving the Linnaean as well as the popular names of each. The first category lists some two dozen, the second three dozen, the third nearly four dozen, and the fourth, twenty-seven. In addition to these, he states, the English found on coming to Virginia tobacco, maize, round potatoes, pumpkins, cymlings, and squash, "but it is not said whether of spontaneous growth or by cultivation only. Most probably they were natives of more southern climates, and handed along the continent from one nation to another of the savages." For further information on "the infinitude of other plants and flowers," he refers the reader to Clayton's *Flora Virginica*. Yet he cannot conclude this section without mentioning what grains the farms produce, what the Virginia garden yields, as well as the produce of the orchards and the grasses native to Virginia.

With the simple statement that "our quadrupeds have been mostly described by Linnaeus and M. de Buffon," Jefferson turns to a subject that was challenging the leading minds of the world at the time and that continued to fascinate him throughout his life. This was the science of palaeontology—more particularly vertebrate palaeontology. It offered everything that most appealed to his philosophical and speculative turn of mind—a "large element of the unknown, the need for constructive imagination, the appeal to other branches of biological and physical investigation for supplementary evidence, and the necessity of constant comparison with the present aspects of nature," as Henry F. Osborn has so aptly described the science. Although the first vertebrate fossils in America had been observed by Europeans as early as 1519, and although mastodon bones had been discovered by LeMoyne in 1739 and taken to Europe for study by Buffon and others, Jefferson was one of the first to encourage the science in this country. More than that, the eminence of his position along with his persistent attempts to collect and bring together material for observation and study did much to advance knowledge in this field.

A large part of this section of the *Notes* is devoted to a certain celebrated controversy. Buffon, and his associate, Daubenton, had made the statement that the animals common to Europe and America were smaller in the latter place, that the animals peculiar to America are small, and that those domesticated on both continents have degenerated in this country. The renowned Abbé Raynal had added fuel to the fire by declaring that European man degenerates when transplanted to America. It would not be in place to go into the details of the discussion here, or to rehearse Buffon's hypotheses which he advanced to substantiate his theories. Jefferson devotes many pages to refuting them. He completely routed his opponent by three impressive tables giving "a comparative view of the quadrupeds of Europe and America." Those marked with an asterisk "are actual weights of particular subjects, deemed among the largest of their species"; those marked with a dagger "are furnished by judicious persons, well acquainted with the species and saying, from conjecture only, what the largest individual they have seen probably would have weighed. The other weights are taken from Messrs. Buffon and Daubenton, and are of such subjects as came casually to their hand for dissection." [44] The first table deals with the aboriginal animals of both continents, the second with those found in one of the two only, and the third, domesticated of both. It must be said that the American creatures come off very handsomely and quite demolish Buffon's theory. The bison, the heaviest American quadruped, leads off with a proud, asterisked 1,800 pounds. The palmated elk topped the scales at 410, whereas his European brother could boast of but a meager 153.7; and the otter, 12 pounds against 8.9. Most impressive of all was the American cow, weighing more than three times the European—2,500 pounds against 763.[45]

Jefferson sent Buffon a copy of his *Notes* on June 7, 1785, at the same time that he gave one to Chastellux. "The other copy I delivered at your hotel," he wrote the Marquis, "was for M. de Buffon. I meant to ask the favor of you to have it sent to him, as I was ignorant how to do it." [46] Four months later, on October 13, he observed to Hogendorp: "I have never yet seen M. de Buffon. He has been in the country all summer. I sent him a copy of the book, and have only heard his sentiments on one particular of it, that of the identity of the mammoth and the elephant. As to this, he retains his opinion that they are the same." [47] They seem to have met not long after this. On December 31 Buffon wrote Jefferson thanking him for a skin Jefferson had sent and inviting him to dinner. "*M. de Buffon,*" the letter reads, "*fait bien de remercîments á Monsieur Jefferson de la peau de l'animal qu'il a eu la bonté de lui envoyer. Si sa santé lui permettoit, M. de Buffon aurait l'honneur d'aller lui temoigner sa reconnaissance, mais comme il ne peut sortir, il espère que Monsieur Jefferson voudra bien venir avec Monsieur de Chastellux diner au jardin [du roi] tel jour qu'il leur conviendra.*"

Even in a dinner invitation, the Count could not resist a reference to his pet theory. "*Ce cougar de Pensilvanie,*" he continues, "*diffère de celui qui a été décrit par M. Colinson que paru qu'il a le corps moins long à peu près dans le rapport de 13 à 16. Il a aussi le queue moins longue, il parait tenir le milieu pour la grandeur entre le cougar de M. Colinson et celui de l'Amérique méridionale. Mille compliments et respects.*" [48]

The meeting must have taken place very shortly, for a week later, on January 7, 1786, Jefferson wrote Archibald Cary, who shared these interests: "In my conversations with the Count de Buffon on the subjects of natural history, I find him absolutely unacquainted with our elk and deer. He has hitherto believed that our deer never had horns more than a foot long, and has, therefore, classed them with the roebuck, which I am sure you know them to be different from." Jefferson now makes a proposal designed surely to win over the reluctant Buffon. "Will you take the trouble to procure for me the largest pair of buck's horns you can," he asks Cary, "and a large skin of each color—that is to say a red and a blue? If it were possible to take these from a buck just killed, to leave all the bones of the head in the skin, with the horns on, to leave the bones of the legs in the skin also, and the hoofs to it, so that, having only made an incision all along the belly and neck, to take the animal out, we could, by sewing up that incision, and stuffing the skin, present the true size and form of the animal, it would be a most precious present." [49]

Not long after he addressed a similar letter to Archibald Stuart, saying: "I have made a particular acquaintance here with M. de Buffon, and have a great desire to give him the best idea I can of our elk." [50] He then makes the same request for a whole animal. That both Colonel Cary and Stuart had failed him, we learn from a letter to Francis Hopkinson in December of this same year. In June Hopkinson had sent Jefferson an account of a most extraordinary bird he had recently come across. "I have lately been in New Jersey," he writes, "and saw a bird which a countryman had shot, and is, I think, a curiosity. This bird is of the heron species and is certainly a stranger among us. It has three long and very white feathers growing out of the top of its head, but they are so formed as to look more like pieces of bobbin, or silk cord, than feathers, and very beautiful. But what I thought most remarkable is, that to the middle of the claw of each foot he had annexed a perfect *small toothed* comb, with which I suppose he combed his elegant plumage. I have got one of the feet and two of the feathers of the crest, which, when a better opportunity offers, I will send to you for M. Buffon, with such a description of the bird as I can give. After all, it is more than probable that this may be no curiosity to so great a natural historian as M. Buffon." [51]

"You must not presume too strongly that your comb-footed bird is known to M. de Buffon," Jefferson replies. "He did not know our panther. I gave him the stripped skin of one I bought in Philadelphia, and it presents him a new species, which will appear in his next volume. I have convinced him that our deer is not a *chevreuil*, and would you believe that many letters to different acquaintances in Virginia, where this animal is so common, have never enabled me to present him with a large pair of horns, a blue and red skin stuffed, to show him their colors, at different seasons? He has never seen the horns of what we call the elk. This would decide whether it be an elk or a deer." [52]

BUFFON. By Houdon

JOHN SULLIVAN. By John Trumbull. (*Courtesy of the Frick Art Reference Library*)

Although Hopkinson was not in a position to send this, he did ship his bird on November 6, 1786. Jefferson acknowledged the receipt of the creature on the first of August the following year. "The leg and feathers of the bird are also arrived," he tells Hopkinson, "but the comb, which you mention as annexed to the foot, has totally disappeared. I suppose this is the effect of its drying. I have not yet had an opportunity of giving it to M. Buffon, but expect to do so soon." [53]

Meanwhile, Jefferson turned once more to the problem of securing the skin and bones of a moose. In 1784 he had written General John Sullivan of New Hampshire for such information as he could furnish in regard to the moose, elk, and caribou. On March 12 Sullivan promised to send him whatever he could find and agreed to consult Jonathan Dore, John McDuffee, and Gilbert Warren, noted local hunters, on the subject. This he did through the Reverend Isaac Hasey, who sent Sullivan a detailed report on the matter. It was duly transmitted to Jefferson and is preserved among his papers. The opinions of the hunters were tabulated, as we see in the loose memoranda concerning the *Notes* preserved in the Massachusetts Historical Society, and subsequently incorporated in the completed work.

On January 7, 1786, after his meeting with Buffon, Jefferson once more wrote Sullivan. "The readiness with which you undertook to endeavor to get for me the skin, the skeleton, and the horns of the moose, the caribou, and the original or elk," he says, "emboldens me to renew my application to you for those objects which would be an acquisition here, more precious than you can imagine. Could I choose the manner of preparing them, it should be to leave the hoof on, to leave the bones of the legs and the thigh if possible in the skin, and to leave also the bones of the head in the skin with the horns on, so that by sewing up the neck and belly of the skin we should have the true form and size of the animal. However, I know they are too rare to be obtained so perfect. Therefore I will pray you to send me the skin, skeleton, and horns just as you can get them, but most especially those of the moose...." [54]

Sullivan took Jefferson at his word. The fire of battle was once more kindled in the General's veins. He was at this time president of New Hampshire. There was no difficulty in calling out troops. As

Jefferson said: "It was my fault that I had not given him a rough idea of the expense I would be willing to incur for them. He had made the acquisition an object of a regular campaign, and that, too, of a winter one. The troops he employed sallied forth, as he writes me, in the month of March—much snow—a herd attacked—one killed—in the wilderness—a road to cut twenty miles—to be drawn by hand from the frontiers to his house—bones to be cleaned, etc., etc., etc. In fine, he puts himself to an infinitude of trouble, more than I meant: he did it cheerfully, and I feel myself really under obligations to him."

When Jefferson wrote this letter to Colonel Smith he was under the impression that all had been in vain. "That the tragedy might not want a proper catastrophe," he concludes, "the box, bones and all, are lost.... But I have written him not to send me another." [55] Within a few days, however, the boxes, which had been shipped from Portsmouth on January 26 under the particular care of Captain Samuel Pierce, turned up. The only blow was the bill. This amounted to forty guineas.

On the first of October Jefferson sent a triumphant letter to Buffon. "I am happy to be able to present you at this moment," he writes, "the bones and skin of a moose, the horns of another individual of the same species, the horns of the caribou, the elk, the deer, the spiked horned buck, and the roebuck of America. They all come from New Hampshire and Massachusetts and were received by me yesterday. I give you their popular names, as it rests with you to decide their real names," he adds with deference to Buffon's position in the scientific world.

After all his expense and trouble, Jefferson was disappointed in the results. "The skin of the moose was dressed with the hair on," he adds, "but a great deal of it has come off, and the rest is ready to drop off. The horns of the elk are remarkably small. I have certainly seen some of them which would have weighed five or six times as much. This is the animal which we call elk in the southern parts of America." So that Buffon might have a more accurate idea, Jefferson continues that he has "taken measures, particularly, to be furnished with large horns of our elk and our deer, and therefore beg of you not to consider those now sent as furnishing a specimen of their ordinary size.

I really suspect you will find that the moose, the round-horned elk, and the American deer are species not existing in Europe. The moose is, perhaps, of a new class. I wish these spoils, Sir," he concludes, "may have the merit of adding anything new to the treaures of nature which have so fortunately come under your observation and of which she seems to have given you the key." [56]

Buffon was, alas, not at home when this noble gift arrived, being doubtless still in the country, as he had been at the same season two years previously when Jefferson sent his *Notes*. Jefferson therefore wrote a note to the Count's associate, Daubenton, saying: "Mr. Jefferson being informed that M. le Comte de Buffon is absent, takes the liberty of recommending to the care of M. Daubenton the objects of natural history which accompany this letter. He leaves the letter to M. de Buffon open, that M. Daubenton may see under what names these objects have come, and he will beg the favor of him to seal and forward the letter when he shall have read it." [57]

Any acknowledgment of the letter or the gift, if there was one in writing, seems not to have been preserved. As the *Biographie Universelle* says of Buffon and his critics: *"C'est le silence que Buffon a toujours gardé envers ses critiques."*

"So far," Jefferson observes, turning from Buffon's theories on animals, "the Count de Buffon has carried this new theory of the tendency of nature to belittle her productions on this side of the Atlantic. Its application to the race of whites, transplanted from Europe, remained for the Abbé Raynal. 'On doit être etonné,' he says, 'que l'Amérique n'ait pas encore produit un bon poète, un habile mathématicien, un homme de génie dans un seul art, ou seule science.'" This was adding insult to injury. Jefferson comes to the defense of his country and countrymen with passion. "When we shall have existed as a people as long as the Greeks did before they produced a Homer, the Romans a Virgil, the French a Racine and Voltaire, the English a Shakespeare and Milton, should this reproach still be true, we will inquire from what unfriendly causes it has proceeded, that the other countries of Europe and quarters of the earth shall not have inscribed any name in the roll of poets." [58] At this point in Jefferson's own copy of the *Notes* he inserted the observation: "Has the world as yet produced more than two poets, acknowledged to be such by all nations? An Englishman only reads Milton with delight, an Italian Tasso, a Frenchman the Henriade; a Portuguese, Camoens; but Homer and Virgil have been the rapture of every age and nation. They are read with enthusiasm in their originals by those who can read the originals and in translations by those who cannot."

Jefferson did not let the vindication of his country go at this. "In war," he writes, "we have produced a Washington, whose memory will be adored while liberty shall have votaries.... In physics we have produced a Franklin, than whom no one of the present age has made more important discoveries, nor has enriched philosophy with more, or more ingenious, solutions of the phenomena of nature. We have supposed Mr. Rittenhouse second to no astronomer living; that in genius he must be the first, because he is self-taught. As an artist he has exhibited as great a proof of mechanical genius as the world has ever produced. He has not indeed made a world; but he has by imitation approached nearer its Maker than any man who has lived from the creation to this day.

"As in philosophy and war, so in government, in oratory, in painting, in the plastic art, we might show that America, though but a child of yesterday, has already given hopeful proofs of genius, as well as of the nobler kinds, which arouse the best feelings of man, which call him into action, which substantiate his freedom, and conduct him to happiness, as of the subordinate, which serve to amuse him only. We therefore suppose that this reproach is as unjust as it is unkind; and that, of the geniuses which adorn the present age, America contributes its full share." [59] The golden pen was still at work.

Of particular interest is Jefferson's discussion of the Indians, a subject of paramount curiosity to Europeans. He had consorted with them since childhood. He had an understanding of them that was vouchsafed to few of his contemporaries. As he wrote John Adams: "In the early part of my life I was very familiar with the Indians, and acquired impressions, attachment, and commiseration for them which have never been obliterated." [60] There are few more affecting public papers than Jefferson's various addresses to these people. They radiate an all-comprehending humanity, an understanding and an acceptance of a psychology alien to the white man. Above all, they meet the red man on his own ground. There is no thought of a smile, no hint of condescension when he is addressed by the Chieftains Crooked-Legs or Stinking Fish, when Three-Legs, a Piankeshaw chief, hands him the white pipe of peace and bids him smoke, or when John Baptist de Coigne, chief of the Wabash and Illinois, salutes "first the Great Spirit, the Master of life, and then you."

It is singular coincidence that Jefferson's valedictory to the governorship, a paper endorsed merely "June, 1781," should have been addressed to De Coigne, bidding him keep peace. To judge by the context of the letter, De Coigne seems recently to have appeared before the legislature, pleading for help for his people in these distressed times. "I am very much pleased with the visit you have made us," Jefferson observes in the fatherly tone that won him the devotion of these people, "and particularly that it has happened when the wise men from all parts of our country were assembled together in council and had an opportunity of hearing the friendly discourse you held to me. We are all sensible of your friendship and of the services you have rendered, and I now, for my countrymen, return you thanks and, most particularly, for your assistance to the garrison which was besieged by the hostile Indians." After a lengthy discussion of the war and its relation to the Indians, he promises to share with them "what little goods we can get," and to send them the schoolmasters De Coigne had requested "to educate your son and the sons of your people. We desire above all things, brother, to instruct you in whatever we know ourselves. We wish to learn you all our arts and to make you wise and wealthy.... This is, brother, what I had to say to you," he concludes. "Repeat it for me to all your people.... Hold fast the chain of friendship which binds us together, keep it bright as the sun, and let them, you and us, live together in perpetual love."[61]

Most striking is Jefferson's defense of the red man against Buffon's charges. These are too long to quote in their entirety but are summed up in his statement: "*Quoique le sauvage du nouveau monde soit à-peu-près de même stature que l'homme de notre monde, cela ne suffit pas pour qu'il puisse faire une exception au fait général du rapetissement de la nature vivante dans tout ce continent; le sauvage est foible et petit par les organes de génération; il n'a ni poil, ni barbe et nulle ardeur pour sa femelle; quoique plus léger que l'Européen, parce qu'il a plus l'habitude à courir, il est cependant beaucoup moins fort de corps; il est aussi bien moins sensible, et cependant plus craintif et plus lâche; il n'a nulle vivacité, nulle activité dans l'âme ... il demeurera en repos sur ses jambes ou couché pendant des jours entiers ... la plus précieuse étincelle du feu de la nature leur a été refusée ... leur coeur est glacé, leur société froide et leur empire dur ... la nature en lui refusant les puissances de l'amour l'a plus maltraité et plus rapetissé qu'aucun des animaux."* [62] These are a few of the charges brought against him.

These words fired Jefferson to an elaborate discourse on the Indian and his good qualities.[63] "An afflicting picture, indeed," he exclaims, "which for the honor of human nature I am glad to believe has no original." After disclaiming any acquaintance with the Indians of South America, he continues: "The Indian of North America being more within our reach, I can speak of him somewhat from my own knowledge, but more from the information of others better acquainted with him, and on whose truth and judgment I can rely. From these sources I am able to say in contradiction to this representation that he is neither more defective in ardor, nor more impotent with his female, than the white reduced to the same diet and exercise; that he is brave, when an enterprise depends on bravery ... that he will defend himself against a host of enemies, always choosing to be killed rather than surrender ... that in other situations, also, he meets death with more deliberation, and endures tortures with a firmness unknown almost to religious enthusiasm with us ... that he is affectionate to his children, careful of them, indulgent in the extreme ... that his friendships are strong and faithful to the uttermost extremity; that his sensibility is keen, even the warriors weeping most bitterly on the loss of their children, though in general they endeavor to appear superior to human events, that his vivacity and activity of mind is equal to ours in the same situation." [64]

After further discussion of the Count's theories, Jefferson comes to the conclusion that "to form a just estimate of their genius and mental powers, more facts are wanting, and great allowance to be made for those circumstances of their situation which call for a display of particular talents only. This done, we shall probably find they are formed in mind as well as in body, on the same module with the 'Homo sapiens Europaeus.' The principles of their society forbidding all compulsion, they are to be led to duty and to enterprise by personal influence and persuasion. Hence eloquence in council, bravery and address in war, become the foundations of all consequence with them. To these acquirements all their faculties are directed. Of their bravery and address in war, we have multiplied proofs, because we have been the subjects on which they were exercised. Of their eminence in oratory we have fewer examples, because it is displayed chiefly in their own councils. Some however, we have of very superior luster." [65]

Jefferson concludes his plea with the deeply moving speech of the chieftain, Logan, to Lord Dunmore when he was governor of Virginia. "I may challenge the whole orations of Demosthenes and Cicero, and of any more eminent orator, if Europe has furnished any more eminent," he exclaims, "to produce a single passage superior to the speech of Logan, a Mingo chief." And Jefferson is right. For simplicity, for a biblical eloquence, for deep human feeling, as well as for dramatic quality, Logan's words are unsurpassed. "I appeal to any white man," they read, "to say if he ever entered Logan's cabin hungry, and he gave him not meat; if ever he came cold and naked, and he clothed him not. During the course of the last long and bloody war Logan remained idle in his cabin, an advocate of peace. Such was my love for the whites that my countrymen pointed as they passed, and said, 'Logan is the friend of white men.' I had even thought to have lived with you but for the injuries of one man. Colonel Cresap, the last spring, in cold blood and unprovoked, murdered all the relations of Logan, not sparing even my women and children. There runs not a drop of my blood in the veins of any living creature. This called on me for revenge. I have sought it. I have killed many: I have fully glutted my vengeance: for my country I rejoice at the beams of peace. But do not harbor a thought that mine is the joy of fear. Logan never felt fear. He will not turn on his heel to save his life. Who is there to mourn for Logan? Not one." [66]

Further aspects of the Indian are discussed in the eleventh query.

"When the first effectual settlement of our colony was made, which was in 1607," Jefferson writes, "the country from the seacoast to the mountains, and from the Potomac to the most southern waters of James River, was occupied by upwards of forty different tribes of Indians." After discussing their organization, their relation to each other, and their history, Jefferson turns to their cultural achievements. "I know of no such thing as an Indian monument," he remarks, "for I would not honor with that name arrow points, stone hatchets, stone pipes, and half-shapen images. Of labor on the large scale, I think there is no remain as respectable as would be a common ditch for the draining of land, unless it would be the barrows, of which many are to be found all over this country. These were of different sizes, some of them constructed of earth and some of loose stones. That they were repositories of the dead has been obvious to all, but on what particular occasion constructed was a matter of doubt."

Jefferson goes into the various theories then prevalent as to whether these were communal sepulchers for the dead of villages presumed once to have existed near by, or whether they were depositories of bones of the dead collected by the Indians at certain periods. He then embarks on a remarkable description of his own activities as an archaeologist. "There being one of these [barrows] in my neighborhood, I wished to satisfy myself whether any, and which of these, opinions were just. For this purpose I determined to open and examine it thoroughly. It was situated on the low grounds of the Rivanna, about two miles above its principal fork, and opposite to some hills on which had been an Indian town.... I first dug superficially in several parts of it and came to collections of human bones, at different depths, from six inches to three feet below the surface." After describing the kind and condition of the bones he tells us: "I proceeded then to make a perpendicular cut through the body of the barrow, that I might examine its internal structure."[67] In the most approved method of the modern archaeologist, Jefferson continued his researches. As has been pointed out,[68] he anticipated by a good hundred years the methods of present-day archaeology, more particularly stratigraphical archaeology, or the study of cultural strata. His approach, furthermore, was that of the contemporary worker in the field who does not seek objects *per se,* but is interested in increasing his knowledge of a problem. It is all the more remarkable when we consider that these observations were, in all probability, made before 1773, the year Jefferson began to become so involved in the Revolutionary movement that he had little thought or time for anything else.

Throughout his life Jefferson took a passionate interest in the language of the Indians. "It is to be lamented, then, very much to be lamented," he writes in the *Notes,* "that we have suffered so many of the Indian tribes already to extinguish, without our having previously collected and deposited in the records of literature, the general rudiments, at least, of the languages they spoke. Were vocabularies found of all the languages spoken in North and South America ... with the inflections of their nouns and verbs, their principles of regimen and concord, and these deposited in all the public libraries, it would furnish opportunities to those skilled in the languages of the Old World to compare them with these, now or at any future time, and hence to construct the best evidence of the derivation of this part of the human race." [69]

Meanwhile, for years Jefferson had been following his own injunction. His collection of Indian vocabularies was ultimately to include that of about forty tribes. No one had hitherto undertaken anything so extensive. He left no stone unturned. He interviewed guides and traders, corresponded with Indian agents, adjured explorers of the western country who went out under his aegis to collect and write down all they could. Thus we learn from his manuscript catalogue of letters written, which he began in 1779, that on December 28, 1783, he wrote Colonel Benjamin Hawkins, a member of Congress and subsequent Indian agent, who was a great friend of the Indians, about Buffon's characterization of them. He likewise addressed a letter to Captain Thomas Hutchins, who had visited most of the tribes, in 1768, to make a census of them, asking for such vocabularies as he had collected. He also, on the same day, appealed to his old friend Bernard Moore for help in regard to the language of the Mattaponies and Pamunkeys, and to his new friend William Short concerning the Nottoways.[70] As he was fond of observing, he had "long considered their language as the only remaining monument of connection with other nations [i.e., of Asia], or the want of it, to which we can now have access. They will likewise show their connections with one another. Very early in life, therefore, I formed a vocabulary of such objects as, being present everywhere, would probably have a name in every language; and my course of life having given me opportunities of obtaining vocabularies of many Indian tribes, I have done so on my original plan, which, though far from being perfect, has the valuable advantage of identity, of thus bringing the languages to the same points of comparison."

Dr. John Sibley, an Indian agent and his correspondent on this occasion, had sent an account of many more tribes than Jefferson had suspected lived "west of the Mississippi and south of the Arkansas." He begs Sibley to collect their languages and encloses "a number of my blank vocabularies, to lessen your troubles as much as I can.... No matter whether the orthography used be English, Spanish, French, or any other, provided it is stated what the orthography is." He states that he already has the vocabularies of two of the tribes in this region, has taken measures to obtain those north of the Arkansas, and already possesses "most of the languages on this side of the Mississippi. A similar work, but on a much greater scale," he concludes, "has been executed under the auspices of the late Empress of Russia as to the red natives of Asia which, however, I have never seen. A comparison of our collection with that will probably decide the sameness or difference of origin, although it will not decide which is the mother country and which the colony." [71]

To another correspondent he wrote that he had seen a report of Volney, the French scholar, on a work entiled *Vocabulaires comparés des langues de toute la terre,* "with a list of 130 words, to which the vocabulary is limited. I find that 73 of these words are common to that and to my vocabulary, and therefore will enable us, by a comparison of language, to make the inquiry so long desired, as to the probability of a common origin among the people of color on the two continents." [72]

The comparison was destined never to be made. Although early in 1800 Jefferson wrote Colonel Hawkins that he was about to print his vocabularies, "lest by some accident it might be lost," [73] he did not get to it during the busy years of his presidency. On his return to Monticello from Washington in the spring of 1809, the trunk containing these valuable papers was stolen by boatmen and destroyed. The papers it contained were scattered in the mud along the banks of the James River. "It may be described as a hair trunk," Jefferson wrote his agent, "about 7 or 8 feet in cubic contents, labeled by a card on the top T I No. 28, containing principally writing papers of different qualties... a pocket telescope... a dynamometer in steel and brass, an instrument for measuring the extensions of draught animals, a collection of vocabularies of the Indian language.... The value was probably about $150, exclusive of the vocabularies, which had been the labor of 30 years in collection for publication." He authorizes a reward of twenty or thirty dollars.[74]

The epilogue is contained in a letter of 1825 to Philip Duponceau, vice-president of the American Philosophical Society, who was likewise deeply interested in the Indian languages. "I now send you the remains of my Indian vocabularies," Jefferson writes, "some of which are perfect. I send them with the fragments of my digest of them, which were gathered up on the banks of the river where they had been strewed by the plunderers of the trunk in which they were. These will merely show the arrangement I had given the vocabularies, according to their affinities and degrees of resemblance or dissimilitude."[75]

Having disposed of these important topics, as well as given particular attention to the charters of the state and its constitution, Jefferson turns his attention, in the fourteenth query, to a consideration of the laws of the state and their revision. He thus comes to the question of slavery—another of the outstanding phases of the *Notes*. That he favored emancipating all slaves born after the passage of a certain proposed act in the revision, educating them in "tillage, arts, or sciences, according to their geniuses" until they reached their majority, then colonizing them "to such place as the circumstances of the time render most proper," is well known. "It will probably be asked," he observes, "why not retain and incorporate the blacks in the state, and thus save the expense of supplying by importation of white settlers, the vacancies they will leave? Deep-rooted prejudices entertained by the whites; ten thousand recollections by the blacks of the injuries they have sustained; new provocations, the real distinctions which nature has made, and many other circumstances will divide us into parties, and produce convulsions, which will probably never end but in the extermination of the one or the other race.

"To these objections, which are political," he adds, "may be added others which are physical and moral. The first difference which strikes us is that of color.... [It] is fixed in nature and is as real as if its seat and cause were better known to us.... Besides those of color, figure, and hair, there are other physical distinctions proving a difference of race." The author enlarges on this point to the great advantage of the white man, concluding: "The circumstance of superior beauty is thought worthy of attention in the propagation of our horses, dogs, and other domestic animals; why not in that of man? Negroes," he continues, "are at least as brave and more adventuresome. But this may perhaps proceed from a want of forethought, which prevents their seeing a danger till it be present. When present they do not go through it with more coolness or steadiness than the whites. They are more ardent after their female, but love with them seems to be more an eager desire than a tender delicate mixture of sentiment and sensation. Their griefs are transient. Those numberless afflictions which render it doubtful whether heaven has given life to us in mercy or in wrath, are less felt and sooner forgotten with them. In general, their existence appears to participate more of sensation than reflection...." [76]

In another section of the *Notes* Jefferson takes up other aspects of slavery. So enlightened were his views, so at variance with those of most of his contemporaries, that he hesitated to make them public. The concept of slavery, both from a philosophical and a practical point of view, was odious to him. To the majority of his fellow Virginians, a large part of whose fortune was in this human commodity, Jefferson's convictions were nothing short of treasonable—treason to his heritage and treason to his class. Who of them was prepared to agree that "the whole commerce between master and slave is a perpetual exercise of the most boisterous passions, the most unremitting despotism on the one part and degrading submissions on the other? ...

The man must be a prodigy who can retain his manners and morals undepraved by such circumstances."

These were strong words, but more vigorous expressions were to come. "With what execrations should the statesman be loaded," Jefferson continues, "who, permitting one-half the citizens thus to trample on the rights of the other, transforms those into despots and these into enemies, destroys the morals of the one part, and the amor patriae of the other. For if a slave can have a country in this world, it must be any other in preference to that in which he is born to live and labor for another.... With the morals of the people, their industry also is destroyed. For in a warm climate, no man will labor for himself who can make another labor for him. This is so true, that of the proprietors of slaves a very small proportion indeed was ever seen to labor. And can the liberties of a nation be thought secure," he cries, "when we have removed their only firm basis, a conviction in the minds of the people that these liberties are the gift of God? That they are not to be violated but by his wrath? Indeed, I tremble for my country when I reflect that God is just; that His justice cannot sleep forever." [77] No people ever had a more eloquent advocate or a more prophetic one.[78]

In view of the complexities of getting established in a new country, the printing of the *Notes* was, very naturally, postponed for some months after his arrival in France. On December 10, 1784, Jefferson wrote Monroe: "I could not get my answers to the queries on Virginia printed in Philadelphia; but I am printing it here and will certainly ask your acceptance of a copy." [79] It was not until May 11, 1785, however, that the printing was completed. On that day Jefferson informed Madison: "They yesterday finished printing my notes. I had 200 copies printed, but do not put them out of my own hands, except two or three copies here, and two which I shall send to America, to yourself and Colonel Monroe, if they can be ready this evening, as promised." [80] They were to go forward in the care of M. Doradour, a Frenchman who was departing to settle in Virginia. That the *Notes* actually were finished on this date, we learn from a subsequent letter from Madison in which he acknowledges their receipt through the agency of that gentleman. On the first of August, 1785, Jefferson settled the bill with his printer. On that date, according to his account book, he paid "Mons. Pierre for printing for myself 1130-4 francs." This was, undoubtedly, Phillipe Denis Pierres, the well-known printer of the rue St. Jacques, who had done work for Franklin and was very likely recommended by him. The edition was a small octavo of 391 pages. The notes contributed by Charles Thomson were printed as an appendix and comprise the last 25 pages of the volume.

Owing to the radical opinions expressed in the work, Jefferson hesitated to have the *Notes* distributed even after they had been printed, until, as he wrote Chastellux, he should "know whether this publication would do more harm than good." His two great objects, he confided to the Marquis, were "the emancipation of their slaves and the settlement of their constitution on a firmer and more permanent basis"—both questions the Virginians of that period preferred not to be prodded into taking under consideration. James Madison was the first to let him know the reaction of his fellow countrymen. In his letter of May 11 Jefferson had said to Madison: "I beg you to peruse it carefully, because I ask your advice on it and ask nobody's else. I wish to put it into the hands of the young men at the college, as well an account of the political as physical parts. But there are sentiments on some subjects which I apprehend might be displeasing to the country, perhaps to the Assembly or to some who lead it.... Communicate it, then, in confidence to those whose judgments and information you would pay respect to, and if you think it will give no offense, I will send a copy to each of the students at William and Mary College, and some others to my friends and to your disposal, otherwise I shall only send over a very few copies to particular friends in confidence and burn the rest." [81]

On November 15, 1785, Madison, who had just returned from a holiday at Montpelier in Orange County, wrote from Richmond: "I have looked them over carefully myself and consulted several judicious friends in confidence. We are all sensible that the *freedom of your strictures* on some *particular measures* and *opinions will displease their respective abettors*. But we equally concur in thinking that this consideration ought not to be weighed against the *utility of your plan*. We think both the facts and the remarks which you have assembled too *valuable* not to be made known." As for presenting a copy to each student, Madison adds: "Mr. Wythe suggested that it might be better to put the number you may allot to the University into the library, rather than to distribute them among the students. In the latter case the stock will be immediately exhausted. In the former, the discretion of the professors will make it serve the students as they successively come in. Perhaps too, an indiscriminate gift might offend some narrow-minded parents." [82]

Meanwhile Jefferson had not been so timid about permitting his friends in Paris to see his work. "I have been obliged to give so many of them here," he complained to Madison on September 1, "that I fear their getting published." [83] His fears proved not without foundation, even though each copy bore on the fly leaf the injunction: "Unwilling to expose these sheets to the public eye, the writer begs the favor of [the recipient] to put them into the hands of no other person on whose care and fidelity he cannot rely to guard them against publication." Through the death of one of the recipients, a Mr. Williamos,[84] a copy fell into the hands of a bookseller, even though, as Jefferson says, "I immediately took every precaution I could to recover this copy." This man was "about publishing a very abominable translation," when early in 1786 the learned and distinguished Abbé Morellet offered to undertake the work himself. Two years before, the Abbé had been elected a member of the Académie Française. As his biographer says, "*l'académie faisait en lui une acquisition précieuse. Peu de ses confrères possédaient au même degré l'habitude et le talent d'analyser les idées de définer les mots, d'y attacher le sens qui leur est propre.*" [85]

"A translation by so able a hand," Jefferson wrote Dumas, the agent of the United States at The Hague, "will lessen the faults of the original instead of their being multiplied by a hireling translator." [86] Morellet proposed the addition of a map, which Jefferson accordingly prepared. "It is on a single sheet 23 inches square," he explained to Edward Bancroft of London on February 26, 1786, in asking him to get an estimate from an engraver for 1,800 copies, "and very closely written. It comprehends from Albemarle Sound to Lake Erie, and from Philadelphia to the mouth of the great Kanhaway, containing Virginia and Pennsylvania, a great part of Maryland, and a part of North Carolina. It is taken from Mitchell, Hutchins, and Fry and Jefferson.... Though it is on a scale of only an inch to 20 miles, it is as particular as the four sheet maps from which it is taken, and I answer for the exactness of the reduction. I have supplied some new places.... Though the first object which induced me to undertake it was to make a map for my book, I soon extended my view to the making as good a map of those countries as my materials would admit.... I shall finish it in about a fortnight, except the divisions of the counties of Virginia, which I cannot do at all until I can get Henry's map of Virginia. This I must trouble you to procure for me and send immediately by the diligence." [87]

Jefferson and Morellet worked industriously on the translation, as proved by a series of letters from the Abbé, hitherto unobserved. Every few days the author sent new passages to be incorporated. In turn, the translator had suggestions of his own to make. He writes on one occasion: "*J'ai été forcé aussi d'adoucir l'endroit des théologiens dans la crainte de nos censeurs qui ne refuseraient la permission d'imprimer des choses trops claires. Vous êtes bien heureux d'être citoyen d'un pays libre et de pouvoir travailler vous même comme vous [voulez].*" [88] How carefully Jefferson went over the translation is indicated in a seven-page memorandum dated January 19, 1787, headed "Errors in the Abbé Morellet's translation of the Notes on Virginia, the correction of which is indispensable," in which he gives the French and English versions of certain passages in parallel columns with the expressions to be corrected, underlined.[89] The *Notes* finally appeared as *Observations sur la Virginie, par M. J. traduit de l'anglais* and included the map. The date given on the title page is 1786, but as the map for it was not yet printed in July 1787,[90] when Jefferson was under obligation to send the plate to Stockdale, it was not until somewhat later that the book actually appeared.

With the appearance of a French edition imminent, it seemed necessary for Jefferson to sponsor a publication in English. As Madison wrote him in May 1786: "Your notes having got into print in France, will inevitably be translated back and published in that form not only in England but in America, unless you give out the original. I think, therefore, that you owe it not only to yourself, but to the place you occupy and the subjects you have handled, to take this precaution."[91] Nevertheless Jefferson hesitated. It was nearly a year after the proposed French edition before he approached Stockdale, the English publisher. There can be no doubt but that Jefferson was sincerely modest in regard to his work. Every copy of the *Notes* he presented, every letter he wrote regarding them, contains words minimizing their importance and deprecating his own ability. Thus he wrote Hopkinson on September 25, 1785, shortly after their appearance: "I have sometimes thought of sending a copy of my *Notes* to the Philosophical Society, as a tribute due to them; but it would seem as if I considered them worth something, which I am conscious they are not."[92]

Hence it was not until February 1, 1787, that Jefferson wrote Stockdale: "You have two or three times proposed to me printing my *Notes on Virginia*. I never did intend having them made public, because they are little interesting to the world; but as a translation of them is coming out, I have concluded to let the original appear also. I have therefore corrected a copy and made some additions. I have, moreover, had a map engraved which is worth more than the book. If you choose to print the work I will send you the corrected copy, and when it shall be nearly printed, I will send the plate of the map. I would not choose that it should be put under a patent, nor that there should be a tittle altered, added, nor omitted."[93]

A fortnight later Stockdale replied with the usual skepticism of the publisher, mingled with a dash of proverbial British dourness. "I shall be happy to receive your corrected copy," he writes, "which shall be neatly and correctly printed and published, according to your desire, without one tittle of alteration, though I know there is some bitter pills relative to our country.... I intend to print 500 copies, which from the merit of the work and the advantage of your name, I hope will be sold, but all things are uncertain."[94]

The corrected copy was dispatched by the diligence of February 28, 1787, with an order for 400 copies. The preceding December Jefferson had already written William Carmichael, American chargé in Spain: "My *Notes on Virginia*, having been hastily written, need abundance of corrections. Two or three of these were so material that I am reprinting a few leaves to substitute for the old." [95] These were pages 52-54 of the original edition, which were struck out of the copies still in Jefferson's hands, and the new ones pasted in.

These corrections were, of course, embodied in the English edition. In the abandoned pages Jefferson had advanced a theory, other than that of a universal deluge, in which John Bartram, Kalm, and other early naturalists had concurred, to explain the incidence of sea shells on mountaintops. He had suggested that, "besides the usual process for generating shells by the elaboration of earth and water in animal vessels, may not nature have provided an equivalent operation, by passing the same materials through the pores of calcareous earths and stones? ... Is it more difficult for nature to shoot the calcareous juice into the form of a shell, than other juices into the form of crystals, plants, animals, according to the construction of the vessels through which they pass? ... Have not naturalists already brought themselves to believe much stranger things?" [96]

This theory seems to have called forth a storm of discussion, sufficient to have caused Jefferson to discard it and substitute the new pages. A survey of the leading scientific periodicals of France, such as the *Journal des Savants* or the *Journal de Physique*, not to mention nonscientific papers such as the *Mercure de France*, for the years 1785-89 inclusive, has failed to disclose any mention of the subject in print. One can only conclude that Jefferson's theory was the subject of conversations between him and the other men of his circle interested in the natural sciences, and that the changes in the *Notes* were the result of this.

In sending his manuscript to Stockdale, Jefferson cautioned him "to have the most particular attention paid to the correcting of the press," as the *Notes* were "filled with tables, which will become absolutely useless if they are not printed with a perfect accuracy.... With respect to the plate of the map, it is impossible to send it at the same time. It was engraved in London, and on examination I found a prodigious number of orthographical errors. Being determined that it shall not go out with a single error, an engraver is now closely employed in correcting them. He promises to have it finished the

THE NOTES ON VIRGINIA

next week, say by the tenth of March; but I suppose you must expect he will not be punctual to a day." [97]

Jefferson little knew what he would have to reckon with in regard to his map. Four days after writing Stockdale he set off on a tour of southern France from which he did not return until June 11. The map was still not available, being in the hands of Barrois, the publisher of Morellet's translation. It was not until three weeks after coming back, and after the most annoying difficulties, described in a letter to the Abbé, that Jefferson was able to send the plate to England. On August 2 he notes having "repaid Mr. Short for de la Haye for correcting my map plate, 123 fr." Finally, on the fourteenth of August, he acknowledged the receipt of a dozen copies of the *Notes*, "in their original form and language." This edition included, aside from the map that had appeared in the French edition, an introductory note, and the three appendices Jefferson had had printed after the book first appeared. It was likewise the first edition to bear the author's name. It was a copy of this edition that Jefferson retained and kept always with him, enriching it enormously by manuscript notes. And it was this volume that formed the basis for the revised edition of the *Notes* published after his death by J. W. Randolph and Co. in 1853.

Jefferson's manuscript additions to his copy reveal the remarkable scope of his reading and the profundity of his learning. There are references to Herodotus, Xenophon, Diodorus Siculus, and other classical writers when the discussion of a certain phenomenon, such as that of a universal deluge, goes back to ancient times. It would appear that he had devoured almost every known work on the New World, from that earliest traveler, Amerigo Vespucci, onward. His *Letters* are frequently quoted. Other early writers referred to are José de Acosta, the Spanish missionary whose *Historia natural y moral de las Indias* was published in 1590, Antonio de Ulloa, another Spaniard, author of *Voyage Historique de l'Amérique*, which appeared in 1752, François Xavier Clavigero, the Mexican Jesuit, author of *Storia antica del Messico*, Corneille de Pauw, whose *Recherches sur les Américains* caused a furore in 1768, Ramusio, the Italian historian, author of *Navigations au Nouveau Monde* published in 1566,

Antoine Herrera, the Spaniard, the French translation of whose work appeared in 1622, the same year as the Spanish, under the title of *Descriptions des Indes occidentales, qu'on appelle aujourd'hui nouveau-monde,* and the more recent traveler, Peter Kalm, friend of Linnaeus, who visited America in 1768 and of whose work we have already spoken.

Jefferson's difficulties with pirated editions of his work were not confined to the threatened French one. On August 3, 1787, Stockdale wrote him: "Just as I was going to ship 400 of your work for Richmond and Philadelphia, I had the disagreeable intelligence to learn that your book was already printed in Philadelphia, and a skeleton of a map added to it, which, though not equal to mine, I am informed, as it comes much cheaper, it will answer their purpose." [98]

This rumor was confirmed in a letter from Alexander Donald, an old friend and associate, written from Richmond on December 15, 1787. Jefferson had sent him some copies of his books and map for distribution. He wrote that they had not yet arrived and observed: "On the whole, I fear I will not be able to acquit myself with [illegible] on this consignment. You may remember that your countrymen in general are not much given to books.... But you will see by the enclosed advertisement that there is an edition of the book just going to be published in Philadelphia, the price of which will be only 7 shillings, 6 pence, Virginia currency." He enclosed an advertisement announcing that there was "Now in press and shortly to be published by Prichard and Hall, Printers, Philadelphia, *Notes on the State of Virginia,* by his Excellency, Thomas Jefferson, Minister Plenipotentiary from the United States of America to the Court of France." After listing the contents, the advertisement announces that "the work will be comprised in a handsome octave volume, with an elegant type and good paper.... Subscriptions are taken at Mr. Davis' printing office in Richmond, where a specimen of the work is left for inspection." [99] Jefferson's papers do not show that he took any steps against the publisher or did anything to try to stop it. There probably was little he could do, especially at such a distance.

That Jefferson's *Notes* met with a warm reception is well known. As the Abbé Morellet wrote Franklin: "The work of your excellent

MARQUIS DE CHASTELLUX. By Charles Willson Peale. (*Courtesy of the National Museum, Independence Hall*)

JEFFERSON'S PORTRAIT OF WASHINGTON. By Joseph Wright.
(*Courtesy of the Massachusetts Historical Society*)

THE NOTES ON VIRGINIA   303

countryman, Mr. Jefferson, which I have translated, has been much liked here. It has been very well received, and I consider its principles very sound and the facts well arranged." [100] Contemporary published comment, however, is not abundant. A mildly condescending notice appeared in the *Monthly Review* of London for 1788. "Virginia is a territory now too generally known to attract much attention," it begins, "except with regard to such circumstances as result from or refer to the late revolution which it has undertaken in common with its neighboring states; and in this view, the representations of the present very intelligent writer afford us much to applaud, as well as some things to which we cannot afford a ready assent.... After vindicating the animals and aboriginal natives of North America against the depreciations of Buffon," it continues, "Mr. Jefferson cannot be supposed to overlook the white inhabitants or English-Americans, of whom he is a warm panegyrist, even to the point of enthusiasm." [101] A brief digest of the *Notes* is given, and certain passages, particularly the one on slavery, are quoted at some length, but no significant comment is made.

A careful reading of the leading scientific journals of France of the time, the *Journal des Savants,* the *Journal de Physique,* in which Chastellux proposed to reprint a section of the *Notes,* but which does not seem to have appeared, as well as the *Journal de Paris,* which contained reviews of the leading books in each issue, and the *Gazette de Paris* have failed to reveal any notice of Jefferson's work. This paucity of reviews, however, is made up to a great extent by a long one, on June 2, 1787, occupying pages 29-40 and 69-81 in the leading periodical of the French capital, the *Mercure de France.* It is concerned with the Abbé Morellet's translation and is unsigned.[102] It has not hitherto been reproduced or brought into conjunction with the *Notes* in modern times. The *Mercure* speaks of the work as *"un exemple bien éclatant de cette réunion de la philosophie avec les talens de l'homme public, et celui que nous avons eu sous nos yeux dans la personne du célèbre Benjamin Franklin.... Ceux qui connaissent l'auteur de l'ouvrage que nous annonçons ici, et qui n' a pas voulu se nommer à la tête de son livre... ne tarderont pas a reconnaître dans les* Observations sur la Virginie *cette heureuse réunion de connaissances qui tendent à un même but, le bonheur des hommes, par les deux routes qui y conduisent, l'étude de la nature et celle de l'homme en société.*

"*Cet ouvrage est du petit nombre de ceux qu'on peut appeler véritablement instructifs. Un grand nombre des faits bien observés et de vérités utiles bien discutées, une grand simplicité, une marche de l'esprit sage et sûr, l'espèce d'eloquence qui tient naturellement au sujet, le sentiment des droits de l'homme, le calm de la conviction avec la chaleur qu'inspire l'amour de la vérité, tels sont les caractères de* Notes on Virginia, Observations sur la Virginie, *titre qu'on trouvera bien modeste, après avoir reconnu tout ce que l'auteur y a repandu de connaissances intéressantes.*"

After discussing the various sections of the *Notes*, the reviewer takes up Jefferson's relation to Buffon. "*De la page 99 à la page 161 M. J. combat la théorie du célèbre auteur d'*Histoire Naturelle *sur le continent de l'Amérique et justifie le nouveau monde du reproche qu'on lui fait de ne produire que des espèces foibles et dégénérées, tant en animaux qu'en hommes. Les questions de ce genre sont d'une discussion difficile,*" the writer observes and launches into a lengthy discourse of the merits of the case, as he sees them.

"*Je finis en laissant entendre l'auteur lui-même,*" the review concludes with a fine tribute to Jefferson, "*parlant avec éloquence, le langage de la raison, de l'humanité et de la saine politique, contre la guerre, ce fléau de genre humain,*" and he gives in translation the concluding passage from the *Notes*—a clarion call to Virginia and to the new nation.

"Young as we are," Jefferson writes, "and with a country before us to fill with people and happiness, we should point in that direction the whole generative force of nature, wasting none of it in efforts of mutual destruction. It should be our endeavor to cultivate the peace and friendship of every nation. . . . Our interest will be to throw open the doors of commerce, and to knock off all its shackles, giving perfect freedom to all persons for the vent of whatever they may choose to bring into our ports and asking the same in theirs. . . . Were the money used by a country to wage war," he concludes, "expended in improving what they already possess, in making roads, opening rivers, building ports, improving the arts, and finding employment for their idle poor, it would render them much stronger, much wealthier and happier. This I hope will be our wisdom." [103]

Jefferson had, alas, reckoned without human nature.

XII. The Darkest Year

THE PERIOD following the writing of his *Notes on Virginia* was one of the darkest in Jefferson's life. It was clouded by the constantly increasing frailty of his wife's health and the certainty that this beloved companion was slipping from him. "A desire to leave public office with a reputation not more blotted than it has deserved," obliged him to go to Richmond in the fall of 1781, as we have seen, at the time the investigation of the conduct of the executive came up. After an attendance of thirteen days, he was excused on December 21 for the rest of the session. Christmas was spent with the Tuckahoe Randolphs, and on the twenty-ninth Jefferson and his family started back to Monticello by way of the Point of Fork.

Jefferson withdrew from public life at this period more completely than would have seemed possible for a man who had devoted the past decade of his life to furthering the good of his country. He assumed the role of private citizen and farmer as though he had never aspired to anything else. On May 8 he notes: "Our daughter Lucy Elizabeth [second of that name] was born at one o'clock A.M." From that moment until the sixth day of September when he inscribed the words, "my dear wife died this day at 11:45 A.M.," life was a long-drawn-out and losing battle with death. Jefferson's marriage and his extraordinary devotion to his wife have been described in Chapter IX of *Jefferson: The Road to Glory*. With her death he sank into a period of despair from which it was all but impossible for him to rouse himself. It was only when he had evolved the philosophy which he later expounded to Madison, when that gentleman's suit was rejected by Miss Floyd of New York, that he was able to find a measure of peace. This was that "firmness of mind and unremitting occupation will not long leave you in pain."[1]

When November found him, as he said, "a little emerging from the stupor of mind which had rendered me as dead to the world as was she whose loss occasioned it," it was clear that henceforth service to his country was to be at once his solace and his vocation. He was at this time still a member of the House of Delegates, but his heart was yet too torn and bewildered for him to attend. The session had been called for Monday, October 21. There was no quorum on that day, or for many days following. On the twenty-fourth the names of those who failed to appear were noted, and it was "ordered that the sergeant at arms attending this House take into his custody Thomas Jefferson and Thomas Walker, Members from Albemarle."[2] As most of the members had failed to attend, the sergeant-at-arms appears to have had a busy time. On the fifth of November Jefferson was again ordered taken into custody, and on the eighth he finally appeared in charge of a "special messenger by Mr. Speaker's warrant." He was discharged from custody and from further duties the same day, "it appearing to the House that he had good cause for his present non-attendance."[3] The following day the Assembly at last convened.

Meanwhile Jefferson's name had kept coming up in Congress. On November 12 James Madison notes in his *Debates of the Congress of the Confederation* Jefferson's reappointment as "minister plenipotentiary for negotiating peace was agreed to unanimously and without a single adverse remark. The act took place in consequence of its being suggested that the death of Mrs. Jefferson had probably changed the sentiments of Mr. Jefferson with regard to public life."[4] The same day he wrote Edmund Randolph: "The resolution passed a few minutes ago.... You will let it be known to Mr. Jefferson as quickly as secrecy will admit. An official notification will follow by the first opportunity. This will prepare him for it. It passed unanimously, and without a single remark adverse to it."[5] On November 19 Madison again informed his correspondent that "Colonel Bland set out on Friday last. He carried with him an official notification to Mr. Jefferson of his appointment."[6]

Jefferson was likewise considered at this time for the post of secretary of foreign affairs. Robert R. Livingston was resigning, and he consulted some of his colleagues as to whether "Mr. Jefferson would prefer the vacancy to his foreign appointment."[7] Madison "answered him in the negative," as he says, but Edmund Randolph put his reply more pithily. "Nothing less than Europe would suit our friend of Monticello," he observes. "However, I will write him on the subject."[8]

What stirrings the news of his appointment aroused in Jefferson's mind, now that he was free to visit the countries he had dreamed of these many years, how grateful he was to fate for removing him from scenes at once dear yet alive with torturing memories, we can only surmise. Again he has left no record of his thoughts or of his emotions, except for the laconic remark, "With the public interest the state of my mind concurred in recommending the change of scene proposed; and I accepted the appointment."[9] On the twenty-sixth he wrote Livingston: "I received yesterday the letter with which you have been pleased to honor me, inclosing the resolution of Congress of the 12th inst. renewing my appointment as one of the ministers plenipotentiary for negotiating a peace, and beg leave through you to return my sincere thanks to that august body for the confidence they are pleased to repose in me.... I will employ in this arduous charge with diligence and integrity, the best of my poor talents, which I am conscious are far short of what it requires.... Your letter finds me at a distance from home, attending my family under inoculation. This will add to the delays which the arrangement of my particular affairs would necessarily occasion. I shall lose no moment, however, in preparing for my departure and shall hope to pay my respects to Congress and yourself at some time between the twentieth and the last of December."[10]

The days following he spent making arrangements for what he believed was to be a long absence from home. On the second of December farewell was said to Colonel Archibald Cary, under whose ample roof the Jefferson children had suffered the woes of inoculation against smallpox. Polly, now four years old, and the infant Lucy Elizabeth were taken to Eppington and put under the care of Mrs.

Jefferson's sister, Elizabeth Eppes. Martha, the eldest, was to have her first view of the great world. She was to accompany her father. The ambition of this eleven-year-old girl, whose horizon had hitherto been bounded by Monticello and Richmond with its adjacent plantations, was, as Crèvecoeur tells us, "to see nine states out of the thirteen." [11] On the fifteenth of December Jefferson sent a notice to the *Virginia Gazette* that "the subscriber having occasion to be absent from the state for some time, has confided the care of his affairs to Francis Eppes, Esq., of Chesterfield, and Colonel Nicholas Lewis of Albemarle, to whom, therefore, he begs leave to refer all persons having business with him." Four days later he notes in his account book: "Set out from Monticello for Philadelphia, France, etc."

It was not until the twenty-seventh that Jefferson and Patsy, as he fondly called Martha, reached Philadelphia, where they put up at the Indian Queen. He immediately plunged into work. "I could not propose to jump into the midst of a negotiation without a single article of previous information," [12] he had written Madison on learning of his appointment, and Madison had duly reported to his crony, Edmund Randolph, on December 30: "Mr. Jefferson arrived here on Friday last and is industriously arming himself for the field of negotiation."

The ten days or so Jefferson had planned to spend in Philadelphia were destined to extend not to weeks but to months. It was a harrowing period, attended by misfortune of every sort, and ending in disappointment. On the fourteenth of January, already long after he had expected to sail, Jefferson wrote Francis Eppes: "You will hardly expect to receive a letter from me at this place, and of so late a date. Yet I have apprehensions of being here ten days or a fortnight longer, for though ready myself, some time since, the vessel on which I go is not ready." [13] The ship on which he expected to sail was the French frigate *Romulus*, on which the French minister, Luzerne, had arranged passage for him.

At the end of January Jefferson determined to proceed to Baltimore with his party. They arrived after a journey of five days, "braving all weather and plunging through thick and thin." Winter cold had suddenly set in, and the Chevalier de Villebrune, in command of the *Romulus*, "was obliged to fall down with his ship and the *Guadeloupe* to about twelve miles below this." In a letter laying his troubles before Madison, Jefferson continues: "The ice has since cut off all correspondence with him till yesterday, when I got a boat and attempted a passage." But fate was against him. The tide rose, "the ice closed in on us on every side and became impenetrable to our little vessel so that we could get neither backwards nor forwards." A sloop finally rescued the party and put it on board the *Romulus*, where the night was spent and where further bad news was in store. Jefferson found himself in the unusual position of being the object of a man-hunt by the British.

"The Chevalier de Villebrune," he continues, "communicated to me several letters of intelligence which deserve weight, by which we are informed that the enemy, having no other employment at New York, have made our little fleet their sole object for some time and have now cruising for us nothing less than 1 ship of 64 guns, 4 of 50, 2 of 40, 18 to 25 frigates from 24 to 30 guns, a most amazing force for such an object." Jefferson lays several alternative plans before his friend, the one he most favors being "to ask a flag for me from the enemy and to charter a vessel here," but he fears this might "be thought injurious to the dignity of the states, or perhaps be thought such a favor as Congress might not choose to expose themselves to the refusal of.... I fear I shall be here long enough to receive many letters from you," he concludes. "My situation is not an agreeable one, and the less so as I contrast it with the pleasing one I left so unnecessarily." [14]

Meanwhile the French minister put at Jefferson's disposal the frigate *Guadeloupe*, which the latter describes as "having laid ten months under water. She got perfectly sobbed, insomuch that she sweats almost continually on the inside, in consequence of which the commander and several of the crew are now laid up with rheumatisms. But this I should have disregarded had it not appeared that it was giving to the enemy the ship and crew of a friend, and delaying myself in fact by endeavoring at too much haste. I therefore have not made use of the liberty given me by the minister." [15]

The same day Jefferson wrote the Secretary of Foreign Affairs, asking his advice. A week later Livingston replied: "I have delayed in answering your favor of the 7th instant until I could obtain the sense of Congress on the matter it contains. I conceive it hardly possible, while the British cruisers retain their present station, for you to elude their vigilance in either of the ships offered to your choice. This concurring with the late advices from England has induced Congress to pass the enclosed resolution." [16] This was to the effect that "the Secretary of Foreign Affairs informs Mr. Jefferson, that it is the pleasure of Congress, considering the advices lately received in America and the probable situation of affairs in Europe, that he do not proceed on his intended voyage until he shall receive their further instructions." [17]

The Chevalier de Villebrune was frankly delighted with the outcome. The prospect of becoming a prisoner of war had not been attractive. "*Je vois avec bien de plaisir,*" he writes Jefferson, "*que vous avez approuvé le parti que nous avons pris de retenir les deux frégates. J'ai parlé ce matin à un homme qui était à bord du* Leon, *il y a dix jours. Il m'a dit que ce vaisseau avec le* Centurion *et plusieurs frégates était en croisière resolu à ne quitter les caps qu' après le départ des deux frégates du Roi et du convoi.*" [18]

The Chevalier enclosed a copy of the king's recent conciliatory speech before Parliament which finally admitted the possibility of negotiating with the colonies. The French minister and James Madison likewise sent copies. These merely contributed to the undecided state of mind in which Jefferson found himself. Conscious that he was only marking time, he again wrote Livingston on February 14 for guidance. Speaking of the king's speech, he says: "We learn that preliminaries between America and Great Britain, among which is one for the acknowledgment of our independency, have been provisionally agreed to on his part.... As considerable progress has been made in the negotiations for peace since the appointment with which Congress was pleased to honor me, it may have become doubtful whether any communications I could make, or any assistance I could yield to the very able gentleman in whose hands the business already is, would compensate the expense of prosecuting my voyage to Europe. I therefore beg leave through you, Sir, to assure Congress that I desire this question to be as open to them now as it was on the day of my appointment, and that I have not a wish of my own either to go or to stay." [19]

Livingston, not unappreciative of Jefferson's embarrassment and "suspense in respect to their final determination," replied that it "cannot long be doubtful, since the negotiations have certainly arrived at such a crisis as either to terminate soon in peace, or a total rupture, in the latter case you will necessarily be obliged to proceed on your voyage, as Congress seems anxious to avail themselves of your abilities and information in the negotiations." [20]

"I am exceedingly fatigued with this place," Jefferson complained to Madison, "as indeed I should be with any other when I had neither occupation nor amusement." The record of his days sounds dreary enough. On arrival he notes buying "play tickets, 22/6," but there was no other diversion. He and Patsy lodged with a Mrs. Langston and apparently had their meals at Mrs. Ball's, with an occasional dinner or supper at Grant's, who had recently opened the "large and elegant" Fountain Inn. There was only one bright spot, the home of the French general who had been commander at Hampton under Rochambeau. "I am very particularly indebted here to the politeness and hospitality of General LaValette," Jefferson tells Madison, "who obliges me to take refuge in his quarters from the tedium of my own the latter half of every day. You are indebted to him too," he adds, with a sly wink at his friend, "as I should make my long letters much longer, and plague you with more cypher, were I confined at home all day." [21]

The pleasure must have been mutual, for LaValette wrote Jefferson, with all the grace and the enthusiasm which the French command: "*C'est à moi, Monsieur, à vous faire des remerciements de m'avoir favorisé de votre bonne et agréable compagnie pendant votre séjour à Baltimore. Elle a fait mon agrément, je me rappellerai toujours avec plaisir ce temps heureux. Il me donne infiniment de regrets de la préférence que vous venez de donner à Philadelphie, mais il faut savoir faire des sacrifices aux personnes qu'on aime....*" [22]

On February 23 Jefferson finally started on the return journey to Philadelphia, not on the twenty-eighth, as is usually stated. On that day he paid 22/6 for crossing the Gunpowder Creek, a scant dozen miles to the north of Baltimore.[23] He arrived in Philadelphia on the twenty-sixth, and another period of waiting began. On March 4 he wrote Francis Eppes that he expected "every hour permission to return home," but no word came. On the thirteenth he once more appealed to Livingston. "Supposing dispatches received by the Washington may have enabled Congress to decide on the expediency of continuing or countermanding my mission to Europe," he writes, "I take the liberty of expressing to you the satisfaction it will give me to receive their ultimate will so soon as other business will permit them to revert to this subject." [24]

It was not until the first of April that Congress finally resolved "that the Secretary of Foreign Affairs inform the Honorable Thomas Jefferson, in answer to his letter of the thirteenth of March, that Congress consider the object of his appointment so far advanced as to render it unnecessary for him to pursue his voyage, and that Congress are well satisfied with the readiness he has shown in undertaking a service which from the present situation of affairs, they apprehend, can be dispensed with." [25]

True to his word that "I shall be here but a very few days after this shall be received," Jefferson and Patsy set off again for Virginia on April 12. Before leaving he lodged with Robert Morris 500 dollars to cover any expenses that might have been incurred in hiring a house for himself in Paris. He wrote John Jay, at this time one of the American commissioners in France, who had undertaken to arrange this for him, explaining his failure to come and taking occasion to congratulate him. There is not the slightest tone of envy or regret that he was deprived of taking part in the important negotiation severing forever the colonies from their dependency on Great Britain, as he writes: "I cannot take my departure without paying to yourself and your worthy colleagues my homage for the good work you have completed for us, and congratulating you on the singular happiness of having borne so distinguished a part both in the earliest and latest transactions of this Revolution. The terms obtained for us are indeed great, and are so deemed by your country." [26]

Jefferson proceeded by way of Baltimore, Upper Marlboro, and Port Royal, where he visited Edmund Pendleton, to Hanover Court House, doubtless less sleepy then than now, and on to Richmond.

He arrived there on the twenty-second. There are no entries in his account book from the twenty-third to the thirtieth, and no letters. It is probable that he hurried first of all to Eppington to see his "dear little ones," of whom, as he says, he had had no word for three months.

On his return to Richmond he lingered another week, in order, he observes, to see some members of the Assembly. He might be momentarily out of office, but he was determined to use his influence in regard to certain measures to come before the legislature. What he had particularly at heart was a proposed bill for remodeling the Virginia constitution, of which he continued to be a bitter opponent. The meeting of the legislature had been called for the fifth of May, but a quorum was not obtained until the tenth. Nevertheless many of the Assemblymen were already in Richmond. "I passed yesterday in association and conversation with as many of them as I could," he writes Madison from Tuckahoe on the seventh, on his way to Albemarle.

It was not until the fifteenth, when the air was heavy with the perfume of locusts and the mountainside glowed with the yellow of Scotch broom, that Jefferson reached Monticello. It was to be a quiet summer, spent in the company of his children and his maiden sister, Anna Scott. There can be no doubt but that the loss of his wife struck him afresh when he reached home and viewed again the scenes they had shared for ten short years. A period of quiescence, of attempted readjustments, ensued. A few exotic plants brought with him were set out. The few entries in his account book again deal almost exclusively with household matters. His farm book is silent after the disaster of Cornwallis, and even the garden book contains but a single notation for 1783, made on September 2 and 3 when a blighting frost struck the garden. Little work was going forward on the mansion, although there are small payments to Will Beck, the mulatto who had been freed by Dr. Thomas Walker and had worked at Monticello since 1769, and although a British deserter was likewise employed as a carpenter and one Joseph Price engaged in that capacity on September 20. Jefferson, in contrast to his usual energetic activity seemed, if not to have lost heart, at least to be willing to let time slip by.

In one respect this was not true—in regard to the reformation of the constitution. Shortly after his return to Monticello he once more attempted to effect it. It will be recalled that when the constitution then in force was framed by the Virginia Convention in 1776, while Jefferson was in Congress, he challenged the right of that body to adopt it, contending that it was not elected for that purpose, but "when independence, and the establishment of a new form of government, were not even yet the objects of the people at large." [27] Now, after having talked with members of the Assembly, he felt that a propitious moment was at hand. He wrote Madison on May 7, 1783: "T. Mason is a meteor whose path cannot be calculated. All the powers of his mind seem at present to be concentrated on a single object, the producing a convention to new model the constitution. This is a subject much agitated, and seems the only one they have to amuse themselves with till they shall receive your propositions." [28]

Fired by the hope that such a convention would be called, Jefferson composed a new constitution for his state between May 15, when he arrived home, and June 17, when he sent a copy of it to Madison. Abandoning the "Bill for new modeling the form of government," which he had written in 1776 and sent posthaste to the Virginia Convention in the hope he might influence their determinations, he completely rewrote it in the light of the experience of the last eight years and of his own broadening views. The long and pitiless indictment of George III which had introduced this bill and been affixed to the constitution of 1776, is omitted. It was no longer necessary to remind the people that the monarch had perverted his kingly office into "a detestable and insupportable tyranny." In its place is given a brief historical résumé of the Revolution and its results, concluding: "It hath pleased the Sovereign Dispenser of all human events to give to this appeal [to arms] an issue favorable to the rights of the states; to enable them to reject forever all dependence on a government which had shown itself so capable of abusing the trusts reposed in it." [29]

It was, of course, necessary to introduce to the public the idea of the necessity of a new constitution. In this Jefferson adopts a somewhat paternal tone. "During the progress of that war, through which we had to labor for the establishment of our rights, the legislature of the commonwealth of Virginia found it necessary to make a temporary organization of government for preventing anarchy, and pointing our efforts to the two important objects of war against our invaders, and peace and happiness among ourselves. But this, like all other acts of legislation, being subject to change by subsequent legislatures possessing equal powers with themselves, it has been thought expedient that it should receive those amendments which time and trial have suggested, and be rendered permanent by a power superior to that of the ordinary legislature." To this end the Assembly recommended to the people of the state to elect delegates to meet in general convention "with powers to form a constitution of government for them to which our laws present and future shall be subordinate." [30]

It would be unsuitable here to attempt a detailed analysis of Jefferson's constitution and the degree in which it varied from the existing one. Of particular interest, however, in view of his experience in that office, are his provisions concerning the governor, as well as the Council. Whereas the existing constitution read that "a governor or chief magistrate shall be chosen annually by a joint ballot of both houses," Jefferson provides that "the executive powers shall be exercised by a governor," chosen the same way, but for a period of five years instead of one, and ineligible for re-election. "By executive powers," he specifies, "we mean no reference to those powers exercised under our former government by the Crown as of its prerogative, nor that these shall be the standard of what may or may not be deemed the rightful powers of the governor. We give them those powers only which are necessary to execute the laws (and administer the government) and which are not in their nature either legislative or judiciary. The application of this idea must be left to reason."

Jefferson proceeds to enumerate the specific powers he would deny the governor, a surprisingly large number, including many he had himself enjoyed. Among them are the "laying of embargoes, of establishing precedence, of retaining within the state or recalling to it any citizen thereof." A new note is injected with the proposal that "the power of declaring war and concluding peace, of contracting alliances, of issuing letters of mark and reprisal, of raising armed forces, of building armed vessels, forts, or strongholds, of coining money or regulating its value, of regulating weights and measures, we leave to be exercised under the authority of the confederation; but in all cases respecting them which are out of the said confederation, they shall be exercised by the governor, under the regulation of such laws as the legislature may think it expedient to pass. The whole military of the state," he concludes, despite his own bitter experience, "whether regular, or of militia, shall be subject to his directions; but he shall leave the execution of those directions to the general officers appointed by the legislature." [31]

The Council of State in Jefferson's constitution is to be chosen by joint ballot of the two houses, for a term of seven years, and be ineligible for re-election. Whereas the existing constitution provided that the Council should "assist in the administration of the government," [32] a relic from the colonial government, Jefferson, having known the evils of this joint responsibility, provides that "their duty shall be to attend and advise the governor when called on by him, and their advice in any case shall be a sanction to him. They shall also have power, and it shall be their duty, to meet at their own will, and to give their advice, though not required by the governor, in cases where they shall think the public good calls for it." [33]

Jefferson sent a copy of his constitution to Madison on June 17, with the comment: "You will have opportunities during your stay in Philadelphia of enquiring into the success of some of the parts of it, which, though new to us, have been tried in other states. I shall only except against your communicating it to anyone of my own country, as I have found prejudices frequently produced against propositions handed to the world without explanation or support. I trust that you will either now, or in some future situation, turn your attention to this subject in time to give your aid when it shall be finally discussed. The paper enclosed may serve as a basis for your amendment, or may suggest amendments to a better groundwork." [34]

The convention was never called, contrary to Jefferson's expectations, but he did not give up hope. "You have seen George Mason, I hope," he writes Madison on December 11, "and had much conversation with him. What are his sentiments as to the amendment of our constitution? What amendment would he approve? Is he determined to sleep on, or will he rouse and be active? I wish to hear from you on this subject." [35] Eventually he carried his constitution with him to Paris and had it printed there in 1786. It was subsequently bound with the *Notes on Virginia*, with a brief statement as to the occasion of its composition.

On the sixth of June, Jefferson had again been elected to Congress. His term was to begin in November. During the latter part of the summer he seems to have rallied himself and begun thinking of the problems and duties ahead. He wrote Madison, at this time in Congress, on August 31: "I propose to set out for Congress about the middle of October.... Either here or in Philadelphia I must ask a perusal of your Congressional notes with leave to take notes from them, as they will better than anything else possess me of the business I am to enter on. What is become of the mutineers?" he asks, referring to the body of soldiers who had driven Congress from Philadelphia in June 1783 and obliged them to find new quarters in Princeton. "What of the secretaryship of foreign affairs? What of the commercial treaty with Great Britain? These and many other questions I hope for the pleasure of having answered by you at Monticello."

After asking Madison to enquire whether he may again lodge with the hospitable Mrs. House and Mrs. Trist, in case Congress returns to Philadelphia, and, if it does not, will Madison find him "a tolerable berth wherever they are," he adds, "A room for myself, if it be but a barrack, is indispensable." He continues: "In either event of my being or not being in Philadelphia, I propose to place Patsy there, and will ask the favor of Mrs. Trist to think for me on that subject, and to advise me as to the person with whom she may be trusted, some boarding school of course, though I am not without objections to her passing more than the day in such a one." [36]

The end of September found Jefferson setting out for the Tidewater to settle business affairs in Richmond and once more to place the youngest children under the care of Mrs. Eppes. He was back at Elk Hill by the third of October and at Monticello shortly after. Horses were bought from Thomas Mann Randolph and Charles

THE DARKEST YEAR 319

Carter. Wine was bottled and stored; the house was prepared for a long absence and left in charge of the steward, John Key, who had been re-engaged for another year on September 24. On October 16, accompanied by Martha in his phaeton, and on horseback by James, that exceptional slave who was to accompany him to Europe, Jefferson "left Monticello for Congress," as he puts in. He went by way of the valley, then in the glory of fall coloring.

In planning the journey there is little doubt but that Jefferson had in mind enriching his *Notes on Virginia.* It was the first time he had made the journey north by this route, and he stopped on the way to visit the famous caverns that distinguish this area. The fifth query in the *Notes* deals with the cascades and caverns of the state, and Jefferson, so far as we know, had never yet seen them. On the eighteenth he records that he "gave Early at the cave 6/." His visit resulted in a sketch entitled "An Eye-draught of Madison's cave," which was embodied in the *Notes* along with a verbal description and an elaborated drawing by another hand. From here Jefferson went on through Woodstock and Winchester to the wonder of Harper's Ferry, which he now saw for the first time. He "ascended the heights behind the tavern," he tells us, where the full view of the scene was spread before him. His mind was dazzled, his spirit bewitched. It was some time before he got his impressions in order and wrote the description, already quoted, which he embodied in the *Notes on Virginia.*[37] On the twenty-ninth he reached Philadelphia and once more lodged at the Indian Queen.

Jefferson gave himself but a few days to settle his personal affairs in Philadelphia. He was in a hurry to be at his post. Patsy, instead of being placed in school, was left temporarily under the care of Mrs. Trist and Mrs. House. On the nineteenth, she went to live with Mrs. Thomas Hopkinson, mother of Jefferson's friend Francis Hopkinson. Here she was to enjoy the best that a large city had to offer a young girl. Her father arranged for her studies to be continued under various tutors. The art of dancing was to be acquired at the academy of Monsieur Cenas, who announced in the *Pennsylvania Gazette* for June 18, 1783, that he had just arrived in the city and had opened a dancing school. For this her parent notes he is to pay £3 a quarter, and the same sum was paid to Mr. Bently each month "for teaching her music." Du Simitière, a popular artist and antiquary of the time, was to be her master in drawing. Within a short time the temperamental Frenchman declined to continue the lessons. "He says he is no schoolmaster and not obliged to go through the drudgery of teaching those who have no capacity." [38] Hopkinson wrote Jefferson, urging him not to pay any more, as Du Simitière had already received a guinea as a so-called entrance fee. In reply Jefferson gently cautioned his child: "I have much at heart your learning to draw, and should be uneasy at your losing this opportunity, which probably is your last." [39] How Patsy's education was conducted we learn from the first of a series of charming and amazing letters which this devoted parent wrote to his gifted child. The first one is dated Annapolis, November 28, 1783, where he had followed Congress.

How difficult it has been for him to leave his daughter we observe in the first sentence. "The conviction that you would be more improved in the situation I have placed you than if still with me," he writes with tenderness, "solaced me in my parting with you, which my love for you has rendered a difficult thing. The acquirements which I hope you will make under the tutors I have provided for you will render you more worthy of my love; and if they cannot increase it, they will prevent its diminution."

To render an already respectful and sensitive child doubly considerate, he admonishes her to "consider the good lady who has taken you under her roof, who has undertaken to see that you perform all your exercises, and to admonish you from all those wanderings from what is right or what is clever, to which your inexperience would expose you. Consider her, I say, as your mother, as the only person to whom, since the loss with which Heaven has pleased to afflict you, you can now look up; and that her displeasure or disapprobation, on any occasion, will be an immense misfortune which, should you be so unhappy to incur by an unguarded act, think no concession too much to regain her good will."

After this excellent advice he suggests how his daughter should improve her time. It is not a diet of tennis, horses, motors, and boys that is recommended, but a strict attention to the arts that will produce a cultivated woman. "The following is what I should approve," he writes. "From 8 to 10, practice music. From 10 to 1, dance one day, draw another. From 1 to 2, draw on the day you dance, and write a letter next day. From 3 to 4, read French. From 4 to 5, exercise yourself in music. Fom 5 till bedtime, read English, write, etc.... I expect you to write me by every post," he continues. "Inform me what books you read, what tunes you learn, and enclose me your best copy of every lesson in drawing. Write also one letter a week either to your Aunt Eppes, your Aunt Skipwith, your Aunt Carr, or the little lady from whom I now enclose a letter. Take care that you never spell a word wrong. It produces great praise to a lady to spell well." [40]

In thanking the Marquis de Marbois for "presenting a French tutor to my daughter," as well for recommending certain books for her to read, Jefferson discusses the principles which guided him in the remarkable education he gave his child. "The plan of reading I have formed for her," he writes, "is considerably different from that which I think would be most proper for her sex in any country but America. I am obliged in it to extend my views beyond herself, and consider her as possibly the head of a little family of her own. The chance that in marriage she will draw a blockhead I calculate to about fourteen to one, and of course that the education of her family will probably rest on her ideas and direction without assistance. With the poets and prose writers I shall therefore combine a certain extent of reading in the graver sciences. However, I scarcely expect to enter her on this till she returns to me. Her time in Philadelphia will be chiefly occupied in acquiring a little taste and execution in such of the fine arts as she could not prosecute to equal advantage in a more retired situation." [41]

Meanwhile Jefferson had received a report on his daughter from Mrs. Trist. "Patsy is very hearty," she writes. "She now and then gives us a call. She seems happy, much more so than I expected. When you write give her a charge about her dress, which will be a hint to Mrs. Hopkinson to be particular with her. Du Simitière complains that his pupil is inattentive. You can be particular in these matters when you write, but don't let her know you heard any complaints. I fancy the old lady [Mrs. Hopkinson was sixty-five at the time] is preparing for the other world, for she conceits the earthquake we had the other night is only a prelude to something dreadful that will happen." [42]

Jefferson devoted a letter full of stark common sense to each of these suggestions, well realizing that they would thus be doubly emphatic. "I hope you will have good sense enough to disregard those foolish predictions that the world is to be at an end soon," he writes on December 11. With irrefutable logic he adds: "The Almighty has never made known to anybody at what time He created it, nor will He tell anybody when He will put an end to it. As to the preparations for that event, the best way is for you always to be prepared for it. The only way to be so," he continues, and he may well have been obliged to Mrs. Hopkinson for the opportunity to deliver this little sermon, "is for you never to say or do a bad thing.... Our Maker has given us all this faithful interval monitor [the conscience], and if you always obey it you will always be prepared for the end of the world, or for a much more certain event, which is death. This must happen to all; it puts an end to the world as to us; and the way to be ready for it is never to do a wrong act." [43]

As one of his Christmas presents, Jefferson sent his daughter a discourse on dress. "I omitted in that letter to advise you on the subject of dress," he writes on December 22, "which I know you are a little apt to neglect. I do not wish you to be gaily clothed at this time of life, but that your wear should be fine of its kind. But above all things, and at all times, let your clothes be neat, whole, and properly put on. Do not fancy you must wear them till dirt is visible to the eye. You will be the last one who is sensible of this. Some ladies think they may, under the privileges of the déshabillé, be loose and negligent in their dress in the morning. But be you, from the moment you rise till you go to bed, as cleanly and properly dressed as at the hour of dinner or tea.... Nothing is so disgusting to our sex as a want of cleanliness and delicacy in yours. I hope, therefore, the moment you rise from bed, your first work will be to dress yourself in such style as you may be seen by any gentleman without his being able to discover a pin amiss, or any other circumstance of neatness wanting." [44]

A more touching appeal by a parent to his child has seldom been voiced than the one with which Jefferson concludes his first letter to his beloved daughter. "I have placed my happiness on seeing you good and accomplished," he writes, "and no distress which this world can now bring me would equal that of your disappointing my hopes. If you love me, then strive to be good under every situation and to all living creatures, and to acquire those accomplishments which I have put in your power." [45] Certain it is that no daughter more loyally fulfilled her father's ardent hopes.

XIII. The Leader of Congress

It is recorded in the *Journal* of Congress for November 4, 1783, that "Mr. Jefferson, a delegate for Virginia, attended and took his seat." Owing to the mutiny of certain troops some months before, which had "in a hostile and threatening manner [proceeded] to the place in which Congress were assembled, and did surround the same with guards,"[1] that body had left Philadelphia and had been sitting in the hamlet of Princeton, New Jersey, since the twenty-sixth of June. The new Congress, of which Jefferson was a member, had begun its "annual existence" on the day before Jefferson's arrival and had elected Thomas Mifflin of Pennsylvania its president. As he observes in his autobiography, Jefferson found it at this time "a very small body and the members very remiss in their attendance on its duties"[2]—a lamentable contrast to the vigorous body of men who had fought so stoutly and so successfully for independence less than a decade before. On the very day of his arrival Congress adjourned until the twenty-sixth of the month, then to meet in Annapolis. Jefferson returned to Philadelphia on the seventh. He remained there, attending to private business, until the twenty-second. On that day he set out again for the new seat of Congress in company with James Madison, who was on his way to Virginia.

Annapolis at this time, according to Samuel Dick, congressman from New Jersey, had much to offer. It is "pleasantly situated," he writes, "on a basin which forms the mouth of the River Severn. They count about 300 houses, some of them superb and magnificent, with corresponding gardens and improvements. A waste space of some hundred acres, unemployed and uncultivated, bounded by pines of short growth, adjoins the town. The whole view resembling an Asiatic picture. . . . Most of the gentlemen in Congress have been liberally educated. Eight of us lodge in one house, and our time at home is spent agreeably enough, while the polite attention of the gentlemen of the town engages all our leisure hours in visits and amusements. The players exhibit twice a week, and there is a brilliant assembly or ball once a fortnight to which we have standing cards of invitation." [3]

So far as we can judge from Jefferson's letters or account book, he did not participate in this gaiety. A contributing cause was his health. "I have had very ill health since I have been here," he wrote Madison six weeks after his arrival, "and am getting lower rather than otherwise." [4] His account book shows that he consulted Dr. Murray, the leading physician of Annapolis, on various occasions. Fond as he was of the theater, he seems not to have bought a single ticket for the play. Although he employed a French maître d'hôtel, his account book of this period reflects largely his activities as a housekeeper, with frequent entries for china, linen, silver, provisions, and similar items. He had with him, as one of his colleagues observed, "a good library of French books," which doubtless stood him in good stead. The interest he took in the "superb and magnificent" houses is attested by a drawing, preserved among his papers, of the beautiful Harwood house, completed only a few years before.

There was one bright spot during this period, however. This was the friendship Jefferson formed with a young Dutchman, Count Gijsbert Karel van Hogendorp, a relative of Peter John van Berckel, the first minister for the Netherlands to the United States. He arrived in November 1783, with a letter of introduction to Charles Thomson from Henry Petersen, an American who was military clothier of the troops stationed at Utrecht. He speaks of Hogendorp as "a young nobleman of this republic of distinguished qualities and deserving of the politest reception. His amiable behavior will bespeak your favor better than all that I can write. He accompanies M. van Berckel, the Minister of his Mightiness to your court." [5]

Thomson was not long in making him acquainted with Jefferson, and the latter in turn gave him a letter of introduction to Washington. Jefferson speaks of the young man—he was twenty-one years old at the time—in the highest terms. "A very particular acquaintance with him here," he writes, "has led me to consider him the best informed man of his age I have ever met. Nature and application seem equally to have concurred in fitting him for important business." [6]

Hogendorp came to Annapolis in March 1784 *"pour voir le Congrès,"* as he writes his mother.[7] The shrewd observations he sent home were not too flattering. "The members of Congress are no longer, in general, men of merit or of distinguished talents," he writes. "For Congress is not respected as formerly.... It is difficult to obtain a majority.... The continual change of members, joined to the causes I have indicated, renders their conduct less uniform. What is even more afflicting is that the members, being to a less extent men who possess the confidence of the nation, than men who are willing to accept the commission, it has come about that Congress is composed of young men, rich and frivolous; or old countrymen uninformed in the affairs of the world ... and very little of men who, endowed with virtuous principles and necessary knowledge, have sufficient patriotism to sacrifice their private views for the public interest."

Of Jefferson, Hogendorp has left a little-known portrait. It is given here in translation from the French. "During my stay at the seat of Congress," he writes, "Mr. Jefferson was a man of many affairs. Retired from the great world, he occupied himself solely with public concerns. He indulges in no amusements but those of belles-lettres. The bad state of his health, he has often said to me, is the reason for his retirement; but it seems to me, rather, that, accustomed to the agreeable society of an amiable wife, he is not attracted to ordinary society now that she is gone. His mind, nurtured on lofty ideas, is averse to idle babble.... He possesses the diffidence of true merit, which embarrasses one at first and which puts at a distance those who seek his acquaintance. Those who really try to know him find a man of letters, an amateur of natural science, of law, and of politics, a philosopher and a friend of humanity." [8]

When Hogendorp left Annapolis, he sent Jefferson a letter as remarkable for what we should tend to consider presumptuousness, were it not that the author was trying to express himself in a language at which he was not at home, as for the unusually frank and informal picture it gives us of Jefferson. The letter has not been published before. "When I came to Annapolis, though I now recollect to have heard your praise at Boston," the young man writes, "yet I was then ignorant of your character and your conduct during the Revolution. Let this not surprise you, for here as in Europe I found it but too frequent that reputation is not in proportion to merit. If since my arrival in America I had been continually entertained of your great qualities, surely that circumstance would not have raised you in my opinion to the smallest degree, after a personal acquaintance which put it in my power to form a judgment according to my own observations, and my own feelings.

"It is because I not only love and esteem you, but am also in hope of having engaged your affection by a similarity in our principles and our pursuits, that I am anxious to cultivate an acquaintance which so happily commenced. For on a hint from the gentleman who introduced me to you, I resolved to pay you a visit. I very soon observed that your conversation bent on serious objects could be more useful to me than that of any gentleman in town I had met with. Your making no hyperfluous compliments, your retired life, made you appear a man of business. Even your cool and reserved behavior prepossessed me in favor of you. I valued so much the more every little mark of esteem that I could perceive in your conversation. You must have observed that I did feel no constraint in your company. . . .

"You have obliged me by your questions respecting the Netherlands. . . . With your writing I went on solitary walks in the wood that looks so beautiful from the little meadow behind your house. At the same time I became acquainted with your state and with yourself. I grew fond of your benevolent character, as much as I admired your extensive learning, your strength of judgment. I pitied your situation, for I thought you unhappy. Why, I did not know; and though you appeared insensible to social enjoyment, yet I was perfectly convinced you could not have been ever so. One evening I talked of love, and then I perceived that you still could feel and express your feelings. . . .

"I shall pass through Annapolis again in order to see you and to talk a little more with you about a correspondence after my returning home. You know that The Hague has been for a long time the center of all negotiations. It is yet the political center of Europe. Therefore in this respect my letters may be interesting to you, whom I find more acquainted with our history and our politics than any gentleman in America that I have conversed with....

"Why is my time limited? Why cannot I go with you this summer to Augusta, or Pittsburg? Why cannot a friendship be established and cemented, which now only a foundation is laid of? ..." [9]

Jefferson was obviously moved by Hogendorp's letter and embarked upon a correspondence that endured for some years. "The sentiments therein expressed are much too partial," Jefferson remarks in a little-known reply to the preceding letter, "and I am sure, had your time permitted you to have ranged a little more through these states, you would have found many others whom they would have better fitted.... Your observation on the situation of my mind is not without foundation, yet I had hoped it was unperceived, as the agreeable conversations into which you led me often induced a temporary inattention to those events which have produced that gloom you remarked. I have been happy and cheerful. I have had many causes of gratitude to heaven; but I have also experienced its rigors. I have known what it is to lose every species of connection which is dear to the human heart—friends, brethren, parents, children. Retired, as I thought myself, to dedicate the residue of life to contemplation and domestic happiness, I have been again thrown by events on the world without an object on which I can place value...." After remarking upon Hogendorp's character and abilities with the same frankness the young man has displayed, Jefferson concludes: "I shall take particular pleasure in administering to your information all future occurrences within my reach," in exchange for "those occurrences in Europe, either political or literary, which may be worthy of note." [10]

A disheartening period followed Jefferson's arrival in Annapolis. Everything was askew, in both public and private life. Arthur Lee, instead of engaging a house for the Virginia delegation, as had been expected, failed to do so. "I rather suppose it is for some particular set of gentlemen with whom he means to join," [11] Jefferson observed to his disappointed colleague, Monroe. He was obliged to put up with "Mrs. Gheeseland," apparently the widow of Judge Beverly Ghiselin of Anne Arundel county court,[12] where his account book tells us, he paid "12/6 pr day for lodging and breakfast, dinner, wood, servant." On the eighth of January he and Monroe engaged other quarters, a "little house" of Mr. Dulaney, according to the accounts, to which they removed on February 25.

The disappointments and disillusionments of public affairs far overshadowed all else. According to the Articles of Confederation, the presence of the delegates from nine states was necessary for the transaction of business, and this seemed almost impossible of achievement. "It is now above a fortnight since we should have met, and only six states appear," Jefferson wrote Madison with some despair on the eleventh of December. "We have some hopes of Rhode Island coming in today, but when two more will be added seems as insusceptible of calculation as when the next earthquake will happen." Business of the utmost importance was awaiting Congress, yet to all appearances that body was prepared to hazard the costly gains of war.

The signing of the definitive treaty of peace was before Congress at this moment. That the faithful members should have been chagrined with the laggards is not surprising. The treaty, signed on behalf of the British government, had been brought to this country on November 20 by John Thaxter, secretary to John Adams, one of the peace commissioners. Two days later he handed it to the president of Congress. That gentleman had immediately notified the governors of the various states and urged them to impress upon the delegates "the necessity of their attending in Congress as soon as possible." But of no avail. On the seventeenth of December Jefferson informed the governor of Virginia that a Congress of seven states had been made up, "but nine being requisite to ratify the treaty, we have been unable to get this done. . . . I am sorry to say I see no prospect of making up nine states, so careless are either the states or their delegates to their particular interets as well as the general good which would require that they all be constantly and fully represented in Congress."[13] On the first day of the New Year the same complaint was reiterated. "We have never yet had more than seven states," he writes Madison, "and very seldom that, as Maryland is scarcely ever present, and we are now without a hope of its attending till February. Consequently, having six states only, we do nothing. Expresses and letters are gone forth to hasten the absent states that we may have nine. . . . The critical situation in which we are like to be, gave birth to the idea that seven might ratify. But it could not be supported."[14]

A violent dispute arose in Congress over the question of the ratification by seven states. The proponents of this idea feared, for one thing, that if the treaty were not signed by March 3, 1784, when the provisional treaty would come to an end, "it would be the option of Great Britain after that time to accept it, or not, as she should think proper."[15] Jefferson had this as much at heart as anyone. He had written the governor of Virginia on December 24: "We have no certain prospect of nine within a given time; chance may bring them in and chance may keep them back, in the meantime only a little over two months remain for their assembling, ratifying, and getting the ratification across the Atlantic to Paris. All that can be said is that it is yet possible."[16]

Arthur Lee led the cohorts in favor of the idea. According to Osgood, he was "very warmly opposed" by Jefferson and his adherents, Monroe, Gerry, Howell, and Ellery. On the twenty-seventh of December Jefferson presented a report outlining his position and that of his colleagues. A heated debate ensued, and on the second of January Jefferson, finding his opponents "very restless under the loss of their motion," offered a resolution which is essentially a compromise with the other faction. It proposes "that the states now present in Congress do declare their approbation and so far as they have power, their ratification of said treaty." It was to be "transmitted to our ministers with instructions to keep the same uncommunicated and to propose to the other contracting party a convention extending the time for the exchange of ratifications three months further; that the said ministers be informed that so soon as nine states shall be present in Congress, the said treaty shall be submitted to them, and their ratification when obtained shall be transmitted also." This motion, says Jefferson, "was debated on the third and fourth, and on the fifth, a vessel being to sail for England from this port, the House directed the president to write our ministers accordingly."[17] Thus the matter rested until the arrival of the missing delegates made ratification possible.

Several pages of Jefferson's autobiography are devoted to this dispute. In a letter written to Madison on February 20, 1784, he sums it up in a few words. "I think I informed you in my last," he writes, "that an attempt had been made to ratify the definitive treaty by seven states only, and to impose this under the sanction of our seal (without letting our actual state appear) on the British Court. Read, Williamson, and Lee were violent for this, and gave notice that when the question should be put, they would call the yeas and nays and show by whose fault the ratification of this important instrument should fail, if it should fail. I prepared the enclosed resolution by way of protest and informed them I would place that also on the journals with the yeas and nays as a justification of those who opposed the proposition. I believe this put a stop to it. They suffered the question to rest undecided till the fourteenth of January, when nine states appeared and ratified.... Being persuaded I shall be misrepresented within my own state, if any difficulties should arise, I enclose you a copy of the protest containing my reasons. Had the question been put, there were but two states who would have voted for a ratification by seven. The others would have been in the negative, or divided." [18]

Meanwhile, despite delays, despite bickering, Jefferson's talents were by no means being wasted. He was now forty years old, and his unusual abilities had reached their full maturity. His contribution to the development of this country during these five months he was in Congress were greater than that of any other single man. He is described by David Howell, a veteran congressman from Rhode Island, as "one of the best members I have ever seen in Congress." [19] That this opinion was general is reflected in the number of committees to which he was appointed, and by his twice being made chairman of Congress in the absence or indisposition of the president.[20] There was not one committee of importance which did not bear his name and which was not to benefit alike by his judgment and his pen. The reports of most of those with which he was connected are in his hand—in fact, in these few months he drafted no less than thirty-one. It would not be in place here to discuss all of them. Aside from those treated in some detail in the following pages, he early draughted a report on the unfinished business of Congress, in an effort to straighten out their muddled agenda. With Elbridge Gerry of Massachusetts and Hugh Williamson of North Carolina he presented a lengthy report on December 20, "On the letters of the Ministers of the United States at Paris," which had accompanied the definitive treaty. This report was ultimately to form the basis of the "Instructions for Ministers Plenipotentiary appointed to negotiate treaties of commerce with European nations," which was passed on May 7, 1784, when Jefferson himself was made a minister. He likewise reported on the reduction of the civil list, was on the committee for negotiating with the Indians, on the grand committee for preparing a report on the arrears of interest on the national debt, on the one for Continental bills of credit, and the one for drafting instructions to the ministers plenipotentiary—to mention the most imporant.

In December Jefferson, with Gerry and James McHenry of Maryland, was put on a committee to devise a suitable ceremonial for General Washington's last public appearance.[21] This was the extraordinary act by which the commander in chief resigned his commission, thus setting at rest the lurking fears of those who dreaded the dominance of the military over the civil government. Washington arrived in Annapolis on the nineteenth. "On the twentieth he signified to Congress his desire to resign his command and retire to private life." On the twenty-second Jefferson outlined the simple yet dignified procedure to be followed, and on the twenty-third "His Excellency was admitted to an audience and addressed Congress." "Congress," says a contemporary account, "were seated and covered, as representatives of the sovereignty of the union; the spectators were uncovered and standing. The general was introduced to a chair by the Secretary, who, after a decent interval, ordered silence. The President then informed the General that 'the United States in Congress assembled were prepared to receive his communication,' on which he rose with great dignity and delivered his address. This was followed by his advancing to the President and resigning his commission. He resumed his place and received in a standing posture the answer of Congress, which the President delivered with eloquence."[22] Jefferson's prescriptions were followed to the letter. He himself reported the occasion to his governor as an "affecting scene." Jefferson had known how to give this secular occasion the dignity and impressiveness of a religious ceremony.

The benefit of Jefferson's judgment was also sought in the famous case of the Society of the Cincinnati. In the spring of 1783 this society, intended to be hereditary, was formed by a group of officers whose purpose it was to keep alive the memory of the war among themselves and their descendants. Opposition to this innocent-sounding organization began immediately. There was an almost pathological fear, readily enough understood, of anything hereditary, as well as of a standing army. "Our late officers having formed themselves into a society by the name of one Cincinnati," Samuel Osgood wrote John Adams, who was always willing to lend an ear to grumbling, when not engaged in it himself, "the institution begins to be attended to, and by many judicious persons it is thought that in time it will be very dangerous.... Surely this country will not consent to a race of hereditary patricians." [23] Elbridge Gerry quotes from a letter and concurs in it as his opinion that "some of our best friends think the order of Cincinnati will eventually divide us into two mighty factions.... The total abolition of this institution must at all events be effected, or we may bid a final adieu to every pretention as free men. ... Should it be suffered to exist in the present form, the constitutional Congress must soon be suspended by the military one; and an existence in any form will furnish an *intriguing court* with a fixed order of them to carry on operations against our constitutions." [24]

The feeling against the Cincinnati ran higher with the months. No one has expressed the objections to it more ably than Jefferson. "They [the opposition] urge that it is against the confederation—against the letter of our constitutions—against the spirit of all of them—that the foundation on which all these are built is the natural equality of man, the denial of every pre-eminence but that annexed to legal office, and particularly the denial of a pre-eminence of birth... that experience has shown that the hereditary branches of modern governments are the patrons of privilege and prerogative, and not of the natural rights of the people whose oppressors they generally are ... that a distinction is to be kept up between the civil and the military, which it is for the happiness of both to obliterate." He concludes his observations, of which there are numerous others, with as handsome a tribute as one man could pay another: ". . . that the moderation and virtue of a single character has probably prevented this Revolution from being closed, as most others have been, by a subversion of that liberty it was intended to establish; that he is not immortal, and his successor, or some of his successors, may be led by false calculations into a less certain road to glory." [25]

Washington at last decided to consult Jefferson on the subject. On April 8 he wrote: "If with frankness and the fullest latitude of a friend, you will give me your opinion upon the institution of the Society of the Cincinnati, it would confer an acceptable favor upon me. If to this opinion you would be so obliging as to add the sentiments, or what you suppose to be the sentiments, of Congress, I would thank you. . . . You may be assured, Sir, that to the good opinion alone which I entertain of your abilities and candor, this liberty is to be attributed." [26]

Washington asked for an immediate reply, and on the sixteenth Jefferson wrote him, although the two men were to meet the following week in Annapolis. "The subject has been at the point of my pen in every letter I have written to you," he says, "but has been still restrained by reflection that you had among your friends more able counsellors, and in yourself one abler than all." He left Washington in no doubt as to his own opinion, observing in almost the first sentence: "As far as you have stood connected with it, [it] has been a matter of anxiety to me . . . because I have wished to see you standing on ground separated from it and that the character which will be handed to future ages at the head of our revolution, may in no instance be compromitted in subordinate altercations. . . ."

As for Congress, "if left to themselves [they] will in my opinion, say nothing on the subject. . . . Their sentiments, if forced from them, will be unfriendly to the institution. If permitted to pursue their own path, they will check it by side blows whenever it comes in their way . . . [and] will give silent preferences to those who are not of the fraternity." He goes on to say that he has had private conversations with members of Congress and among them has "as yet found but one who is not opposed to the institution and that with an anguish of mind, though covered under a guarded silence, which I have not seen produced by any circumstance before." [27]

It is undoubtedly largely due to this letter that Gerry, the vociferous opponent of the Society, was able to write Samuel Adams on May 7: "George Washington, on his way to meeting of the Cincinnati at Philadelphia, passed through this place, and I am confidentially informed that he is opposed to the plan and is determined to recommend the dropping of it altogether." [28] A week later he reported the news from Philadelphia that there was absolutely no reason to doubt the report, "the members being generally very sick of the business." [29]

Meanwhile, the signing of the definitive treaty of peace had, as we have seen, been awaiting the arrival of the proper number of delegates before it could be concluded. Jefferson's colleagues on the committee for the ratification were Elbridge Gerry, William Ellery of Rhode Island, Jacob Read of South Carolina, and Benjamin Hawkins of North Carolina. On the sixteenth of December, three days after Congress finally convened at Annapolis, Jefferson hopefully presented a report on the treaty, resolving that it be ratified by Congress and that a proclamation immediately be issued "to the several states of the union and requiring their observance thereof." This was read and entered, but not passed until the fourteenth of January. It was only then that the president of Congress was able triumphantly to announce that "this day nine states being represented in Congress, viz., Massachusetts, Rhode Island, Connecticut, Pennsylvania, Delaware, Maryland, Virginia, North Carolina, and South Carolina, together with one member from New Hampshire and one member from New Jersey, the treaty of peace was unanimously ratified by those present. This being done, Congress, by a unanimous vote, ordered a proclamation to be issued." [30]

The ratification itself is a brief document of some twenty lines, affirming that the "United States in Congress assembled having seen and considered the definitive articles, aforesaid, have approved, ratified, and confirmed and by these presents do approve, ratify, and confirm the said articles, and every part and clause thereof, engaging and promising that we will sincerely and faithfully perform and observe the same, and never suffer them to be violated by anyone, or transgressed in any manner, as far as lies in our power." [31] Likewise in Jefferson's hand is a draught of the proclamation to the citizens of the various states. After announcing the ratification, it continues in tones more muted than those of the Declaration: "... and being sincerely disposed to carry the said articles into execution truly, honestly, and with good faith ... we have thought proper by these presents to notify the premises to all the good citizens of these states, hereby requiring and enjoining all bodies of magistracy, legislative, executive, and judiciary, all persons bearing office, civil or military, of whatever rank, degree, or powers, and all others, the good citizens of these states of every vocation and condition, that reverencing those stipulations entered into on their behalf under the authority of that federal bond by which their existence as an independent people is bound up together and is known and acknowledged by the nations of the world ... they carry into effect the said definitive articles." [32]

Fate would have it that the man who had phrased the paper which had ignited the Revolution should pen the one announcing its successful conclusion. It is no paean of joy, no passionate and relentless document, as was the Declaration—no ebullition of fierce emotional conflict. Neither is that tone to be found in any of the letters written by the various delegates to their friends and families, as had been the case in 1776. Jacob Read, to be sure, made a motion that "Congress do on Wednesday next the twenty-first celebrate the ratification of the definitive treaty of peace, and that a public entertainment be given on the same day," and Philadelphia voted £600 for the erection of the triumphal arch "to be embellished with illuminated paintings and inscriptions," executed by Charles Willson Peale, which came to such a disastrous end on the night of the illumination,[33] but on the whole the *feux de joie* were few.

Two days after the signing, when the irregular post from Virginia unexpectedly arrived, Jefferson sent a copy of the proclamation to the governor. He enclosed it in a letter reflecting his continued discouragement with Congress and its dilatory manner of dealing with the immediate problems of the new nation. "The important subjects now before Congress," he writes, "are: 1. authorizing our foreign ministers to enter into treaties of alliance and commerce with the several nations who have desired it. 2. Arranging the domestic administration. 3. Establishing arsenals within the states, and posts on our frontier. 4. Disposing of the western territory. 5. Treaties of peace and purchase with the Indians. 6. Money"—a formidable agenda under any circumstances.

"Your Excellency will perceive," he continues, "that these are questions of such difficulty as must produce differences of opinion, and of such importance as forbid a sacrifice of judgment to one another. We have but nine states present, seven of which are represented by only two members each. There are fourteen gentlemen then, any one of which differing from the rest, stops our proceeding, for all these questions require the concurrence of nine states. We shall proceed in a day or two to take them up, and it is my expectation that, after having tried several of them successively and finding it impossible to obtain a single determination, Congress will find it necessary to adjourn till the spring...." [34]

Congress did not adjourn, as Jefferson had predicted. Perhaps it would have been better had it done so, for it was a sorry body. "The enemy are not at our gates to stimulate union and dispatch," [35] one member remarked, and he uttered a bitter truth. "The situation of Congress is truly alarming," wrote James Tilton of Delaware. "The most important business pending and not states enough to take it up, while those present are fatigued into resentment and also into despair with loitering away their time to little purpose." [36] To those members who had given lavishly of their time, their strength, and their spirit, the situation was more bitter than gall and wormwood. "Considering what a deep share I have taken in this controversy," wrote Charles Thomson at this time, "and how anxious I have ever been not only for the success of our cause, but for the honor and dignity of the United States, you will readily conceive that a recollection of the events which have taken place these six months past must give me the most pungent pain. During the contest I have been witness to scenes which gave me extreme uneasiness and distress, but I had this consolation, that we had an object which engaged the attention of foreign nations, an army, and a general struggling with difficulties, and in spite of cold, hunger, and nakedness, bearing up against and checking a powerful invading foe. ... But now that the war is closed with honor and success, the eyes of all Europe are turned upon that Council which it was supposed directed the measures of this continent, in high expectation of seeing traits of wisdom, dignity, and prudence, and what a scene have they exhibited? Oh, that it could be obliterated from the annals of America and utterly effaced from my memory!" [37]

Jefferson devotes several pages of his autobiography to a description of the discussions and the bickering that distinguished Congress during this period, from which he emerges on the lonely eminence of silence. "Our body was little numerous, but very contentious," he writes. "Day after day was wasted on the most unimportant questions. A member, one of those afflicted with the morbid rage of debate, of an ardent mind, prompt imagination, and copious flow of words, who heard with impatience any logic which was not his own, sitting near me on some occasion of a trifling but wordy debate, asked me how I could sit in silence, hearing so much false reasoning, which a word should refute? I observed to him that to refute indeed was easy, but to silence was impossible; that in measures I brought forward by myself, I took the laboring oar, as was incumbent on me, but that in general I was willing to listen." He concludes with the observation that a repetition of what has already been said by others "is a waste and abuse of the time and patience of the House which could not be justified. And I believe that if the members of deliberate bodies were to observe this course generally, they would do in a day what takes them a week." [38]

Jefferson's letters at this time are a series of complaints. "We cannot make up a Congress at all," he writes Madison on the twentieth of February. "There are eight states in town, six of which are represented by two members only. Of these, two members of different states are confined by the gout, so that we cannot make a house. We have not sat above three days, I believe, in as many weeks. Admonition after admonition has been sent to the states, to no effect. We have sent one today. If it fails, it seems as well we should all retire." [39]

On the first of March the spell was finally broken, "a gentleman having this day arrived from New Hampshire.... Nine states being on the floor, we are once more enabled to proceed with the important business of the union," [40] Jacob Read of South Carolina wrote his governor. Even Jefferson's hopes rose, although a thorough schooling in human nature kept him from being too optimistic. "I am not without hope that we shall be able by the first of May to adjourn till November," he confided to Benjamin Harrison. "Nothing could prevent it but the loss of votes sometimes by divisions of the states, eight of the eleven being represented by two members only, any three of the sixteen members can still defeat our endeavors, and your knowledge of men will suggest to you the possibility of three dissenting voices out of sixteen on any question." [41]

The most important business before Congress on this morning was consideration of the cession by Virginia of her lands lying to the north and west of the Ohio. It was a matter over which Congress had haggled with Virginia several years, as well as with the other states which had western claims. Virginia's original cession, fathered by Jefferson, had been passed by the Assembly in its hectic meeting on January 2, 1781, as we have seen. The conditions, however, were unacceptable to Congress, and in October of the following year that body refused to accept it. Many more months of discussion ensued, and on September 13, 1783, Congress outlined terms which would be agreeable. In the fall meeting of the Assembly that year an attempt was made by the friends of the measure to make it conform to congressional demands. A series of letters from Joseph Jones to Madison and Jefferson during this period keeps them informed of the progress of the bill through the House and the Senate.[42] It was finally passed and sent to Congress. "We have received the act of our Assembly ceding the lands north of Ohio and are about executing a deed for it," Jefferson writes Madison on February 20, 1784.[43] The draught of the deed is in Jefferson's hand.

In a letter to Governor Harrison, written on the third of March, Jefferson describes the passage of this important bill. "On receiving the act of Assembly for the western cession," he writes, "our delegation agreed on the form of a deed,[44] we then delivered to Congress a copy of the act, and the form of the deed we were ready to execute whenever they should think proper to declare they would accept it.

They referred the act and deed to a committee, who reported the act of Assembly to comport perfectly with the propositions of Congress, and the deed was proper in its form, and that Congress ought to accept the same." He goes on to describe in detail the difficulties encountered and the objections raised by the representatives of certain states. "We meddled not at all, therefore, and showed a perfect indifference," he continues. "We told them we were not authorized to admit any conditions or provisions, that their acceptance must be simple, absolute, and unqualified, or we could not execute." [45] Finally the dissenting Pennsylvanian received permission "to change his no into aye, the vote then passed, and we executed the deed." [46] "Virginia has completed her cession of territory to the United States," Williamson of North Carolina exulted to his governor, "by which we may be enabled to pay off no small part of the national debt. . . . An object which holds out the prospect of sinking near half of our national debt certainly claims the most serious attention." [47]

The exact boundaries of the ceded territory had not yet been determined. Jefferson, naturally, considered them a matter of the utmost importance and did everything in his power to promote his views. "I think the territory will be laid out by passing a meridian through the western cape of the mouth of the Great Kanhaway from the Ohio to Lake Erie," he writes Madison, "and another through the rapids of Ohio from the same river to Michigan. . . . We hope North Carolina will cede all beyond the same meridian of Kanhaway, and Virginia also. For God's sake push this at the next session of Assembly." [48]

To George Washington he likewise confided this hope and his vision for a great empire for his "country." "Further she cannot govern; so far is necessary for her own well-being," he writes. "The reasons which call for this boundary" he enumerates under seven heads: The lead mines are within this territory, the Kanhaway "traverses our whole latitude and offers to every part of it a channel for navigation and commerce to the western country . . . this river and its waters forms a band of good land passing along our whole frontier . . ." and finally he unfolds his vision of making the Potomac, united with the upper waters of the Cheat and Yohogany rivers, the great gateway to the west. "Nature," he says, "has declared in favor of the Potomac, and through that channel offers to pour into our lap the whole commerce of the western world." Jefferson could not, of course, foresee the developments of the nineteenth century which outmoded his line of reasoning, but nothing can outmode the philosophy behind his ideas. "All the world is becoming commercial," he observes. "Was it practicable to keep our new empire separated from them, we might indulge ourselves in speculating whether commerce contributes to the happiness of mankind. But we cannot separate ourselves from them. Our citizens have had too full a taste of the comforts furnished by the arts and manufactures to be debarred the use of them. We must then in our defense endeavor to share as large a portion as we can of this modern source of wealth and power." [49]

Immediately after the cession of the western territory, a committee, of which Jefferson was chairman, and which included Chase and Howell, handed in a report on a "Temporary Government of Western Country." It was read on the third and recommitted on the seventeenth. The document, again in Jefferson's hand, provides for the formation of states, for the meeting together of "their free males of full age... for the purpose of establishing a temporary government," and lays down the principles upon which both temporary and permanent governments are to be established. The feature most frequently commented upon is the names Jefferson suggested for the proposed states, the boundaries of which he outlined—Sylvania, Michigania, Cherronesus, Assenisipia, Metropotamia, Illinoia, Saratoga, Polypotamia, Pelisipia. Only the one called Washington had a familiar ring.

Congress was not satisfied with the proposal. On March 22 a revised plan of government was submitted by the original committee. It was assigned for consideration on the twenty-fourth, debated in Congress for three days in April, amended, and finally passed on the twenty-third of that month, every state but South Carolina voting for it. It is virtually the same as the preliminary draught, except for a change in the fourth paragraph regarding the admission of new states and the omission of Jefferson's ten proposed states, with the "hard names left out," [50] as one of the members observed. This document, as has long been recognized, is one of the most important from Jefferson's pen. Essentially every provision of the more celebrated Ordinance of 1787 is foreshadowed in it. It embodies the wholly revolutionary principle that the inhabitants of this new territory were not, as has been said, "to be held as subject colonists, but were to be given equal rights with the parent state." [51] Two days after the passage of the act, Jefferson sent a copy to Madison with the remark: "You will observe two clauses struck out of the report, the first respecting hereditary honors, the second slavery. The first was done not from an approbation of such honors, but because it was thought an improper place to encounter them. The second was lost by an individual vote only. Ten states were present. The four eastern states, New York and Pennsylvania, were for the clause. Jersey would have been for it, but there were two members, one of whom was sick in his chambers. South Carolina, Maryland, and ! Virginia! voted against it. North Carolina was divided, as would have been Virginia, had not one of its delegates been sick in bed." [52]

The clause which caused such high feeling and which came so near being embodied as one of the fundamental principles upon which the government of this new territory was to be based, reads: "...that after the year 1800 of the Christian era, there shall be neither slavery nor involuntary servitude in any of the said states, otherwise than in punishment for crimes, whereof the party shall have been convicted to have been personally guilty." [53] Thus was lost one of the most enlightened provisions of the act, one which would well have affected the whole history of this country. Thus was defeated Jefferson's second revolutionary attempt to stamp out the blight of slavery.

A second problem posed by the newly acquired western territory was the disposition of the lands. On the thirtieth of April a committee, of which Jefferson was chairman, reported an "Ordinance for ascertaining the mode of locating and disposing of lands in the Western Territory," with elaborate provisions for dividing it into hundreds, of ten square miles each, then into smaller units, with provisions for a survey and a register to be appointed by Congress. There were likewise provisions for the printing of warrants giving a right to one lot of a square mile, and other details. The report was read a first time on May 7, according to the *Journals* of Congress, and "Monday next assigned for a second reading." On the twenty-eighth of May, after Jefferson had left Congress, it was again considered but was defeated, only one state and two individual votes being in its favor. Nevertheless Jefferson's ideas formed the basis for the revised ordinance which was adopted a year later.

That Jefferson was nettled by this defeat is obvious in an ironical letter he wrote Hopkinson on May 3, in which he comments sarcastically on most of the bills he fostered: "In the scheme for disposing of the soil, an happy opportunity offers of introducing into general use the geometrical mile, in such a manner that it cannot possibly fail of forcing its way on the people. However, this bearing some relation to astronomy and to science in general, which certainly have nothing to do with legislation, I doubt whether it can be carried through." [54]

Shortly after Congress met in Annapolis, Jefferson was appointed to the so-called Committee of States, along with Samuel Osgood of Massachusetts and Roger Sherman of Connecticut. Once more Jefferson was the penman. At the time of the formation of the Articles of Confederation, this committee had been substituted therein for the proposed Council of State. As Congress had been obliged to remain constantly in session during the Revolution, the committee had never functioned. Now, with attendance becoming ever more dilatory and the members more irresponsible, the need of an executive committee when Congress was not in session became more acute. In July 1783 five men had been named "to consider and devise the powers with which a Committee of the States shall be vested during a recess of Congress," and their report was ultimately read on January 23, 1784. The matter, however, was referred to a new committee, of which Jefferson was the chairman.

One week later he presented his report. From the draught preserved among his papers, it is obvious how much he had ruminated on the subject and how important he considered this first gesture towards an executive. It was no secret that Congress was restive and eager for a recess. The members had promised themselves one as soon as peace was declared. Now, in the spring of 1784, it was not possible to keep them together much longer. The increasing diminution in attendance, the caliber of the delegates, which led Thomson to exclaim, "I wish the states would send forward men of enlarged minds and conciliating tempers that matters might not be precipitated and that time might be given for consolidating and strengthening the confederacy," [55] were indicative of their eagerness to be released. What would be the effect on the feeble union when there was no longer a visible administrative head of government, was the grave question that troubled Jefferson and many another serious patriot.

His solution was in the report on the Committee of States, to which he proposed to give very substantial executive and administrative powers, withholding from it only the greater powers of making war, entering on treaties or alliances, coining or borrowing money, sending or receiving ambassadors, and certain others. In his rough draught of the report he considers in great detail, and in his favorite tabulated form, the powers that should and should not be allotted the executive. It occupies four full pages. It is endorsed as having been delivered January 30, entered and read May 27, and passed on May 29.

As revised, it was compressed into one succinct page. The committee was divested of most of the powers Jefferson had given it, and what was left was much more general in character. It was to consist of a representative from each state, "pursuant to the 9th Article of Confederation and perpetual union, to sit in the recess of Congress for transacting the business of the United States." It was to "possess all the powers which may be exercised by seven states in Congress assembled," with six exceptions; no questions, excepting daily adjournment, could be determined without the full nine votes.

That the report was put aside for four months was doubtless not too pleasing to its author. He evidently considered it more or less dead, for in March he wrote Pendleton: "I think it will be prudent immediately to define the powers of a Committee of the States, that if we are left in the lurch again, as we have been, there may be some power to place at the head of affairs till the states can be made sensible of the necessity of sending on full delegations." [56] April came and still there was no settlement. "We talk of adjourning in May," Arthur Lee writes, "and leaving a Committee of the States. It will, I think, be wrong; but some members are so afraid of the southern climate in the summer, that they take it for granted they shall die unless they adjourn." [57]

Jefferson had left Congress by the time the bill was finally passed. That the Committee of the States was to fail completely when called into being on June 4, after Congress had recessed, and that it was to come to an inglorious end when three disgruntled members called for their horses and rode away, he could not foresee. But he might have been tempted to echo the words of his fellow delegate, John Mercer, who questioned whether it was not "a prostitution of the name of government to apply it to such a vagabond, strolling, contemptible crew as Congress." [58]

The impression such conduct was to make on foreign governments, the spectacle of a state with no "visible head," to use Jefferson's words, at all, is contained in a letter of June 18 of the Chevalier de la Luzerne, the retiring French minister. "Congress dispersed on the third of this month, with great precipitation," he writes, "leaving a vast amount of business in suspense and a committee whose powers are extremely limited. . . . It scattered almost immediately, and I think it will not be easy to reassemble them. Behold, then, the body representing the sovereignty of the confederation, without activity, and, so to say, annihilated, and the essential branch of the sovereign power retrenched at least six months." [59] It was, indeed, not a pretty picture.

Jefferson was concerned with two other committees of first importance, and his influence was to be felt long after he had left Congress to go to Europe. These were the committee to determine a permanent seat of government and the one to decide on the coinage of the United States. The question of a suitable residence for Congress had long been discussed, but after the removal from Philadelphia in the summer of 1783, it became acute. "As the United States in Congress assembled represent the sovereignty of the whole union," to use Jefferson's words, it was obvious to all that it should have a seat of its own, with jurisdiction over it. Likewise, "as the residence of Congress will necessarily give added weight to that state in which they shall be permanently fixed," the inevitable struggle began among the various states to secure the coveted prize. There was a party, to be sure, which feared that such a "dominion" was in danger of becoming "the hiding place of all the scoundrels upon the continent and, like the churches of Italy, a refuge from justice," [60] but it was much in the minority. Most of the states offered "prospect of sugar plums," as Richard Peters observed, in the hope of ensnaring Congress. "Many states have been bidding for them," John Armstrong, Jr., secretary of the Council of Pennsylvania writes. "Maryland has set the highest value upon their importance. She gives up her State House for their public deliberations, her Mansion House for their president, and makes them a present of £30,000 for the purpose of building 12 hotels, public offices, etc." [61] New York offered "the little village of Esopus upon the cold banks of the Hudson, a legislative authority for 5 miles about, and a judicial for 15." [62]

On his arrival in Philadelphia in the fall of 1783, Jefferson sent an account of the situation to the governor of Virginia. "Congress, it seems," he writes, "thought it best to generalize their first determination by putting questions on the several rivers on which it had been proposed that they should fix their residence. Hudson River, the Delaware and Potomac, were accordingly offered to the vote. The first obtained scarcely any voices; the Delaware obtained seven. This, of course, put the Potomac out of the way." Although the Delaware had thus been decided upon and the falls seemed to be favored, Pennsylvania held out for Germantown, and Delaware for Wilmington. The southern states now took new hope, "brought on a reconsideration of the question, and obtained a determination that Congress should set one-half of their time at Georgetown, and that, till accommodations should be provided there, Annapolis should be substituted in its place." The fate of the nation's capital thus wavered according to the representation of the various states at a given time. "What will be its final decision can only be conjectured," Jefferson concludes.

After summing up the alignment as it then stood, he considers the attitude of his own state. "Virginia, every place southward of Potomac being disregarded by the states, as every place north of the Delaware, saw it would be useless to consider her interests as to more southern positions. The falls of the Potomac will therefore probably unite the wishes of the whole state.... Those who respect commercial advantages more than the convenience of individuals, will probably think that every position on the bay of Chesapeake, or any of its waters, is to be dreaded by Virginia, as it may attract the trade of that bay and make us with respect to Maryland what Delaware state is to Pennsylvania. Considering the residence of Congress therefore as it may influence trade, if we cannot obtain it on the Potomac, it seems to be our interest to bring it past all the waters of the Chesapeake Bay." [63]

Several more months of discussion brought home to Jefferson the apparent hopelessness of the situation. In February he wrote Madison: "Georgetown languishes. The smile is hardly covered now when the federal towns are spoken of. I fear that our chance is at this time desperate. Our object must therefore be if we fail in an effort to remove to Georgetown, to endeavor then to get some place off the waters of the Chesapeake where we may be ensured against Congress considering themselves as fixed." [64]

In April, when it was obvious that adjournment was only a matter of weeks and when every member was aware that Congress was fast becoming the laughing stock of the country with its "vagabondizing from one paltry village to another," as Charles Thomson put it, the question of a permanent seat for the national government was at last seriously debated.

We find that again Jefferson had prepared some "Notes" on the subject. It is a curious document, but one to which he had obviously given much consideration. It would seem to be, in part, memoranda used by Jefferson in the discussions in Congress, in part rebuttal of objections raised. The three principal sites, the North River, falls of Potomac, and falls of Delaware, are weighed, with the advantages of each. It was but natural that the second should have the most to recommend it in Jefferson's eyes—geographical centrality, proximity to western country already ceded, inducement to further cessions from the Carolinas and Georgia, remoteness from the influence of any overgrown commercial city. The cities considered as temporary sites for the capital each receive a well-considered paragraph. He then turns to tabulating the advantages common to all the states, to the southern states, to Virginia and Maryland and "peculiar to Virginia," should the capital be placed at Georgetown. He concludes with a table giving the distance of the various states from Philadelphia, Trenton, and

Georgetown. It is clear even to the most slow-witted where Jefferson had determined the capital of the United States should be situated.

With this in view, Jefferson draughted two resolutions for the conduct of the affairs of the new seat of government. One is printed as "Resolutions for the Legislatures of Maryland and Virginia," [65] and deals with the appointment of commissioners from each state "who shall have powers to purchase sufficient ground, to agree on the buildings necessary to be erected, to have them erected without delay, and to call for and apply moneys by way of payment or of advance for the same." The second, headed "Resolve on Continental Congress," takes up the question of the proposed jurisdiction of Congress over the seat of government. This question had been raised as early as July 1783 and the usual committee appointed to consider it. A report was brought in, discussed, and referred to a Committee of the Whole. Although September 25 was set as the date for debate, nothing further was done until the spring of 1784. In the general house-cleaning of reports that then took place, prior to adjournment, this was one of the matters scheduled to be referred to the next Congress. It was at this time that Jefferson prepared his resolution. Its provisions are, in essence, those that were eventually adopted.

Jefferson's name is associated with the coinage of this country from its very earliest days. On April 19, 1776, before the colonies had declared their independence, a committee had been appointed by the Continental Congress "to examine and ascertain the value of the several species of gold and silver coins current in these colonies, and the proportions they ought to bear to Spanish milled dollars." Jefferson was added to this committee on July 24. He presented a report on September 2. It was ordered to lie on the table, where it remained. There were at this time, and before, nearly as many monetary systems as there were colonies. Trade with Britain was carried on in pounds and shillings, but for everyday use, so to speak, the Spanish dollar was largely employed among the colonies. The necessity of being able to translate the money of exchange into that of account, and vice versa, led to the practice of counting the dollar at so many shillings. As Robert Morris said in his report to Congress: "Various coins which have circulated in America have undergone different changes in value,

THE LEADER OF CONGRESS

so that there is hardly any which can be considered as a general standard, unless it be the Spanish dollar. These pass in Georgia at 5 shillings, in North Carolina and New York at 8, in Virginia and the four eastern states at 6, and all other states except South Carolina at 7 shillings 6 pence." In South Carolina the rate was 32 shillings 6 pence.[66] The Articles of Confederation had added to the confusion by permitting each state to coin money, although it reserved "the sole and exclusive right and power of regulating the alloy and value of coin struck."

During the anxious years of the war, no regularizing action was taken. The financial situation of the states degenerated to such an extent that depreciated paper money was practically the only currency in circulation. Early in 1782, Congress undertook the task of attempting to create some sort of order out of this chaos. On January 4 a committee was appointed "to ascertain the value and weights at which all foreign coins shall be received in taxes by the Treasurer of these United States and to form such ordinance or ordinances as may be necessary to regulate the currency of the same." [67] Three days later, Robert Morris, the superintendent of finance, was directed to prepare a table of such rates. Morris interpreted this directive as he saw fit, and on the fifteenth addressed the letter which we have just quoted to the president of Congress. Jefferson, who credits Gouverneur Morris, Robert Morris's second in command, with having written it,[68] describes it as "an able and elaborate statement of the denominations of money current in the several states, and of the comparative value of the foreign coins chiefly in circulation with us. He went into the consideration of the necessity of establishing a standard of value with us, and of the adoption of a money unit. He proposed for that unit such a fraction of pure silver as would be a common measure of the penny of every state without leaving a fraction. This common divisor he found to be 1/1440 of a dollar, or 1/1600 of the crown sterling." [69] In addition Morris recommended the establishment of a mint, and also "that it was desirable that money should be increased in the decimal ratio, because by that means all calculations of interest, exchange, insurance, and the like are rendered much more simple and accurate." [70]

Jefferson criticized Morris's scheme as being "too minute for ordinary use, too laborious for computation, either by the head or in figures. The price of a loaf of bread 1/20 of a dollar, would be 72 units, ... a horse or bullock of eighty-dollar value would require a notation of six figures, ... the public debt, suppose of eighty millions, would require twelve figures, to wit 115,200,000,000 units"[71]—a truly astronomical number for that time. The month after his report Morris was instructed to prepare a plan for the establishment of a mint, but he did not respond in any way for ten months, when he asked for a committee to consult with him. From then on the matter lagged in committee after committee, the reports of which were merely "entered and read."

In April of 1784 Jefferson was put on a committee to consider the questions of a mint and a money unit. Paying little attention to the former, he concentrated his efforts on the establishment of a unit of currency. On the twenty-sixth he wrote Robert Morris asking for a copy of the report the latter had made, which had become lost, "so that those who have attended the present year only cannot have the benefit of your then communications.... The Secretary told me he would endeavor to recover it by writing to the former members of the committee, but his endeavors have proved ineffectual, and the session of Congress drawing to a close, I thought it necessary that the business should be put into a train of preparation before they separate, that it may be ready for final discussion when they meet again. I have therefore," he adds, "thrown my own thoughts together on the inclosed paper, with a design of asking your revisal of them and corrections before any proposition be made to Congress.... The impatience of Congress to separate renders it necessary to propose this subject within a few days."[72]

These "Notes," which were handled so casually, became the basis of the currency of the United States as we know it today. Jefferson proposed, as he says, "to adopt the dollar as our unit of account and payment, and that its divisions and subdivisions should be in the decimal ratio." He speaks of submitting his notes to Morris and adds, "I received his answer and adherence to his general system, only agreeing to take for his unit one hundred of those he first proposed, so that a dollar should be 14⁴⁶⁄₁₀₀, and a crown 16 units." Jefferson, wise in the ways of politics, concludes, "I replied to this, and printed my notes in a flying sheet, which I put in the hands of the members of Congress for consideration, and the committee agreed to report on my principle. This was adopted the ensuing year, and is the system which now prevails." [73]

Irked by the usual endless discussion of this subject, Jefferson took satisfaction in ridiculing his own ideas to Francis Hopkinson, in the letter already referred to. "I have hopes that the same care to preserve an 'athletic sense of calculation,' " he writes (he has been discussing the subdivision of a mile), "will not permit us to lose the pound as a money unit and its subdivision into 20ths, 240ths, and 960ths, as now generally practiced. Certain innovators have been wishing to banish all this cunning learning, to adopt the dollar for our unit, to divide that into 10ths, 100ths, etc., and to have a gold coin of the value of 10 dollars, a silver coin of the value of a dollar, another of the value of ¹⁄₁₀ of a dollar, or the Spanish bit, and a copper one equal to ¹⁄₁₀₀ of a dollar. Intermediate silver coins are also proposed for convenience: to wit, the half-dollar or ⁵⁄₁₀, the Pistereen ²⁄₁₀, and the halfbit, ⁵⁄₁₀₀. Thus in a sum of money expressed in these figures 3472, every figure expresses the number of pieces of the several coins which will pay off the sum: to wit, 3 golden pieces, 4 units, 7 bits, and 2 coppers.

"This is surely an age of innovation," he adds with uncanny foresight, "and America the focus of it!" [74]

XIV. Farewell to America

THE SEVENTH DAY OF MAY, 1784, proved to be one of the most important in Jefferson's life. It would not have been surprising had he failed to believe that fate was at last prepared to smile upon him. For the last three years she had pursued him with afflictions. These years had witnessed the disastrous end of his governorship and the breaking up of his home through the death of his beloved wife. The solace of a European mission had been within his grasp, had then been withdrawn. Life had settled down to a routine of hard work, a determination on Jefferson's part to do his utmost in molding the new nation.

On this May morning Congress had concluded its discussion and completed, as Gerry writes, a "business which has been long before them, their instructions to their ministers for negotiating treaties of commerce. To those, which are to extend to almost every commercial power in Europe, are added propositions for treaties of amity with the Emperor of Morocco and other Barbary powers."[1] Jefferson, his memory still fresh with the miseries of war, had been able to introduce into these instructions certain of his humane and, for the time, revolutionary views, such as that "if war should hereafter arise between the two contracting parties, the merchants of either country then residing in the other ... shall be allowed to remain nine months to collect their debts and settle their affairs." Furthermore, "all fishermen, all cultivators of the earth, and all artisans or manufacturers, unarmed and inhabiting unfortified towns, villages, or places, who labor for the common subsistence and benefit of mankind ... shall be allowed to continue the same, and shall not be molested by the armed forces of the enemy ... and all merchants and traders, exchanging the products of different places, and thereby rendering the necessaries, conveniences, and comforts of human life more easy to obtain and more general, shall be allowed to pass free and unmolested; and neither of the contracting powers shall grant or issue any commission to any private armed vessels empowering them to take or destroy such trading ships, or interrupt such commerce." [2] This was, indeed, a new language in which to write treaties.

During this morning a letter arrived from Benjamin Franklin confirming the news that John Jay was sailing for the United States. Congress immediately appointed him to the long vacant post of secretary of state, and, "on the motion of Mr. Hardy, seconded by Mr. Gerry, resolved that a minister plenipotentiary be appointed in addition to Mr. John Adams and Mr. Benjamin Franklin for the purpose of negotiating treaties of commerce. Congress proceeded to the election and the ballots being taken, Mr. Thomas Jefferson was elected, having previously been nominated by Mr. Hardy." [3] Dramatically, Jefferson thus made his exit from Congress.

Jefferson sent two letters to the governor of Virginia on the seventh concerning the state of affairs in Congress, but he does not mention his own appointment. It was not until the thirteenth of May that the other delegates, Hardy, Mercer, and Lee, informed the governor what had happened. "On the 7th inst.," they write, "Congress agreed to a plan for forming commercial treaties with the maritime powers of Europe and those of Africa bordering on the Mediterranean. To a measure ardently solicited by the mercantile part of America and warmly espoused by a large majority of Congress, we did not choose to withhold our assent ... and to suspend the final decision on the measure, until Mr. Jefferson had been joined in the commission for these negotiations to Mr. Adams and Dr. Franklin." [4]

Jefferson's own reaction to his appointment is lost in the impenetrable mist that obscures almost every detail of his private life. It is only by turning to the list of letters written and received, which he began keeping in 1779, that we can glimpse some tiniest ray of the excitement that transported him, of the thousand plans that crowded his mind. He thought first of all of Monticello and his family, as very naturally he would. On this May evening of the seventh, already crowded with the long debates in Congress, he sat down to write those nearest him. It is obvious that his appointment was not wholly unexpected, that tentative arrangements for a long absence had already been made, and that these letters were only to seal the agreements. First there was one to William Short, with whom he had some time since discussed an idea of being private secretary. Jefferson's notation reads: "Short. notice of my appointment to Europe. To join me at Philadelphia on the 25th and bring James [a servant]." Next he wrote James Key, the steward at Monticello, "to send James." Turning to his family, he wrote a letter to Mrs. Eppes labeled "valedictory," and to Mrs. Carr, his own widowed sister, Martha, whose boys were now in need of masculine oversight, to "consign Peter Carr to Mr. Madison. Dabney also. Invite to pass hot season at Monticello." To Mrs. Skipwith, his wife's sister Ann Wayles, a "valedictory," and to "Mr. Skipwith ditto, invitation to pass hot weather at Monticello." A similar letter went to his unmarried sister, Anna Scott Jefferson. The following day and the next, he notes writing valedictories to his closest friends, Bellini, Madison, James McClurg, who had been in college with him, Mazzei, George Grimes, John Walker, Nicholas Lewis, enclosing power of attorney, David Ross, and Dr. Currie, offering "a welcome to my quarters in Paris." There was likewise a letter to the governor with a "tender of service to state."

Jefferson lost no time in leaving Annapolis. Dr. Murray, who had attended him on the several occasions when he had been ill, was "paid in full £35-4." Partout, a Frenchman who acted as majordomo in the household of Jefferson and Monroe, was paid "his wages from April 1 to May 11, at 30 guineas a year, £5-18." The "household things and books" were sold to Colonel Monroe, who was "to pay Mr. Dulaney my house rent, £5-6-9, and Fraser stable rent £6." Other business was concluded, and on the eleventh Jefferson set out with a high heart, we cannot doubt. He took a boat across Chesapeake Bay which landed him at Rockhall, about twenty miles up. There he spent the night at Spencer's tavern and left the next morning for Chestertown. Worral's inn was his stopping place that night, and on the thirteenth he came to the lovely old town of Newcastle, Delaware, which until lately was sleeping so peacefully and far removed from the bustle of this world. The following day he reached Philadelphia and celebrated his arrival by attending "the playhouse." Two weeks of intense activity ensued, in which further preparations for the trip were made and old accounts settled. Mrs. Hopkinson was paid £22/10/6 in full for looking after Patsy, Mrs. House, with whom Jefferson had lodged before, received £7/12, Hiltzheimer, the stableman, £7/17/6.

Before leaving Philadelphia Jefferson was to gratify one of his great desires. This was to witness a balloon ascension. Some time previously he and Francis Hopkinson had started a correspondence on this subject. Scarcely a year before, in June 1783, Joseph Montgolfier and his brother Jacques had succeeded in sending up a balloon thirty-six feet in diameter at Armonoy. The news traveled quickly from France to America. It captured the imagination of all scientists and near-scientists. "What think you of these ballons?" Jefferson asked Hopkinson on February 18, 1784. "The Chevalier Luzerne communicated to me a letter received from his brother, who mentions one he had seen himself. The person who ascended in it regulated its height at about 3,000 feet, and passed with the wind about 6 miles in 20 minutes, when they chose to let themselves down, though they could have traveled triple the distance."

Jefferson's next words electrify the reader. His uncanny clairvoyance, in view of the developments of the last years, is nothing short of phenomenal. "This discovery seems to threaten the prostration of fortified works," he writes, "unless they can be closed above, the destruction of fleets, and what not.... Inland countries may become maritime states, unless you choose rather to call them aerial ones, as their commerce is in future to be carried on through that element.... We shall soar sublime above the clouds." [5]

It was not long before the Philadelphians were experimenting with balloons, and on the twelfth of May Hopkinson wrote Jefferson about the first actual ascension. "We have been amusing ourselves with raising air balloons made of paper," he writes. "The first that mounted our atmosphere was made by Dr. Foulk and sent up from the garden of the minister of Holland the day before yesterday. Yesterday forenoon, the same balloon was raised from Mr. Morris's garden... to the great amusement of the spectators.... I am contriving a better method of filling them." [6]

This was something Jefferson was bound to see, no matter how great his hurry. He was deep in the subject and had just completed a study of the latest book on aeronautics by Saint-Fond. A detailed report had been sent to his nephew, Philip Turpin, whose education he had directed, "as to the reality and extent of the late discovery of traversing the air in balloons." [7] He was scarcely back in Philadelphia before he notes, on May 17, "pd. for 2 tickets to see balon 15/." Whether he took his little daughter to view this modern wonder, or whether his companion was Francis Hopkinson, we have no way of knowing. In any case, he exulted to Monroe a few days later: "I have had the pleasure of seeing three balloons here. The largest was 8 feet in diameter and ascended about 300 feet." [8]

Two entries in Jefferson's account book before he left Philadelphia are of particular interest. On May 20 there is the rather unusual item of "pd. for a panther skin 45/." It was not as fantastic as it seemed, however, for Jefferson had a purpose in buying it. Already he was planning to get the better of a certain celebrated Frenchman and his mistaken ideas about the New World with a visible and demonstrative actuality. Many years later, in relating various anecdotes of his life to Daniel Webster, he remarked that, "being about to embark from Philadelphia for France, I observed an uncommonly large panther skin at the door of a hatter's shop. I bought it for half a Jo [sixteen dollars] on the spot, determining to carry it to France, to convince M. Buffon of his mistake in relation to this animal, which he had confounded with the cougar. He acknowledged his mistake and said he would correct it in his next volume." [9]

The second entry, the last before he left Philadelphia, concerns £17/10 which he left with Francis Hopkinson "for Wright for drawing General Washington." The artist who was to paint this portrait was Joseph Wright, an American, who had studied with Hoppner and West in England. He was at this time settled in Philadelphia. Before coming there, in the late summer of 1783 he had painted portraits of both George and Martha Washington at the General's headquarters at Rocky Hill, near Princeton. Washington referred to

Wright, shortly after, as "a gentleman who is thought...to have taken a better likeness of me than any other painter has done." It was doubtless a replica of this portrait that Wright undertook to paint for Jefferson, as there is no record of other sittings.

On the thirtieth of May Hopkinson wrote: "Mr. Wright has made a most excellent copy of the General's head; he is much pleased with it himself, and I think it rather more like the original. In order to admit of its being packed up at all, he has been obliged to expose it all this day in the sun. The consequence is that the colors will sink in, as the painters call it—that is, will look dead and without brilliancy or gloss. This is the case with all pictures, till the colors are brought out again by a varnish. This operation must be performed in France, as it cannot be done till the picture is thoroughly dry, for which you know there is no time in the present case." [10]

The picture was duly packed and added to Jefferson's peculiar assortment of baggage. It is a half-length with the left hand resting on a sword. The face is a rosy salmon, the coat dark blue with gold epaulets and buff facing. The waistcoat, emphasizing the portliness of the subject, is likewise of buff, with gold buttons. Whether Jefferson commissioned this portrait solely to adorn his residence in Paris, or as a model for a figure of Washington, is not certain. In the years following the close of the Revolution, there had been various discussions concerning a suitable memorial to Washington, and on June 22, 1784, the legislature of Virginia resolved that "the Executive be requested to take measures for procuring a statue of General Washington to be of the finest marble and best workmanship, with the following inscription on its pedestal: 'The General Assembly of the Commonwealth of Virginia have caused this statue to be erected as a monument of affection and gratitude to George Washington who, uniting to the endowments of the hero the virtues of the patriot, and exerting both in establishing the liberties of his country, has rendered his name dear to his fellow citizens and given the world an immortal example of true glory.'" [11] In July Jefferson was requested to secure a sculptor to model such a figure. He had, of course, as his correspondence with Short shows, known of the enterprise, and it is possible that he carried the portrait with him for this purpose.

On the twenty-eighth of May, after last farewells, Jefferson and his young daughter set out. The world beckoned him as never before, not since his early youth. Conscious that, except for a brief trip to New York nearly twenty years ago, his knowledge of the United States was limited to Virginia, Maryland, and Pennsylvania, he determined to extend it. He wrote Edmund Pendleton a few days before he started: "I mean to go through the Eastern [New England] states in hopes of deriving some knowledge of them from actual inspection and inquiry which may enable me to discharge my duty to them somewhat better." Thus he and Patsy, with their servants, headed north. Colonel David Humphreys had been appointed secretary of the commission on May 12. Jefferson met him in Philadelphia, and they made plans to travel to Europe together, plans which did not eventuate. Ezra Stiles mentions that he was with Jefferson in New Haven, but we do not know whether he accompanied Jefferson on his whole New England trip.

Jefferson and his party crossed the green and listless Neshaminy, some ten miles out of Philadelphia, dined at Bristol, and spent the night at Trenton. There was breakfast at Princeton next day, dinner at Brunswick, and lodging at Woodbridge. A "second river" was crossed on the third day, then the wide blue Hackensack, ambling through the Jersey meadows. On the thirtieth the passage was made from Paulus Hook, now lost in the maze of Jersey City, to New York.

Six busy days were spent there. Although the city was not the metropolis it is today, there was temptation enough to buy books, maps, chessmen, a hat, and various other necessities. On the fifth of June, after paying "Mrs. Ellsworth 6 days' lodging, etc. 17-3-4," the travelers were off again towards New England. The first night was passed at Fort Washington, the rocky promontory which then guarded the upper reaches of the Hudson, but from which now springs the noble span of the George Washington Bridge. The following day breakfast and dinner were enjoyed at Mrs. Haviland's, in Rye, Westchester County. The party lodged with Mrs. Wells, in Stamford, that night. The next day, passing along the old highway which Benjamin Franklin had marked with milestones from Boston to New York in

1753, they reached Fairfield. This village, which had been burned by the British in 1779 when some 200 houses were destroyed, still showed the scars of its ordeal. Jefferson and Martha breakfasted there, then proceeded to New Haven, where they arrived after dinner on the seventh.

The following day Jefferson called upon Ezra Stiles, president of Yale College. He came with a letter from Roger Sherman, who introduced him as "a gentleman of much philosophical as well as political knowledge—and I doubt not you will be very agreeably entertained with his conversations." The reverend gentleman comments on the visit in his diary, giving an account of Jefferson's accomplishments and education. He seems more interested in the state of the College of William and Mary, as was perhaps natural with a college president, than in any other phase of their conversation. "He tells me," Stiles observes somewhat smugly, "President Madison's salary and perquisites are about £400 per annum." He speaks of the reformation of the college, stimulated by Jefferson, and is somewhat horror-struck, as well he might be, that "they made it unnecessary to learn any Latin or Greek in order to admission into the College." Further topics of conversation are reflected in Stiles's statement that "Governor Jefferson says the total inhabitants of the state of Virginia is nearly 380,000 souls, whites, and 250,000 blacks . . . that property is so diffused through the state that five-sixths of the whites possess 100 acres land and upwards to large landholders, and that the plebeian interest will prevail over the old aristocratical interest in that state."

The impression made upon him by Jefferson is that of "a most ingenious naturalist and philosopher, a truly scientific and learned man, and every way excellent. . . . Governor Jefferson has seen many of the great bones dug up on the Ohio. He has a thighbone *three feet long* and a tooth weighing *sixteen pounds*." [12]

The ninth saw Jefferson on his way again. It would be futile to follow him from place to place. Except for a single letter, we have only his account book to give us any information. This is largely a record of the minor mishaps of the trip—how much was paid for mending the harness, the phaeton, or a broken axletree—accidents which occurred all too frequently. Just before sailing, Jefferson wrote

Madison in farewell, apologizing for not sending him any "particular communications," and observing: "Indeed there are few I should have to make, unless I were to enter into a detail which would be too lengthy, as to the country and people I have visited." This is, alas, just what is lacking.

Going by way of Hartford, Norwich, and New London, Jefferson passed into "Rhode Island state," where a broken axletree kept him overnight at the hamlet of South Kingston. Two days were spent in Newport, not so long ago evacuated by the French, one at Providence, and on the eighteenth he reached Boston. Here he found that Abigail Adams was "within thirty-six hours of sailing." Great as was his desire to have her company on the long crossing, he was obliged to forego it. It was impossible to make the necessary preparations in time. As it was, he allowed himself only three days in Boston before setting out on a side trip to the north which was to take him to the leading ports of New England.

The fruit of this was a report on the state of New Hampshire made in answer to certain queries of young Van Hogendorp. Jefferson discusses ten points: the government, the price of labor, shipbuilding, navigation, the fisheries, exports, imports, freight, manufactures, and the "balance with Great Britain." Although dated "New Hampshire, June, 1784," the notes were not cast into final form and sent Hogendorp until November 20, 1784, when Jefferson was already established in Paris.[13]

Jefferson had, as he wrote Elbridge Gerry, determined to take the first ship available, "but, hearing of no vessel going from any eastern port to France, I had in contemplation to return to New York and take my passage in the French packet which was to sail on the 15th [of July] inst., but it was suggested to me that I could with certainty get ashore on the coast of France, somewhere, from any vessel bound for London, and Mr. Tracy had a vessel to sail from hence the third, which would save twelve days in the outset, and probably as many more in the run. I engaged my passage on her, and with the more pleasure as he was to go himself on her."

The Mr. Tracy mentioned by Jefferson was Nathaniel Tracy of Newburyport, a graduate of Harvard in the class of 1769, described as "merchant, philanthropist, patriot, and financier of the Revolution." [14] He was a man of great means, who during the course of the war had fitted out numerous cruisers which were charged with preying on British vessels and capturing men, ammunition, and supplies. He likewise contributed large sums of money to the government. The handsome brick house, which now serves as a library, was where he entertained visiting dignitaries, and it was there that Jefferson stayed with him on his New England tour.

"The intermediate time," Jefferson continues, "I have employed in a trip to Portsmouth, in order to gather in that state, as I had endeavored to do in the others through which I had passed, such information of their commerce and other circumstances as might in some degree enable me to answer the purposes of my mission. No small part of the time, too, has been occupied by the hospitality and civilities of this place, which I have experienced in the highest degree. These, with the preparations for my voyage, have left me scarcely a spare moment; and, receiving assurances from every quarter that I might derive from Mr. Tracy the fullest information as to the commerce of this state, I have deferred much of the inquiries I wished to make to the vacant hours of our voyage." [15]

Jefferson concludes his letter by saying that he is leaving for Gerry, with whom he had been closely associated in Congress for years, "a token of my friendship for you, which will remind you of me sometimes while you have pen in hand and which, therefore, you must keep as a monitor on my behalf." [16] The gift, according to Gerry's biographer, was a "portable writing desk of a fashion then not common in the United States." On May 23, before leaving Philadelphia, Jefferson had paid a silversmith 30 shillings for work on a "traveling box," and it is not impossible that this was the "elegant traveling desk which I value most highly as a pledge of your friendship," for which Gerry thanked him on his return to Boston.

Jefferson was back from his excursion to Portsmouth on the twenty-sixth. En route he had visited Salem, Ipswich, Marblehead, and Newbury, Massachusetts, and gone as far as Exeter, New Hampshire. His ship was due to sail on July 3, and the last days were harried. He sold his horse, "Assurcagoa, to Neil Jameson for £30. He is to bear expenses of Bob and the horses to New York, to furnish him there with 30 dollars to carry him home, to send some porter, fish, etc., to F. Eppes and remit the balance to James Buchanan for me." [17] Purchases for the voyage were made. Four dozen bottles of hock, apples, oranges, bedding for on shipboard, to the extent of £9/12/7, a chamber pot, a table and chair are the outstanding items. Colonel Ingersoll was paid £22/17 for lodging while Jefferson was in Boston. Bob was started back to Virginia on the first. Finally, on the fourth, Jefferson paid "ferriage to Charleston 1/3" and boarded the *Ceres* under the command of Captain St. Barbe. He notes that they sailed from Boston on July 5 at 4 o'clock in the morning.

What thoughts filled Jefferson's mind as he stood on deck early in the summer morning watching the sun rise over the rugged Boston harbor, is something we can only surmise. It was the eighth anniversary of the Declaration of Independence. Although the final form of government was not yet established, although there was still a maze of problems both gigantic and picayune, through which its leaders must find their way, Jefferson's new country was already standing firmly established. As he turned for a last farewell to the fast receding shore, the sentiments to which he was later to give voice may well have filled his mind: "If there be any among us who would wish to dissolve this union, or to change its republican form, let them stand undisturbed as monuments of the safety with which error of opinion may be tolerated, where reason is left free to combat it. I know, indeed, that some men fear that a republican government cannot be strong; that this government is not strong enough.... I believe this, on the contrary, the strongest government on earth. I believe it is the only one where every man at the call of the laws, would fly to the standard of the law, and would meet invasions of the public order, as his own personal concern." [18]

Notes

Except in quotations from certain illiterates, the spelling and punctuation of all quotations has been modernized.

CHAPTER I

1 Edmund Cody Burnett, *The Continental Congress*, p. 214.
2 A. E. Lipscomb and A. E. Bergh, *The Writings of Thomas Jefferson* (cited henceforth as Lipscomb), vol. 16, p. 116.
3 *Ibid.*, vol. 1, p. 53.
4 Moncure Conway, *Edmund Randolph*, p. 29.
5 Peter Force, *American Archives*, 4th series, vol. 6, p. 1524.
6 Lipscomb, vol. 4, pp. 253-6.
7 Paul Leicester Ford, *The Writings of Thomas Jefferson* (cited henceforth as Ford), vol. 2, p. 7.
8 Pp. 284-90.
9 Lipscomb, vol. 16, p. 116.
10 James Curtis Ballagh, *The Letters of Richard Henry Lee* (cited henceforth as Ballagh), vol. 1, p. 203.
11 *Ibid.*, p. 205.
12 Lipscomb, vol. 2, p. 160.
13 *Idem.*
14 *Ibid.*, vol. 4, pp. 259-60.
15 Edmund Cody Burnett, *Letters of Members of the Continental Congress* (cited henceforth as *Letters Members Continental Congress*), vol. 2, p. 28.
16 Jefferson Papers, Library of Congress.
17 *Idem.*
18 *Letters Members Continental Congress*, vol. 2, p. lxxiii.
19 *Journals of the Continental Congress*, vol. 15, p. 433.
20 *Letters Members Continental Congress*, vol. 2, p. 129.
21 Ballagh, vol. 1, p. 218.
22 Ford, vol. 2, pp. 91-2.
23 Lipscomb, vol. 1, p. 62.
24 *Idem.*
25 *Journal of the House of Delegates*, vol. for 1776, p. 41.
26 Pp. 209-28.

363

27 Ford, vol. 2, pp. 99-100.
28 Lipscomb, vol. 1, p. 62.
29 *Report of the Committee of Revisors*, chap. LXXIX. Reprinted in Ford, vol. 2, p. 220 *ff*.
30 *Idem*.
31 Lipscomb, vol. 1, p. 71.
32 Ford, vol. 2, p. 232. "Report of Revisors," chap. LXXX.
33 *Idem*.
34 *Ibid.*, p. 233.
35 Lipscomb, vol. 1, p. 66.
36 Ford, vol. 2, pp. 195-6.
37 *Journal of the House of Delegates*, pp. 56-7.
38 Lipscomb, vol. 5, p. 181.

CHAPTER II

1 Henry S. Randall, *Life of Thomas Jefferson* (cited henceforth as Randall), vol. 1, p. 235.
2 Jefferson Papers, Library of Congress.
3 *Memoirs of the Life of Philip Mazzei*, translated by H. R. Marraro, p. 284.
4 *Ibid.*, p. 194.
5 *Ibid.*, p. 203.
6 Ford, vol. 3, p. 425.
7 Lipscomb, vol. 5, p. 152.
8 *William and Mary Quarterly*, series 2, vol. 5, p. 3.
9 *Ibid.*, p. 12.
10 Mazzei erroneously gives his age as "not yet fifteen." The *Enciclopedia Italiana* says the date of his birth was 1752.
11 Mazzei, *Memoirs*, pp. 185-6.
12 Jefferson Papers, Library of Congress.
13 Lipscomb, vol. 4, pp. 38-42. A portion of this letter has been quoted in the author's *Jefferson: The Road to Glory*, pp. 54 and 57. In the letter as printed in the various editions of Jefferson's works, no superscription is given.
14 *Journals of the Continental Congress*, vol. 14, p. 899. The spelling of the gentleman's name is variously given as d'Anmours, d'Anemours, D'Anmours, and Danmours. There is a variation in the way he signs his own letters.
15 *Official Letters of the Governors of Virginia* (cited henceforth as *Official Letters*), vol. 2, p. 68.
16 Virginia State Archives, printed in *The Researcher*, vol. 1, pp. 142-3.

17 *Journal of the House of Delegates*, Dec. 8, 1779, p. 82.
18 *Virginia Gazette*, Jan. 1, 1780, quoted in *Official Letters*, vol. 2, pp. 84-5.
19 Ballagh, vol. 2, p. 148.
20 Jefferson Papers, Library of Congress.
21 *Idem.*
22 *Idem.*
23 *Virginia Gazette*, Sept. 11, 1779.
24 Mazzei, *Memoirs*, p. 225.
25 Lipscomb, vol. 4, p. 57.
26 *Ibid.*, vol. 4, pp. 45-59.
27 Jefferson Account Book, Library of Congress, under dates of April 22, 29, and July 21, 1779.
28 Jefferson Papers, Library of Congress.
29 *Idem.*
30 *Idem.*
31 *Idem.*
32 *Idem.*
33 Ford, vol. 2, p. 303.
34 Jefferson Papers, Library of Congress.
35 Jefferson Papers, Missouri Historical Society.
36 Jefferson Papers, Library of Congress.
37 Lipscomb, vol. 4, pp. 138-9.
38 Jefferson Papers, Library of Congress.
39 *Idem.*
40 Mazzei, *Memoirs*, p. 226.
41 Jefferson Papers, Library of Congress.
42 *Idem.*
43 Lipscomb, vol. 5, pp. 127-9.
44 Jefferson Papers, Library of Congress.
45 *Idem.*
46 *Idem.*
47 Lipscomb, vol. 19, pp. 71-2.

CHAPTER III

1 Johann David Schoepf, *Travels in the Confederation* (1911 ed.), vol. 1, p. 55.
2 *Journal of the House of Delegates*, reprinted in Ford, vol. 2, pp. 186-7.
3 Jefferson Papers, Library of Congress.
4 Ford, vol. 2, p. 187.
5 Ballagh, vol. 2, p. 82.

6 *Bland Papers*, vol. 2, p. 11 (June 6, 1779).
7 Ford, vol. 2, p. 245.
8 *Ibid.*, p. 192.
9 Constitution of 1776, reprinted in Armistead R. Long, *The Constitution of Virginia, an Annotated Edition*, p. 114.
10 *Virginia Magazine*, vol. 44, p. 48.
11 Long, *Constitution of Virginia*, p. 114.
12 *Journal of the House of Delegates*, p. 107 (Dec. 21, 1776).
13 Lipscomb, vol. 2, pp. 173-4.
14 William Wirt Henry, *Patrick Henry*, vol. 2, pp. 48-9.
15 Figures from W. W. Hening, *Statutes at Large* (cited henceforth as Hening), vol. 9, pp. 485, 521; vol. 10, pp. 118, 219.
16 Hening, vol. 9, p. 292. For the draught, in Jefferson's hand, see Ford, vol. 2, p. 123.
17 John Adams, *Works*, vol. 9, p. 465.
18 *Letters of Joseph Jones*, edited by Worthington C. Ford, p. 1.
19 *Official Letters*, vol. 2, p. 14.
20 *Bland Papers*, vol. 2, p. 11.
21 *Journal of the House of Delegates*, May 1779, p. 15.
22 Ford, vol. 2, p. 188.
23 Robert K. Brock, *Archibald Cary of Ampthill*, p. 157.
24 Fiske Kimball, *Thomas Jefferson, Architect*, pp. 139-41, plates 101-6. See also his *Thomas Jefferson and the First Monument of the Classical Revival in America*.
25 Hening, vol. 10, p. 86.
26 *Cf.* Jefferson's map of Richmond in Fiske Kimball, *Thomas Jefferson, Architect*, pp. 139-40 and figs. 102, 103.
27 Hening, vol. 10, p. 317.
28 *Calendar of Virginia State Papers*, vol. 3, p. 418.
29 Jefferson Papers, Library of Congress.
30 *Cf.* letter to John Jay, quoted from the papers of the Continental Congress in *Official Letters*, vol. 2, pp. 38-9.
31 Only a portion of Jefferson's letters as governor survive. These fill a stout volume of some 530 pages. The books in which his letters were transcribed from June 1, 1779, until January 5, 1781, when Richmond was captured by the British, were carried off by Arnold. The British Museum possesses one for the period July 27-September 18, 1780.
32 Hening, vol. 9, pp. 377-80.
33 *Ibid.*, vol. 10, p. 67.
34 *Williamsburg Gazette*, July 3, 1779. Quoted in *Official Letters*, vol. 2, p. 19.

NOTES

35 *Official Letters,* vol. 2, pp. 4-5.
36 *Ibid.,* vol. 2, pp. 47-8.
37 Ballagh, vol. 1, pp. 451-2.
38 Hening, vol. 10, p. 125.
39 Ballagh, vol. 2, p. 65.
40 Lipscomb, vol. 4, p. 298.
41 Hening, vol. 10, p. 241 *ff.*
42 *Ibid.,* pp. 279-80.
43 *Ibid.,* pp. 280-6.
44 *Ibid,* p. 347.
45 *Ibid.,* p. 399.
46 "Edmund Randolph's Essay," in *Virginia Magazine,* vol. 44, pp. 313-4.
47 J. C. Fitzpatrick, *Writings of Washington* (cited henceforth as Fitzpatrick), vol. 17, pp. 75-6.
48 *Official Letters,* vol. 2, pp. 70-1.
49 *Journal of the House of Delegates,* Nov. 26, 1779.
50 Hening, vol. 10, p. 17.
51 *Ibid.,* p. 291.
52 *Official Letters,* vol. 2, pp. 78-9.
53 Fitzpatrick, vol. 6, pp. 163-8.
54 Hening, vol. 9, pp. 267-8.
55 *Ibid.,* p. 292.
56 *Ibid.,* p. 117.
57 Lipscomb, vol. 2, p. 125.
58 Hening, vol. 10, p. 83.
59 *Ibid,* p. 18.
60 Fitzpatrick, vol. 6, p. 164.
61 Ballagh, vol. 2, p. 158.
62 *Virginia Magazine,* vol. 44, p. 318.
63 Ballagh, vol. 2, pp. 73-4.
64 Hening, vol. 10, p. 214.
65 Hening, vol. 9, p. 150.
66 *Ibid.,* p. 196.
67 Henry, *Patrick Henry,* vol. 2, p. 278.
68 *Virginia Gazette,* Sept. 25, 1779. Quoted by R. A. Stewart, *The History of Virginia's Navy of the Revolution,* pp. 73-6.
69 Jefferson Papers, Library of Congress. (The *Journal of the House of Delegates,* however, lists 16 ships on November 30, 1779. Both lists except the prisonship *Gloucester.*)
70 Ballagh, vol. 2, pp. 83-5.
71 Published through the courtesy of the owner, Stanley F. Horn.

72 *Official Letters*, vol. 2, p. 18.
73 Hening, vol. 10, p. 123.
74 Quoted by H. J. Eckenrode, *The Revolution in Virginia*, p. 203, from *Executive Communications*, 1779.
75 *Journal of the House of Delegates*, Nov. 30, 1779; Hening, vol. 10, p. 217.
76 *Official Letters*, vol. 2, p. 15.
77 *Virginia Gazette*, Dec. 11, 1779.
78 Fitzpatrick, vol. 17, p. 246.
79 *Ibid.*, p. 317.
80 *Official Letters*, vol. 2, pp. 80-1.

CHAPTER IV

1 Quoted from the *Journal* of the Reverend David Jones, in William Hayden English, *Conquest of the Country Northwest of the River Ohio* (cited henceforth as English), vol. 1, p. 60.
2 *Ibid.*, p. 66.
3 *Illinois Historical Collections, George Rogers Clark Papers*, vol. 8, p. 209. The punctuation and spelling of the Clark documents have been modernized.
4 *Idem.*
5 *Ibid.*, p. 118.
6 *Official Letters*, vol. 1, p. 33.
7 "Clark's Memoir," *Illinois Historical Collections*, vol. 8, pp. 217-8.
8 *Ibid.*, p. 218.
9 *Ohio Valley Historical Series*, no. 3, *Clark's Campaign in the Illinois*, with an introduction by Henry Pirth, p. 2.
10 Cf. *Official Letters*, vol. 2, p. 87.
11 *Journals of the Council of the State of Virginia* (cited henceforth as *Journals of Council*), vol. 2, p. 56.
12 *Illinois Historical Collections*, vol. 8, p. 219 (quoted in English, p. 467).
13 Quoted in Henry, *Patrick Henry*, vol. 1, p. 586.
14 *Illinois Historical Collections*, vol. 8, p. 123.
15 *Ibid.*, p. 170.
16 *Ibid.*, p. 97.
17 *Ibid.*, p. 140.
18 *Ibid.*, p. 139.
19 *Official Letters*, vol. 1, pp. 371, 372.
20 *Ibid.*, vol. 2, pp. 9-11.
21 *Ibid.*, pp. 10-11.

22 Ford, vol. 2, pp. 246-7.
23 Fitzpatrick, vol. 16, p. 68.
24 *Ibid.*, p. 272.
25 Quoted from the *Virginia Gazette* in *Official Letters*, vol. 2, p. 40.
26 *Ibid.*, p. 41.
27 *Ibid.*, p. 42.
28 *Ibid.*, pp. 41-4.
29 Fitzpatrick, vol. 19, pp. 500-1.
30 *Official Letters*, vol. 2, pp. 210-1.
31 Ford, vol. 2, pp. 64-5.
32 *Ibid.*, pp. 65-6.
33 *Illinois Historical Collections*, vol. 8, p. 220.
34 *Official Letters*, vol. 1, p. 280.
35 *Journal of the House of Delegates*, Dec. 9, 1778.
36 *Idem.*
37 *Official Letters*, vol. 2, p. 36n.
38 *Pennsylvania Archives*, vol. 8, p. 46 (quoted in *Official Letters*, vol. 2, p. 37).
39 *Official Letters*, vol. 2, p. 98n.
40 *Ibid.*, p. 100.
41 *Ibid.*, pp. 447-8.
42 *Ibid.*, p. 481.
43 *Ibid.*, p. 520.
44 *State Records of North Carolina*, vol. 14, p. 220; *Official Letters*, vol. 2, pp. 62-3.
45 *Official Letters*, vol. 2, p. 63.

CHAPTER V

1 *Official Letters*, vol. 2, pp. 126-7.
2 *Ibid.*, pp. 127-8.
3 Jefferson Papers, Library of Congress.
4 Hening, vol. 10, pp. 309-10.
5 *Ibid.*, p. 312.
6 *Idem.*
7 *Idem.*
8 *Bland Papers*, vol. 2, p. 40.
9 Gates Papers, New York Historical Society.
10 *Idem.*
11 Fitzpatrick, vol. 20, p. 248.
12 Jefferson Papers, Library of Congress.
13 *Official Letters*, vol. 2, pp. 150-1.

14 See *Official Letters,* vol. 2, pp. 117-8 for this letter.
15 *Official Letters,* vol. 2, pp. 127-8.
16 Gates Papers, New York Historical Society.
17 Jefferson Papers, Library of Congress.
18 *Magazine of American History,* vol. 5, p. 241 *ff.* Quotations are from pages 303 and 304.
19 *Official Letters,* vol. 2, p. 204.
20 "Edmund Randolph's Essay," *Virginia Magazine,* vol. 44, p. 316.
21 Jefferson Papers, Library of Congress.
22 *Official Letters,* vol. 2, pp. 186-7.
23 *Ibid.,* pp. 183-4.
24 *Ibid.,* p. 183.
25 *Ibid.,* pp. 187-90.
26 *Ibid.,* pp. 204-5.
27 *Ibid.,* p. 202.
28 *Ibid.,* p. 204.
29 Fitzpatrick, vol. 20, pp. 30-1.
30 *Bland Papers,* vol. 2, p. 36.
31 *Official Letters,* vol. 2, pp. 221-2.
32 *Ibid.,* p. 222.
33 *Ibid.,* p. 226.
34 *Ibid.,* p. 223.
35 *Ibid.,* p. 227.
36 *Ibid.,* p. 230.
37 *Ibid.,* pp. 224-5.
38 *Ibid.,* p. 236.
39 *Ibid.,* p. 224.
40 *Calendar of Virginia State Papers,* vol. 2, p. 122.
41 *Official Letters,* vol. 2, p. 229.
42 *Ibid.,* p. 232n.
43 *Ibid.,* p. 234.
44 Nelson Letters, Historical Society of Pennsylvania.
45 *Official Letters,* vol. 2, p. 234.
46 *Ibid.,* pp. 236-7.
47 *Ibid.,* p. 240.
48 *Bland Papers,* vol. 2, p. 51.
49 *Official Letters,* vol. 2, p. 250.
50 *Ibid.,* p. 108.
51 Fitzpatrick, vol. 18, p. 74.
52 *Official Letters,* vol. 2, p. 211.
53 Fitzpatrick, vol. 20, pp. 148-9.

NOTES

54 *Official Letters*, vol. 2, pp. 241-3.
55 The letters to the county lieutenants, differing slightly in terms and phraseology, are to be found in *Official Letters*, vol. 2, pp. 245-8.
56 Fitzpatrick, vol. 21, pp. 23-4.
57 *Official Letters*, vol. 2, pp. 250-3.
58 *Calendar of Virginia State Papers*, vol. 1, p. 441.
59 *Ibid.*, p. 502.
60 *Ibid.*, p. 572.

CHAPTER VI

1 *Official Letters*, vol. 2, pp. 276-7.
2 *Ibid.*, p. 254.
3 *Idem.*
4 Steuben Papers, New York Historical Society, noted in John McAuley Palmer, *General von Steuben* (cited henceforth as Palmer), pp. 246-7.
5 Henry Lee, *Memoirs of the War in the Southern Department*, p. 316. Also Lipscomb, vol. 16, p. 175.
6 *Official Letters*, vol. 2, p. 256.
7 Steuben Papers, New York Historical Society.
8 *Official Letters*, vol. 2, p. 259.
9 Lipscomb, vol. 16, p. 174.
10 *Journals of Council*, vol. 2, pp. 173-4.
11 *Official Letters*, vol. 2, p. 260.
12 *Ibid.*, p. 258.
13 Steuben Papers, New York Historical Society.
14 *Official Letters*, vol. 2, p. 369.
15 *Journals of Council*, vol. 2, p. 270.
16 *Official Letters*, vol. 2, p. 206.
17 *Ibid.*, p. 225.
18 *Ibid.*, p. 304.
19 *Ibid.*, p. 402.
20 *Journal of the House of Delegates.*
21 *Ibid.*, November 6, 1780.
22 Lipscomb, vol. 17, p. 5.
23 Steuben Papers, New York Historical Society.
24 Dreer Collection, Historical Society of Pennsylvania.
25 Steuben Papers, New York Historical Society.
26 Lipscomb, vol. 17, p. 2.
27 *Ibid.*, pp. 1-4.
28 *Official Letters*, vol. 2, pp. 266-8.

29 John Graves Simcoe, *Journal of the Operations of the Queen's Rangers* (cited henceforth as Simcoe), pp. 161-2.
30 Jefferson Papers, Library of Congress.
31 *Calendar of Virginia State Papers*, vol. 1, p. 420.
32 Steuben Papers, New York Historical Society.
33 *Calendar of Virginia State Papers*, vol. 1, p. 423.
34 *Ibid.*, p. 430.
35 *Ibid.*, p. 447.
36 Jefferson Papers, Library of Congress. Printed in *William and Mary Quarterly*, series 2, vol. 6, p. 132.
37 *Official Letters*, vol. 2, p. 265.
38 Lipscomb, vol. 17, pp. 3-4.
39 *Official Letters*, vol. 2, p. 261.
40 Freidrich Kapp, *The Life of Frederick William von Steuben* (cited henceforth as Kapp), p. 372.
41 *Ibid.*, pp. 376, 378.
42 *Official Letters*, vol. 2, p. 287.
43 Palmer, p. 251.
44 Steuben Papers, New York Historical Society.
45 Dreer Collection, Historical Society of Pennsylvania.
46 *Calendar of Virginia State Papers*, vol. 1, p. 440.
47 *Ibid.*, pp. 420-1.
48 Steuben Papers, New York Historical Society.
49 Kapp, pp. 376-7.
50 *Ibid.*, p. 378.
51 Nelson to Jefferson, Historical Society of Pennsylvania.
52 Dreer Collection, Historical Society of Pennsylvania.
53 *Official Letters*, vol. 2, pp. 285-6.
54 *Ibid.*, pp. 152-3.
55 *Ibid.*, pp. 162, 396.
56 Hening, vol. 10, pp. 379, 381, 382, 467.
57 *Ibid.*, pp. 379-380. *Journal of the House of Delegates*, Dec. 9, 1780.
58 Hening, vol. 10, p. 377.
59 *Bland Papers*, vol. 2, pp. 57-8.
60 *Calendar of Virginia State Papers*, vol. 1, p. 409.
61 *Official Letters*, vol. 2, p. 283.
62 *Ibid.*, p. 341.
63 *Ibid.*, p. 342.
64 *Ibid.*, p. 312. This letter was erroneously stated by Ford to have been written to George Rogers Clark.

CHAPTER VII

1. *Official Letters,* vol. 2, pp. 80-1.
2. *Ibid.,* p. 273.
3. *Ibid.,* p. 287.
4. *Ibid.,* p. 294.
5. *Ibid.,* p. 269.
6. *Cf.* letter to Major John Winston, *Ibid.,* p. 300.
7. *Journals of Council,* vol. 2, p. 273.
8. *Calendar of Virginia State Papers,* vol. 1, p. 444.
9. These were chiefly Colonel William Davies, Colonel James Innes, Major Richard Claiborne.
10. Steuben Papers, New York Historical Society.
11. *Idem.*
12. *Official Letters,* vol. 2, pp. 268-9.
13. Historical Society of Pennsylvania.
14. Steuben Papers, New York Historical Society.
15. *Official Letters,* vol. 2, pp. 269-70.
16. *Ibid.,* pp. 271-2.
17. Steuben Papers, New York Historical Society.
18. *Calendar of Virginia State Papers,* vol. 1, p. 416.
19. *Official Letters,* vol. 2, pp. 275-6.
20. Steuben Papers, New York Historical Society.
21. John Christian Senf, a German military engineer, had been appointed a colonel of engineers in South Carolina in February 1779. He came to Virginia in October 1780. In February 1781 he was appointed engineer to the Commonwealth of Virginia with the rank of lieutenant colonel.
22. Steuben Papers, New York Historical Society.
23. *Official Letters,* vol. 2, pp. 333-34.
24. *Ibid.,* pp. 344-45.
25. *Ibid.,* p. 348.
26. *Ibid.,* pp. 469-70.
27. Steuben Papers, New York Historical Society.
28. *Official Letters,* vol. 2, pp. 511-2.
29. Kapp, p. 367.
30. *Ibid.,* p. 360.
31. The statutes authorized the governor, with the advice of Council, "to appoint one or more fit and able persons to act as quartermasters to the militia drawn into actual service." Further, "the commanding officer of any detachment of militia drawn out into actual service shall,

if necessary, appoint a commissary or contractor to procure provisions for the said detachment." Hening, vol. 10, p. 296.
32 *Calendar of Virginia State Papers*, vol. 1, pp. 420-1.
33 *Official Letters*, vol. 2, p. 264.
34 *Calendar of Virginia State Papers*, vol. 1, p. 414.
35 *Ibid.*, p. 44.
36 *Official Letters*, vol. 2, p. 279.
37 *Ibid.*, pp. 301-2.
38 Fitzpatrick, vol. 21, p. 191.
39 Burk, *History of Virginia*, vol. 4, p. 456.
40 Kapp, p. 361.
41 *Ibid.*, pp. 356-7.
42 Palmer, p. 246.
43 *Official Letters*, vol. 2, p. 298.
44 *Bland Papers*, vol. 2, p. 40.
45 *Journal of the House of Delegates*, p. 67.
46 *Ibid.*, p. 78.
47 *Ibid.*, p. 80.
48 *Official Letters*, vol. 2, pp. 284-5.
49 Ballagh, vol. 2, p. 214.
50 Fitzpatrick, vol. 17, pp. 246, 317. For Jefferson's proposed measures of defense, see *Official Letters*, vol. 2, pp. 80, 81.
51 Fitzpatrick, vol. 20, pp. 30-1.
52 *Ibid.*, p. 325.
53 Cf. *Official Letters*, vol. 2, p. 284. Letter to Captain Maxwell.
54 Fitzpatrick, vol. 20, p. 447.
55 *Calendar of Virginia State Papers*, vol. 1, p. 409.
56 *Ibid.*, pp. 454-5.
57 *Virginia Historical Register*, vol. 4, p. 195.
58 Jefferson Papers, Library of Congress. Quoted in *William and Mary Quarterly*, series 1, vol. 6, p. 131.
59 Lipscomb, vol. 16, pp. 176-7.

CHAPTER VIII

1 *Official Letters*, vol. 2, p. 277.
2 *Ibid.*, pp. 278-9.
3 *Journals of Council*, vol. 2, p. 273.
4 *Official Letters*, vol. 2, p. 412.
5 *Journals of Council*, vol. 2, pp. 274-5.
6 *Ibid.*, p. 275.
7 Steuben Papers, New York Historical Society.

NOTES

8 *Journal of the House of Delegates*, in *Bulletin of the Virginia State Library*, vol. 17, p. 45.
9 *Official Letters*, vol. 2, p. 429.
10 *Ibid.*, p. 430.
11 *Calendar of Virginia State Papers*, vol. 2, pp. 14-5.
12 *Idem.*
13 *Official Letters*, vol. 2, pp. 291-3.
14 Historical Society of Pennsylvania.
15 *Official Letters*, vol. 2, pp. 298-9.
16 Fitzpatrick, vol. 3, p. 450.
17 *Calendar of Virginia State Papers*, vol. 1, pp. 523-4.
18 This document, too complicated to print here in full, is to be found in the *Official Letters*, vol. 2, pp. 306-7.
19 *Journals of the Continental Congress*, vol. 19, pp. 177-8.
20 Ms. letter in Gribbel sale (1945).
21 *Calendar of Virginia State Papers*, vol. 1, pp. 526-7. For further details of Harrison's mission, see *Letters Members Continental Congress*, nos. 540, 610, 647, 649, 652, 661; *Journals of the Continental Congress*; and *Calendar of Virginia State Papers*, vol. 1, pp. 492, 500, 503, 509, 511.
22 Fitzpatrick, vol. 21, pp. 380-3.
23 *Official Letters*, vol. 2, p. 329.
24 *Ibid.*, pp. 331-2.
25 Benjamin F. Stevens, *Clinton-Cornwallis Controversy*, vol. 1, p. 355.
26 *Idem.*
27 George W. Greene, *Life of Nathanael Greene*, vol. 3, pp. 174, 175.
28 *Official Letters*, vol. 2, p. 335.
29 *Ibid.*, p. 345.
30 *Ibid.*, pp. 353-4.
31 *Ibid.*, pp. 359-60.
32 Greene Papers, Clements Library.
33 *Calendar of Virginia State Papers*, vol. 1, p. 551.
34 These letters are printed in the *Calendar of Virginia State Papers*, vol. 1, pp. 551, 555, 563, 566-7, 570, 574, 581.
35 Hening, vol. 10, p. 570; *Official Letters*, vol. 2, p. 377.
36 *Bulletin of the Virginia State Library*, vol. 17, pp. 3-52.
37 Fitzpatrick, vol. 21, p. 270.
38 *Lafayette in Virginia*. Institut Français de Washington, p. 2.
39 *Official Letters*, vol. 2, pp. 382-3.
40 *Ibid.*, p. 401.
41 *Ibid.*, p. 393.
42 *Letters Members Continental Congress*, vol. 1, p. 566.

43 *Official Letters*, vol. 2, p. 349.
44 *Ibid.*, p. 347.
45 *Ibid.*, p. 375.
46 Steuben Papers, New York Historical Society.
47 *Official Letters*, vol. 2, p. 386.
48 *Ibid.*, p. 402-3.
49 *Ibid.*, p. 408-9.
50 *Calendar of Virginia State Papers*, vol. 1, p. 573. A complete list of the ships lying at Turkey Island, under Mitchell, is to be found on p. 588 of the same volume.
51 *Ibid.*, p. 572.
52 *Ibid.*, vol. 2, pp. 74-5.
53 *Official Letters*, vol. 2, p. 420.
54 *Calendar of Virginia State Papers*, vol. 1, p. 577.
55 *Official Letters*, vol. 2, p. 439.
56 *Ibid.*, pp. 511-2.
57 *Calendar of Virginia State Papers*, vol. 1, p. 583.
58 *Journals of Council*, vol. 2, p. 314.
59 *Ibid.*, p. 315.
60 *Official Letters*, vol. 2, pp. 424-5.
61 *Calendar of Virginia State Papers*, vol. 1, p. 593.
62 *Idem.*
63 Steuben Papers, New York Historical Society.
64 *Journals of Council*, vol. 2, p. 322.
65 *Official Letters*, vol. 2, pp. 440-1.
66 *Journals of Council*, vol. 2, p. 318.
67 *Ibid.*, pp. 442, 443, 444.
68 *Official Letters*, vol. 2, p. 445.
69 *Ibid.*, pp. 458-9.
70 *Ibid.*, pp. 467-8.
71 *Ibid.*, p. 460.
72 *Ibid.*, pp. 471-2.
73 Ballagh, vol. 2, p. 476.
74 *Official Letters*, vol. 2, p. 478.
75 *Ibid.*, pp. 476-7.
76 Steuben Papers, New York Historical Society.

CHAPTER IX

1 Steuben Papers, New York Historical Society. The *Journals of the Council* states that copies of Innes's letters to Jefferson were sent to Steuben. With rare exceptions, the wording of the Innes letters in the

NOTES

Steuben Papers is not identical, thus indicating that Innes wrote him independently.

2 *Journals of Council*, vol. 2, pp. 337-8.
3 See letter to Col. William Preston, *Official Letters*, vol. 2, p. 489.
4 *Calendar of Virginia State Papers*, vol. 2, p. 78.
5 *Official Letters*, vol. 2, p. 490.
6 *Ibid.*, p. 492.
7 Kapp, p. 424.
8 *Calendar of Virginia State Papers*, vol. 2, p. 59.
9 Steuben Papers, New York Historical Society. Abstract in *Calendar of Virginia State Papers*, vol. 2, p. 59.
10 *Calendar of Virginia State Papers*, vol. 2, pp. 59-60.
11 Simcoe (1844 ed.), pp. 190-1.
12 Steuben Papers, New York Historical Society.
13 These three letters are in the Steuben Papers, New York Historical Society.
14 Simcoe (1844 ed.), pp. 191-2.
15 *Official Letters*, vol. 2, p. 495.
16 *Idem*. A similar letter to Jefferson is published in the *Calendar of Virginia State Papers*, vol. 2, p. 65.
17 Steuben Papers, New York Historical Society.
18 *Calendar of Virginia State Papers*, vol. 2, p. 69.
19 Steuben Papers, New York Historical Society.
20 *Official Letters*, vol. 2, p. 497.
21 *Bland Papers*, vol. 2, pp. 68-9.
22 *Official Letters*, vol. 2, p. 509.
23 Kapp, pp. 425-6.
24 Steuben Papers, New York Historical Society.
25 Madison, *Writings*, vol. 2, p. 146.
26 I. N. Arnold, *Life of Benedict Arnold*, p. 345. Simcoe, in his *Journal*, pp. 194-201, gives a spirited description of the destruction of the ships, as well as of the skirmish at Petersburg.
27 *Official Letters*, vol. 2, p. 494.
28 *Bland Papers*, vol. 2, p. 69.
29 Charlemagne Tower, *Lafayette* (cited henceforth as Tower), vol. 2, p. 294.
30 *Official Letters*, vol. 2, p. 510.
31 *Ibid.*, p. 498.
32 *Kapp*, p. 429.
33 G. W. Greene, *Life of Nathanael Greene*, vol. 3, p. 221.
34 *Calendar of Virginia State Papers*, vol. 2, p. 111.
35 *Ibid.*, p. 107.

36 *Ibid.*, p. 93.
37 *Ibid.*, p. 40.
38 *Official Letters*, vol. 2, pp. 499-500.
39 *Ibid.*, p. 503.
40 *Ibid.*, p. 515.
41 *Ibid.*, p. 523.
42 *Journal of the House of Delegates.*
43 *Official Letters*, vol. 2, p. 512.
44 *Ibid.*, p. 507.
45 *Calendar of Virginia State Papers*, vol. 2, p. 92. The aide's name is erroneously given as Langborn in this source.
46 *Official Letters*, vol. 2, p. 517.
47 *Ibid.*, p. 518.
48 *Ibid.*, p. 510.
49 *Idem.*
50 *Ibid.*, pp. 506-7.
51 Banastre Tarleton, *History of the Campaigns of 1780 and 1781* (cited henceforth as Tarleton), p. 338.
52 *American Historical Review*, vol. 20, pp. 596-7.
53 Tarleton, p. 339.
54 Tower, vol. 2, p. 310.
55 *Ibid.*, p. 308.
56 *Official Letters*, vol. 2, pp. 518-9.
57 *Ibid.*, p. 526.
58 Ballagh, vol. 2, p. 235.
59 *Official Letters*, vol. 2, pp. 526-7.
60 *Ibid.*, p. 529.
61 James Graham, *Life of General Daniel Morgan*, p. 376. The figure given by Lafayette is at startling variance with that of Colonel John Banister who in a letter to Theoderick Bland, dated merely 1781, but which, from the context, was written after the skirmish at Petersburg, says: "I am engaged in a regiment of volunteer horse, pretty well mounted and equipped, in General Lawson's corps of volunteers, the whole of which, including horse and foot, amount to about 600 men." *Bland Papers*, vol. 2, pp. 62-3.
62 Greene, *Life of Nathanael Greene*, vol. 3, pp. 556-7.
63 *Idem.*
64 Tower, vol. 2, p. 315.
65 *Idem.*
66 *American Historical Review*, vol. 20, p. 601.
67 *Official Letters*, vol. 2, p. 523.
68 Tarleton, p. 292.

69 Maycocks was the seat of David Meade Randolph. It was on the south side of the James, a little below Westover.
70 *Calendar of Virginia State Papers*, vol. 2, p. 122.
71 Tarleton, p. 293.
72 *Ibid.*, p. 343.
73 *Ibid.*, p. 294.
74 *Ibid.*, p. 294-5.
75 Ms. letter in Gribbel sale (1945).
76 *Calendar of Virginia State Papers*, vol. 2, p. 112.
77 *Bland Papers*, vol. 2, p. 65.
78 Lafayette, *Memoires*, American edition, pp. 416-8.
79 John C. Hamilton, *Works of Alexander Hamilton*, vol. 1, p. 264.
80 *Official Letters*, vol. 2, p. 527.
81 *Ibid.*, pp. 524-5.
82 *Calendar of Virginia State Papers*, vol. 2, pp. 141-2.
83 *Official Letters*, vol. 2, pp. 524-5.
84 *Ibid.*, pp. 500-1.
85 *Journal of the House of Delegates.*
86 *Official Letters*, vol. 2, p. 516.
87 *Ibid.*, p. 515.
88 *Calendar of Virginia State Papers*, vol. 2, p. 126.
89 Ballagh, vol. 2, pp. 233-5.
90 Fitzpatrick, vol. 22, p. 383.
91 *Ibid.*, p. 189.
92 *Official Letters*, vol. 2, p. 523.
93 *Ibid.*, p. 525.
94 Fitzpatrick, vol. 22, p. 190.

CHAPTER X

1 Pendleton Letters, Mays Collection, Library of Congress. Quoted in M. H. Woodfin, "Contemporary Opinion in Virginia of Thomas Jefferson," in *Essays in Honor of W. E. Dodd,* edited by Avery Craven.
2 Jefferson Papers, Library of Congress.
3 Lipscomb, vol. 6, p. 427.
4 *Ibid.*, vol. 9, p. 354.
5 *Ibid.*, p. 352.
6 Watson was recommended to him by William Fleming who knew Jefferson's needs and chanced upon the man at Culpeper. Jefferson Papers, Library of Congress.
7 *Official Letters*, vol. 2, p. 479.

8 *Journals of Council*, vol. 2, p. 333.
9 *Calendar of Virginia State Papers*, vol. 2, p. 78.
10 *Ibid.*, p. 92.
11 *Official Letters*, vol. 2, p. 516.
12 *Idem.*
13 Lipscomb, vol. 4, p. 190.
14 *Virginia Magazine*, vol. 8, p. 116.
15 Jefferson Papers, Library of Congress.
16 *Idem.*
17 *Idem.*
18 *Idem.*
19 Steuben Papers, New York Historical Society.
20 *Calendar of Virginia State Papers*, vol. 2, p. 151.
21 *Ibid.*, p. 444.
22 *Journal of the House of Delegates.*
23 *Idem.*
24 *Idem.*
25 Lipscomb, vol. 17, pp. 17-8.
26 *Journal of the House of Delegates.*
27 *Calendar of Virginia State Papers*, vol. 2, p. 152, and note. See also *Virginia Historical Magazine*, vol. 44, p. 321.
28 *Journals of the Council*, vol. 2, p. 356.
29 Jefferson Papers, Library of Congress.
30 *Idem.*
31 *Idem.*
32 Lipscomb, vol. 17, pp. 20-1.
33 *Ibid.*, pp. 6-10.
34 *Ibid.*, p. 10.
35 *Journal of the House of Delegates.*
36 Lipscomb, vol. 4, p. 187.
37 Postscript in letter to James Monroe, Sept. 16, 1781. The letter is printed in Lipscomb, vol. 4, pp. 186-7, but the postscript is omitted.
38 James Monroe, *Writings*, vol. 1, p. 11.
39 *Virginia Magazine*, vol. 36, p. 168.
40 Tarleton, p. 297.
41 Lipscomb, vol. 1, p. 75.
42 Tarleton, p. 297.
43 See letter to Madison, March 24, 1782, Lipscomb, vol. 4, p. 190.
44 Lipscomb, vol. 17, p. 19.
45 *Ibid.*, vol. 7, p. 67.
46 *Ibid.*, vol. 17, p. 19.
47 Pocket Account Book, 1781, Jefferson Papers, Library of Congress.

48 Lipscomb, vol. 7, p. 68.
49 *Idem.*
50 *Ibid.*, p. 68-9.
51 *Ibid.*, p. 69.
52 Jefferson Papers, Library of Congress.
53 *Idem.*
54 *Idem.*
55 *Journal of the House of Delegates.*
56 *Idem.*
57 *Massachusetts Historical Society Proceedings*, series 2, vol. 19, p. 144.
58 Madison, *Writings*, edited by Gaillard Hunt, vol. 1, p. 167.
59 *Journal of the House of Delegates.*
60 Lipscomb, vol. 17, p. 10.
61 *Virginia Magazine*, vol. 44, p. 321.
62 *Journal of the House of Delegates.*
63 Madison, *Writings*, vol. 1, p. 166.
64 *Massachusetts Historical Society Proceedings*, 2nd series, vol. 19, pp. 144-5.

CHAPTER XI

1 *Letters Members Continental Congress*, vol. 6, pp. 120-1.
2 Jefferson Papers, Library of Congress. The reply itself is in the Papers of the Continental Congress, quoted in *Letters Members Continental Congress*, vol. 6, 190n.
3 Ford, vol. 3, pp. 48-9.
4 Jefferson Papers, Library of Congress.
5 *Letters Members Continental Congress*, vol. 6, p. 211.
6 *Ibid.*, vol. 6, p. 50.
7 *Ibid.*, p. 49.
8 *Ibid.*, pp. 235-6.
9 Madison, *Writings*, vol. 1, pp. 207-8.
10 *Letters Members Continental Congress*, vol. 6, p. 153.
11 *Ibid.*, vol. 5, p. 499.
12 Lipscomb, vol. 4, p. 165.
13 *Ibid.*, vol. 1, pp. 90-1.
14 *Ibid.*, vol. 4, p. 40.
15 *American Historical Review*, vol. 12, p. 76.
16 Jefferson appears to have been elected a member of the Philosophical Society on January 21, 1780, according to a notice in the *Pennsylvania Packet* of January 27, 1780. He was a member of the Council of the Society from 1781-85 and again from 1818-26. He was president from January 1797 to his resignation in November 1814.

17 Thomson Papers, Library of Congress, for 1765-84. This letter seems not to have been published previously.
18 *Ibid.* Also in the Jefferson Papers, Library of Congress.
19 A reproduction of the edition printed at Frankfurt in 1590, made for the Holbein Society, is in the Library Company of Philadelphia.
20 *Philosophical Transactions of the Royal Society*, London, 1693, vol. 17, p. 942.
21 *Neu gefundenes Eden*, p. 73.
22 See *Thomas Hutchins, A Topographical Description*, edited by F. C. Hicks, and *The Courses of the Ohio River*, edited by B. W. Bond, Jr.
23 Ford, vol. 3, p. 29.
24 Jefferson's manuscript catalogue of books of 1783 shows that he owned Clayton's *Flora Virginica* as well as *Clayton's Flora Virginica* by Gronovius.
25 Lipscomb, vol. 7, p. 325.
26 G. E. Hastings, *Life and Works of Francis Hopkinson*, pp. 333-4.
27 This last sentence is omitted in both Ford and Lipscomb.
28 Lipscomb, vol. 4, pp. 201-2. This letter is printed, addressed to Clark, in the *Illinois Historical Collections*, vol. 19, pp. 155-6.
29 Ford, vol. 5, p. 159.
30 The only manuscript copy of the *Notes* that has as yet come to light is the one in the Coolidge Collection at the Massachusetts Historical Society. It is complete with text, tables, and many footnotes. It likewise includes Thomson's manuscript notes printed as an appendix to the *Notes*, as well as Jefferson's *Draught for a Fundamental Constitution for Virginia* (untitled), which he had printed as a pamphlet in Paris, in the same format as the *Notes*, and later added as an appendix to the copies he still had. A careful comparison of this manuscript with the original edition and with the English one of 1787 indicates that it was not the completed manuscript for either one. It seems rather to have been the manuscript Jefferson retained, from which he probably made a fair copy for the printer. At first glance it would seem identical. The title page is the same, and for some pages the text is identical with the original edition, except for occasional marginal notes. There are careful interlineations such as a manuscript is likely to have, and these are embodied in the printed version. Beginning with page 8 and 9, however, it becomes obvious that this is a draught. There are no less than four versions of these pages, each on separate sheets, with the new version either pasted over the old, or laid in. This is likewise true of pages 28 and 29, where there are two duplicate pages, although it involved the laborious copying of an elaborate table—the one comparing the quadrupeds of Europe and America.

NOTES

There are four varying copies of pages 44 and 45, two of 58 and 59, after which there is an unnumbered page. From page 60-80 the text runs along smoothly without a break. Various additions and changes are made after this, notes again written in, often upside down on the page, and there are two versions of pages 108-109 and 114-115.

In addition to many notes and queries to himself, preliminary tables, notes for corrections and additions, there are certain papers from other hands. There is a two-page description of the Indian, phrases from which Jefferson incorporated, notes by an unidentified correspondent on the size and weights of wild animals, later incorporated in the *Notes*, and a letter, dated Tuckahoe, October 12, 1783, comparing European and American animals, wild and domestic.

31 Lipscomb, vol. 5, p. 180.
32 *Ibid.*, p. 200.
33 *Ibid.*, vol. 4, p. 455.
34 Sullivan's answer to Marbois's queries (preserved in the Huntington Library) are to be found in the *Letters and Papers of Major-General John Sullivan*, vol. 3, pp. 229-39. A canvas of the libraries and historical societies of most of the other 13 states has failed to reveal any similar replies.
35 *New York Historical Society Collections*, vol. for 1878, pp. 199-200.
36 Ford, vol. 3, p. 91.
37 *Ibid.*, p. 92.
38 *Ibid.*, p. 91.
39 *Ibid.*, p. 93.
40 *Ibid.*, p. 92.
41 *Ibid.*, p. 102.
42 *Ibid.*, pp. 109-10. In Jefferson's own copy of the *Notes*, the edition printed in England in 1787, with his additions, corrections, and changes, which is preserved in the Alderman Library of the University of Virginia, Jefferson has crossed out the passage immediately following the word "headache" and changed it to read "this painful sensation is relieved by a short but pleasing view of the Blue Ridge downwards, and upwards by that of the Short hills, which with the Purgatory mountain is a divergence from the North ridge; and descending then to the valley below the sensation becomes delightful in the extreme." It then continues: "... it is impossible for the emotions, etc." This passage was not included in the 1853 edition of the *Notes*, which supposedly contained all Jefferson's corrections (which it does not) or noted by Ford, vol. 3, p. 110.

43 Jefferson acquired the Natural Bridge by royal grant July 4, 1774. In the first of his account books, that for August 18-December 24, 1767, the first page contains a diagram of the bridge and matter-of-fact notes describing its size, extent, the kind of stone of which it is formed, the trees that grow there, and so on.
44 Ford, vol. 3, pp. 139-42.
45 The question was further discussed in a letter to Chastellux dated June 7, 1785. *Ibid.*, p. 137n.
46 Lipscomb, vol. 5, p. 4.
47 *Ibid.*, pp. 180-1.
48 Jefferson Papers, Library of Congress.
49 Lipscomb, vol. 5, pp. 244-5.
50 *Ibid.*, p. 260.
51 Jefferson Papers, Library of Congress.
52 Lipscomb, vol. 6, p. 21.
53 *Ibid.*, pp. 206-7.
54 Jefferson Papers, Library of Congress.
55 Lipscomb, vol. 6, pp. 324-5.
56 *Ibid.*, pp. 325-7. Lipscomb gives the date October 3, but it is October 1 in the original letter.
57 Jefferson Papers, Library of Congress.
58 Ford, vol. 3, p. 168.
59 *Ibid.*, pp. 168-9.
60 *Ibid.*, vol. 9, p. 358.
61 Lipscomb, vol. 16, pp. 371-7.
62 Among the miscellaneous memoranda concerning the *Notes* in the Massachusetts Historical Society, is an acute two page account of the Indian by an unidentified correspondent. Jefferson has used various phrases from this in his description.
63 Quoted in Ford, vol. 3, pp. 150-1.
64 Ford, vol. 3, pp. 151-2.
65 *Ibid.*, pp. 155-7.
66 *Ibid.*, pp. 156-7. The controversy over Logan's speech which arose some years after the publication of the *Notes* is discussed in Ford, vol. 3, p. 157-64n. George Rogers Clark's discussion of it is in the *Illinois Historical Collections*, vol. 8, pp. 3-9.
67 For a complete description of his activities see Ford, vol. 3, pp. 201-5.
68 See Karl Lehman, "Thomas Jefferson, Archaeologist," in *American Journal of Archaeology*, vol. 47, pp. 161-3.
69 Ford, vol. 3, p. 207.
70 Jefferson Papers, "Index, Chronological letters written and received 1779-1814," Library of Congress.

NOTES

71 Lipscomb, vol. 11, p. 79-81.
72 *Ibid.*, pp. 102-3.
73 *Ibid.*, vol. 10, pp. 161, 162.
74 Jefferson Papers, Massachusetts Historical Society.
75 *Ibid.*
76 Ford, vol. 3, pp. 243-5.
77 *Ibid.*, pp. 266-7.
78 In some manuscript comments on the *Notes*, preserved among his papers, Francis Hopkinson observes, *à propos* of slavery, "Among the blacks is misery enough but no poetry. You seem to be too severe on the character of the Negroes. That Buffon might upon inquiry perhaps find instances sufficient to retort your censure on his character of the Indians. People born in slavery and habituated to misery cannot be expected to have any poetical disposition. It is the contrast between a state of enjoyment and [illegible] that can suggest poetical ideas.

"The comparison of the treatment of slaves in Virginia with those of ancient Rome," he continues, "is no more than placing one bad thing alongside of a worse in order to justify it. After all it is very difficult to prove (if not impossible) that nature has really made any material distinction other than what may be accounted for by climate, education, civilization, freedom or slavery, etc. etc. There are manifest differences indeed between individuals as to [illegible] powers, but even these perhaps, could they be minutely traced, would be found to originate in mechanical causes and not in any real difference of souls." (Photostat in Historical Society of Pennsylvania).
79 Ford, vol. 4, p. 20.
80 *Ibid.*, p. 46.
81 *Ibid.*, p. 47.
82 Madison, *Writings*, vol. 2, p. 215.
83 Lipscomb, vol. 5, p. 110.
84 Williamos is a somewhat nebulous character—a man professionally at outs with the world. There is a letter from him preserved in the Jefferson papers, written from Paris on July 8, 1783, in which he speaks of having served under General Lee in the Revolution. On June 4, 1784, the last entry in his account book on leaving Boston, Jefferson notes "gave Mr. Williamos for servants at Ingersoll's 12/." On November 8, 1785, there is another notation of having given "Mayer for support of Williamos, 120 francs."
85 *Biographie Universelle*, vol. 30, p. 121.
86 Lipscomb, vol. 5, p. 274.
87 Ford, vol. 3, p. 74.

88 Jefferson Papers, Library of Congress.
89 *Ibid.*
90 See letter to Morellet, July 2, 1787, Ford, vol. 3, pp. 77-8.
91 *Writings*, Madison, vol. 2, p. 236.
92 Lipscomb, vol. 5, p. 148.
93 Ford, vol. 3, p. 76.
94 *Massachusetts Historical Society Collections*, 7th series, vol. 1, p. 25.
95 Lipscomb, vol. 6, p. 29.
96 Ford, vol. 3, pp. 118-9.
97 *Ibid.*, p. 77.
98 *Massachusetts Historical Society Collections*, 7th series, vol. 1, p. 29.
99 Jefferson Papers, Library of Congress.
100 Jared Sparks, *Works of Franklin*, vol. 10, p. 317.
101 *The Monthly Review*, vol. 77, pp. 377-82; 459-64.
102 Jefferson's map is mentioned in the review. It thus seems plausible that the reviewer had seen proofs of it, as the book itself did not appear until somewhat later.
103 Ford, vol. 3, pp. 278-9.

CHAPTER XII

1 Ford, vol. 3, p. 338.
2 *Journal of the House of Delegates.*
3 *Idem.*
4 Madison, *Writings*, vol. 1, p. 259.
5 *Idem.*, note.
6 *Ibid.*, p. 261.
7 *Letters Members Continental Congress*, vol. 6, p. 551.
8 *Idem.*
9 Lipscomb, vol. 1, p. 76.
10 Ford, vol. 3, pp. 61-2.
11 Crèvecoeur to Jefferson, September 1, 1784, Jefferson Papers, Library of Congress.
12 Ford, vol. 3, p. 66.
13 *Ibid.*, p. 296.
14 The quotations from the letters to Madison are to be found in Ford, vol. 3, pp. 300-4.
15 *Ibid.*, pp. 301-2.
16 *Ibid.*, p. 307.
17 *Idem.*
18 Jefferson Papers, Library of Congress.
19 Ford, vol. 3, p. 308.

20 *Ibid.*, p. 309n.
21 *Ibid.*, p. 312.
22 Jefferson Papers, Massachusetts Historical Society.
23 Pocket Account Book for 1783.
24 Ford, vol. 3, p. 315.
25 *Idem.*
26 Lipscomb, vol. 4, p. 214.
27 *Notes on Virginia*, Query 13, no. 5, Ford, vol. 3, p. 225.
28 *Ibid.*, p. 318.
29 *Ibid.*, p. 321.
30 *Ibid.*, pp. 321-2.
31 *Ibid.*, pp. 325-6.
32 Hening, vol. 9, p. 116.
33 Ford, vol. 3, p. 327.
34 *Ibid.*, p. 334.
35 *Ibid.*, p. 347.
36 *Ibid.*, pp. 338-9.
37 See letter to Horatio Spafford, Lipscomb, vol. 12, p. 280.
38 George E. Hastings, *The Life and Works of Francis Hopkinson*, p. 334.
39 Sarah Randolph, *The Domestic Life of Thomas Jefferson* (cited henceforth as *Domestic Life*), p. 72.
40 *Ibid.*, pp. 69-70.
41 *American Historical Review*, vol. 12, pp. 76-7.
42 *Domestic Life*, p. 45n.
43 *Ibid.* This is an extract of the letter of that date. A search of all known letters of this period has failed to reveal the complete letter.
44 *Ibid.*, pp. 45-6.
45 *Ibid.*, pp. 44-5.

CHAPTER XIII

1 Proclamation of President of Congress. *Letters Members Continental Congress*, vol. 7, p. 196.
2 Lipscomb, vol. 1, p. 77.
3 *Letters Members Continental Congress*, vol. 7, p. 472.
4 Ford, vol. 3, p. 369.
5 Jefferson Papers, Library of Congress.
6 Lipscomb, vol. 4, p. 449.
7 Gijsbert Karel van Hogendorp, *Brieven en Gedenkschriften*, Eerste Deel, pp. 333-9.
8 *Ibid.*, pp. 346-7.

9 Jefferson Papers, Library of Congress.
10 Hogendorp, *Brieven*, pp. 359-60.
11 Ford, vol. 3, p. 347.
12 *Maryland Historical Magazine*, June 1946, p. 118.
13 Ford, vol. 3, p. 347.
14 *Ibid.*, p. 371.
15 *Letters Members Continental Congress*, vol. 7, p. 414.
16 Ford, vol. 3, p. 365.
17 Lipscomb, vol. 1, p. 88.
18 Ford, vol. 3, pp. 397-8.
19 *Letters Members Continental Congress*, vol. 7, p. 451.
20 *Journals of the Continental Congress*, vol. 26, pp. 133, 172.
21 The report, as printed in the *Journals of Congress*, is in Gerry's writing.
22 *Letters Members Continental Congress*, vol. 7, p. 395n.
23 *Ibid.*, p. 416.
24 *Ibid.*, p. 522.
25 Ford, vol. 3, pp. 466-7.
26 Fitzpatrick, vol. 27, pp. 388-9.
27 This letter is published in its entirety in Ford, vol. 3, pp. 464-70.
28 *Letters Members Continental Congress*, vol. 7, p. 516.
29 *Ibid.*, p. 526.
30 *Ibid.*, p. 411.
31 Ford, vol. 3, p. 376.
32 *Ibid.*, p. 377.
33 For an account of this occasion see the *Philadelphia Journal*, January 21 and 24, 1784.
34 Ford, vol. 3, p. 379-80.
35 *Letters Members Continental Congress*, vol. 7, p. 510.
36 *Ibid.*, p. 443.
37 *Ibid.*, p. 421.
38 Lipscomb, vol. 1, pp. 86-7.
39 Ford, vol. 3, p. 399. For the "admonition" see *Letters Members Continental Congress*, vol. 7, p. 444.
40 *Letters Members Continental Congress*, vol. 7, pp. 456-7.
41 Ford, vol. 3, p. 444.
42 See *Letters of Joseph Jones*, edited by Worthington C. Ford, pp. 132-8.
43 Ford, vol. 3, p. 400.
44 The Virginia delegation to Congress consisted at this time, aside from Jefferson, of Thomas Hardy, Arthur Lee, James Monroe, and John Frances Mercer, who was absent.

45 Ford, vol. 3, pp. 411-2.
46 *Letters Members Continental Congress*, vol. 7, p. 475.
47 *Idem.*
48 Ford, vol. 3, pp. 400-1.
49 *Ibid.* The letter to Washington occupies pages 420-5 of vol. 3.
50 *Letters Members Continental Congress*, vol. 7, p. 511.
51 Ford, vol. 1, p. xxx.
52 *Ibid.*, p. 471.
53 *Ibid.*, p. 432.
54 *Letters Members Continental Congress*, vol. 7, p. 512.
55 *Ibid.*, p. 531.
56 *Ibid.*, p. 458.
57 *Ibid.*, p. 486.
58 *Ibid.*, p. 591.
59 *Ibid.*, p. 557n.
60 *Ibid.*, p. 183n.
61 *Ibid.*, p. 182n.
62 *Ibid.*, p. 183n.
63 Ford, vol. 3, pp. 341-3.
64 *Ibid.*, p. 400.
65 *Ibid.*, p. 462.
66 Francis Wharton, *Revolutionary Diplomatic Correspondence*, vol. 5, p. 104.
67 *Journals of the Continental Congress*, vol. 22, p. 8.
68 Jared Sparks, in his *Life of Gouverneur Morris*, says "... the estimates and calculations on which the letter is founded, still exist in his [G. Morris's] handwriting."
69 Lipscomb, vol. 1, p. 78.
70 Wharton, *Revolutionary Diplomatic Correspondence*, vol. 5, pp. 108-9.
71 *Ibid.*, pp. 78-9.
72 *Letters Members Continental Congress*, vol. 7, pp. 502-3. Jefferson adds: "... an insurmountable aversion to copying obliges me also to desire a return of the inclosed papers of which I retain no copy."
73 Lipscomb, vol. 1, p. 79.
74 *Letters Members Continental Congress*, vol. 7, p. 512.

CHAPTER XIV

1 *Letters Members Continental Congress*, vol. 7, p. 516.
2 Ford, vol. 3, pp. 489-93.
3 *Journals of the Continental Congress*, vol. 26, p. 356.

4 *Ibid.*, pp. 524-5.
5 George E. Hastings, *Life and Works of Francis Hopkinson*, p. 336.
6 *Ibid.*, p. 337.
7 *Thomas Jefferson to his Relatives, the Turpins*, edited by Marie Dickore.
8 Lipscomb, vol. 4, p. 453.
9 Fletcher Webster, *The Private Correspondence of Daniel Webster*, vol. 1, p. 371.
10 Quoted in Fiske Kimball, "Joseph Wright and His Portraits of Washington," in *Antiques*, vol. 15, no. 5, pp. 371-82.
11 Hening, vol. 11, p. 552.
12 Franklin B. Dexter, *The Literary Diary of Ezra Stiles*, vol. 3, pp. 124-7.
13 Hogendorp, *Brieven*, Erste Deel, pp. 361-5.
14 *Dictionary of American Biography*, vol. 18, p. 64.
15 Austin, *Life of Elbridge Gerry*, vol. 1, pp. 452-4.
16 *Idem.*
17 Pocket Account Book, June 30, 1784.
18 Ford, vol. 8, p. 3.

INDEX

The index includes all references to what may be called the *dramatis personae* and scenes of this biography, both major and minor, but not to persons or places mentioned but casually and incidentally.

Adams, John, 4, 5, 6, 259, 286, 333, 353
———, Samuel, 169, 335
American Philosophical Society, 264-265, 293, 299, 381
Ampthill, 138, 214, 221
Animals, 270-273, 280-285, 303, 350, 356, 483
Annapolis, 23, 320, 324-325, 354
Appomattox River, 143, 194, 210-213, 224, 228, 266
Archaeology, 290-291
Arnold, Benedict, 177, 178, 187, 197, 206, 213, 214, 217, 223, 224, 227, 250, 255; invasion of Virginia, 125-151, 172-174, 247

Baloons, 355-356
Baltimore, 309-312
Bancroft, Edward, 297
Banister, John, 110, 211, 215, 229, 256, 378
Barbé-Marbois, *see* Marbois
Barracks, The, 19, 20, 33, 35, 107
Barron, James, 196, 205
Battersea, 211
Bear, 270, 271, 272
Beck, Will, 314

Bellini, Carlo, 18, 23-24, 354
Berkeley, 140, 145, 156
Birds, 266, 270-271, 276, 282-283
Bland, Theodorick, 47, 100, 110, 117, 148, 167, 170, 172, 192, 211, 229, 307, 378
Blenheim, 36-37, 252
Blue Ridge, 21, 278
Botany, 266-268, 270, 279
Boundaries, 9, 90-94, 275
Brandon, 132, 221, 222, 223
Brickell, John, "North Carolina," 267
Buffalo, 270, 272, 280
Buffon, Comte de, 268, 279, 280-286, 287-288, 291, 303, 307, 356, 385

Camden, battle of, 105-107
Caribou, 283
Carr, Dabney, 354
———, Martha Jefferson, 321, 354
———, Peter, 354
Carriages, 44-45
Carter's Mountain, 251, 252
Cary, Archibald, 6, 214, 221, 228, 270, 281-282, 308
Caverns, 319
Charles City Court House, 140, 155

391

Charleston, S. C., 96, 97, 98
Charlottesville, 219, 233-234, 240, 242, 243, 244, 253
Chastellux, Marquis de, 18, 273-274, 281, 296, 303
Chesapeake Bay, 109, 125, 147, 148, 187, 190, 194, 197, 199, 201
Chesterfield Court House, 133, 141, 164, 204, 207, 211, 214, 217, 228, 347
Chicahominy River, 155, 207-210, 223, 228
Cincinnati, Society, 333-335
City Point, 210, 221
Claiborne, Richard, 138, 152, 202
Clark, George Rogers, 78-85, 91, 118-124, 143-144, 145-146, 269-270, 276, 277
Clayton, John, of Virginia, *Flora Virginica*, 268, 279
——, John, of Yorkshire, "Virginia," 265-266
Climate, 263, 271
Clinton, Sir Henry, 97, 98, 106, 197, 223, 228
Coigne, Jean Baptist de, 287
Colle, 22, 23, 33, 34, 36, 37, 251
Collier, Sir George, 53-54
Collinson, Peter, 268, 281
Commerce, treaties of, 332, 352-353
Commissaries, 374
Confederation, Articles of, 4
Congress, Continental, 4-9, 10-11, 148, 182-183, 190, 199, 201, 216, 256, 259, 261, 307, 311, 313, 318-320, 324, 351
Convention troops, 18, 32-35, 38, 76, 102, 107, 130-131, 175-176

Cornwallis, Lord, 98, 103, 105, 106, 114, 130, 184-187, 198, 201, 221-229, 231, 251-254
Cougar, 281
Cowpens, battle of, 185
Criminal law, 14
Currency, U. S., 5, 337, 348-351
Currie, James, 139, 354

Dancing, 319, 321
D'Anmours, Chevalier, 18, 27-32
Daubenton, Louis, 280, 285
Davies, William, 66, 139, 164, 243
Debt, national, 332
Declaration of Independence, 3, 12
Deer, 270, 271, 273, 280, 281, 283, 284-285
De Kalb, Baron, 103, 104
Delaware River, 346-347
Deluge, the, 300, 301
Detroit, 118-123
Dickinson, John, 4
Digges, Dudley, 153, 216, 222, 235, 242
Drummond, Mrs., 10
Duponceau, Philip, 293
Durand, *Voyage d'un français*, 266
Du Simitière, Pierre Eugène, 320, 321

Education, plan for, 14-15
Elizabeth River, 54, 110, 115, 187, 193, 276
Elk, 270, 271, 272, 273, 280, 281, 282, 283

INDEX

Elk Hill, 19, 55, 239, 240, 253-254, 318
Encyclopedias, 31-32, 238
Entails, abolition of, 12-13
Eppes, Elizabeth Wayles, 309, 318, 321, 354
———, Francis, 131, 309, 313, 362
Eppington, 131, 308, 314
Excavation, 290-291
Extraterritoriality, 28-29

Fabbroni, Giovanni, 25-27, 263
Fine Creek, 134, 140
Fleming, William, 47, 53, 61, 239, 242, 379
Forest, The, 10, 55, 140
Frankfort on the Main, 44
Franklin, Benjamin, 4, 5, 10, 11, 286, 302, 303, 353
Frederick, Md., 9
Fredericksburg, 14, 146, 157, 221
French fleet, 30, 31, 183, 187, 192-194, 196, 197, 200, 229, 231, 248

Gates, Horatio, 100, 102, 103, 105-107, 187
Geismar, Baron von, 18, 19, 20, 38, 40-45
Gerry, Elbridge, 330, 332, 333, 335, 352, 353, 360, 361
Gilmer, George, 9, 39, 242
Girardin, Louis, 166, 251
Great Lakes, 276, 277
Greene, Nathanael, 141, 142, 163, 185-188, 198, 200, 201, 214, 215, 216, 219, 226, 228, 229, 247

Gronovius, 268
Guilford Court House, battle of, 188

Hamilton, Alexander, 227, 230
———, Henry, 78, 84-90
Hampton, 113, 125, 194, 196
Hampton Roads, 53, 110, 144, 203
Hanau, 42, 44
Hancock, John, 11
Harper's Ferry, 278, 319
Harpsichord, 20
Harriot, Thomas, "Virginia," 265
Harrison, Benjamin, 127, 182-183, 339, 354
Hartford, 360
Harvard College, 268
Hawkins, Benjamin, 291, 292
Henry, Patrick, 6, 8, 48, 51, 55, 67, 80, 81, 82, 91, 134, 245, 256
Hesse-Cassel, 42, 44
Hessians, 5, 18, 19, 20, 33-35, 211
Hogendorp, Count van, 17, 273, 281, 325-328, 360
Hood's, 132, 143-144, 145, 157, 159-162, 194, 195, 210
Hopkinson, Francis, 269, 282-283, 319, 320, 343, 351, 355, 356, 385
Hopkinson, Mrs. Thomas, 319-322
Howell, David, 330, 331
Humphreys, David, 358
Hutchins, Thomas, "Virginia," 267, 276, 291, 298

Illinois River, 81, 83, 276, 277
Impressment, 53, 103, 179, 193, 194, 196, 198, 217-218, 220-221

Indians, 5, 77, 78, 84, 94-95, 117-118, 279, 286-293, 332, 337, 383, 384
Innes, James, 127, 130, 203, 204, 205, 206, 207, 208, 209

James River, 127-146, 157, 159-162, 165, 175, 193, 194-196, 203-209, 223, 224, 225, 253, 266, 276
Jamestown, 205, 206, 207
Jay, John, 313, 353
Jefferson, Anna Scott, 314, 354
——, Lucy Elizabeth, 114, 238; 2d. 306, 308
——, Maria (Polly), 19, 55, 134, 308
——, Martha (Patsy), 10, 19, 36, 39, 55, 309, 312, 313, 318, 319-323, 355, 358
——, Martha Wayles, wife of Thomas, 9, 10, 19, 20, 22, 36, 37, 55, 114, 134, 239, 306
Jefferson, Thomas, in Continental Congress, 1776, 4-9; offered post as commissioner to France, 1776, 10; in Virginia House of Delegates, 1776-1779, 12-17; Governor of Virginia, first term, 46-96; second term, 96-242; retirement from public life, 236-238, 240-242; in House of Delegates, 1781, 250, 257; 1782, 307; offered post as commissioner to negotiate peace, 1781, 259; elected to Congress, 1781, 256; appointed commissioner to negotiate peace, 1782, 308; in Congress, 1783-1784, 318, 324-351; appointed minister to negotiate treaties of commerce, 352-353; in New England, 358-362; sails for France, 362
"Notes on Virginia," 31, 262-305, 314, 327; map of Virginia, 267, 297-298, 299, 300, 301, 386
Books, 39, 267, 268, 301-302, 325; health, 23, 262, 325, 354; horses, 361; servants, 319, 325, 354; slaves, 240, 319, 354, 362
Joel, B. Edgar, 149-150
Jones, Joseph, 262, 263, 339
Jouett, Jack, 262

Kaskasia, 82, 83, 277
Kentucky, 79, 81

Lafayette, Marquis de, 151, 178, 190-192, 196, 198, 214-215, 219-231, 234, 240, 259
Lancaster, Pa., 9
Languages, Indian, 291-293
La Valette, General, 312
Lee, Arthur, 328, 330-331, 344
——, Henry ("Light-Horse Harry"), 6, 97, 113, 126, 142, 163, 173
——, Richard Henry, 6, 7, 8, 9, 11, 47, 48, 62, 69, 70, 72, 100, 148, 167, 169, 201, 225, 234, 242
——, Thomas Ludwell, 7, 13
Leslie, Alexander, 110-115
Lewis, Nicholas, 309, 354
——, William, 194, 195, 243
Linnaeus, 268, 279
Livingston, Robert R., 308, 311-313
Logan, 289
Loyalists, *see* Tories
Luzerne, Chevalier de la, 199, 223, 227, 260, 309-311, 345, 355
Lyn(n)haven Bay, 198

Madison, James, 170, 213, 238, 240, 256, 257, 261, 295, 296-297, 298,

INDEX

306, 307, 308, 309, 311-312, 314, 315, 319, 324, 325, 329, 331, 337, 339, 340, 342, 347, 354, 360

Madison's Cave, 319

Magill, Charles, 187-188

Manchester, 134, 137, 138, 140, 155, 204, 205, 207, 210, 214-215, 216

Marbois, Marquis de Barbé-, 31, 262-265, 273, 274-275, 321

Mason and Dixon line, 92, 94

Mason, George, 7, 8, 13, 62, 75, 82, 231, 317

——, Thompson, 315

Mastodon, 280, 281

Mathews, Sampson, 88, 157, 270

Maxwell, James, 126, 147, 148, 192, 193, 194, 210

Mazzei, Philip, 18-25, 29, 33, 213, 354

McClurg, James, 354

Meade, Richard, 163

Mercure de France, 300, 303-305

Meteorology, 241, 263, 271

Mifflin, Thomas, 324

Militia, 53, 67-69, 76, 99, 105-110, 119, 122, 128-129, 131, 132, 133, 134, 142, 143, 145, 166, 170, 179-180, 181-182, 189, 191, 204, 205, 207, 212, 217-219, 221, 224, 227, 235, 248-249, 255

Milton, 251

Ministers, instructions to, 332, 336, 352-353

Mississippi River, 276-277

Missouri River, 276-277

Mitchell, William, 194, 195, 198

Monroe, James, 53, 251, 295, 328-329, 330, 354, 356

Monthly Review, 303

Monticello, 9, 19, 20, 23, 55, 238, 240, 242, 251-253, 262, 306, 314, 318-319, 353, 354

Montpelier, Va., 296

Moore, Bernard, 291

Moose, 283-285

Morellet, Abbé, 297-298, 301, 302, 303

Morgan, Daniel, 226

Morris, Gouverneur, 349

——, Robert, 313, 348-350, 355

Mounds, Indian, 290

Mühlenberg, John Peter Gabriel, 111, 112, 115, 150, 204

Music, 18, 20, 26-27, 36, 41, 45, 320, 321

Muter, George, 66, 139

Natural Bridge, 274, 278

Natural history, 263, 267, 268, 270, 274, 285

Navy Yard, 54

Negroes, 293-295, 385

Nelson, Thomas, 4, 46, 107, 111, 113, 115, 125, 126, 128, 132, 133, 137, 140, 141, 142-146, 149, 154-157, 158, 175, 180, 193, 198, 203, 215, 242, 243, 244, 249, 250

Neu gefundenes Eden, 266

New England, tour in, 358

New Hampshire, 360

New Haven, 359

New Kent road, 205, 206, 209, 210

Newport News, 110, 111, 113, 144, 146, 203, 205

New York, 169, 170, 182, 201, 226, 235, 358

Nicholas, George, 245-248, 251, 256, 257

——, John, 134, 140, 153, 154-155

——, Robert Carter, 6, 8, 13

Norfolk, 54

North Carolina, 94-95, 97, 116, 175, 183, 185-187, 198, 200, 215, 218, 227, 267

Northwest, *see* West

Ochs, J. N., "Carolina," 267

Ohio Company, 79

Ohio River, 82, 122, 200, 267, 276, 277

Osborne's, 138, 140, 210, 213-214, 215, 221, 223, 224

Page, John, 7, 46, 47, 172, 241-242, 256

Paleontology, 266, 269-270, 279-280, 359

Panther, 271, 282, 350

Paris, 274

Paroles, 177-178

Peace, negotiations of, 311-312, 313; treaty, 329-331, 335-336

Pendleton, Edmund, 7, 9, 13, 14, 237, 256, 257-258, 313, 344, 358

Pennsylvania boundary, 90-94

Petersburg, 103, 128, 138, 143, 204, 210-213, 221, 223, 224, 227, 228, 377, 378

Philadelphia, 4, 9, 182, 199, 269, 274, 302, 309, 312-313, 318, 319-321, 324, 336, 345, 354, 355-358

Phillips, William, 19, 33, 36-37, 86, 170, 178, 179; invasion of Virginia, 197-221, 223

Philology, comparative, 291-293

Pianoforte, 20, 36

Pierres, Phillipe Denis, 296

Pittsburg, 118, 121

Point of Fork, 239, 253, 306

Poplar Forest, 251, 253, 259

Portsmouth, N. H., 284, 361

Portsmouth, Va., 54, 110, 114-115, 144, 151, 175, 178, 184, 192, 197, 198, 199, 201, 250

Potomac River, 9, 201, 202, 276, 277, 278, 340, 346-347

Primogeniture, abolition of, 14

Princeton, 318, 324, 358

Quartermasters, 373

Randolph, Edmund, 6, 49, 64, 69, 106, 245, 250, 251, 257, 261, 307, 308-309

——, Isham, 268

——, Thomas Mann, 318

Raynal, Abbé, 280, 285

Recruiting, 53, 64-67, 70, 76, 99, 102-104, 107, 108, 117, 179-180, 189, 217; *see also* Militia

Religious freedom, statute for, 3, 13-14

Revisal, *see* Virginia, revisal of laws

Revolution, war of, 52-55, 96-98, 103, 110-115, 125-151, 185-188, 190-231, 251-254

Richmond, 12, 55-57, 125, 128, 133, 134-135, 136-141, 164, 172-173, 207, 215-216, 223, 224, 228, 233, 238, 248-249, 255, 302, 313, 314, 318

INDEX

Riedesel, Baron von, 18, 19, 33-34, 35-38, 48
Rio Norte (Grande), 277
Rittenhouse, David, 269, 286
Rivers, 266-267, 275-277; *see also* single names
Rodney, Commodore, 110
Rübsamen, Jacob, 20
Rutledge, Edward (Jr.), 41

Salem, 361
Santa Fe, 277
Science, 25, 263, 269; *see also* special topics
Seal of The United States, 5-6
Seat of government, permanent, 345-348
Senf, John Christian, 152, 159, 160, 161, 162, 193, 373
Shells, 300
Shippen, Thomas, 41
Shipyard, 194, 197, 208-209, 210
Short, William, 291, 301, 354, 357
Sibley, John, 292
Silver, 32, 36
Simcoe, John Graves, 136, 206, 215, 223
Skipwith, Anne Wayles, 321, 354
Slavery, 293-295, 296, 303, 342, 385
Smallwood, General, 143, 145, 154
Smithfield, 144
South Carolina, 94-95, 97-99, 105-107, 116, 170, 175, 185, 201, 215, 218
Staunton, 219, 244
Steuben, Baron von, 117, 126, 127, 132, 133, 134, 136, 137, 138, 140, 141-146, 153, 154-164, 165, 166, 177, 180, 183, 185, 190-193, 198, 202-205, 207, 209-211, 215, 216; 224, 243, 249
Stevens, Edward, 101-102, 105-107, 109, 111, 112
Stiles, Ezra, 358, 359
Stockdale, John, 298-299, 300, 302
Stuart, Archibald, 282
Suffolk, 54
Sullivan, John, 262, 269, 274, 283-284
Supply, military, 53, 66-67, 97-103, 107, 108, 111-112, 162-163, 164-165, 175, 179-180, 182-183, 189, 192, 219-221

Taliaferro family, 25
Tarleton, Banastre, 105, 186, 188, 223, 228, 229, 251-253
Theater, 312, 325, 355
Thomson, Charles, 264, 269, 270, 274, 275, 296, 325, 337, 347, 382
Tilly, Commodore de, 192, 194
Tories, 59-61, 99, 105, 177, 227
Tracy, Nathaniel, 360-361
Transylvania Company, 79
Trist, Mrs., 318, 319, 321
Tuckahoe, 55, 134, 239, 240, 306, 314
Tucker, St. George, 47, 57
Turpin, Philip, 356
———, Thomas, 57
Tyler, John, 252, 256

Unger, Jean Louis de, 18, 19, 20, 38-40

Valley of Virginia, 319
Van Hogendorp, *see* Hogendorp
Villebrune, Chevalier de, 309-311
Vincennes, 83, 84-85, 277
Violin, 20, 41
Virginia, Assembly, 12-17, 48, 127, 128, 130-131, 153, 167-168, 180-181, 189-190, 196, 219, 220, 225, 233-234, 242-245, 255-257, 307, 314, 317, 357; Board of War, 66, 102, 249; Commissioner of War, 66, 139; Constitution, 6-8, 293, 314, 315-318; Convention, 6-8; Council, 49, 128, 130, 153, 169, 175-176, 193, 197, 199, 203, 216, 222, 239, 240, 242-243, 245-246, 317; currency, 51-52, 61-64, 238; Navy, 71-75, 109, 146-149, 193-197, Commissioner of, 126, 147, 192; revisal of laws, 3, 12-17, 293; taxes, 52, 61, 63, 64; war in, invasions of Collier, 53-55, Leslie, 110-115, Arnold, 125-151, 172-174, Phillips, 196-221, Cornwallis, 221-231, 251-254
Vocabularies, Indian, 291-293
Volney, Comte de, 292

Wabash, 81, 82, 122
Walker, John, 141, 158, 225, 354
———, Thomas, 270
Waltersdorff, Baron de, 41-42
Washington, George, 65, 67, 69, 75-76, 86-89, 97, 110, 111, 118-121, 151, 165-166, 169-170, 183-184, 187, 190, 208, 211, 221, 225, 229, 231, 232, 234-236, 248, 286, 325, 332, 334-335, 340; portrait, 357
Wayne, Anthony, 222, 224
Webster, Daniel, 356
Weedon, George, 111, 146, 155, 156, 157, 158, 198
West, conquest of the, 78-95; territory, 168-169, 337, 339-343
Westham, 132, 133, 134-135, 139, 140, 158, 172
Westover, 132, 133, 134, 136, 140, 145, 154, 175, 210, 221, 228
William and Mary, College of, 14-16, 23, 359
Williamos, Mr., 297, 385
Williamsburg, 10, 12, 16, 20, 21, 23, 47, 55, 131, 137, 157, 197, 204-209, 228, 248; Palace, 55, 57-58, 63; Wythe house, 10
Wilton, 137, 224, 226
Wine, 22, 44, 319, 362
Wright, Joseph, 357
Wythe, George, 7, 10, 13, 16, 17, 25, 82, 297

Yale College, **358-359**
York, Pa., 9
York River, 276
Yorktown, 193, 195, **208**, **250**

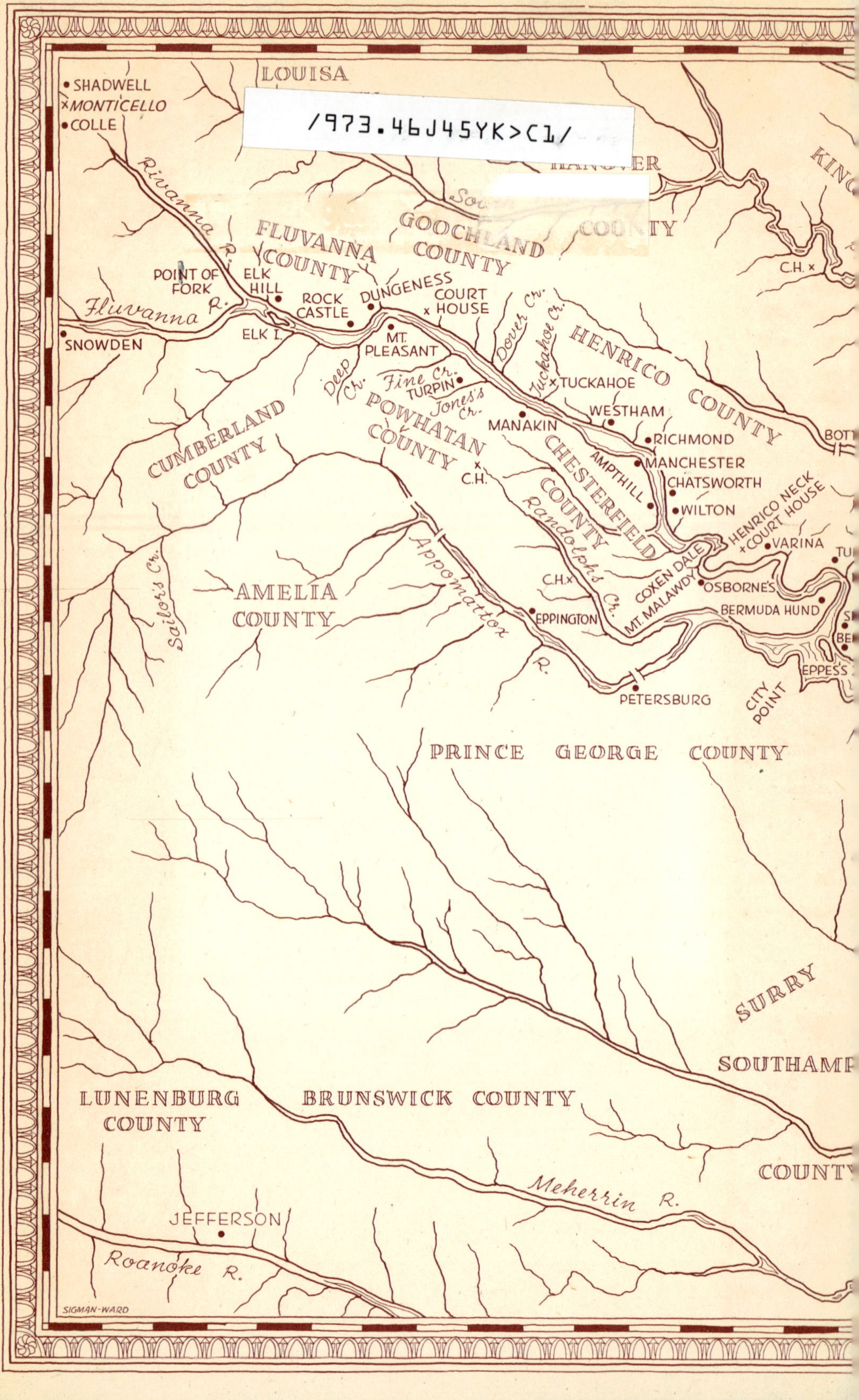

LOUISA
SHADWELL
MONTICELLO
COLLE
HANOVER
COUNTY
KING
Rivanna R.
FLUVANNA COUNTY
GOOCHLAND COUNTY
C.H.
POINT OF FORK
ELK HILL
ROCK CASTLE
DUNGENESS
COURT HOUSE
Fluvanna R.
SNOWDEN
ELK I.
MT. PLEASANT
Dover Cr.
Tuckahoe Cr.
HENRICO COUNTY
Deep Cr.
Fine Cr.
TURPIN
TUCKAHOE
Jones's Cr.
POWHATAN COUNTY
MANAKIN
WESTHAM
CUMBERLAND COUNTY
C.H.
RICHMOND
AMPTHILL
MANCHESTER
CHESTERFIELD COUNTY
CHATSWORTH
WILTON
HENRICO NECK
COURT HOUSE
VARINA
Randolphs Cr.
Appomattox R.
Sailor's Cr.
AMELIA COUNTY
C.H.
COXEN DALE
MT. MALAWDY
OSBORNE'S
EPPINGTON
BERMUDA HUND
EPPES'S
PETERSBURG
CITY POINT
PRINCE GEORGE COUNTY
SURRY
SOUTHAMP
LUNENBURG COUNTY
BRUNSWICK COUNTY
COUNTY
Meherrin R.
JEFFERSON
Roanoke R.
SIGMAN-WARD